W9-DFM-874

Birth Certificate

Also by Mark Thompson

A Paper House: The Ending of Yugoslavia

Forging War: The Media in Serbia, Croatia, Bosnia and Herzegovina

The White War: Life and Death on the Italian Front 1915–1919

BIRTH CERTIFICATE

The Story of
Danilo Kiš

MARK THOMPSON

CORNELL UNIVERSITY PRESS
Ithaca & London

First published 2013 by Cornell University Press
Printed in the United States of America

Library of Congress Cataloging-in-Publication Data

Thompson, Mark, 1959–
    Birth certificate : the story of Danilo Kiš / Mark Thompson.
        p. cm.
    Includes bibliographical references and index.
    ISBN 978-0-8014-4888-1 (cloth : alk. paper)
    1. Kiš, Danilo, 1935–1989.   2. Authors, Serbian—20th century—Biography.   I. Title.
    PG1419.21.I8Z896   2013
        891.8'2354—dc23
    [B]   2012027625

Cornell University Press strives to use environmentally responsible suppliers and materials to the fullest extent possible in the publishing of its books. Such materials include vegetable-based, low-VOC inks and acid-free papers that are recycled, totally chlorine-free, or partly composed of nonwood fibers. For further information, visit our website at www.cornellpress.cornell.edu.

Cloth printing   10 9 8 7 6 5 4 3 2 1

To Sanja–

> Ti si duša duše moje,
> Ti si srce srca moga
>
> –Anon., Bay of Kotor, c. 1750

and to Divna

Contents

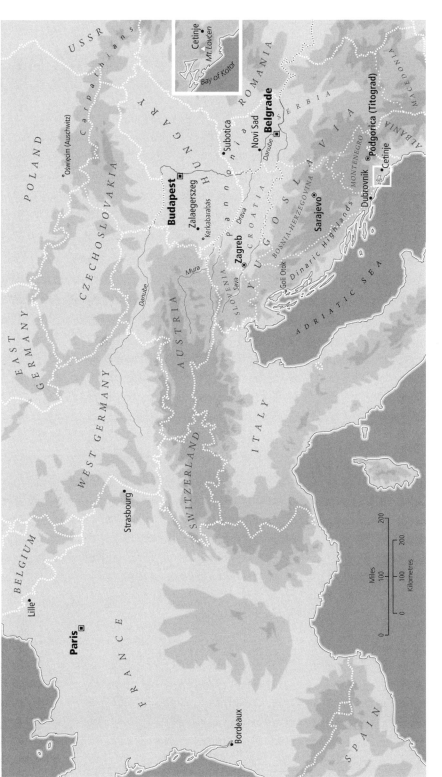

"We travelled for days through a snowy wasteland, blank as the ocean, losing all sense of direction" – GARDEN, ASHES

Map by Louis Mackay

Great and Invisible

> The death of Danilo Kiš . . . wrenchingly cut short one of the most important journeys
> in literature made by any writer during the second half of the twentieth century.
> —Susan Sontag

Obsessed with writing, politics and art's freedom from politics, passionately anti-communist and anti-nationalist, Danilo Kiš was a man of liberal convictions and violent emotions. An ethnic anomaly, a secular half-Jewish gnostic, a creature of instinct and appetite haunted by loss, a bohemian whom nothing but his vocation could make orderly: from these quarrels with himself and his society, Kiš distilled four or five superlative books, writing and revising in solitary rapture, condensing to the utmost, becoming "the genius of a particular time, experience and place".

He was given to superstitious awe of the printed word: its power to nourish the imagination and harm the world. If history is a prison and biographical data are fate—as Kiš felt they were—then literature is a form of freedom which most shows itself in its enemies' embrace. His work carries an echo, the sonar resonance of literature seeking a frontier with its opposites: encyclopaedias, police files, casualty lists, birth certificates, railway timetables, gazetteers. He tests fiction's possibilities, not by slighting our desire for stories but rather by drawing that desire into zones of history where it cuts against our hunger for truth, unadorned. Nobody did more to prove that Europe's twentieth-century experiments in fiction can take the measure of its experiments in totalitarianism, without curbing the liberties of the one or blurring the crimes of the other.

The degree-zero purity of this achievement chills as it exhilarates, but if you get a taste for Kiš's work, nothing quite takes its place. His books have been translated into more than twenty languages. In the mid-1980s, he was considered for the Nobel Prize. Yet he has no measurable readership in English today, despite admirers who include Susan Sontag, Nadine Gordimer, Joseph Brodsky, Salman Rushdie, and Milan Kundera, who acclaims Kiš as "great and invisible", the writer who turned the Stalinist terror, the struggle against Nazism, and the Holocaust into great poetry: "the only one who never sacrificed so much as a phrase of his books to political commonplaces." A decade ago, Rushdie listed a baker's dozen of Europe's great novelists since 1945. Among these, only Kiš was and is out of print in Britain, and is nearly so in the United States.

> "You think my Wednesday people ever heard of this Danilo Kiš? You carry on
> about him, but they never heard of him."

For the irritable editor in Cynthia Ozick's novel, Kiš is worse than unfamiliar; he is—the implication goes—justly neglected, and efforts to alter this condition are worse than doomed: they give offence.

In his own language, his books are classics, widely available, much written-about, revered for their beauty, wit, and compassion. For their zest and their generous welcome to the wider world; for rejecting the nationalist plea (veiling a threat) to prefer local references and traditions; and for leading readers down to the wellsprings of art. Yet his status is also contested in Serbia, his fame still resented as the Western world's reward to a purveyor of flashy techniques.

"He was a very rooted writer, but also completely cosmopolitan," Sontag recalled, "which is the most wonderful combination." To his admirers, Kiš's books are wholly of their place and language, yet better than that place and language otherwise produced; hence a cause for pride and regret. Nobody except Ivo Andrić matters as much to readers across the Bosnian, Croatian, Montenegrin, and Serbian language area, between the Danube and the Adriatic. His aspiration and achievement make him a touchstone of value. Never the most characteristic writer from Yugoslavia, he became the most essential.

Critics praise the intelligence and density of his prose, bursting the premodern epic-realist mould, shunning the topical without veering into abstraction or cutting out the rich murmurs of its native language-world. Yet that world, with its intricate compacted differences, is dauntingly remote. Slavonic orthography is part of the problem. Anglophones flinch at diacritical marks and clotted consonants. How to read a writer if you cannot say his name? Kiš believed there were three great modern authors in his language. Miroslav Krleža, the Croatian colossus, does not exist in English, no matter that he invented the existentialist novel before Sartre or Camus. Miloš Crnjanski, a Serb, is almost unknown. Only Ivo Andrić, the Nobel laureate from Bosnia, scrapes through this test.

What is more, Kiš's books do not—with a partial exception: *A Tomb for Boris Davidovich*—offer the pleasure that translated fiction from communist Europe provided during the Cold War: a veiled commentary, witnessing political depravity in narratives etched with satire; a gallery of black-comic portraits, generic evocations of rural life, and interludes of earthy sex. Most of these elements are sometimes present in Kiš, but not in simple enough forms or doses to sell. Readers who prefer literature as surrogate sociology, reportage or travel writing, a political *roman à clef*, entertainment, or compensation—meaning all of us some of the time and most of us all the time—may not find much reward.

Kiš knew the Balkans were seen as a realm of tourism and atrocity: sun-kissed coastlines fronting a "vast area of tribes and nationalities where the two worst wars in history, and the cold war, began and ended in the lifetimes of our parents and grandparents"— as someone said who knew better.

Literature tells about places whether it speaks openly about them or not, recording "the secret history of nations", as Balzac believed. Kiš died two years before his own place was destroyed in a convulsion that lasted for a decade and cost scores of thousands of lives. The word *Yugoslavia* is mentioned only once in his fiction. National themes or mythemes occur only ironically, subversively. He does not inform us about his country or region, in the way that realist literature provides opinions, information, and local colour. On the contrary, he wrote against realist, ethnic, or politicised literature. This makes him doubly remote. To foreign readers, even his cosmopolitanism is exotic; for every cosmopolitanism is moulded like a plaster mask on the features of its sectarian twin.

By defining himself as a Yugoslav writer contributing to Serbian literature in the Serbo-Croatian language, Kiš teased the pedantry of societies where labels matter more than the baggage. His principal affinities were elective, not fated, more influenced by French and Russian writers than by the overlapping cultures clustered as on a microscope slide between Vienna and Athens. ("I don't have close ties to the Yugoslav tradition," he admitted in 1965.) Apart from Krleža and Andrić, he belongs in the company of Jorge Luis Borges and Vladimir Nabokov, Italo Calvino, Georges Perec, Bruno Schulz and Joseph Brodsky.

The biographer of a neglected writer feels futility dragging. Kiš's books are worth the risk and effort, but what sort of effort should it be? No-one, presuming to publish anything literary, is exempt from what he called "the permanent search for form". He was proud of his creative restlessness, each book a fresh departure, yet the continuities are unmissable. They are markers along his journey in literature. To have a chance of being truthful, a study of Kiš should be experimental, encyclopaedic in style, with a flavour of pastiche. Here it is: an extended commentary on a miniature autobiography which he wrote for an American reference work that was never published. He printed the text elsewhere, urged friends to read it, and recited it in public. Like his best books, it blooms under a magnifying lens.

Note on Pronunciation

The 'ˇ' perching on the *s* in Kiš is called a hachek. He told his French students to think of it as a bird. It softens *s* to *sh*, so 'Kiš' is part *kiss* and part *quiche*. Other Slavonic diacriticals turn *z* to *zh* and *c* to *ch*. Unaccented, *c* is hard, like *ts*. Đ and đ sound like a soft *g* (as in *George*). And *j* is always like the English *y*.

Birth Certificate

Izvod iz knjige rođenih
(kratka autobiografija)

Moj je otac ugledao sveta u zapadnoj Madjarskoj a završio
je trgovačku akademiju u mestu rodjenja izvesnog gospodina Viraga
koji će, milošću gospodina Džojsa, postati slavnu Leopold Blum (Bloom)
Mislim da je izvesna liberalna politika Franje Josipa II, kao i
želja za integracijom, navela moga dedu da svom još meloletnom sinu
madjarizuje prezime; mnoge pojedinosti iz porodične hronike ostaće,
medjutim, zauvek nerazjašnjene: godine 1944, moj otac kao i ~~skoro~~
svi naši rodjaci biće odvedeni u Aušvic, odakle ~~nik~~ se skoro niko
od njih neće vratiti.

Medju mojim precima s majčine strane nalazi se jedan legendar-
ni crnogorski junak, koji će se opismeniti u svojoj pedesetoj godini
i slavi svoga mača dodati slavu pera, kao i jedna "amazonka", koja
je iz osvete posekla glavu turskom nasilniku. Etnografska retkost
koju predstavljam izumrećí, dakle, sa mnom.

U mojoj četvrtoj godini (1939), u vreme donošenja antijevrej-
skih zakona u Madjarskoj, roditelji su me krstili u Uspenskoj crkvi
u Novom Sadu u pravoslavnu veru, što mi je spaslo život. Do svoje tri-
naeste godine živeo sam u Madjarskoj, u očevom rodnom kraju, gde smo
pobegli ~~posle~~ 1942, posle novosadskog pokolja. Radio sam kao sluga
kod bogatih seljaka, a u školi sam slušao katehizis i katoličku
biblijsku egzegezu. "Uznemirujuća različnost", ono što Frojd naziva
Heimlichkeit, biće moj~~im~~ osnovnim ~~prvim~~ književnim i metafizičkim poticajem;
u svojoj devetoj godini napisao sam prve pesme, na madjarskom; jedna
je govorila o gladi, druga je bila ljubavna pesma par excellence.

Od svoje sam majke nasledio sklonost ka pripovedačku ~~mešivanu~~ mešavinu
fakata i legende, a od svoga oca poetiku i ironiju. Za moj odnos
prema književnosti nije bez značaja činjenica da je moj otac bio
pisac medjunarodnog reda vožnje: to je čitavo kosmopolitsko književ-
no nasledje.

Birth Certificate (A Short Autobiography)

by Danilo Kiš

My father came into the world in western Hungary and was educated at the commercial college in the birthplace of a certain Mr Virág, who would, by the grace of Mr Joyce, eventually become the famous Leopold Bloom. I believe it was the liberal policy of Franz Josef II together with a desire for integration that led my grandfather to Magyarise the surname of his underage son. Many details of the family chronicle will, though, remain forever obscure: in 1944 my father and all our relatives were taken away to Auschwitz, whence almost none returned.

Among my ancestors on my mother's side is a legendary Montenegrin hero who learned to read and write at the age of fifty, adding the glory of the pen to the glory of his sword, as well as an 'Amazon' who took revenge on a Turkish brute by cutting off his head. The ethnographic rarity I represent will, therefore, die out with me.

In 1939, in my fourth year, when anti-Jewish laws were being promulgated in Hungary, my parents had me baptised in the Orthodox faith at the Church of the Assumption in Novi Sad. This saved my life. I lived until my thirteenth year in my father's native region of Hungary, to which we fled in 1942 after the Novi Sad massacre. I worked as a servant for rich peasants, and in school I listened to the catechism and Catholic Bible study. The 'troubling dissimilarity' that Freud calls *Heimlichkeit* was to be my basic literary and metaphysical stimulus; in my ninth year I wrote my first poems, in Hungarian: one was about hunger, the other was a love poem *par excellence*.

From my mother I inherited a propensity for telling tales with a mixture of fact and legend; from my father—pathos and irony. And it was not without significance for my relationship to literature that my father was the author of an international

1

railway timetable: an entire cosmopolitan and literary legacy in itself.

My mother read novels until her twentieth year, when she realised, not without regret, that novels are 'made up' and rejected them once and for all. This aversion to 'sheer fabrication' is latent in me as well.

In 1947 we were repatriated by the Red Cross to Cetinje where lived my uncle, a well-known historian and a biographer of and commentator on Njegoš. Immediately after we arrived, I took the art-school entrance examination. (The admissions committee included Petar Lubarda and Milo Milunović.) The bust of Voltaire we were asked to draw—a plaster cast of Houdon's statue—reminded me of an old German woman I had known in Novi Sad, and that is how I drew him. I was accepted nonetheless, probably on the basis of other work. I had to wait a year or two in order to get the necessary academic qualifications. Meanwhile I decided to finish secondary school after all.

For two years I learned violin at the music school, where I was taught by Simonuti Senior, whom we called 'Paganini' not only for his appearance but because he loved tremolos. Just when I reached the second position, the music school moved to Kotor. I went on playing by ear—Gypsy music, Hungarian romances, and the tango and 'English' waltzes at school dances.

At the secondary school I continued to write poetry. I also translated Hungarian, Russian, and French poets, primarily as stylistic and linguistic exercises: I was training to be a poet, learning the craft of literature. We were taught Russian by White Army officers, émigrés from the Twenties who substituted for absent teachers and were equally at home with mathematics, physics, chemistry, French and Latin.

From the Gymnasium I entered the University of Belgrade, where I was the first student to graduate from the newly created Department of Comparative Literature.

As a lector for Serbo-Croatian language and literature I have taught in Strasbourg, Bordeaux and Lille. For the last few years I have been living in Paris, in the tenth *arrondissement*, and am not homesick; sometimes I wake up not knowing where I am: I hear our countrymen calling to one another, and an accordion blaring from the cassette player in a car parked under my window.

(1983)

Birth Certificate

A Short Autobiography

B irth certificates do not look like this, and the text under the title confirms a mismatch. It does not even tell us the author's name or his parent's names, where he was born or when. But it does speak of his origins and early life, the parental legacy of traits and ancestral influence, expressing a settled conviction about their formative power. The subtitle underlines the point; a life comes down to family, early encounters, moments, scenes, episodes: nothing that takes longer than four minutes and twenty-five seconds to summarise.[1] Birth certificates determine our autobiographies, which are always short. The title is literally wrong, yet right.

The mismatch and its implications generate the vital friction called irony, stirring us into active readership. An active, sceptical reader was the only sort worth being and, for a writer, the only sort worth having. Even opportunities like this title should be taken, our habits are so lazy and blinding.

Kiš traced the motivation behind his writing to the pressure in early adulthood to understand the catastrophe that broke over his family in the Second World War, starting in the Yugoslav city of Novi Sad, where Kiš's father Eduard narrowly escaped death in January 1942. Eduard then led his wife Milica and two children (nine-year-old Danica and seven-year-old Danilo) to the remote village in Hungary where he was born and his relatives still lived. The family was living there in penury when Eduard was deported to Auschwitz in 1944.

The three survivors were rescued in 1947 by Kiš's uncle, who took them to Montenegro, the homeland of Kiš's mother. His father's surviving papers would spur Danilo's imagination and shape his conception of literature. For many years, his main endeavour was to retrieve his father—and his own origins—in fiction. His masterpiece, *Hourglass*, is a maze-like commentary on a quarrelsome, incensed letter that Kiš's father wrote in 1942 to his sister, Danilo's aunt.

Kiš believed that documents are imbued with invisible, unsuspected literary power. When a writer uses or imitates a document, its original (official) purpose

---

1 This is the duration of Kiš's recording of this *Birth Certificate*, which can be heard at http://www.kis.org.yu/web/Acitav/A/index.htm.

merges into a new meaning. His writing thrives on the ironies and energies that find release when documents or documentary forms are freed from their function. This power is more abundant in documents such as certificates of birth, marriage, and death, which are universal and singular, marking the contours of a unique life.

My father

His father was to Kiš what Dublin was to James Joyce, courage to Hemingway, or exile to Vladimir Nabokov: a spur to creativity and often its subject. He stands at the heart of Kiš's early poems and emerges as the central figure in most of his fiction.

Even when he wasn't writing about his father, filiation was Kiš's theme: a daughter's discovery of her late father's biography gives the plot of "The Encyclopaedia of the Dead", his finest story. His cycle of stories about Soviet tyranny centres on Stalin, present as a picture on the wall of an interrogator's office—the ultimate bad parent, a source of cruel illusion, a false god. "Miksha looked up at that portrait, at that good-natured, smiling face, the kind face of a wise old man, so much like his grandfather's; he looked up at him pleadingly, and with reverence."

Yet Kiš's first published works were heartfelt poems about the loss of his other parent, who died of cancer when he was sixteen. His debut was called "Farewell to Mother". Its first line was: "Mother! Your glassy gaze agitates my soul". After four simple ABAB rhyming stanzas, the poem ends by invoking the "tender love of a mother who's no more!" Kiš's anguish was expressed too directly, with too little craft, for the result to be more than a cry of pain. It is mawkish, made somehow memorable by the poet's determination to tackle the most searing experience by force of sincerity.

At eighteen years old, Kiš was not a precocious talent. Where his gift showed was in the speed of learning by trial and error. In 1953, two years after their mother's death, his sister Danica married and moved to a town on the coast of Montenegro, where she had lived as a student. Again, loss sparked poetry:

The Wedding Party

The wedding party
leaves my home
Black, they took
my mother
and sister,
white
My heart shudders alike

5

at tolling bells
or pistols' peal
The wedding party
leaves my home

The twenty-year-old Kiš had learned that unmastered truth and strength of feeling do not produce true and strong writing; for creativity needs distance from pain. The naked urgency has gone, replaced by a pattern of paired opposites that circles around to its start. (Circular form would fascinate him to the end of his life.) Above all, he had grasped the value of selection and compression: every word is judged and syllable weighed.

This was the last poem with any allusion to his mother. In one of those coincidences that strew his biography—and help explain his sense that "nothing in a writer's life is accidental"—it was printed in a magazine in 1955, alongside the first text he published about his father.

Biography

A wonderful drunk was Eduard Kon.
Behind glasses with glistening lenses, he
     watched the world as through a rainbow.

1.

Even as a child he had to pee after the others
    at school, because he was circumcised.
Once he loved the baker's daughter and was a bit happy.
When she found out he was circumcised, it seemed to her
    she could never share his bed.
Then on, he loved sticking money in the fiddler's bow
    and kissing gypsies.
Afterwards—for comfort—he fell for Delirium, who
    wrapped him in a true embrace.

2.

The wind scattered his ashes above the narrow chimney
    of the crematorium, high, high . . .
        up to the rainbow.

Where the mother figured as an immense archetype, named, venerated, and mourned, the father prompts a narrative (a man's life), history (the extermination of the

Jews), politics (racism), and poetics (tropes, tragicomedy, allegory, irony). "The Wedding Party" was a tidier poem, but "Biography" held richer promise for a writer whose future lay with prose.

These three poems about his mother, father, and sister form a miniature triptych, marking out the terrain that he would spend nearly twenty years mapping in fiction. With his father emerging as his subject, Kiš was groping towards literary correlatives for primordial experiences and for the large questions that stemmed from them. The quest had begun for form—what he called the *grace of form*.

Eduard Mendel (or Emanuel) Kohn was born on 11 July 1889 in the village of Kerkabarabás, near the town of Zalaegerszeg in south-western Hungary. He was the sixth of seven children born to Miksa Kohn (b. 1840) and Regina (*née* Fürst, 1850), the only Jewish family in the village.

Miksa (full name: Max or Mihaily) owned a general store and some nearby woodland. His ancestors may have been goose-feather merchants who came to Hungary as refugees from Alsace. At some point the woods were lost. "The wood in the forests he owned was burned to make potash, used in the manufacture of tile stoves and cooking ware," Kiš said. "Whether he was ruined by a fire or by competition from Bohemian porcelain, which greatly reduced the demand for potash, I don't know." Later in life, Eduard bore a grievance against some of his siblings in connection with the lost forests, convinced that they had conspired to stop him inheriting his share.

Eduard attended a secondary school some 20 kilometres away in Lendava, a market town then in Hungary, later in Yugoslavia, and now in a green corner of Slovenia. In 1903, he enrolled at the Commercial Academy in Zalaegerszeg as Eduard Kiss. What he did between summer 1906 and joining the railways in September 1907 is not clear. Danilo believed that he was involved in unsuccessful business ventures—something he would repeat after retirement.

Eduard settled in Subotica in July 1920. Before the First World War, Subotica was Szabadka, a Hungarian town with handsome Art Nouveau buildings testifying to its prosperity. The synagogue is almost worthy of Gaudí's Barcelona. The postwar settlement put Szabadka in the new state of the South Slavs, a few kilometres from the border. To dilute the ethnic Hungarian population in this sensitive zone, the government granted land around the town to hundreds of Montenegrins.

This was probably not the reason why Milica Dragićević (b. 1903) found herself in Subotica in 1930, on her first trip away from her native Montenegro. For she was visiting her sister Draginja, who worked for the Yugoslav railways alongside her husband Milutin Malović, also Montenegrin. How Milica came to meet Eduard is not known. Danilo Kiš would call it "a rare encounter, perhaps unique at that time." We shall say more about this unlikely union in chapter 13; it suffices to note here that Montenegro had no Jewish population and anti-Semitism was hardly known there. Eduard was probably the first Jew Milica had met. More to the point, his Jewishness probably signified very little to her.

The courtship that followed is equally obscure. They married the following October, when Eduard was forty-two. A wedding photograph shows a solemn couple, no longer young, gazing at the camera side by side, touching at the temple. Wide-eyed behind rimless spectacles, with a wing collar and striped tie, he looks resolute but surprised. Milica's pale flowered dress contrasts with her thick black hair, brushed back from a strikingly beautiful face with eyes that expect to suffer.

Danica was born in August 1932 in Zagreb—the capital city of Croatia—as the parents returned from a visit to Eduard's brother Adolf, who lived in Trieste with his Italian wife. The second child was born in Subotica on 22 February 1935: *Danilo / male / Jew* reads the entry in the town's registry of births. Danica and Danilo are Montenegrin names.

Eduard's was a troubled personality. He spent three months in a psychiatric hospital near Belgrade in 1934, and two shorter spells there in 1939. Danilo never forgot visiting his father in September 1939. Eduard asked Milica for a pair of scissors "to cut short his suffering: it's late summer, autumn rust is starting to eat away at plane-tree leaves, and my father is sitting in his hospital pyjamas on a wooden bench in the hospital grounds, an absent look in his eyes."

Young Eduard Kiss—"Those high celluloid collars lent the body a certain dignity, imposing discipline, holding the head proud, idealistically aloft . . ." (*Garden, Ashes*)

Danilo grew up believing that alcohol was the cause of his father's illness. He discovered only much later that the drinking had been a symptom of a deeper malaise. When he learned in "the early Seventies" that Eduard's diagnosis in 1934 was not delirium tremens, as he had expected, but the condition called anxiety neurosis, it struck him as "a revelation".

> After reading up on psychopathology and anxiety neurosis, I started seeing all kinds of things more clearly. I learned first that anxiety neurosis had long been thought an endemic condition of the Jewish intelligentsia of Central Europe; second, that patients often took to drink to drown their latent fears; and third, that the disorder was congenital in 10 to 20 per cent of cases, according to some scholars, and in 70 to 90 per cent according to others. At last I was able to account for the traumatic fears that had plagued me on two or three occasions in my youth but that fortunately lasted for only a few days. . . . The suffering was hideous. A kind of "metaphysical fear", fear and trembling. All of a sudden, with no visible exterior cause, the defence mechanism that lets you live with the knowledge of human mortality goes to pieces, and a menacing lucidity comes over you—an absolute lucidity, I would call it. I've described it—that condition of an intense inner trembling—in a chapter of *Hourglass*.[2]

The revelation enlarged Danilo's view of his father, letting him see Eduard, despite his eccentricities or because of them, as a generic figure, typical of educated Central European Jews who were unhinged by the looming threat of fascism.

Between his son's birth and his later spells in hospital, Eduard edited the *Yugoslav National and International Travel Guide* for 1938. Danilo would make a cult of this 150-page compendium of bus, ship, train, and air timetables (see chapter 22). He said it gave him his literary credentials, a vocational ancestry. It allowed him to claim professional kinship with his father: thanks to this book, he was "the son of a 'writer', of an authentic wanderer and traveller from Kakania."[3]

Eduard's other written legacy was a collection of personal papers that were left behind when he was taken off to the ghetto in Zalaegerszeg in spring 1944 and then to Auschwitz, transported, as Danilo would tell a friend, over the same railway network that he had served. When Milica took the children with her to Montenegro in 1947, Danilo made sure his father's papers came too. Twenty years or so later, he 'transposed' this scene in a fictional account of the family's departure from Kerkabarabás:

> We get on the train with our absurd baggage, dragging the tent of our wanderings behind us, the sad legacy of my childhood. Our historic suitcase, badly

---

2 This is chapter 53 of *Hourglass,* discussed in chapter 19 of this book.
3 "Kakania" was the Austrian novelist Robert Musil's naughty name for the Habsburg Empire. It was adapted from "k.u.k.", a ubiquitous official acronym in the empire that stood for *kaiserlich und königlich* (imperial and royal).

frayed, with clasps ready to burst any moment with a rusty crack like flintlocks, had navigated the flood empty and alone, like a coffin. Now, like ashes in an urn, it only holds my father's pitiful remains: his photographs and papers. Here are his birth certificate, his school diploma, those incredible torahs covered with the script of a distant, almost mythical past, precious testimony of a dead poet, the archives of his affliction: transcripts of court cases, documents from a Subotica brush factory (that went bankrupt due to him), injunctions, work permits, his promotion to station master, and finally two of his letters—the "Great and Small Testaments"—and his discharge from the hospital at Kovin. . . .

What was it that led me to smuggle this wonderful archive into our suitcase, hiding it from our mother? No doubt it was the early awareness that this would be the sole legacy of my childhood, the only material proof that I ever existed and my father ever existed. For without all that, without those manuscripts and those photographs, I would certainly be convinced today that none of it ever happened, that it was all a story I had dreamed up afterwards as a consolation. My father's face would have been wiped from my memory like so many others, and if I held out my hand I would grasp at a void. I would think I'm dreaming.

Along with these papers, he stowed a few exercise books, a children's Bible, a Shorter Catechism, a German textbook, a favourite novel (*The Captain of the Silver Bell*), and then,

Wedding day, Subotica, 1931—"That same evening, Eduard Sam noticed a woman among the company at the next table: an extraordinarily beautiful woman." (*Garden, Ashes*)

last but first of all, the gem of the archive: the *Yugoslav National and International Travel Guide* for 1938, with my father as the editor-in-chief (and which would take on a new life, undergoing a wonderful metamorphosis, an Assumption, in one of my books). I put the *Travel Guide* among my own things, *my* books, as a precious heirloom.

———

When interviewers asked if his father died in Auschwitz, Kiš said no, he had "disappeared". The distinction was fundamental. Disappearance was all he knew of his father's fate, and it was mysterious, incomprehensible. As a boy, he needed to make sense of it and could not do so, because it was too huge to be understood. "In this way his absence became stronger than my mother's presence", he remembered. "Who was this man whom I had seen little enough of before, often drunk or in hospital, and who had suddenly vanished forever? This is how my father became a mythical image for me, a writer—the more so as he was shadowed by his own mythology, that of the Jewish people, whose martyrdom I suffered alike."

He told an interviewer that his memories of his father "are negatives in a sense, images of his absence. To this day I picture him climbing into cars, cabs, trains or trams. We are either waiting for him or seeing him off. . . . Or before our last visit, in 1944, to the improvised ghetto in Zalaegerszeg, from which he never returned. That accounts for my need to reconstitute his image". As he had hardly known his father, memory could not help much with this task. While this troubled him in boyhood, it became an asset. For it meant that he was free to invent him. As he said, "the father who appears in my works under the name of Eduard Sam, or E.S., is an idealised projection unencumbered by the solid, homogeneous mass of realities and memories. He is therefore doubly negative as a literary hero. He is an invalid, an alcoholic, a neurasthenic, and a Jew—in a word, ideal material for a literary character."

came into the world

This is the first metaphor. As Kiš once said, with relish, "when we're among metaphors, we're amid—literature."

What he writes here is "*ugledao sveta*", literally saw or glimpsed the world. It is a common figure of speech, without much personal or stylistic stamp. But a stamp there is. Provided the writer has not transgressed by bringing his "non-narrative I" into a story, Kiš said, metaphors and similes reveal "the maker's invisible and unseen mark". The relationship between the two parts of a simile creates a writer's identity. This is why the *like* or *as* of a simile "announces his presence like a knocking at the door. Like the rapping on the wooden table at a spiritualist séance: *I'm here.*"

He said on another occasion that the wonder of metaphors is how they "discover" a reality which they "transpose" at the same moment. The reality discovered and transposed here is that Kiš's father was not only born in western Hungary: he first *saw the world* there. The encounter with everything outside himself began in a particular place, as it had to.

The metaphor activates his father: rather than offering him as the object of a passive construction ('was born'), Kiš hints at his awakening consciousness, pointing to the moment when the first perceptions will be imprinted from a universe beyond the touch of starfish hands, flexing.

Which is why "saw the light of day" might be a better translation.

in western Hungary

There was a sea here long ago, so the books say . . .

Đorđe Balašević, *"Pannonian Sailor"*

Eduard's ancestors may have reached Hungary around the time of Emperor Josef II's Edict of Tolerance (1782), which acknowledged the right of Jews to be permanent residents of Vienna, Lower Austria, Moravia, and Hungary. (Even under economic pressure after the eastward exodus from Alsace, Louis XVI and his regime could not bring themselves to emancipate the Alsatian Jews.) Or perhaps they emigrated after Napoleon's "Infamous Decree" of 1808 had restricted the Alsatian Jews' freedom of movement and choice of trade. This last alternative would fit with Kiš's own impression, gleaned from his father's papers, that their Hungarian ancestors were feather merchants expelled from Alsace.

Kiš was chary of naming states in his fiction. Yugoslavia is mentioned only once, and even Hungary, where much of his work is located and which seems less burdened as a name, scarcely features. These words were too saturated in politics to be safe for literature or redeemable by it. By contrast, Montenegro was sufficiently tested by time and redolent of legend ("rough rock-throne of freedom!") to be admissible.

There was an older name for this part of the world, encompassing Hungary, which he did accept. This was "Pannonia", which occurs more than a dozen times in *Hourglass* as a shorthand for the entire geographical and cultural space where the action takes place, a triangle with vertices at Novi Sad, Kerkabarabás, and Budapest. The name appealed to Kiš because its antique sheen made it mysterious and evocative, like Thomas Hardy's "Wessex". Insulated against politics, it could not be abused or resurrected by nationalists of any stripe, because any claim to the Pannonian legacy (whatever that might amount to) could be countered by rival claims, equally plausible.

During the Pliocene era, a shallow sea covered what became the Pannonian plain, now extending over Hungary and into Croatia, Slovakia, Austria, Romania, Ukraine, and Serbia. The deposits left by these waters are 3 or 4 kilometres deep.

The name was Roman. For four centuries, the province of Pannonia lay at the frontiers of the empire. In current terms, it covered most of Croatia, much of Slovenia, parts of northern Serbia, a sliver of eastern Austria (including Vienna), and most of western Hungary. From the fourth century B.C., Greek and Roman historians identified numerous tribes in this "contact zone between Illyrians, Thracians and Celts", in András Mócsy's phrase—or migrating across it, under the fading dominion of the Celts. **15**

The Scordisci, Eravisci, and Daci; the Cimbri, Boii, and Taurisci; the Breuci and the An-
dizetes; the Colapiani, Iasi, Oseriates, Amantini, and the Cornacates; the Osi, the Cotini,
and the Anartii were all designated "Pannonians" by Polybius in a fragment dating from
the second century B.C.

The Scordisci were the mightiest tribe—Polybius believed they drank from human skulls—until Scipio Asiagenus defeated them around 85 B.C., opening the way
to the Danube. Emperor Augustus sent the young Tiberius to pacify these regions, and
the tribes succumbed one by one. (Appian: "The Pannonians do not live in towns, but
in villages and hamlets organised on the basis of clans. They do not assemble in joint
councils, nor do they have joint leaders who are supreme; 100,000 of them are capable
of bearing arms, but because of the prevailing anarchy they never assemble as a combined
force.") According to Edward Gibbon, Pannonia was "one of the last and most difficult
conquests of the Romans." The territory was annexed in 11 B.C. Garrisons and fortresses
were erected. Roman traders moved in. A major colony was established at Savaria, now
Szombathely. After the province expanded eastwards to the Danube a hundred years
later, observation posts sprouted along the river where sentries could monitor the movements of peoples in "the woods and marshes of Barbaricum".

The province made its living from the imperial budget: soldiers' pay, civil servants'
salaries, infrastructure projects. Its fortunes changed in the third century, under Emperor
Septimius Severus, a former governor of Pannonia who knew how much he owed its
legions. Around 200 A.D., the province "became attractive to many easterners, Syrians,
Jews, Greeks from Asia Minor and Egyptians, who appeared in large numbers everywhere".

This heyday ended with the first Vandal attacks around 259. The Sarmatian Roxo-
lani, the Quadi, and the peoples of the lower Danube razed many towns. Yet the province
recovered, and later Roman sources described it as rich and cheerful, though Gibbon
believed the Pannonians retained "their original ferocity" beneath "the tame resemblance
of Roman provincials". Marshland was reclaimed. Large estates dotted the fertile plains.
The *Expositio totius mundus*, a survey of the known world compiled by a Syrian in the
fourth century, stated that Pannonia was "a country in all respects rich", benefiting from
busy trade in corn, cattle, and slaves, who may have been prisoners taken in wars beyond
the Danube.

Goth attacks began in the third century. When the Quadi invaded Pannonia in
375, Gibbon wrote, they arrived during the harvest and "unmercifully destroyed every
object of plunder which they could not easily transport; and either disregarded or demolished the empty fortifications." Fritigern, king of the Visigoths, led his hordes across the
lower Danube in 376. They were accommodated but not appeased, and quickly settled in
large numbers, "paralysing economic life and the functioning of the administration over
large areas". Laments over the loss of Pannonia began to be heard in Rome.

The Visigoths and Vandals returned in the new century: Alaric and then Radagai-
sus led armies through "the warlike and hostile country of Pannonia" (Gibbon) on their
way to Italy. By 425, according to Marcellinus, parts of Pannonia were controlled by the

Huns. Roman reconquest in 433 hardly affected the situation. In 441, Attila seized the Roman holdings along the Danube. According to the Byzantine historian Procopius, in the sixth century, Pannonia was a desert devoid of people. Around 790, the territory was absorbed into the empire of Charlemagne, who "retaliated on the Avars, or Huns of Pannonia, the same calamities which they had inflicted on the nations." (Gibbon again.) Slavic and Magyar tribes moved in, and stayed.

Magyar and Croat humanists turned Pannonia into a cultural legacy in the fifteenth century.[4] Styling themselves forlornly as Pannonians, they claimed links to ancient Rome and the revival of learning in Renaissance Italy. In modern times, interest in Pannonia was limited to classical scholars, cartographers, and archaeologists but also anthropologists and ethnographers. Folktales and ballads, wedding rituals, feast-days, vernacular architecture, and even the forms of industrialisation across "the Pannonian space" were scrutinised for shared patterns and motifs. Jovan Cvijić, father of Yugoslav human geography or political ethnography (see chapter 13), claimed Pannonia as a "psychic geography" inhabited by a specific human type, one of several components of the South Slav (Yugoslav) ethnic identity. After the Great War, Miroslav Krleža alluded to Pannonia in his novels and journalism as an emblem of imperial ruination, provincial irrelevance, and human despair.

Cvijić's version of Pannonia was political, where Krleža's was dystopian. In Tito's Yugoslavia, however, Cvijić's ethnographical pseudo-science was discredited and Krleža stopped using the evocative old name. It persisted as a poetic strand in the music of Vojvodina, a brand name for Hungarian processed cheese, and cheap wine ('Treasure of Pannonia'). When Kiš reclaimed "my Pannonia" in the 1960s and 1970s, he was, in the words of a recent critic, reviving "a cultural space whose boundaries were more durable than traditional ethnic, national, religious, and ideological ones." This carried its own anti-political message; for "Pannonia challenged the authority of nationalist and Marxist discourses, proposing in their place an alternative history of continuous historical destruction, and the homelessness of the individual."

Pannonia's function in *Hourglass* is suggested in an early chapter, tipping off the readers, providing guidance for the journey they have begun—both vertical and horizontal, through time as well as space:

---

4 The most distinguished of these remote figures was Ivan Česmički or Janus Pannonius (1434–1472). Born in Slavonia, schooled in Ferrara and Padua, author of satirical epigrams and anti-clerical squibs, and later the bishop of Pécs in Hungary, this wandering scholar died in Zagreb. Near the end of his life he wrote a long poem, "Of the Great Flood". According to Czigány, this poem projects "personal fears" onto "the outside world: a great, almost cosmic deluge comes to destroy the nations and culture of Europe. The subject draws on his memories of the great floods of 1468; a comet was seen before that natural disaster, and the omen was interpreted by contemporaries as indicating a catastrophic ending to the world. Janus, worried by the Bohemian war of King Matthias, and submerged in his own anxieties which were augmented by his astrological studies, depicted all these horrors in one long and awesome vision of devastation." Kiš nowhere mentions this predecessor in the imagination of biblical calamity (see chapter 18). Writing in autumn 1942, when the seven-year-old Kiš was surviving in deepest Pannonia, Miroslav Krleža hailed Janus Pannonius as a genuine poet unjustly neglected, "unknown and forgotten. . . . waiting more than 400 years for revaluation [and] liberation from reactionary prejudices". If the name of Janus Pannonius endures today, it is thanks to his fictionalised role in a story by Jorge Luis Borges, "The Theologians".

If a man endowed with a dog's hearing were to put his ear to the ground at the right moment, he would hear a soft, barely audible gurgling, as when water is poured from one pitcher to another or when sand sifts through an hourglass, that's what he might hear, that's what you are likely to hear if you lay your head on the ground, press your ear to the earth, and let your thoughts bore into the depths of the earth, through geological strata to the Mesozoic and Paleozoic, through layers of sand and dense clay, boring like the roots of some giant tree through layers of mud and rock, through layers of quartz and gypsum, layers of snails and empty shells, layers of peat and fish bones and fish scales, through the bones of turtles and starfish, of sea horses and sea monsters, through layers of amber and fine sand, layers of seaweed and humus, dense layers of algae and nacreous shells, dense deposits of lime, layers of coal, layers of salt and lignite, tin and copper, of skulls and shoulder blades, layers of silver and gold, layers of zinc and pyrites, because somewhere down there, at a depth of a few hundred metres, lies the corpse of the Pannonian Sea, not quite dead yet, just smothered, crushed beneath ever-new layers of earth and rock, clay and muck, animal corpses and human corpses, corpses of human beings and human works, just immobilised, that's all, for it is still breathing, has been for thousands of years, through the stalks of waving wheat fields, through swamp reeds, through the roots of potatoes, not entirely dead, just crushed by the Mesozoic and Paleozoic strata, yes indeed, it has been breathing now for several hours, several minutes (in terms of earth time), breathing heavily, asthmatically, like a miner wedged in by beams and struts and great blocks of sweating coal. If you lay your head on the earth, if you glue your ear to the moist clay, especially on these quiet nights, you'll hear its breathing, its long death rattle.

Hourglass is about the permanent eclipse of a world—the world of Central European Jews, who belong to the past as definitively as the fossilised strata deep underground. Kiš said it was no coincidence that everything in the novel took place on the seabed, as it were, and all the ideas and materials and things mentioned in the book seemed to have been hauled into the daylight from the depths, exhumed "like unique archaeological finds". In this sense, he said, *Hourglass* was an "anthropological novel". *Ulysses* has been called the last Habsburg novel; perhaps *Hourglass* is the epitaph.

The quoted passage also pays ambivalent homage to Ivo Andrić and his vision of Yugoslavia as the culmination of a grim but meaningful history. For it echoes a celebrated passage in *Travnik Chronicle* (1945), where a young French diplomat describes a glimpse into Bosnia's remote past:

Today as I was riding towards Kalibunar, I saw a place where the rain had eroded the soil under the path. To a depth of some dozen feet you could see, like geological layers, one on top of the other, the traces of former roads that had passed through this same valley. At the bottom were heavy paving stones, the remains of a Roman road, six feet above them the remnants of a mediaeval cobbled way and, finally, the gravel surface of the Turkish road where we walk today. So, in a chance cross-section, I was shown 2,000 years of human history, and in them three epochs, each of which buried the other.

If Andrić—who when young had fought for a united Yugoslavia—hints here (and elsewhere) at a consoling teleology, Kiš's revelation of what has been lost offers nothing beyond its truthfulness and beauty.

Kiš's attachment to Pannonia predisposed him to share the enthusiasm for a cultural concept of Central Europe, which stirred keen interest in the early 1980s. This enthusiasm had nothing to do with the old pan-Germanic, geopolitical concept of *Mitteleuropa*. Rather, it pointed out the overlapping cultural traditions that united and distinguished the nations between the German anvil and the Russian hammer.

The countries always included in this virtual zone were Poland, Hungary, and Czechoslovakia. The new entity had many spokespersons—writers such as the Lithuanian-born Polish poet Czesław Miłosz and the Hungarian György Konrád, liberal dissidents like Václav Havel in Prague—but no ministries, banners, officials, or borders. Many books, but no slogans. Many sympathisers, and one overarching foe: the Soviet Union, which had absorbed these lands after 1945, crushed periodic revolts, and now, many feared, threatened to obliterate its manifold identities altogether.

The key expression of this fear was a superb polemic by the Czech novelist, Milan Kundera, called "The Tragedy of Central Europe" (1984). Kiš is the only Yugoslav writer mentioned in this manifesto for that part of Europe "situated geographically in the centre, culturally in the West and politically in the East". In this sense, 'Central Europe' signified a multicoloured resistance movement to the grey oblivion of Soviet power. With hindsight, the enthusiasm for Central Europe was a portent of Soviet communism's collapse. At the time, it was an exciting recovery of pre-communist values and traditions, sometimes rashly acclaimed as inherently pluralist and democratic. Reminders that shared Central European values had included rabid nationalism, fascism, and communism itself were not allowed to poison the atmosphere. And indeed, the new concept of Central Europe was anti-nationalist as well as anti-communist, for it championed the shared cultural inheritance and cross-currents that made the region more than the sum of its parts.

Even Pannonia's Roman legacy could be turned to account. Writing around 1980, the Hungarian Jenő Fitz affirmed that the "development of a Pannonian consciousness played a great part in the formation of a unified society" in the third century, though he failed to demonstrate that there was a unified society or to produce evidence of a "Pannonian consciousness" beyond an alleged "nostalgia for complete Romanisation". While conceding that, of the "great variety of gods and symbols" unearthed by archaeologists in the region, "none was original", Fitz claims to have found "reinterpretations" of "types" drawn from classical and Middle Eastern cults, "as if" these were "united in a pantheistic synthesis." In short, Fitz offered a Roman Pannonia customised for the anti-Soviet 1980s.

Kiš welcomed the West's "belated discovery" of Central Europe "as a single great cultural complex", while warning that it came too late. Refusing to sentimentalise the fate of the countries affected, he pointed out that they had done "almost nothing" to stop their own cultural decline, leaving émigrés like Kundera to sound the alarm.

By the mid-1980s, with Czesław Miłosz as well as Kundera naming him among the Central European writers, interviewers were asking Kiš about Central Europe. After decades of resistance to defining himself in national, ethnic, or political terms, he found the new designation spacious and vague enough to fit. Anyway, he was giving up hope that Yugoslav writers could be dissuaded from sliding into nationalist boasting and mutual recrimination; it was a relief to turn from this to 'Central Europe'. While insisting that he was "a *European* writer in the first place", he agreed that he was "a Central European writer to the core". His partly Hungarian identity gave him the keys to Central Europe, and he had always, he pointed out, written about Central European themes. Even *A Tomb for Boris Davidovich* was Central European, since the revolutionaries who made the pilgrimage to the Soviet Union and were swallowed up there were Central European themselves, for the most part.

'Central Europe' appealed to his anti-nationalist as well as his anti-communist principles. In a tantalising reflection, he suggested that, "if there is a style and a sensibility that separate me from Serbian and Yugoslav literatures, then they belong to something that could be called the Central European complex"—the same complex that, in his view, had produced Krleža, Andrić, and Crnjanski.

This was provocative. If Krleža, Andrić, and Crnjanski were truly Central European, what was left for Yugoslav literature? Krleža himself, raised in the struggle against the Habsburg Empire before 1914, had been hostile to the notion of Central European cultural identity, seeing it as a stalking horse for pan-Germanism. And Serbian nationalist circles—which were busy reviving some very different cultural myths in the mid-1980s (see chapter 33)—saw the fashion for Central Europe as another German-led endeavour, all too predictably endorsed by duplicitous Slovenians and Croatians, to belittle the achievements of Serbian Orthodox culture.

Kiš was aware of his compatriots' doubts and deplored them. Despite the fact that their only literary giants had their origins in this same Central Europe, they were too closed and separated from Europe to "take this opportunity" to promote their culture before the outside world. Yugoslav writers would have a better chance of escaping from cultural autism if they accepted larger, more inclusive literary identities. When Latin American literature became fashionable, he pointed out that foreign readers neither knew nor cared whether a writer was Bolivian or Argentinean, and what was more, the writers themselves were ready to present themselves "brilliantly" as "representing an entire continent". He contrasted this with Yugoslav writers' dedication to "home-made, private and privatised stories that look meaningless even from a slightly wider perspective".

"Variations on Central European Themes", written in 1986, is one of his richest essays. It starts with Kiš distancing himself from the euphoric utopianism of some celebrants of Central Europe. It was, he said, "risky" to claim that Central Europe was geopolitically or culturally homogeneous. The antagonisms among Central European countries and cultures are "more alive than the agreements", and anyway, "[a]ll positive cultural contacts among them date from the Middle Ages or the Renaissance". As for the Habsburg Empire, with its "reluctant absolutism", he advised against nostalgia; the old Austro-Hungarian monarchy was a phantom even in its heyday, as its best writers had shown. The cultural unity claimed for the Empire was "an oversimplification" wrought by hindsight. He quoted Robert Musil: "the whole myth of our [Austro-Hungarian] culture is empty romanticism". In literary terms, moreover, the dead writers of Central Europe had belonged firmly to the European tradition, not to a Central European variant.

On the fatal role played by the Soviet Union, Kiš echoed Kundera. "A new geopolitical division of Europe has separated Vienna from her former colonies . . . making today's Budapest, Prague, Warsaw, and Bucharest closer to Moscow than to her." Consequently, Central European culture had become "nostalgia for Europe"; for Europe as it was defined in the mid-1980s had no space for its central nations and cultures. "Waking from a long ideological hibernation, the European West discovered that part of its own cultural heritage was missing and that it was much the poorer for it." But this awakening had come too late: " 'Central Europe' as a cultural and historical phenomenon had become a thing of the past." Indeed, the very "notion of a Central European sphere of culture may well be felt more strongly in the West than in the countries that ought logically to constitute it."

Turning to Yugoslavia, which was usually absent from these debates, Kiš reminded readers that the cultures and literatures of Central Europe had "based their autonomy not only on reciprocal differences and reciprocal repulsions . . . but also and primarily on a rejection of Vienna and the Viennese cultural sphere." Croatian intellectuals in the early twentieth century had despised Vienna as a reactionary backwater. They turned instead to Paris, as did some Serbs. Other Serbs looked to Russia as Serbian culture's traditional " 'window on the world', one where two myths coincide: Pan-Slavism (Orthodoxy) and revolution, Dostoevsky and the Comintern."[5]

When he dwelled on the meaning of Central Europe for contemporary writers, Kiš's remarks applied to himself as much as to anyone. "Writers whom others call Central European or who describe themselves as such . . . come to realise that their nonconformity stems from a certain reserve and an almost unconscious yearning for broader, more democratic European horizons".[6] Such writers have, he continued, "long been trapped

5 By linking Serbian nationalism to Stalinism, this clause was too much for the editors of a Belgrade literary journal who reprinted the essay in 1990, the apogee of Serbia's nationalist revival under Slobodan Milošević: so they deleted it.

6 The Romanian novelist Norman Manea (b. 1936) expressed a debt to Kiš's account of the Central European writer, for whom "consciousness of belonging to Central Europe is itself in the end a kind of dissidence". "As an 'outsider' I had found my condition best described in Danilo Kiš's concept of the European".

between two kinds of reductionism: ideological and nationalistic. Though tempted by both, they have realised that the ideals of an 'open society' lie in neither, and find their ultimate legitimacy exclusively in language and literature". Yet, like all honourable commitments, this one too was fraught with uncertainty. For "no one abandons a community without regret. Betting on eternity is as vain as betting on the present. Hence the constant sense of 'inauthenticity'." When he wrote this essay, Kiš had already abandoned his own community by moving to Paris.

Despite these doubts, Kiš claimed to find evidence of "a Central European poetic" in certain writers from Poland and Hungary. "What is the tone, the vibration that situates a work within that magnetic field? Above all, the inherent *presence of culture* by way of allusion, reminiscence or reference to the whole European heritage, an awareness of the work itself that does not destroy its spontaneity, a careful balance between ironic pathos and lyrical flight. This is not much. It is everything." Everything, too, that Kiš wanted his work to achieve.

Ten days after Kiš's death, in October 1989, Mikhail Gorbachev's spokesman told the world that the Brezhnev Doctrine had been replaced by the Sinatra Doctrine: no longer would the Soviet Union claim the right to intervene in neighbouring countries when 'socialism' was threatened. As the Cold War came to an end, the concept of Central Europe first triumphed, then withered. By 2004, when most countries of the region entered the European Union, the Soviet Union was a fading memory and wider interest in the cultural identities of this region had faded with it. Politics giveth, and politics taketh away. The younger generation of Central Europeans cannot feel their parents' loyalties as their own or easily share the passion of writers like Kiš or Zagajewski, for whom literature is an ark of European culture; or their fear that, in Kundera's words, "we have come to the era of post-art, in a world where art is dying because the need for art, the sensitivity and the love for it, are dying".

Then again, as a realm of imagination, a psychogeography, Central Europe could never have taken solid form. It remains as a mythic name for several kinds of nostalgia, tradition, and potentiality. When Wittgenstein explained that he was "not interested in constructing a building, so much as in having a perspicuous view of the foundations of possible buildings", he wrote as a Central European in this mythic sense. Likewise Claudio Magris from Trieste, when he commented on the sense of "something unrealised" about the cities of Central Europe, "as if they possess something that could have made them truly great and marvellous", holding out a promise which nothing can fulfil. And Kiš is never more Central European than when he inspires disappointment that he failed to achieve even more. For the enlarged sense of artistic possibility that radiates from his work, like a beam sweeping the horizon, is his own creation.[7]

---

7 As the critic Guy Scarpetta finely remarks, Kiš created his own genealogy: Rabelais, Bruno Schulz, Broch, Borges, and the nouveau roman are linked in his writing—and nowhere else.

and was educated at the commercial college in

. . . Zalaegerszeg, the nearest proper town to Kerkabarabás, some 25 kilometres away. Eduard entered the Commercial Academy in 1903 and passed his final examination in 1906. From September of the following year, he was employed on the imperial and royal railways. He was promoted several times, rising to the rank of senior controller in 1923 and, five years later, to senior inspector. "As a result, until 1942 we travelled free of charge in first-class compartments," Danilo claimed to recall, "and the guards saluted him as if he were a general."

A portrait photograph in Budapest in 1919 shows the thirty-year-old Eduard in a dark jacket, high collar, and elegant patterned necktie, sporting a trimmed beard and moustache. His hair is neatly parted on the left. His eyes are wide-set and purposeful, the nose impressive over a wide, shapely mouth. The following year he was photographed in the same jacket, collar, and tie, but the impression is different: gone are the beard and moustache, his hair is centre-parted, he looks closer to twenty than thirty, and his expression is withdrawn.

That same year, 1920, after the disintegration of the Austro-Hungarian Empire, Eduard applied to join the state railway of the new Yugoslav state and was accepted. On 20 July, he transferred to Subotica. The following month he swore an oath of loyalty, swearing "by Almighty God to be loyal to the reigning King, to uphold the constitution of the Kingdom of Serbs, Croats and Slovenes . . . [and] conscientiously uphold the regulations concerning the security of railway traffic . . . So help me God." He was granted citizenship of the new kingdom in 1925 and took early retirement three years later, in circumstances that are—like much else in his biography—obscure. Perhaps on grounds of ill health, due to early symptoms of the psychiatric disorder that became acute in the 1930s. Or perhaps, as a Hungarian Jew, he was an automatic candidate for removal.

the birthplace of a certain Mr Virág, who would

Twenty-odd words into the *Birth Certificate*, before he has told us anything directly about himself, Kiš starts weaving literature into the facts, as if his father's education and the 'birth' of a fictional character—from James Joyce's *Ulysses*—were equal events in his own biography.

He writes as if Virág really existed before Joyce transposed him into fiction. Or as if Bloom were the fictional face of a real coin whose other side was Virág. Either way, Kiš is paying tribute to Joyce's creative powers in a way that casts Joyce in a rather Kiš-like light. For it implies that Joyce's fictional Virág stands to his equally fictional Bloom as Danilo's real father stands to his fictional version, "E.S.". Mildly confused? You are meant to be. This not-quite-seamless confounding of fiction and reality is Kiš's hallmark.

Why, then, if this connection matters so much, does Kiš make a double gaffe? For it was Leopold Bloom's father, Rudolf Virág, who was born in Hungary, not Leopold himself. And Eduard Kis went to college in Zalaegerszeg, while the Virág family hailed from Szombathely, a city some 50 kilometres to the north.[8]

Perhaps Kiš doctored the evidence, or simply forgot (suppressed) the truth, in order to strengthen the real coincidences. For it was in Zalaegerszeg ghetto that he saw his father for the last time, in spring 1944. Simply, Kiš wants Bloom to have his roots there, and he conflates the two Blooms for the same reason.

Or he is dropping a refined clue that this *document* is not what it seems to be.

Our uncertainty about his motives is a sure sign we are in the "*presence of culture*", amid the liberating uncertainty of literature.

---

8 Kiš would have found more than coincidence in Joyce's decision to locate Bloom's Hungarian roots in a town that—as a local survivor recalled—"according to Jewish encyclopaedias, was notorious as the most anti-Semitic in the country."

by the grace

Kiš's second metaphor links to something essential.
        Beyond the fancy bow to Joyce lies the theological concept of grace, resting on the idea of a divine favour or mercy that can be sought but never with certainty of success. No believer himself (see chapter 26), Kiš borrowed the language of belief to convey the impossibility of accounting for the miracle of art. With this meaning in play, we catch the idolatrous hint that Joyce's creative powers were virtually divine. For he had metamorphosed perishable Virág into perennial Bloom.

This hint implies something more: nothing outside an artwork can guarantee its value. Writers may be inspired by the best models, study their craft assiduously, and be moved by the finest intentions; yet this is all unavailing if their work does not convince us. Otherwise, Virág stays trapped in the bud. For writing, as Kiš proposed in his *Anatomy Lesson*, is "an alchemical process",

> a transmutation, and the ideal metaphor and even a possible definition of the creative act involved might well be the one applied to alchemy itself: "Alchemy is the *art of transmuting* metal for the purpose of procuring gold." . . . The very process of writing, much like the processes of alchemy, is both mystery and mystification: everything develops in the creator's secret laboratory, that alchemist's workshop where the guild's magic formulas are not merely preserved (*salve et coagula*: purify and integrate) but enriched with personal discovery, the secret beyond secrets. For the ultimate goal is a spiritual transformation, a way to reach the absolute, and that is the domain of the esoteric. "He who fails to obtain gold," says Liu Hsiang, "fails for lack of spiritual preparation."
>
> Even when a writer parades the "secrets" of his workshop, his authorial confessions, that, too, is part of the mystification process: for they are a bogus recipe lacking a single, essential ingredient, the one he believes will turn metal or stone into gold, the one that makes him burn with excitement in his solitude.

Authors can bestow form on their work, while the grace of form may be only invoked, not compelled to attend, unless by genius on a Joycean scale. Trying to pin down this elusive quality of "self-immanence", his favourite definition was "the grace   **27** of form", a phrase Kiš used again and again to account for the unaccountable, unbiddable power that converts inert text into literature to create a living communion of writer and reader. "If a story attains the grace of form," he wrote, "it ceases to convey explicit ideas of whatever kind, it is neither news nor the bearer of news, whether false or true (stories aren't newspapers). For a story is one of the possible perspectives on and feelings about the world, and this possibility . . . is creative freedom in its most elementary form." Commenting for the umpteenth time on the enigmas of his novel *Hourglass*, Kiš called it "a polyphonic whole" which, "like any novel that has attained the grace of form", outgrows its formal and technical features and "stands before us as a sovereign work". And it is not only fiction that needs this benediction. "Any biography, especially a biography of a writer," Kiš warned a journalist, "is sheer reductionism if it has not experienced the grace of form."

The phrase occurs in his fiction from the start. In an early story, "Shoes", the narrator "dreams of Paris and of the books that I'll write, in which all my past and present will experience the grace of form." Near the end of his first novel, *The Garret*, the nameless narrator examines a list of the other tenants in his building. By the flickering light of a match, he peers at the names of "the crowd of characters who are awaiting the grace of form". The disciple in "The Story of the Master and the Disciple", a late story, fears—all too rightly—that his manuscript may have "failed to attain the grace of form".

In this sense, Kiš's little metaphor drills through the crust of secularism into the reservoirs of Christian tradition, accumulated over centuries of faith. Like so much modern art, Kiš's work borrowed more from that tradition than it could repay. Unlike many artists who drew freely on the religious myth-kitty, however, he acknowledged the debt and suffered from it.

Although he lost any religious belief—or belief in such belief—as a teenager, after his mother's death, he did not become an atheist. Lack of belief left a faith-shaped hole that literature could delineate but not fill. He shared the traditional believer's sense of dependence on supernatural powers, but without a believer's scope for appeal to those powers, let alone any faith in their dispensation of justice. Epicurean comforts—women, wine, tobacco, and song—eased the pain or tedium of divine absenteeism. Yet coincidence and serendipity were, perhaps, evidence of some nameless higher order, or simply of fate. This evidence could no more be summoned than could the grace of form itself. It, too, was neither random nor separable from creative work. One important coincidence impressed him while he worked on *A Tomb for Boris Davidovich*:

> Some time in February-March 1976, if I'm not wrong,[9] in my flat in the Rue de Carros in Bordeaux, in blessed solitude and leisure, I finished the story called "A Tomb for Boris Davidovich": an occasion to celebrate! The next day, or two days later, still at the pitch of creativity that poets call "inspired", a

---

9 He was wrong, as often when dates were involved: the year was 1975.

word that I find sacrilegious and would swap for the term concentration or joy of creation (and this is nothing other than the end of idiosyncrasies,[10] an ironic relationship with the world and art, and in the last analysis, with one-self), hence in this condition I go into a bookshop. . . . Around the shelves of books about magic and the occult, multiplying as they always do in deca-dent times, I come across a book about the Inquisition and discover on the contents page, randomly, the history of a certain Baruch and quickly realise that he is like a brother to Boris Davidovich. Like someone delaying the moment of bliss, intellectual or sensual, I put the book aside, pick out some other books as well, slowly, but feverishly in a way, radiantly in a way, before I've even grasped that my own story's sequel is hiding in this history, in the shadow of this pyre . . . I take the books home, read the history of Baruch and already know what I shall do with it and how . . . God's part in creativity! *La part de Dieu.*

———

The emergence of form begins, for Kiš, with the imagination's discovery (or projec-tion) of meaning in randomness or disorder. These are signal moments in his work. The narrator of *Early Sorrows* describes his mother's needlework like this: "when you blew on the downy surface of her angora knitting, to smooth it a little, you would see wondrous patterns like those on Oriental rugs". In *The Garret*, the narrator interprets damp spots in his sordid room: "The damp had covered the walls with wondrous designs of flora and fauna that only thrive and bloom in dreams. The birth of the world was depicted on the ceiling, emerging from rosy sleep and green reality". This scene recurs in *Garden, Ashes*: "The moisture on the ceiling has traced a giant who has become a good spirit, the guard-ian of our house: full-bearded like the Jewish prophets, holding the tablets in his right hand, and in his left, our lamp with the porcelain shield that looks like an upside-down spittoon—a simile that the flies took literally." It culminates in *Hourglass*, where E.S. remembers how his old house in Novi Sad collapsed moments after he exited with the family belongings:

As he followed the movers out of the house, what did E.S. turn to look at?
　The walls.
　What did he see on them?
　Squares of dust in the places formerly covered by family photographs, a re-production of the Mona Lisa cut out of a newspaper, and a colour lithograph . . .; little splotches of liquid on the ceiling suggesting an explosion of anti-aircraft shells; a grease spot on the wall where he had leaned his head while lying in bed;

---

10 By 'idiosyncrasies', he meant the clutter of personal fidgets and concerns from which literature releases us.

traces of green mildew; Chinese silhouettes in places where the plaster had fallen off; designs traced by damp.

What was he thinking about?

About the possibility of reading fate from blotches on the wall, something like a Rorschach test; the patient in his room or cell looks at the blotches on the wall and reads them in the presence of his doctors.

For example?

What do you see in that blotch? The ocean. And what else? A ship on the high seas . . . a toad . . . a black butterfly . . . a vagina . . . the gaping jaws of a dog . . . a vagina (I already said that).

Go on. What else do you see in that blotch, Mr E.S.?

A snapshot of my pelvis at the moment of conception.

Conception! What kind of conception?

Intellectual.

And what does your intellect conceive?

Death, sir.

With his mind running on this theme, E.S. fantasises that he would be recognised as "the founder of muromancy, the science of reading the blotches on walls", which he knew was not a science at all, rather "an obscure branch of magic". Any reader of *Hourglass* has to practise this kind of sorcery, inferring patterns among Kiš's fragments.

Linked to this is the motif of small, lit, inhabited spaces amid wastes. Noah's Ark is the paradigm (see chapter 18). In *Garden, Ashes*, after the father's disappearance, Andi listens to his mother's stories about Montenegro "in the pale glow of the oil lamp", as the rain lashes their hut. And consider the solitary nocturnal figures reading or writing by uncertain light, so that physical confinement contrasts with the infinite reach of language and imagination. In *The Garret*, Kiš evokes an ark-like space where the narrator writes by candlelight, amid cosmic darkness: "The room was like the hold of one of those little boats that rock on the open sea, lost in the dark night." A decade later, that little image seeded Kiš's vision of a cabin-like room where E.S. writes his letter: "The waves of night dash against the sides of the room-boat." In the god-like narration of *Hourglass*, the figure of E.S. emerges, bent over his letter by the light of his lamp, "the only bright spot in the vast darkness". Another decade on, and we are in the dungeon-like chamber that houses *The Encyclopaedia of the Dead*, where the nameless narrator reads her father's biography by lamplight. "The guard escorted me to an enormous door, which he unlocked, and then switched on a dim light and left me alone. I heard the key turn in the lock behind me."

———

Formlessness can hold the promise of form, as Darwin's warm little pond held the promise of life, or as the young Kiš's "awareness of the relativity of all national myths ripened in me spontaneously, like a fruit". But it may also hold a threat, portending fatal kinds of growth which will, unchecked, destroy all form.

Young Andi, in despair at rumours that his father had died a coward's death in Auschwitz, likens him to "a woman with an eternal false pregnancy like a huge tumour." There is a fascinated simile in the "Rubbish Dump" poem (see chapter 22): "Clusters of lilac that disintegrate magnificently / like a smoker's excised lung". In a 1973 interview, he described how he tried to surround words with enough space "so they can be afflicted by different misfortunes, morbid luxuriance, malignant tumours, which often spread beyond my own control." Reading Nabokov in 1983 led him, as he told a friend, to want "to kill this unnecessary, tongue-tied, political beast inside me, that devours me like an illness, like cancer, devouring in the first place its double—homo poeticus!" In his essay on Central Europe, shortly before his own fatal diagnosis, Kiš described anti-Semitism as having formed and grown "like a tumour" in the Habsburg Empire. In the last interview before that diagnosis, he rejected the idea that the novel was in terminal decline: on the contrary, he said, in a disturbingly inapt effort at reassurance, "it's multiplying, even becoming a kind of cancer, but there's no crisis."

Kiš's most memorable and terrible image of form destroyed by formlessness comes at the end of the title story, in *The Encyclopaedia of the Dead*. As if reversing his hopeful vision of "the birth of the world" in *The Garret*, he shows the narrator's uncanny dream-discovery that her father had foreknown the shape of the cancer that would kill him:

> I noticed a flower, one unusual flower, that I first took for a vignette or the schematic drawing of a plant preserved in the world of the dead as an example of extinct flora. The caption, however, indicated that it was the basic floral pattern in my father's drawings. My hands trembling, I began to copy it. More than anything it resembled a gigantic peeled and cloven orange, crisscrossed with fine red lines like capillaries. For a moment I was disappointed. I was familiar with all the drawings my father had done in his leisure time on walls, boards, bottles and boxes, and none was anything like this one. . . . And then, after copying the gigantic peeled orange into my notebook, I read the concluding paragraph and let out a scream. . . .
>
> Do you know what was in the last paragraph? That D.M. took up painting at the time the first symptoms of cancer appeared. And that therefore his obsession with floral patterns coincided with the progress of the disease.
>
> When I showed the drawing to Dr Petrović, he confirmed, with some surprise, that it looked exactly like the sarcoma in my father's intestine. And that the efflorescence had doubtless gone on for years.[11]

---

11 The British writer Gilbert Adair observed in the 1980s that "We are haunted by twin phantasmagorias, one internal, the other external: death by cancer and nuclear annihilation . . . their iconographies neatly overlapping in the coincidence of form between a malignant tumour and a nuclear cloud (the mushroom thus becomes the great cryptic motif of the Eighties). . . . All roads lead to cancer."

of Mr Joyce, eventually become
the famous Leopold Bloom.

No writer meant more to the young Kiš than Joyce, nor any book more than *Ulysses*. He read excerpts from *A Portrait of the Artist as a Young Man* as student, between 1954 and 1958, because it was a set text in his degree course at Belgrade University. Probably he read *Dubliners* when it appeared in translation in Belgrade in 1957, the same year that a translation of *Ulysses* was published in Zagreb.

We know that *Ulysses* mattered most because of three stories Kiš published in 1959. The first story, "Mr Poppy Takes a Walk", starts with the hero putting down his copy of *Ulysses* and setting off for the seaside "to recreate his spirits" and "resolve some doubts". Returning, he reports on his experiences. Fussy and chatty in the style of the Eumaeus episode, Mr Poppy decides against "a Joycean analysis of his (sub)conscious", preferring to describe facts rather than circumstances. Why so? Because a detailed description of even a moment of consciousness would lead to chaos. "The effort to integrate all the associations that occurred to my consciousness and my unconscious while my gaze was wandering around the seashore, from the sea to the clouds, to a bird, etc.—that would be such anarchy that I'm ready to give up in advance."

Even if all the associations could be registered, would the result be art? No, says Mr Poppy, groping towards an insight: "Art is above all the selection of associations, the audacity to destroy thoughts at source. No leniency, thank you." Only those associations should be admitted which are "functional" in the text. Without saying that *Ulysses* fell short of this standard, Mr Poppy warns that Joyce's experimentalism does not release writing from the duty to select—and hence, he implies, to compress and condense.

The argument now shifts to the scale and scope of literary endeavour. Universality—a proper ambition for art—is not achieved by "registering every atom of consciousness and unconsciousness". The secret lies in isolating the atom, or series of atoms, that has universal associations. For "the universal" may, he notes, consist of three apples on Cézanne's table.

Mr Poppy adds a twist: "If I didn't have anything to tell you that you hadn't noticed or felt for yourselves, I would not want to bother you." Kiš is on the cusp, here, of a defining conviction: avoiding the commonplace is a courtesy so important in the etiquette between writer and reader that it amounts to an ethical principle.

33

In the second story, "Mr Poppy Enjoys Himself", Kiš explores what he calls the "barely transparent darkness" of *Ulysses*, initially by attacking the same fictional traditions that Joyce himself had rejected. He complains about the "very boring consistency" of "so-called" realist writing, which has spent two centuries "stubbornly serving up events in the external world. The philistine filtering of facts. The filtering of philistine facts." There is, however, a world elsewhere: the "world within" that had been sketched by Freud, Jung, Bergson, and so forth. This world gives another view of reality, albeit—cautions Kiš—a view that is not immune to the flaw of "one-sidedness" that has made the realist conventions of writers like Galsworthy, with their "objective omniscience", so "depressing".

As if he is now ready to challenge Joyce, Kiš begins to interrogate the great book. "What does *Ulysses* have too much of?" he asks, imitating the master's catechistical format. The answer comes back:

Too much form.
> What else?
> Too much language. Too much subconscious, stream of consciousness, which can all be condensed into an effort of consciousness.
> What else is there too much of?
> Too much subtext. Too much sex. Too much text. Too many tests . . .

In short, too much of everything—and not enough compression or "destruction". He does not complain that Joyce's miraculous patterning of narrative "atoms" fails at any point. Simply, there is *too much*. With this caveat entered, Kiš resumes his praise. *Ulysses* is

> A parody of everything. Of the novel (without a novel), of Ulysses, of life, death, art, philosophy, metempsychosis, the process of writing, Daedalus, Dublin, Aryans, Jews, Irishmen, Englishmen, Consciousness, the Unconscious, sex, text, polyglottism, the Tower of Babel, earth, sea, mankind, womankind, the Church, me, you, him, us, them, a parody of Everything and Nothing. And then a parody of parodies. That's the whole point.

After musing whether Joyce had written the Divine Comedy for our time (but "wilder, less inhibited" than Dante's), Kiš ends with a stern axiom: "Parody is unavoidable and ineluctable if we are to subdue objectivity with the subjective caprices of language."

The last piece in the series is quite different. "Noah's Ark (from Mr Poppy's Notebook)" is inspired by Joyce rather than commenting on him; a blueprint design for a bridge across the gulf between nineteenth-century externality—the fiction of objective omniscience—and modern internality. Kiš turns the hackneyed metaphor of external and internal worlds, used in the second sketch, into an enigmatic narrative. This sketch—published in December 1959—reads like a gloss on Kiš's own first book, *The Garret*, which was written over the winter of 1959–1960. It also marked Kiš's discovery of the Old Testament myth of Noah, of *doubles* and the *uncanny*, all of which would—as motifs and mood—become fundamental to his purposes.[12]

The relish and wonder that Joyce's book stirred in Kiš are palpable in these texts. Nothing else ever drew this sort of response from him. Like T. S. Eliot before him, he was exhilarated to discover that *Ulysses* had "destroyed the whole of the Nineteenth Century". Fiction could never be the same again, because Joyce had upended the convention that fiction could be written and read as if its material—language—was a cipher, a glassy noiseless vehicle for something else—ideas, characters, history, sensations. In so doing, he had produced a novel that was a playbook for novel writing, an encyclopaedia of fictional craft, the reinvention of totality. And parody was a cardinal resource.

Ulysses crowned an intuition Kiš had already had: that the literary and the literal were in contradiction. By parody, he did not mean satirical commentary on the contemporary scene. He meant the use of style, convention, and situation in ways that recognise their usual purposes and meanings—what he called their "associative fields"—without inhabiting them. Alerted to their customary ways of swallowing fictional bait, readers come to see the received meanings and connotations as ingredients of a new meaning.

To take an example: the sunset in *Hourglass* refers to an actual sunset over the sea that E.S. had watched in Montenegro in August 1939, before the war. As a remembered event that haunts his mind, it signals the plangent yearning for lost happiness that is a cliché of sentimental poetry; it also prefigures the extinction of E.S. himself and the Jews of Central Europe (which is why his mind interrogates the image for premonitions); and finally, it forms a motif in the novel's structure. Parody shapes at least two of these functions.

This hyperconscious refinement of fiction's raw material gives Kiš's work its beguiling double echo, its reflexive intelligence, as if he were quoting even when he is not.[13] He told an interviewer that *Hourglass* could not have been written without the example of *Ulysses*. For him, Joyce was always a supreme artificer, a master of omnipotent narrative. This view, widespread in the 1950s, was sealed at the end of the decade by Richard Ellmann's monumental biography. Kiš did not keep abreast of the Joyce industry as it grew over his lifetime. We can be sure, however, that he would have disliked the attempts since the 1980s to read Joyce through the optic of one or another political identity; these would have struck him as reductive, clipping the artist's all-powerful wings.

Joyce was, he argued, the "final product" of the "age of doubt" in literature that had dawned with Gustave Flaubert and eventually produced Borges. Doubt led to searching,

---

12 See chapter 19, which includes a translation of "Noah's Ark (from Mr Poppy's Notebook)".
13 For Kiš, a late high modernist, parody was a mode of intelligence. Thirty years after the Mr Poppy stories, he remarked apropos Rabelais that the "only way to convey knowledge is in the form of parody." Not to *obtain* knowledge but to communicate it in literature. (And is not that axiomatic "only" a parody of critical certitude?)

which culminated in Joyce's quest "for absolute form". Reconciled to the loss of a universality that cannot be regained, but nostalgic for it nonetheless, these "decadent" writers try to assemble a "comprehensive vision of the world and humanity" with the only resources available—fragments of the vanished unity that were once found outside the text. This lost unity cannot be reproduced or mimetically described in literature; it has to be evoked by style, measured by a work's internal harmony and coherence, the balance and beauty of its sentences. Hence Flaubert's mighty struggle to purify his style, Joyce's iron grid of correspondences, and Borges's impossible objects, places, persons, and moments that encapsulate *all* objects, places, persons, and moments. Hence, too, Kiš's scrupulous structures and lyrical inventories.[14]

As the founder of this tradition, Flaubert was unable to break completely with "narrative omniscience and psychological portraiture, those most pernicious and persistent of literary conventions". It fell to Joyce to complete the liberation from realism. While he loved the intricacy of *Ulysses,* it is likely that Kiš also responded to its central simplicity—the story about love at the core of Joyce's labyrinth. He would also have been moved by Joyce's liberal ethical or political commitment, his loathing of what he called "the old pap of racial hatred". As a recent critic has said of Joyce, "no writer tried, with more success, to rid his fiction of the straightjacket of semitic racial oppositions which poisoned the language of the first half of the twentieth century".

Above all, Kiš would have taken heart from Joyce's success in turning a marginal Jewish Irishman, of obscure Central European extraction, into modern literature's one and only immortal Everyman. If Bloom—"a perverted Jew from some place in Hungary", as a fellow Dubliner witheringly calls him (maybe intending 'converted')—could be universal, might not something similar be done for "Eduard Kon", wayward, drunk, peering at the world through glistening lenses before he went up in smoke?

In 1963, Saul Bellow deprecated Joyce for turning away "from the individualism of the romantics and the humanists" towards an "everybody". This grand allegorising ambition was what Kiš admired. For him, Bloom was "the quintessence of the average": a phrase that he scribbled in his copy of Lukács's anti-Joycean broadside, *The Meaning of Contemporary Realism.* Thinking of his own ambitions, he did not want to endow his dead father with a bunch of partly remembered, largely imagined characteristics that would say more about sagging realist conventions than about a unique individual. Joyce, on the other hand, was fascinated by how we fantasise about our own lives as we are living them. When exactly do we do it, under which compulsions or temptations, and in whose terms? *Ulysses* showed Kiš that literature can grow out of attention to these transi-

---

14 Was Kiš aware of Hugh Kenner's study of Flaubert, Joyce, and Beckett, *The Stoic Comedians* (1962)? Kenner is eloquent about these writers' inventiveness in "courting a dead end but discovering how not to die." Kiš would fit this grouping, whose family traits include the expert imitation of clichés, "the comedy of the Inventory, the comedy of exhaustion", and ironic homage to encyclopaedic learning. Kenner's version of stoicism—defined as acceptance, "with neither panic nor indifference, that the field of possibilities available is large perhaps, or small perhaps, but closed"—seems a truer and better umbrella-concept than Kiš's "decadence".

tions and oscillations, between (outer) reality and (inner) fantasy. With Joyce's help, he could invent his father's consciousness.

Yet *Ulysses* was more to Kiš than a literary paragon. His veneration had a deeply personal foundation. Consider:

—Leopold Bloom is not only the most famous Jew in modern literature: his Jewish origins lie in south-western Hungary, very close to Eduard Kis's birthplace.

—Leopold's father Rudolf changes his surname to Bloom, as Eduard's surname was changed to Kis or Kiss.

—Leopold's identity is blurred much as Danilo's was. Both were Jewish on their fathers' side, Christian on their mothers'; both lived in non-Jewish milieus and were seen as Jewish by others even though they were not Jews by Orthodox definition. ("Is he a jew or a gentile or a holy Roman or a swaddler or what the hell is he?" asks one of Bloom's acquaintances. "What is this he is?" asks another. His identity is enigmatic even to himself; when he starts to write a message on the sand, he gets no farther than "I . . . AM.A.")

—Little Leopold is baptised as a Protestant, as Danilo was baptised in the Orthodox Church.

—Like Eduard Kis and Danilo Kiš, Leopold Bloom is married to a Gentile; like Danilo, his mother was also a Gentile.

—Danilo was Eduard's only son, as Leopold was Rudolf Bloom's "only born male substantial heir".

—Their sons saw Eduard and Rudolf, posthumously, as Wandering Jews. The six-year-old Leopold pored over a map of Europe, tracing his father's bachelor wanderings (Vienna, Budapest, Milan, Florence), as the adult Kiš traced his father's wanderings in his books.

—For agnostic Bloom as for gnostic Kiš, the loss of the father created the only *felt* ties to Judaism—ties of remorse in Bloom's case, and in Kiš's, of filial loyalty and a quest for origins. Bloom preserves his father's Haggadah and suicide note. Kiš kept the sheaf of documents that his father left behind.

—Kiš the author and only son searches for his late father. Bloom the father, whose only son died in infancy, searches for a living son—while young Stephen Daedalus suffers for lack of a father figure.

—Bloom is peripatetic around Dublin. In *Hourglass*, E.S. is peripatetic around Pannonia.

There were also some striking biographical resemblances between the two writers:

—Their fathers were boozy eccentrics with fine singing voices. They led their families from one home to another, each worse than the last, as their fortunes plummeted.

—Their mothers died of cancer when the sons were in early manhood.

—Both men refused their dying mothers' pleas: in Joyce's case to confess and take communion, in Kiš's case to disown his Jewishness (see chapter 14).

—They disliked literary talk, were superstitious, and drank to excess. Joyce "was abstemious during the day, and drank only at night", says his biographer. Kiš followed the same regime (see chapter 30).

—They chose voluntary exile in Paris, where Joyce found a unique "atmosphere of spiritual effort", while Kiš praised the "excitement, movement, arguments".

And literary parallels (where Joyce likely influenced Kiš or encouraged him):

—As an artist, Joyce was more fascinated by family bonds than by romantic or sexual ones.

—Both writers were determined to make it new and welcomed experimentation to avoid stimulating 'stock responses' in their readers.

—Joyce called *Ulysses* "a sort of encyclopædia". Kiš's literary "ideal" was "a work that, after the first time round, can be read as an encyclopædia".

—Joyce told Djuna Barnes that writers "should never write about the extraordinary. That is for the journalist." Kiš agreed that "people with 'something to say' should leave literature alone and write for the papers".

—George Bernard Shaw called *Ulysses* "the outcome of a passion for documentation". Kiš entirely shared this passion.

—Likewise, Joyce was obsessed with fidelity to fact, something equally true of Kiš (despite his avowed fear of "the weight of fact").

And cultural parallels:

—Joyce's difficult relationship with what he called "belated" Ireland, and Kiš's relationship with Yugoslavia. (Kiš was a follower of Krleža, who had warned in a famous pre-war essay that "The hands on our literary clock tower are stuck at the symbol of gloomy and ignoble belatedness.")

—Their strong cosmopolitan, anti-nationalist precepts. Joyce called Europe "his spiritual father"; Kiš spoke of "our European matrix". Joyce detested the nationalist "trolls" in Ireland. "When patriotism has laid hold of the writer", he said, he "has no care then to create anything according to the art of literature". Given his hostility to nationalism, Kiš must have relished the confrontation in *Ulysses* between the Citizen, Joyce's spokesman of ethnic identity, and Bloom, who speaks up for civic values:

> What is your nation if I may ask, says the citizen.
> Ireland, says Bloom. I was born here. Ireland.

—Linked with this was their respect for voluntary exile as a spiritual choice, an emblematic modern condition. Joyce told a reader "You have to be in exile to understand me." Kiš said that his move to Paris in 1979 was "a Joycean exile, a self-imposed exile".

Given all this, it seems surprising that Kiš often emphasised the *cost* of Joyce's peerless achievement. "We moderns all came not from under Joyce's overcoat, but out of Joyce's nightmare," he told an interviewer. "The modern European and American novel is really doing nothing but trying to turn Joyce's magnificent defeat into little individual victories. We all halt before Joyce's abyss of ambiguity and linguistic nightmare, craning cautiously over the chasm of dizzying possibilities that our Great Teacher plunged into!"[15]

Kiš's source for 'defeat' was Virginia Woolf, who had called *Ulysses* "a memorable catastrophe—immense in daring, terrific in disaster". Admiration wrestled with envy in her complex response to *Ulysses*, but she never called it a defeat. In some notes dating from the early 1980s, Kiš explained that by "defeat", he was "thinking of the impossibility of eradicating banality completely, because human life is woven from banality; when you score a literary victory (it's still Joyce I'm thinking of), you are still left with the banality of living as your certain defeat". By this despairing logic, Joyce was beaten by his failure to expunge all banality from his work (even the *Wake*?) and, ultimately, by his failure to die on publication day, in February 1922. More than Joyce, the focus of these grim remarks was his own predicament: living in Paris with no secure income, divorced, resentful at the trumped-up scandal over his book *A Tomb for Boris Davidovich*, unsure if he would ever write another.

In this self-scathing mood, he rubbed salt in his wounds, writing the brutal verb "eradicate" when transformation by irony and metaphor was the issue. For banality is not merely kitsch by another name. (Perhaps kitsch is banality unredeemed by form.) There was more wisdom in a remark by another Central European writer in voluntary Parisian exile, E. M. Cioran, that "no true art" can exist "without a strong dose of banality." At their best, Joyce and Kiš both knew this—and proved it in their fiction.

Even before he loaded the odds against himself, Kiš always wrestled with the conundrum: how to purge his work of commonplaces without losing the vital spark of readerly appeal? Silence was the only certain answer. Restlessness and distrust of fiction led eventually to frosty heights where the air was very thin, nearly fatal to story-telling as such.

---

15 On another occasion, he said: "Joyce's wonderful defeat was really nothing less than the first (and probably last) attempt to condense and express this conception of the novel as an all-encompassing unique genre into a single book: in this respect, *Ulysses* and *Finnegans Wake* mark the border between the classical and, in the broadest sense of the term, the modern novel."

{FIRST INTERLUDE}

The Garret and *Psalm 44 (1962)*

> I know not whether more is to be dreaded from streets filled with soldiers accustomed to plunder, or from garrets filled with scribblers accustomed to lie.
>
> —Samuel Johnson (1709–1784)

Kiš's essays and stories from the late 1950s show his veneration of the novel as a literary form—one that he meant to attempt when the time came. In November 1959, a few weeks after returning from Paris (see chapter 32), he started to write *The Garret*, reading it aloud to close friends, longhand page after page, halting to scribble changes, until the book was finished the following May. One of those friends, Boško Mijanović, felt Kiš's excitement at what he was doing and marvelled at the strange evocation of their shared student lives, complete with their vehement conversations, foul digs, life-changing encounters, and wild emotions.

The first lines express a new voice:

I listened as invisible trains wept in the night and shrivelled leaves gripped the frozen, hard ground with their nails. Packs of ravenous, bedraggled dogs came to meet us. They emerged from dark gateways and squeezed between narrow fence-posts. They shadowed us in great silent packs. Now and again they lifted their sad and sombre eyes to look at us.

None of Kiš's earlier stories sounds like this: like a writer letting images bud and grow, leading his pen. An aura of risk keeps the writing still fresh. Kiš is learning, in the act, how to write without the safety net of realism; seeking a fictional language for the encounter between imagination and experience. The narrative is episodic and baffling, lucid at sentence and paragraph levels, implying a story while denying an explanatory framework that would let a reader relax.

The dream-like opening segues to an anxious dialogue between the nameless narrator and his girlfriend or lover. He is so beset by brainy-naïve questions about the meaning of life and swamped by literary fantasies that he can hardly communicate with the woman, whom he calls Eurydice. He feels this failure keenly but cannot remedy it.

He and his room-mate *Jarac-Mudrijaš* (barely translatable as Billy Goat Wise-Guy) rent a room at the top of a building "on the outskirts of the city". They hope that being closer to the stars will aid their powers of thought: an ambition that is mocked by their cockroach-infested garret, "smelling of damp and urine". The date is, we learn, 1956. The place, we infer, is Belgrade. And the emergent satirical theme is the cultural myth of the poet in a garret, with his self-deceiving head in the clouds and his feet in squalor.

The narrator is essaying a novel about his predicament and quotes from the manuscript, which is called—of course—*The Garret*. Wanting to impress Eurydice, he warns her that he has to travel far away. He sends her letters of pastiche anthropology from somewhere called the Bay of Dolphins, teasing the realist novel's ambition to report on exotic societies.

Back home again, he learns that his room-mate is writing a novel about the other tenants in the building, including the concierge, who is thrilled at the prospect of becoming "the *prototype* of all concierges". The two men have an ongoing dialogue about novel-writing and life that is comic in a mannered way and at their own expense: revealing their fear of the experiences which they crave and despise. Kiš's *Garret* seems to merge with the narrator's homonymous work-in-progress. A dialogue with Eurydice turns into an extended quotation from Thomas Mann's *Magic Mountain*: the narrator filters love through his reading. He boasts of singing Eurydice into existence, but is nonplussed by her actual presence.

Then the friends decide to buy a tavern in a harbour town, so they can learn about life from their motley customers. "Everything that we had ever imagined became reality." When the two students quarrel bitterly, the narrator is forced to reckon with his own fantasies and idealism. In the middle of the night, he abandons his work-in-progress and walks downstairs to examine the list of tenants in the entrance hall. Lighting his way with a match, he peers at the list, framed behind grimy glass which reflects his face back at him or, rather, "the ghost of my face". It is an uncanny moment, authentic Kiš. "All at once I realised, not without revulsion, that it was precisely my face which had hidden the whole garret, the whole six-storey world, from me until now." The book ends with the narrator standing in the courtyard of the building in broad daylight, noting how the sun dries the damp walls; how the laundry sways on the lines strung between the upper floors; how a child cries "somewhere on the fourth floor"; how a woman leans out of an upper window, singing, in a thin blouse, so that her breasts swell into view. The narrator looks, turns, and walks away, and the book ends on this note of ambiguous reconciliation with the visible world.

Kiš said in 1965 that he wrote *The Garret* in despair over a love affair. "I started writing it in the form of the diary of a suicidal youth, annotating his consciousness so to speak with images and sounds that came to me in spasms." If he was to interrogate this mood, instead of merely expressing it like a romantic poet, he had to find an ironic perspective. So he turned his narrator into an archetype, what Isaiah Berlin called "the popular image of the artist in his garret, wild-eyed, wild-haired, poor, solitary, mocked-at, but independent, free, spiritually superior to his philistine tormentors".

In what may have been the key to the book's development, and even to his career, Kiš turned the writing of the book into a theme within it. The narrator's solipsism is perfectly reflected by his obsession with writing about the situation that traps him. Dubravka Ugrešić has suggested that *The Garret* was influenced by a brilliant early work of André Gide, *Paludes* (1895). Kiš owned a Serbo-Croatian translation, published when he was a student, and read it with pen in hand, underscoring the epigraphic sentence: "Before I explain my book to others, I am waiting for others to explain it to me." *Paludes* is about a writer's imagination working and reworking the incoming material of his life in real time. The narrative is formed of the narrator's dreams and conversations, often involving his vain affection for a woman, Angela, along with his efforts to write a book called (of course) *Paludes*. Excerpts from this work-in-progress are quoted. He has an alter-ego figure, Hubert, a practical man with practical employment and his feet on the ground, and who also likes or loves Angela. The structure lets readers enjoy the illusion that the book is being written before their eyes, so to speak: that writing and reading form a single act.

If Gide's book has a serious undercurrent, it is the narrator's craving for experience, fear of experience, and addiction to—and disgust with—imaginary experience. Decisiveness and practicality are somehow the enemies of his writing; what's required is a state of tentative and irresolute, melancholic but complacent yearning. Gide delivers a feathery satire on the writer-narrator's pretensions, his ambition to make his friends more interesting for the sake of his book, absurdly overrating the significance of what he does. The writer Edmund White has praised *Paludes* for foreshadowing, "in the lightest, most Parisian way, the twentieth-century preoccupation with intertextuality, books-within-books, perilously shifting levels of reality and the blurring between genres—between autobiography and fiction, for instance. . . . long before anyone else he explored the ambiguities of autofiction, one of the most fertile genres of our day."

Kiš never mentioned *Paludes* in connection with *The Garret*, but we know that Gide was on his mind in September 1959, when he praised his technical mastery. Instead, he encouraged readers to find something contemporary in the book's paranoid tone. He said it had a trippy feel, but without the drugs. This is true. Compare the first sentence of William Burroughs's *Naked Lunch* (1959): "I can feel the heat closing in, feel them out there making their moves, making their moves, setting up their devil doll stool pigeons. . . ." Or Samuel Beckett's *Malone Dies* (1956): "The sound I liked best had nothing noble about it. It was the barking of the dogs, at night, in the clusters of hovels up in the hills, where the stone-cutters lived. . . . The dogs of the valley replied with their gross bay all fangs and jaws and foam." Or *Lolita* (1955): "And sometimes trains would cry in the monstrously hot and humid night with heartrending and ominous plangency, mingling power and hysteria in one desperate scream."

Kiš typed up the book and sent it to Oskar Davičo (1909–1989), a Serbian writer of Jewish extraction who had belonged to Belgrade's pre-war surrealist movement. An unruly communist, Davičo was drawn into the circle around Miroslav Krleža, a leftist who opposed Stalinist cultural policies. He went on to join Tito's partisan army and became an influential figure in the postwar cultural scene, as well as a garlanded novelist and poet.

Davičo responded generously. *The Garret* was witty, lucid and fresh. Its shortcoming lay in the plot, which neither conveyed a real meaning nor achieved a conclusion. It lacked the conflict needed for dramatic tension. "You wear yourself out playing with one particular state of mind, which is more pubescent and student-ish than youthful." This state of mind should frame the story, not provide its substance. As for the satirical element: "at whom are you firing your darts?" (*At myself*, Kiš would have answered.) The hero runs away from every difficulty; his despair lacks any convincing cause. He is too immature to see the truth about himself and the world, or himself in the world.

Despite these misgivings, Davičo commended the book to a publisher as "the first book about our postwar generation" which was written not to flatter but to reveal. "It discovers a dimension of reality that we take little account of (and that little, incompetently)." When the book was published in autumn 1962, the reception was cool. One reviewer objected to the setting—a smelly garret instead of the gleaming new student halls of residence "in Belgrade, Zagreb, Ljubljana, Sarajevo"—and to the book's dearth of "optimism". Kiš never forgot these put-downs, but they did not dampen the thrill of publication. When Wladimir Krysinski met him in Strasbourg, in October 1962 (see chapter 31), Kiš revealed after only a few minutes that

> his new book *The Garret* was just published in Belgrade and he showed it to me. He was obviously proud of it and excited. I asked him to describe the form of his narration. I understood that *The Garret* was a satirical book which used a sort of ironic method. The author incarnates different roles in the narration and thus relativizes both literature and life, has an adventurous 'studentesque' existence and gives pretentious literary descriptions of passionate love. I grasped Danilo's intention in the following way: he was striving to show that everything is a false representation and that irony is both the tool and the target of his writing.

Kiš retained an affection for *The Garret*, rightly seeing it as his first authentic work. Approaching it by way of his best writing, recent critics have praised its "profoundly touching power and grace" (Milan M. Ćirković) and its "ironic dialogue with literary conventions and traditions", even claiming that it gave a fresh start to "Serbian prose" (Jasmina Ahmetagić). One patriotic critic states, grotesquely, that *The Garret* shows Kiš already working within the bounds of "national Serbian literature as determined by language, tradition and poetics". Two things, however, are undeniable: *The Garret* offered a first tentative outing for Kiš's methods and motifs, with charming glimpses of his later power. And if he had never published anything else, only scholars would read it today.

The Belgrade publisher who accepted *The Garret* asked if Kiš had anything more to bulk out the slim volume. With some misgiving, he offered a short novel that he had written in 1960. This was *Psalm 44*, his second apprenticeship, composed in a few weeks for a competition by the Jewish community. He won the prize, but had no illusions then or later about the novel's qualities, deploring its "fatal lack of ironic detachment" and excluding it from his selected works.

Inspired by a newspaper cutting, *Psalm 44* tells the story of a prisoner in Auschwitz who conceives and gives birth there, in 1944. The baby boy survives in secrecy. Marija, the mother, manages to escape with the baby. The father is Jakob, a Jewish doctor who works in the camp hospital; he also escapes. Six years later, the couple take their son Jan to visit the Auschwitz museum, where they meet Maks, a former kapo. Maks, their unseen saviour in the camp, is now a tour guide.

As historical fiction, *Psalm 44* is implausible and oddly disengaged. The inmates are inexplicably healthy and sleep on sheets. "Dr. Nietzsche", a Mengele figure, tells Jakob that the Germans planned "genocide" against the Jews—an unthinkable usage at that time, in that place. The book is rife with clotted sentences and random tonal breaks. A lecture by Marija's father against racial hatred is dropped raw into the story. (The father, called Eduard, is a drinker and a wayward, cross-grained fellow.) The literary allusions feel inappropriate ("as Horace declared of old"). Marija's flashback to the killing in Novi Sad in 1942 is an experiment, never repeated, in the graphic narration of extreme violence: murder, rape, dismemberment. The writing finds its voice when Kiš gives rein to his fascination with the flicker of consciousness, patterning sensation and memory, catching the compacted vividness of remembered time as a painter renders the play of light. There is a fine account of Marija's meandering thoughts, hiding in a cupboard while Jakob speaks with Dr. Nietzsche. (As so often, confinement was Kiš's muse.)

Psalm 44 is a fictional meditation on survival, anti-Semitism, dissimilarity, hope and resignation, and—finally—on Kiš's connection and commitment to the

Holocaust. When Marija and Jakob take the six-year-old Jan to visit Auschwitz, Marija feels apprehensive but also proud; for "she was proud of this mission: to communicate to Jan the joy of those who could create life out of death and love. To grant him the bitter joy of suffering that he had not felt and never would feel on his own skin, but that had to be present in him as a warning, as joy—as a cenotaph."

Ignorant of his mother's intentions, the boy wanders around the dreadful exhibits without understanding: "Jan looks at the heap of incomprehensible, fantastical objects and does not dare to ask anything at all." But it is his destiny to relate his parents' experience to the postwar world, and he makes a start in the museum, asking Marija if the spectacles in the pile of twisted, rusty frames and broken lenses are "the same" as the ones that another visitor is wearing. She nods.

By writing *Psalm 44*, Kiš learned the invaluable lesson that his ideal of delicate, reflexive craftsmanship was incompatible with megaphonic words like Auschwitz, genocide, or FÜR JUDEN VERBOTEN, and with stenographic descriptions of obscene brutality, cornering a reader with implicit—and spurious—claims to authentic testimony ("he sliced her mouth open with two strokes all the way to her ears and pounded on her gold molars with his rifle butt"). Perhaps the circumstance of the competition gave Kiš a licence to explore Jewish themes directly. If so, the licence turned out to authorise a subtle subordination of literature, one that did not tempt him again. In future, he would acknowledge history's careless power without compromising the sovereignty of art.

I believe it was the liberal policy of Franz Josef II

The status of Jews in Hungary improved during Franz Josef's long reign as Habsburg emperor (1848–1916).[16] A few months before the abdication of his predecessor, Ferdinand I, the parliament passed an act of partial emancipation that removed residential restrictions. This acknowledged the strong Jewish support for the 1848 revolution against Austrian rule. In a pattern that was to repeat over the following century, however, the Jews' proven loyalty to the Hungarian state had not impressed local anti-Semites, who used the revolution as cover for pogroms.

After Franz Josef crushed the Hungarian rebels in 1849, Jews who had supported the Magyar cause were treated harshly. Nevertheless, Jewish schools multiplied from some 50 to 250 over the next decade. From 1860, these schools provided lessons in the Hungarian language, bolstering the acculturation and assimilation of a generation whose parents had mostly used German, the lingua franca of Central Europe since the Enlightenment, or its vernacular cousin, Yiddish.

After Hungary gained autonomy under the Habsburg dynasty in 1867, the parliament granted unconditional equality to all the "Israelite inhabitants of the country" (rather than only to those born there). Sweeping away all legal discrimination based on religion, this was boldly progressive.[17] It drove a wedge between Jewish secularists and conservatives, intensifying a rivalry that the conservatives roundly lost. In 1895, civil marriage was introduced, and Judaism gained the status of a recognised religion, on a par with the Christian denominations.

Compared with the only other compact community of Habsburg Jews, in Galicia (modern-day Poland), Hungarian Jews were more urban, secular, educated, and open. Orthodoxy was confined to the eastern part of the country. In the centre and west, Jewish lay leaders opted for Reform Judaism, seeing the Jews' best prospects in a liberal Magyar

---

16 Born in 1830, he became Emperor Franz Josef I of Austria. By calling him Franz Josef II, Kiš—whose pains over style and emotional truth contrast with carelessness over impersonal facts—confused him with his modernising ancestor, Josef II (1765–1790), or perhaps with Franz II (1768–1835), the last holy Roman emperor (1792–1806), who became Franz I, emperor of Austria (1804–1835).

17 Unlike in Austria, however, people could not declare themselves as having no religion (*konfessionslos*). Somebody born as a Jew who did not want to remain part of the Jewish community was obliged to convert to Christianity. It was another reminder of the limits of secularism and civic politics.

state. Jewish life in the cities prospered: the communities straddled most classes of society and economic sectors, with newspapers, music societies, and youth organisations. Life for Jewish families like the Kohns, who were scattered in rural areas—usually the ratio was one family per village—lacked such amenities, but they were not barred from advancement.

In the 1880s and 1890s, Budapest grew at rates unmatched by other European capitals. Seizing the new opportunities in business and industry, Jews boosted Hungarian modernisation, perhaps decisively. Their flourishing was reflected in the demographic boom. By 1910, Hungary had the third largest Jewish community in the world: 910,000, which was double the total in 1868. They formed 5 per cent of the population, concentrated in urban areas (23 per cent in Budapest), where they dominated in the law, medicine, journalism, trade, and finance. This was the golden age for Hungarian Jews.

Inevitably, where liberal nationalism was the engine of modernisation and the route to freedom and progress lay through assimilation, many Jews discovered Hungarian nationalism. The better educated they were, the more prone they were to share the euphoria of awakening Magyar identity. In the course of a few decades, a historian writes, "hundreds of thousands of Jews" had turned into "passionate Magyar patriots". By 1908, the leading British commentator on Central Europe, Seton Watson, could claim that the Jews and the Catholic Church formed the "two chief bulwarks of Magyar chauvinism."

Yet the ethnic offspring of the ancient race were more likely to see their Jewish compatriots as obstacles to the realisation of national goals than as allies. For the identity of the ethnic nation, and hence of the state, remained indelibly Christian. The unprecedented advances since 1848 duly produced their reaction. At best, the outcome was a profound ambivalence. In its liberal variant, this was expressed by Hungary's great statesman of the mid-century, Count István Széchenyi (1791–1860), who worried that the Jews, possessing "more intelligence and more industriousness" than the Magyars, would accelerate the development of the nation at the cost of corrupting its purity and integrity.

The worse outcome was political anti-Semitism, which emerged in the 1870s and gained ground in the 1880s, encouraged by the Russian pogroms of 1881. Jewish prosperity threatened non-Jews, Jews harboured separatist ambitions, Jews were rootless cosmopolitans with no real loyalty to Hungary: these allegations circulated and would intensify after the First World War. Reactionaries saw the Jews as a force behind the rise of liberal ideas and rampant capitalism, destroying Hungary's immemorial aristocratic, semi-feudal order. A local definition of anti-Semitism became well known: "The anti-Semite is a man who detests Jews more than is reasonable."

A "Christian awakening", proclaimed around 1900, gained significant support. Nevertheless, Jews were benignly treated. Whether this attitude veiled envy or contempt was something into which the Jews themselves did not much care to inquire, though wise Theodor Herzl, born in Budapest in 1860, saw the truth: that the Jews remained alien *even* in Hungary.

This story of successful assimilation, fringed with dislike and shadowed by unease, ended with Hungary's disastrous defeat in 1918, two years after the death of the aged emperor. Jewish prominence in the short-lived Hungarian Soviet Republic (March to August 1919) fanned the flames of anti-Semitism. Yet the dream persisted, even after several thousand Jews were murdered during the reactionary White Terror (1919–1920). Joseph Roth noted in the mid-1920s that most Hungarian Jews were still Magyar nationalists, even under the Miklós Horthy regime.

together with a desire for integration that led
my grandfather to Magyarise the surname of his
underage son.

Magyarisation of Jewish surnames was commonplace among Hungarian Jews in
the late nineteenth and early twentieth centuries. The Ministry of Internal Affairs set the rules. Sometimes the alterations preserved the literal meaning of
the original name; Klein (Small) became Kiss or Kis, and Kopf (Head) became Fejes.
Or they adapted the name of the place where they lived. Usually the new name began
with the same letter as the original. Owners of the very widespread name Kohn are recorded as having changed it to Kürti (i.e. from Kürt), Kalmár, Kálmán, Komlós (from
Komló), Kelemen, and Todor, as well as to Kis or Kiss.

A scholar's recent judgement that the taking of non-Jewish names, common
throughout Central Europe in that era, was "a disguised but none the less telling example
of Jewish self-hatred" is less historical than political, and heartless to boot. Most Hungarian Jews wanted to assimilate. Nothing Kiš wrote or said about his grandparents or
his father, born in the high noon of Hungarian Jewry, indicated that they felt otherwise.
Living in the isolation of Kerkabarabás, they may have felt less bound by the ties of communal Jewish identity than Jews who lived in towns and cities.

Eduard's father, Miksa Kohn, obtained permission from the ministry to change the
boy's surname to the common Magyar Kiss or Kis in 1902: presumably to smooth his
path in Hungarian society. The same was done for Eduard's brother Adolf, but not for
their sisters, who would have been expected to marry and take their husbands' names.
Whether Eduard was "underage" is not so clear. In traditional Jewish law, the age of majority is thirteen. Miksa applied for the change of surname in August 1902, a month after
the boy's thirteenth birthday. Approval came from the ministry the following month.

Eduard Sam and E.S., in Kiš's books, were not and could not be Eduard Kis. "A proper
name is an extremely important thing in a novel, a *capital thing*," Flaubert had advised a correspondent. "You can no more change a character's name than you can change his skin. It
would be like trying to turn a negro white." Life, of course, is another matter: people change
their names all the time. But are their old names effaced beyond the reach of ministries to
hunt them down? Hungarian Eduard Kis could not escape from Jewish Eduard Kon.

A passage in *Hourglass* can be read as a savage satire on the dream of assimilation. It
occurs during E.S.'s "nightmarish memory" of being chased by a pack of slavering dogs
that have scented the butcher's meat in his briefcase. **51**

How did man and dogs perceive one another?

They by smell, hearing, and sight; he by hearing alone.

What thought did fear inspire in him?

The thought not only of possible mimicry but also of identification; that, by changing the prescription of his glasses, he could become a dog.

What did his well-known instinct for promotion make him think of?

It is within your power to become at will a dog, cat, a horse, or a bird. By E.S.-brand magic glasses. You will be able to see the world through the eyes of the animal of your choice.

What advertisement did he mentally formulate?

Would you like to see your faithful watchdog or your pet cat as they see you, through their eyes? Would you like to go hunting with the eyes of a dog? Or see the public at the races through the eyes of a horse? Become a horse, a dog or a cat for only ten pengő. The wings of a bird you cannot buy, but you can see the world through an eagle's eye, thanks to the most recent optical, psychological, biological, ophthalmological research. E.S. Optics supplies illustrated catalogues free of charge.

Many details of the family chronicle will, though, remain forever obscure: in 1944 my father and all our relatives were taken away to Auschwitz, whence almost none returned.

By early 1944, Hungary was an increasingly restive member of the Axis. Hitler was determined to keep the Hungarians in the war and enraged by what he called their failure "to settle the Jewish question". On 19 March, two German divisions marched into Hungary. It was, a survivor would recall, "a lovely Sunday morning in Budapest".

At this point, although some 60,000 Hungarian Jews had already been killed for various reasons, 760,000 were still alive—including a hundred thousand converts to Christianity—and able to exist in conditions that were not unrecognisably abnormal. The Hungarian regent, Admiral Horthy, agreed to let Heinrich Himmler's SS take 100,000 Jews for forced labour, or what the German Foreign Ministry termed "relocation in the eastern territories". By this point, a historian writes, the Hungarian leaders "had absolute proof about the realities" of Nazi death camps, so they knew what these terms meant. "Yet they failed either to inform the Jewish masses or to enlighten the Christian population about the impending fate of the deportees."

The Nazis were determined to exterminate the Hungarian Jews. Preparations for a huge influx had begun at Auschwitz months before the occupation. The officer entrusted with overseeing the Final Solution in Hungary was SS Colonel Adolf Eichmann, who would be captured by Israeli agents in Buenos Aires in 1960. At his trial in Jerusalem, Eichmann explained that his orders had been to "ship all Jews out of the country in as short a time as possible." For Himmler had made it clear "that he wanted Hungary combed with a tremendous thoroughness before the Jews there could really wake up to our plans and organise partisan resistance." Eichmann recalled that everything went according to plan, without hindrance: "like a dream", as he repeatedly told the chamber.

Another factor behind Eichmann's success was the quality of local support. According to the Holocaust Museum in Budapest, "the entire state apparatus of wartime Hungary, save the army—that is, from cabinet ministers down to the lowliest clerk of the smallest village—was actively engaged in organising the despoliation and expulsion of Jews." When he learned of its scale, Winston Churchill called the liquidation of Hungary's Jews "probably the greatest and most horrible crime ever committed in the history of the world."

Until March 1944, the Jews were more secure in Hungary than in any other Axis-controlled country. They had not been ghettoised or forced to wear the yellow star. According to survivors such as Trude Levi, from Szombathely, the Jews had heard stories of German savagery in other countries without quite believing them. Besides, "March 1944 was almost the end of the war—or so we thought. In 1941 and 1942 we had expected Hungary to be occupied by the Germans, but not in 1944." For their part, the Jewish authorities urged "strict and conscientious" compliance. The Budapest Jewish Council, appointed by the Nazis, stated that "all the instructions, orders, decisions and decrees . . . will have to be carried out exactly and without any complaint or grumbling." Organised resistance was on a very small scale. Jewish compliance owed much to the fact that, hitherto, the Hungarian authorities had rejected Nazi pressure to hand over the Jews.

The yellow star became compulsory on 5 April. Stars had to be 10 centimetres in diameter, canary yellow, and sewn above the heart. The country was divided into half a dozen districts, "matching the regional organisation of the gendarmerie", Hungary's military police. The Jews were rounded up and concentrated in ghettos around the country. Deportations began on 15 May and continued for almost two months, until Horthy—"deluged with protests from neutral countries and from the Vatican", as well as being pressured by Franklin Roosevelt and Allied air raids on Budapest—called a halt. By 7 July, 437,000 Jews had been deported to Auschwitz. The provinces were now effectively *judenrein*, leaving some 230,000 Jews in Budapest, "in daily terror of their lives", as one of them, Ernő Szép, recalled.

Some Jews took solace in fantasies of salvation: the Soviet army would sweep in from the east, the SS and the Wehrmacht would turn on each other, Germany would collapse, last-minute conversion might still avert the worst. . . . When Kiš wrote about his father's fictional double, E.S., in *Hourglass*, it was important to his conception of E.S.'s liberating lucidity that he was not deceived by these fantasies; that, even in April 1942, his mind did not flinch from foreseeing what would happen:

> . . . even if you don't believe in visions, you could at least believe in the plain (positivistic) facts you find in the newspapers. These facts and these newspapers make it clear that our goose is cooked and that before the Allies can lift a finger the Horsemen of the Apocalypse will be upon us—unless we perish first. Of hunger, despair, fear. Maybe you'll ask me what these famous Horsemen of the Apocalypse of mine, these monstrous figments of my maddened brain, look like. . . . they will be four handsome gendarmes on white horses, armed with rifles and bayonets, handsome moustachioed provincial gendarmes on horseback, with cockerel's feathers stuck in their black hats. Maybe there won't be four of them, as in a deck of cards, but only two. And maybe their horses won't be white. Maybe they won't even come on horseback but on shiny bicycles, or on foot for that matter. But come they will, of that you can be sure. Already they are twirling their moustaches and fixing shiny bayonets on their rifles. I hear the neighing of their horses and I hear the feathers snap and flutter on their black hats.

The gendarmes in Zala county, where Kerkabarabás was located, were especially zealous: 84 per cent of the Jews from Zala died during the war.[18] Only five of Hungary's twenty-five provincial counties suffered worse rates of destruction. It was probably late April or early May when Eduard Kis was taken to the improvised ghetto in Zalaegerszeg, where the guards were reckoned to be especially brutal, in Gendarmerie District III. By early July, the ghetto held 3,209 Jews, most from rural communities. Deportation was carried out on 5 July, only two days before transports were suspended. At least fifteen members of Kiš's family died in Auschwitz, including five of Eduard's six siblings.

In *Garden, Ashes*, Kiš imagined a memory of accompanying his mother to visit his father, deluded and remote in his "small single room in the depths of the ghetto":

> It was a hot summer's day. My father was in shirtsleeves. He kept fiddling with his trouser braces, which always slipped off when he was not wearing a coat.
>
> "I was called to the Office today," he said gleefully, rubbing his hands together. "They put a cross against my name. Schmutz told me. He knows people in the Office."
>
> I hardly recognised him. As he had been wholly and irrevocably liquidated at home, and his smell had completely evaporated over the past fortnight, there could not be the least trace of doubt about the finality of his absence, and I gazed at my own father in disbelief, as if he were someone who could only interest us outside the circle of our most private concerns. There is no question that he realised this himself. This is why he was no longer performing for us, no longer demonstrating his power over the phenomena of life, parading his erudition or raising his voice in prophetic exaltation. For he was bitterly aware of the finality of his removal and the fact that, consequently, we were paying a visit as though he were some acquaintance to whom all has been forgiven, or as one visits the cemetery, once a year, on All Saints' Day.

What Kiš would not do, as a writer, was to follow his relatives into the death camps. In his television play *Night and Fog*, a character says "In Auschwitz, we. . .", then—says the stage direction—"his voice fades away, he disappears into the rain." Indeed, he would not even follow E.S. to the bank of the Danube in January 1942, where he almost died during the Novi Sad massacre. In chapter 53 of *Hourglass*, when E.S. recalls that episode, Kiš leaves a line blank, with a footnote: "Incomplete. A page is missing."

(The sole exception is a terrible, hallucinatory passage in *Early Sorrows*, where Andi Sam fears that one of his aunts who survived Auschwitz wants him to know how shamefully his father met his end, moaning and collapsing beneath the guards' blows, "weeping like a child" as the women around him bore him up, amid the stench of "his treacherous bowels".)

---

18 Eduard's chances of surviving in Vojvodina—had he remained in Novi Sad—would have been no better: for the eventual "loss of Jews from the Hungarian-annexed areas was . . . close to 85 per cent of the total."

Kiš's discretion was ethical as well as an aesthetic choice. For the purpose of contrast, consider another, incomparably more famous and esteemed modernist who specialised in images of suffering humanity. In 1965, Francis Bacon "painted a triptych entitled *Crucifixion* that included a figure with a red armband bearing a swastika". When quizzed about this explosive reference, the artist shrugged; the armband was a purely formal motif "to break the continuity of the arm", in his disingenuous words.[19]

Another reason for Kiš's restraint emerges from his only published comments on art and the Holocaust. When Alain Resnais's documentary film about the death camps, *Night and Fog* (1955), was shown in Belgrade in 1960, Kiš reviewed it for a student newspaper. Appalled by the amnesia that already concealed the worst horrors of the Second World War, mantling it "like grass", Resnais was—Kiš said—determined to expose the "crime of forgetting". His "apocalyptic" film constructed a vision in which everyone was a killer or a corpse, accused or victim.

The price of this "ruthlessness" was, however, unacceptably high. For Resnais's montage technique, using Allied archive film, was impressive in a horrifying way: it succeeded in "reanimating corpses". Kiš wondered whether any artist had the right to deprive us of "the mercy of forgetfulness". Do we not have the right to expect catharsis from art? Obsessed by his mission, Resnais had failed to provide this "essential" relief and so violated our "right to oblivion". Kiš's critique reflected a survivor's need to escape the burden of his own memories (and to justify that need). Yet it was more than this. He was staking out the bounds between art and history, protecting the sovereignty of one against the other's seductive and bullying righteousness.

---

19 The Anglo-Hungarian poet George Szirtes (b. 1948) held his mother's experience of a concentration camp in the same respect. "When I was writing my own long poem *Metro,*" Szirtes has said, "I took my mother to the gates of Ravensbrück, but did not follow her in. There were places I did not feel entitled to go."

Among my ancestors on my mother's side is a legendary Montenegrin hero who learned to read and write at the age of fifty, adding the glory of the pen to the glory of his sword, as well as an 'Amazon' who took revenge on a Turkish brute by cutting off his head.

After Hungarian Jews being "taken away to Auschwitz", we have Montenegrins fighting for glory and revenge. Kiš habitually thought about his parents in antithetical terms. His mother was Milica Dragićević, born near Podgorica in 1903. She had two sisters, Draginja and Milosava, and two brothers, Luka and Risto. Their parents were Jakov Dragićević and Borika Brajović.

The 'Amazon' was Marica, the aunt of Kiš's maternal grandfather, Jakov. At Grahovac, in April 1858, she slew a pasha who had killed her brother in a previous battle. After the Ottoman forces were routed, Marica cut off the pasha's head and offered it to Prince Danilo Petrović, her sovereign, along with the dead man's horse, sword, and belt, embellished with gold. Danilo accepted these tributes and had a silver belt fashioned for Marica as a prize.

The other ancestor was Marko Miljanov. (Jakov's father, Bajo, had married Marko's niece—his brother's daughter.) Born in 1833 to a Montenegrin father and an Albanian mother, in a remote part of the country that he called "a crucified wilderness", young Marko joined the service of Prince Danilo in the 1850s, when the population of Montenegro numbered only some 80,000. He soon proved his worth. A famous victory over the Turks at the battle of Fundina, in 1876, sealed his reputation as the greatest warrior of his age.

Noble, fearless, but also judicious, Marko was the epitome of heroic virtue. In all, he slew more than eighty "Turks", meaning Slavic Montenegrins whose ancestors had converted to Islam under Ottoman pressure. Like the Spartans of old, Marko took feminine care over the combing of his long hair. He had a gift for sententious eloquence ("The hero leads the wise man's horse"). He once described Montenegro as being so small that not even a dead man had room to stretch out his legs.

When Danilo's successor, Prince Nikola, intrigued against him in 1882, Marko resigned from the senate and left the miniature capital of Cetinje, which at the time "had no more than 100 single-storey stone houses". In his clan fastness, he taught himself to read and write. According to Kiš, Marko's "handwriting was square and firm, and because he used neither paragraphs nor punctuation his manuscripts looks like clay tablets." While Nikola modernised his destitute country, granting concessions to foreign traders, reorganising the army, and marrying off his daughters to Serbian, Russian, and Italian 57 royalty, Marko kept a distance. Portraits in his old age show a handsome brow over eagle eyes, shaggy grey moustaches, and an embroidered waistcoat stacked with medals. He lived until 1901: long enough to become the last link to the golden age of Montenegrin valour. In a testamentary letter, he urged his countrymen to do as much for others as conditions allowed. Mountaineers and peasants may not have much to give, but everyone can do right by his conscience. "Generosity is shown in small as in great things. By carrying out little acts of kindness, the large acts will be done when they may be done."

In retirement, the old solder wanted to preserve the deeds of dead heroes in a casebook of ethical ideals, homilies for the benefit of his people. "The flame of truth demands to be remembered but nobody sees it," Marko explained. "Whence my sense of indebtedness to these heroes whom I knew personally or heard speak of. . . . Judge for yourself, my brother, if it is just to forget the acts of true heroes" when "the pen has ventured into hell itself and the nimble intelligence creates novels and what does not exist. . .". *Examples of Humanity and Heroism* (1901) can still be found on the shelves of houses with few if any other books. Miljanov's style is not at all literary: rough, colloquial, homespun. The *Examples* focus on ethical choices and decisions. They reflect the Montenegrin cult of liberty, revenge, and steadfastness in the struggle against Ottoman power. They champion generosity towards the weak, truthfulness with the enemy, and utter commitment to one's word as one's bond—the currency of honour. Dvorniković (see chapter 13) called him the Plutarch of Montenegrin patriarchalism.

The characters in the *Examples* are real people: Tomo Petrov Popović from Medun; Adži and Šaban Mujo, two brothers from Fundina (both Muslim names: Marko had no prejudice in favour of Eastern Orthodox Christians); Risto Božanin of the Vasojević clan; and so forth. Apart from the occasional laconic judgement or opinion, these men do not discuss ethical principles; they act them out. Many of the stories turn on the complex obligations created by the spoken word. In one episode, Osman tells his friend Alija that, owing to a feud, he has been hiding from a certain family for two weeks. "If I don't go out tomorrow," he says, "my honour will be lost beyond recovery." Very well, says his friend, I will be there with you when you go out tomorrow; "we shall die together." By sharing his difficulty with Alija, Osman has obliged him to help; whether he asks for help is irrelevant. Alija's heroism is revealed by his unhesitating acceptance of this moral law. Honour makes a demand which is unconditional, regardless of the cost.

One of the few foreigners to meet Marko was Josef Holeček, a Czech journalist who was fascinated by Montenegro. Marko asked the Czech how people lived in Europe: were they free, did they bear arms, how did they dress, what sort of schools did they go to, were their women attractive, how were they governed? He was baffled and appalled by the power of money in the society that Holeček described and expressed pity for people who had to live their lives wrestling with this force that could not be subdued. At one point, he roused himself from melancholy thoughts on this subject with a promise to his "Czech brother" that "We will come and liberate you."

During one of their conversations, Marko avowed that, "For me, my morality is the supreme law. I consider that I am allowed to do whatever my morality does not forbid." The journalist retorted glibly, "Well, your conscience won't keep you out of prison, but a good lawyer can get you out." Marko had to ask "What's a lawyer?" and was shocked to hear that men were richly rewarded to defend people of whose guilt there was no doubt. "What a wretched way of living," he exclaimed, "a calling worthy of all contempt! If I had been born in your land, I would do everything in my power to expose those blackguards, to compel them to choose a worthier and more honest way of living. I would travel from village to village, urging people to live as brothers, to resolve their differences by common agreement and not to pay a penny to any man who treats the law like trading horses." When Holeček ventured that even Marko Miljanov would pay up to save himself from prison, let alone the rope, Marko was fierce in rebuttal: "Never, on my life! If I am guilty, then I'm ready to pay the price, whatever it may be. Anyone who shirks responsibility for his actions is not a man." After this exchange, Marko felt unaccountably saddened and— so he said—"almost fearful". (This, from a man who had never lost a battle or a duel.) "What a terrible condition it must be," he mused, "for a man never to know if something he does, or a word that he utters, has transgressed the law."

This exchange opens a window on to the world of heroic values as it was being swallowed by bureaucracy and alienation—the world of Holeček's compatriot Franz Kafka, who was born around the time that this conversation took place. Is it fanciful to see Miljanov's bafflement as the ancestral precursor of Kiš's own reactions to foreign literary institutions, reputations, and customs? Although he won international acclaim in the 1970s and 1980s, Kiš remained an outsider in Paris, where he lived in the 1980s, in large part because he would not or could not compromise with French social customs (see chapter 33).

Like Marko, Kiš had a strongly moral sense of the obligations of language and the responsibilities of a writer. Also like him, he held a mystical view of the creative power of language to fire and mould the imagination and—in occult ways—to shape our unliterary lives. There was another resemblance, too. Marko Miljanov once said that, learning to write at fifty meant he had no familiarity with the pen, and "there was no harmony between my thoughts, the paper, the pen and the ink; each looked out for itself, and they all fled from each other." Kiš, too, was in some ways like a child before the written word. A sense of the strangeness of writing and a suspicion that we *make* what we write about, literally: these never left him.

Despite his immense reading, the breadth of his horizons, his apparent worldliness, Kiš was not sophisticated. There is, around him and his books, always a primordial sense that he and they come from a background which has little to do with literature in the academic sense and nothing to do with popular culture in its mass forms. In his last interview, Kiš said "My point of departure is that we know nothing. Metaphysics is a form of poetry in prose. Mankind is an unknown quantity. We don't know where we come from, where we are going, or why we exist. We live in the unknown, as at the beginning of the world or the beginning of human existence." This utterance bespeaks a cosmic solitude and a simplicity which Marko Miljanov could have owned—though Marko never sounded so bereft.

The pride in his extraordinary ancestors that glows faintly in this sentence found almost no other expression in Kiš's work. Marica and Marko were *too* heroic, and probably too picturesque, for him to write about them. Kiš always resisted the conventions of hero worship in Yugoslavia, along with the art which expressed those conventions. He was never drawn to the monumental in any genre, let alone the gigantic political sculpture of Ivan Meštrović, Yugoslavia's best-known artist, or its postwar literary equivalents: the 'epic' novels about the Second World War—called the People's Liberation Struggle—with their schematic plot cycles of bloodshed, sacrifice, and eventual triumph of good (incarnated by the communist-led partisans) over (fascist) evil. Reviewing a war novel in 1959, he thought the best thing about it was precisely its rejection of the familiar black-and-white moral structure. "No longer are there only commissars and commanders, heroes and fighters *par excellence*, but rather people with all their frailties and vices, sometimes bestial, at other times like overgrown children."

Kiš was impelled to write about the victims of atrocity, much more than about its perpetrators or even their opponents. He once defined the "essence" of his writing as "those mysterious vanished people", meaning his father and other relatives who were taken away during his childhood, but by implication also the millions who had shared a similar fate in camps of one kind or another. Fascinated by the challenge of writing about unheroic people, he was bored by the tainted pretentiousness of heroism, its simplifying poetics—its magnetic affinity with violence, power, and success.

Marko Miljanov presented a further problem. For he was associated with traditional patriarchy and 'national literature': values to which Kiš was allergic, for they formed part of the environment that he defined himself against. Jovan Skerlić (1877–1914), the father of Serbian literary studies, had praised the physical and moral healthiness of Marko's book: just the sort of compliment that was certain to alienate Kiš. Marko and his world were as remote from his preoccupations as ancient Mesopotamia—the world of Gilgamesh, the epic poem inscribed on slabs of baked mud. Unlike Mesopotamia, however, the values of archaic Montenegro were not safely dead: they had been preserved and recycled in communist Yugoslavia as elements of the official culture.

A Yugoslav writer who loved European modernism and experimentation might well feel he could not compromise with these oppressive traditions, even—or especially—if his own ancestors had personified those values and regardless of whether courage and honour were crucial values for himself, as they were for Kiš.

A comparison with Borges throws this into relief. Borges was not bored by the Argentine culture of mythic machismo, with its "gaucho values", nor did he feel threatened by his links to that culture. On the contrary, he was fascinated by his forebears Colonel

Isidoro Suárez and Colonel Francisco Borges, men almost unimaginably unlike himself yet linked by blood. The sheer unlikeness—or "dissimilarity"—spurred his poetry: "Here was his home—in the thick of battle. / In his epic world, riding on his horse, / I leave him untouched by my verse." And again: "Shadow / Or final ash, do you hear me now or do / You ignore this voice in your bronze sleep?"

Kiš's indifference to his own epic forebears meant that he was less than just to Marko Miljanov's achievement until late in his own life. He owned no copy of *Examples of Humanity and Heroism* and may not even have read them until the 1980s, at the urging of his Montenegrin friend Stanko Cerović in Paris, when he was thrilled by their concision and directness. There will be more to say about Kiš's relationship to Montenegrin tradition in chapter 24.

The ethnographic rarity I represent will, therefore, die out with me.

Kiš added this sentence by hand to the typescript *Birth Certificate*, presumably as an afterthought. And what a sentence it is. He offers himself as a prize specimen for a science or pseudo-science that he despises, turning us into naturalists peering at a singular genus. Why, we wonder, is he lending credence to disreputable collectivist concepts? What has *he* to do with talk of "ethnographic rarities"?

Yet the offer is ironic, not to say mocking. (As usual, Kiš's narrative choreography is exquisite, laying traps for the unwary and distracting the enemy.) To whom does he "represent" an ethnographic rarity, or—as he put it on another occasion—a "strange race"? Implicitly, to the legions of his compatriots who did not find such terms absurd, let alone dangerous, because nations and not individuals were always the basis of political and cultural life in Yugoslavia.

Kiš has to do with "ethnographic rarities" because such concepts had been part and parcel of Yugoslav culture since the Kingdom of Serbs, Croats, and Slovenes was formed at the end of the First World War. That same year, 1918, saw the publication of *La péninsule balkanique. Géographie humaine*, the most influential work of social science by any Yugoslav writer. In this book, Jovan Cvijić (1865–1927), a geographer who advised the Serbian delegation to the peace talks at Versailles, provided an ethnographic typology of the Yugoslav peoples: the "Dinaric Type" (most Serbs and Croats), the "Central Type" (Macedonians and some others), the "Pannonian Type" (Slovenes, Slavonians, and Vojvodinans), and the "East Balkan Type" (Bulgarians).

The Dinaric personality was the most violent and irrational, but also the most admirable and promising. Named after the chain of mountains linking inland Dalmatia, south-western Serbia, much of Bosnia and Herzegovina, and Montenegro, this type "has an ardent desire to avenge [the 1389 battle of] Kosovo . . . and to resuscitate the Serbian Empire. . . . Betrayed by circumstances and events, abandoned by all, he has never renounced his national and social ideal." This was a political definition; the Serbian Empire meant nothing to the Catholics of Dalmatia or the Muslims of Bosnia. As for the Macedonians, he argued that they could be "Serbianised".

By the same token, Cvijić believed the centuries of Ottoman occupation had inculcated negative traits in the subject population, including "the worship of authorities, pragmatism, egoism, submissiveness, servility, resentment, and moral mimicry". His characterisation of the Ottomanised Bulgars became notorious ("their cold egoism, their restless and constant search for profit . . . and total absence of magnanimity"). For Cvijić, it has been said, "the higher the altitude, the nobler the character". As well as praising the democratic consciousness of the Dinaric type, he was broadly positive about the conservative patriarchal culture of the Dinaric regions.

The opposite of the Dinaric was the Pannonian type, the essential lowlander, who had collaborated with his Habsburg masters. These opposites merged in Kiš's parental legacy. A purer ethnographic antisyzygy cannot be conceived.

Cvijić's political aim was to prove that the South Slavs were tough, self-confident, and capable of state-building under Serbian leadership. Qualities of self-determination were associated with enclaves of resistance to foreign domination. Hence the Serbian government's decision to subsidise the book's publication in French, a language that its wartime allies in Paris, London, and Washington, D.C., could read, to convince them to support a unified Yugoslav state.

The typology was refined by Vladimir Dvorniković, a Croat, Cvijić's most distinguished follower, and author of *The Characterology of the Yugoslavs* (1939). Where Cvijić wanted to prove the Serbs' entitlement to expand their state, Dvorniković wanted to show that the South Slavic peoples collectively were neither "unhistorical" nor incapable of building a modern state. His goal was different, but no less dedicated to Yugoslav unity. He maintained that the Yugoslavs were distinguished by "dynamism, rhythm, strong temperament, strong expressiveness, and the constructive ability of fantasy". Their "fighting strength" and "love of freedom" were other traits, and epic poetry was their "most characteristic collective spiritual creation".

Over time, these ethno-psychological definitions became embedded in popular and academic self-understanding. Even when Cvijić was accused by Croatian ethnographers of being "the outstanding theorist of Serbian imperialism", their criticism inverted the values which he had attached to highlanders and lowlanders; it did not attack the intellectual basis for these typologies. As a result, one scholar points out, "lowlanders could be seen as rational, pragmatic, cultivated on one hand, or degenerate, soft, and submissive on the other; the highlanders, as brave, proud, of superior mettle, or obversely, as violent, primitive, and arrogant." As late as the 1960s, American anthropologists in the field could judge that the stereotypes were "fairly accurate", though whether because people were really like that or because they were living up to their "role models" was impossible to say.

The problem is not that Cvijić, Dvorniković and their followers were writing nonsense. It is that this school of thought was poisoned from the outset by political motives. It verged, quite logically, into eugenics and atrocity. The history of Yugoslav ethnography is inseparable from political misuse, most recently during the wars of the 1990s, when warlords and journalists alike prattled about the ethno-psychological sources of mass violence. Kiš's contempt for this pseudo-science was clear in one of his last stories, where a Central European writer in the 1930s reflects on his mixed origins:

If I were to rummage through my ancestors and have my blood analysed—a very fashionable science among nationalists these days—there I would find, like layers in a river bed, traces of Tzintzar, Armenian, and perhaps also Gypsy and Jewish blood. But I do not recognise this science of spectral blood tests, a science of wholly dubious value, dangerous and inhumane, especially in these times and these parts—where that dangerous theory of blood and soil merely creates suspicion and hatred, and where that 'spectral analysis of blood and origins' is performed by preference in a very spectacular and primitive way, with knife and revolver.

And yet, and yet: below the discursive irony, there are traces of private pathos in this sentence of the *Birth Certificate*, a lament that is almost a boast, which crosses the line into something else—but what? Not self-pity. Rather, a childlike solipsism. (What about his sister Danica, married in Montenegro with children and grandchildren?) The young narrator of *Garden, Ashes* ponders "my eschatological conviction that my end is the end of everything". Decades later, the adult author retains a taproot into the childhood sense of his own uniqueness.

We might leave it there, but for one further consideration: Kiš could not have children. This sentence in his *Birth Certificate* was also a coded message for the few people who knew this and understood its burden. Medical confirmation of infertility came in 1973; he was told that no remedy was possible. The diagnosis was not a complete surprise; he had apparently suspected as much, and blamed a bout of mumps during his military service in 1961, when life in the provincial barracks with other draftees, most of them manual workers or peasants, many of them illiterate, would have heightened his sense of being different, perhaps to the point of freakishness. It seems quite possible that the mumps—with the attendant crude jokes at his expense—added a new vulnerability to the perennial tension around his identity. Fatherless since 1944, was he now also doomed to childlessness?

Only one piece of writing by Kiš survives from his first months in uniform. It is a poem, datelined August 1961 and found among his papers; a turbid, troubled work, self-communing like a dream diary, and titled "Golden Rain" after the Greek myth about Zeus impregnating the captive Danaë as a shower of golden rain. Telling an obscure story of abortion, delivery and death, the poem hatches a brood of fearsome but partly familiar creatures: "some strange little monster comes into the world / my son or father or / brother twin the devil / only knows / a sort of slimy toad . . . no eyes, no face . . . a wingless bird" and so forth, and finally "a monster of the mind in no way / like me and so / close to my / blood / conceived in the pleura around my lungs". If these images are proof of poetic power, it is a gift that brings no joy or consolation. Dread, rather, and despair. For these creatures are figures of biological isolation, "ethnographic rarities" stripped of sympathy.

Even if Kiš had grown accustomed to the real possibility that he was infertile, confirmation may have dealt an enduring blow. He rarely spoke about these matters even with his closest companions, who remain reluctant to discuss them, though they report that Kiš doted on children and had periods of intense longing for fatherhood. But perhaps the real evidence of abiding hurt has always been on view, in his books; for the sensuousness of *Garden, Ashes* with its seeds and arks, and the formal exuberance of *Hourglass* are nowhere found in his later writing, replaced by the caustic ironies of *Boris Davidovich*, the ferocious wit of *The Anatomy Lesson*, and the dry-eyed grief of *The Encyclopaedia of the Dead*.

There has to be a connection between Kiš's sense of uniqueness and his pursuit of generality as a writer. Literature promised salvation from the overpowering specificity of his own experience and the multiplicity of his ethnic identities, by removing and transposing these threats into communicable, indeed beautiful form. Hence his definition of literature as "an attempt at a global vision of reality". This, more than anything, powered his resistance to realist conventions. The descriptive, psychological minutiae of realist fiction were no better than newspapers for fusing recognition and difference in those blissful ways that poetry can achieve within a line or two.

He rejected the false—because arbitrary—coherence of psychological realism (with its omniscient narrators and psychological description) in favour of the true—because accountable—coherence of structure, legend and document. This is why his writing quickens around images that can be called archetypal. Tropes of form and formlessness are discussed in chapter 7; arks and floods are examined in chapter 18. Consider, as well, the motifs of stars, mirrors, sunsets, trains, and packs of dogs, or singular images such as the woman with snow in her hair, in *Hourglass*: "She shakes the snow off her head and he clearly sees her abundant curly hair gathered in a high bun, on which snowflakes settle." Perhaps this glimpse lingered in the mind of his friend Mirko Kovač, when he recalled a sighting of Kiš in the early 1960s: "he was wrapped up in a scarf, you could hardly see his face, while his hair, that great bouquet on his head, was festively sprinkled with snowflakes, like confetti." And in Vesna Goldsworthy's memory of Kiš in the mid-1970s: "I remember seeing him walk along Belgrade's Knez Mihajlova Street through a thick curtain of snow, with snowflakes melting in his dark curls." Kiš's archetypes have the power to seed themselves and create literature at one remove, so people remember the author in terms that he himself created.

In 1939, in my fourth year, when anti-Jewish laws were being promulgated in Hungary,

After the Numerus Clausus bill was adopted in 1920, there was no further anti-Jewish legislation in Hungary until the late 1930s. In March 1938, Prime Minister Kálmán Darányi stigmatised the Jews' "quite disproportionate role" in parts of the economy, and called for a "solution" to ensure that Christians would have a "just share" in industry, business, and finance. He argued slyly that this would undercut "anti-Semitism and the propagation of extremist and intolerant movements".

Two months later, a bill titled "For a More Effective Safeguard of Equilibrium in Social and Economic Life" passed into law. Known as the Jewish Law, this set a 20 per cent limit on Jews working in the economy and the professions. Jews who had converted to Christianity since 1 August 1919 were still Jewish by law. It was the first of twenty-one acts of parliament and hundreds of decrees that would, over six years, strip Jewish and partly Jewish citizens of their rights.

Although the government said there would be no further anti-Jewish legislation, its foreign policy ambitions pointed in another direction. Besides, this was not a promise that right-wing groups or public opinion had any respect for or interest in supporting. In September 1938, Darányi's successor as prime minister, Béla Imrédy, had a meeting with Hitler. A month later, in the course of discussing policy adjustments to bring Hungary into line with the Axis, Imrédy—a rabid anti-Semite—mentioned the necessity for a new Jewish law. A bill was drafted, adopted by the governing party, and passed to the parliament.

The overt purpose was to reduce the 20 per cent ceiling to just 6 per cent, so that, in Imrédy's words, "capital in Hungary should work under Christian direction". The ulterior aim was to drive as many Jews as possible into emigration. Breaking with Hungarian tradition, the bill established race rather than religion as the criterion of Jewishness under law. On this premiss, the bill could deny the validity of conversion. If the bill was to succeed in unstitching the tissue of assimilation, converted Jews could not escape.

Apart from their symbolic significance to blood-and-soil racists, these converts had become a substantial grouping. The communist revolution in 1919 and the Trianon treaty of 1920, when Hungary lost two-thirds of its pre-war territory, turned the trickle of Jewish conversions into a stream. Over 10,000 cases were recorded between 1919 and 1922. (Some 10 per cent later reverted to Judaism.) This surge then fell away until the **67** shock of the first Jewish Law led almost 9,000 Jews to convert in 1938 alone. That year, the total number of baptised Jews in Hungary was estimated at around 35,000.

A few days after Kiš's pre-emptive baptism in Novi Sad (see chapter 15), the principal Jewish communities in Hungary overcame their sectarian differences to issue a joint statement about the bill. After explaining why it was unconstitutional and against Hungary's true interests, the statement reaffirmed Jewish loyalty:

> If this bill becomes law, it will result in the compulsion of hundreds of thousands of us and of our children to be banished from our homes. We may change our homes but we shall never change our homeland. . . . nothing can deprive us of our Hungarian motherland. . . . we shall never be deterred from our devotion to our Hungarian motherland. Neither fire nor water, neither scaffolds nor handcuffs could deter us; we will cling with the same determination to our Hungarian homeland, whose language is our language, whose history is our life.

As testimony to a tragic illusion, this response has indelible pathos. In practical terms, it was completely unavailing.

Imrédy was forced to resign early in 1939 by rumours that one of his great-grandfathers was a converted Jew. He was succeeded by Count Pál Teleki, a doctrinaire racist whose first administration had passed the Numerus Clausus nearly two decades earlier. Teleki now steered the bill through parliament, rebutting efforts to moderate the bill's harshness. Its passage into law was slowed by disagreement over the definition of a Jew. Adopted on 3 May, the law was implemented on 22 August 1939.

Hungary's head of state was Regent Miklós Horthy, a conventional anti-Semite rather than a fascist racist. He worried privately that the Second Law was too radical ("We cannot kill the cow that we want to milk"). For many others, it was not radical enough. Dissatisfaction with the letter and implementation of the law stoked pressure to adopt an even more inclusive basis for persecution. The third piece of anti-Jewish legislation was adopted two years later, in 1941. Modelled on the Nazi Nuremberg Laws, it widened the definition of Jewishness (to catch more converts, now totalling 100,000) and prohibited intermarriage or sexual relations between the races. Unlike the two previous bills, the Race Protection Law, as it was known, brought no material advantage to non-Jews. It was purely ideological, to appease critics of the Second Law. Completing the legal reversal of Jewish assimilation that had begun in 1920, it paved the way for the 1942 law that expropriated Jewish property and for the annihilation that followed in 1944.

Kiš's entire relationship to Judaism and Jewishness is summarised by the linkage, here in the *Birth Certificate*, of 'Jewish' with the threatening prefix 'anti-'.

As the son of an assimilated Habsburg Hungarian Jew who had no religious faith, never attended synagogue, contracted a civil marriage with a non-Jew, did not have his own son circumcised, gave both his children Montenegrin names, and had them baptised in the Eastern Orthodox Church, yet even so was—together with his siblings and their children—persecuted and murdered as a Jew, Kiš naturally enough saw oppression as intrinsic to Jewish identity. He once told an interviewer, "I am half-Jewish, or Jewish, if you prefer". The amendment was not casual; Kiš agreed with Jean-Paul Sartre that Jews are created by anti-Semitism; the power of definition rested with others. For, as he explained, "I am a Jew insofar as others think of me as one." He saw his father Eduard in these terms, as an "inauthentic Jew" who only became Jewish "by the will of others".

He insisted that Jewishness meant suffering, a condition both dolorous and inalienable. Raised "in a Jewish family in which the Jewish religion practically did not exist", Kiš found that Jewishness could only be understood as a fateful brand, a history and mythology of persecution, not as a way of life or set of values, ritual, or dogma, still less as a supportive community. There was not even a supportive family: Eduard and his siblings were at odds, split by bitter quarrels that no outsider—not even Kiš himself, when he tried in later life—could fathom. This is why there is no Jewish domesticity in Kiš's books; the interior is defined by the (Christian) mother's warmth and fearfulness. The Jewish element is banished to the external world where the father wanders, unprotected against History. This sets his writing apart from much American Jewish writing, for example, where the domestic world and the outside world are counterpointed.

Jewishness was decisive in matters of life and death, yet also contingent. As a boy in Hungary and Montenegro, Kiš spoke the same language(s) as his playmates, sat in the same classes, joined their activities and games. Yet he could never be quite one of them. Why was *he* fated to carry the Jewish burden of "fear, hunger and injustice", and not the boy at the next desk? The question had no answer, and indeed no sense. "My fate is to be a wandering Jew," he said. "I cannot do anything about this, that is how it is." Jewishness was the principle of difference: the ultimate, irreducible source of anxiety, the seal of his "troubling dissimilarity".

The Yugoslavia to which Kiš returned in 1947 was a state where racial persecution was banned and assimilation had no place in official ideology. The policy on national identity was "to guarantee each citizen full freedom to express his membership of a nationality, or not to declare his national origin, if he so chooses." Meanwhile, "acts conducive to national inequality and inciting national, racial or religious hatred or intolerance" were punishable. "In contrast to all former states, empires and regimes under which they had lived," the Jewish community could claim in 1989, "Jews in postwar Yugoslavia were not to be subjugated by any restrictions by law or exposed to propaganda campaigns. On the contrary, they had attained full equality in every respect."

The Jews who could enjoy these benefits were pitifully few. Having lost 80 per cent of its members in the war, the community numbered fewer than 15,000; by 1952, emigration to the newly created state of Israel would leave only 6,500. Did young Danilo belong to this group? Not in a formal sense, but history and blood-lines were what they were. After a year or two in Cetinje, he was tempted to throw off the burden, perhaps by presenting himself as Montenegrin or generically 'Yugoslav'. His mother, as she lay dying of cancer, encouraged him to reject his Jewish inheritance. "A year before she died [in 1951], when I was fifteen, she urged me to tear up my birth certificate from the synagogue in Subotica, because being Jewish meant nothing but trouble.[20] Although I agreed, I did not want to cheat with my own life and disown the suffering of an entire world. A vanished world." Even on her deathbed, Milica did not give up; in a makeshift will, she instructed Kiš to burn all the documents connected with his father. (Danica has no memory of her mother making any such plea. It would be characteristic of Kiš to spare his sister such a distressing theme and deny himself the relief of sharing it with her.)

The refusal to disown the burden of Jewishness was an ethical matter for Kiš: an index of integrity (readiness to *be* who one *is*) and a source of honour. Ethical in a different—public—way, was his decision, despite his dislike of political activism, to denounce anti-Semitic outbursts in the Yugoslav press. Such outbursts were impossible until 1967, when Tito broke off diplomatic relations with Israel after the Six-Day War. Official anti-Zionism then gave cover for public anti-Semitism.

The family, 1936

---

20 No birth certificate from the synagogue has survived.

Until the early 1970s, when he finished his 'family cycle' of books, Kiš took little intellectual interest in Jewishness; Sartre and Albert Memmi had given him what he needed to grasp his own experience and be true to it in his evolving art.[21] He was not drawn to qualify that experience by setting it within wider perspectives. When the Talmud was published in Serbo-Croatian in 1982, he read the translator's presentation copy with close attention. He had already read the same translator's version of Gershom Scholem's *On the Kabbalah and Its Symbolism,* which he possessed in French, noting the warning of Rabbi Yishmael that a copyist of the Torah who omits or adds a single letter will destroy the world. He also underlined the Talmudic lesson that the survival of the world depends on thirty-six just men in every generation—a legend that found its way into one of his stories.

In another guide to the Kabbalah, Kiš underlined the statement that a true kabbalist does not search for the truth: he *makes* it. In yet another, he noted the remark that the Apocalypse forms "an important element in Jewish mysticism". And he learned from Scholem that the Zohar was full of invented quotations and fake bibliographical references. He marked this passage and scribbled *Borges* in the margin.

As a young man, Kiš had some contact with the official Jewish organisation in Belgrade and entered one of its literary competitions.[22] If he distanced himself in later life from the Jewish community, it was because he did not want to be limited by identification with any national group or minority. (To be a Yugoslav writing in Serbo-Croatian was limiting enough.) With the exception of his old friend Filip David, he was not eager to discuss Jewishness with Jews; Kiš's publisher Slavko Goldstein, for decades a leading member of Croatia's Jewish community, found that he positively avoided Jewish topics. He never called himself a Holocaust survivor or a Jewish writer, nor took much interest in Jewish literature as such; typically, he was more intrigued by anti-Jewish texts, such as the novels of Céline or the *Protocols of the Elders of Zion*. Yet Gabi Gleichmann, a Jewish friend in Sweden, thought Kiš was "proud of his Jewishness in a way. As an enlightened intellectual, he regarded all religion as atavistic, but he thought Jewishness was an honourable heritage: Jews never persecuted anyone."

Kiš could have been charged, as Hannah Arendt famously was by Gershom Scholem, with lacking "love of the Jewish people"; in which case he would have agreed, as

---

21 He owned two copies of Sartre's *Réflexions sur la question juive* (1954) and annotated both. In his (1969) edition of *Portrait d'un Juif* (1962), Kiš marked Memmi's caustic account of the Jewish family ("tends of necessity to be overwhelming, coercive and castrating") and of the father in particular: "See, then, by what miracle the Jew, often so wretched, defeated, humiliated and excluded, is a majestic patriarch within the family circle. This is his just revenge, acknowledged and consolidated by his own kin. What a paradox that even today the Jewish father can loom so terribly, though he is socially so weak, which is why the work of Jewish writers almost always perpetuates a conflict with the father." Traces of such a conflict do animate *Garden, Ashes,* whereas *Hourglass* gets its energy from conflict within and around the father.

22 His entry won the prize; it is a short novel called *Psalm 44,* his only realist narrative, about a couple and their baby in Auschwitz (see the first interlude).

she did, on the ground that he had "never 'loved' any people or collective". Perhaps this explains why his work receives little attention from scholars of Jewish literature. Another reason may be the anti-Semitic element in *Hourglass*, where E.S. suspects that a Jewish rat was responsible for destroying his house in Novi Sad and describes an Orthodox Jewish acquaintance as "an old synagogue rat". Kiš refused to idealise the victim; fascist propaganda is swirling in the depths of E.S.'s mind; he has partly internalised the evil of the system that will kill him.

Kiš's despairing sense of Jewish identity can be faulted, though not securely. According to a recent critic, "To confine them [Jews] within the gaze of the anti-Semitic Other and that Other's rejection of them is a way of situating them outside history". Kiš would turn that on its head: his perception of Jewish identity was as rooted in history as anything could be. This critic's concession that Jewish suffering "does at least create identity and a sense of collective belonging" would draw a hollow laugh and a shake of the leonine head.

Nor did he care much to discuss the Jewishness of his own writing. To the French critic Guy Scarpetta, he admitted there was "something inadvertently Jewish in what I write, at times almost kabbalistic." Scarpetta agrees, seeing *Hourglass* as a secular 'transposition' of Talmudic textual practices: the impassioned construal of objects as signs, the focus on a father figure, flights of intellectual speculation, spinning stories out of an enigmatic primary text. Staying with *Hourglass*, it seems fair to ask if there is not something midrashic about the exfoliation of his father's wartime letter—what Maimonides called the use of "witty poetical conceit" to instil "a noble moral quality", or what Cynthia Ozick termed the literature of fictive commentary.

Standing back from this or that book and motif (such as the Wandering Jew), is there something Jewish about his overall endeavour and achievement? If it is true, as Marshall Berman proposes, that a form of story which "Jews tell well" is the 'family romance', in which "basic family relationships are loaded with metaphysical intensity, and are felt to form the ultimate core of being", then Kiš is very much a Jewish storyteller. And whether or not "lack of fixity, leading to innovation" has been the key to Jewish creativity, as Eric Hobsbawm contends, it was certainly the rubric of Kiš's journey in literature. And if Jewishness means "self-questioning and uncomfortable truth-telling . . . [a] quality of awkwardness and dissent . . . [making us] the most unforgiving critics of our own [conventions]" (Tony Judt), then Kiš's work qualifies. The intertextual sense of tradition and the vocation to find a true homeland in literature: these too may be distinctively Jewish. Likewise the ready sense of guilt over creativity, as if fiction were a form of idolatry, violating the Second Commandment; this, the dark side of his faith in literature, fed his terrible intuition after 1986 that cancer was his punishment meted for "playing the Creator, competing with God" in his story about a man whose own cancer is expressed obsessively by drawing flower-like motifs (see chapter 7). Kiš was aghast when his oncologist said that his cancer would have dated from the time when he wrote that story. "Although I am no mystic, I believe that you cannot write such things and not be punished."

With Kiš in mind, let us recall the critic who argued that the "re-emergence of Jewish wisdom and Jewish intellect in the European vernaculars is one of the glories of twentieth-century literature", and listed the qualities of that wisdom and intellect: "power of abstraction, profound scepticism, respect for learning, love of wordplay, rectitude of judgement and readiness to indignation, family solidarity". Of all the Jewish writers who have committed heart and soul to literature as a source of existential meaning, an arena of humane understanding where innovation and tradition inform each other, has any done so with greater urgency or flair?

my parents had me baptised in the Orthodox faith at the
Church of the Assumption in Novi Sad.

On 4 January 1939 by the Julian calendar,[23] with the Second Jewish Bill before the parliament in Budapest, Danilo was baptised in the Church of the Assumption of the Holy Mother of God, an eighteenth-century baroque edifice in the centre of Novi Sad. He was a month short of his fourth birthday. More than forty years later, he imagined the scene:

> the priest pouring water over my head as I look all around for my mother—who has entrusted me for the moment to my godfather—the smell of incense, the chant of the priest, the flicker of the candles, the faces of the saints on the icons.

(His sister Danica already possessed this safeguard. She had been baptised in Subotica in 1933, two days before her first birthday, following the custom that daughters took the mother's confession.)

Hungary was another country, but Eduard's origins lay there and most of his family still lived there. He would be aware of the ominous political trends in Budapest. Anyway Hungary's territorial appetites were no secret, and its anti-Semitic policies were in keeping with the trend across Axis-dominated Central Europe.

The shadow was falling across Yugoslavia, too: although no anti-Jewish legislation had been passed, the government had broken with Yugoslavia's previous pro-British, pro-French alignment and leaned towards Germany and Italy. There had been cases of organised anti-Semitism during the 1920s and 1930s: a Muslim boycott of Jewish retailers in Bosnia, a blood libel accusation in Vojvodina, a failed attempt by the Jewish community to stop publication of the *Protocols of the Elders of Zion*. Now, in 1939, the government banned Jewish Hungarians from entering Yugoslavia as tourists. Anti-Jewish legislation followed in October 1940, starting with a "Statute on the Registration of Jews", limiting the numbers of Jews who could be admitted to secondary schools and universities. With hindsight, the parents' decision looks like common sense. In fact, it showed real presence and independence of mind.

---

23 The Julian calendar, used by Orthodox Churches, is 13 days behind the Gregorian calendar. Hence, Kiš was baptised on 22 December 1938 by usual reckoning.

At a later date, Eduard obtained Danilo's certificate of baptism from the Church in Novi Sad. This event features in *Hourglass*, in one of the long interrogations that "E.S." undergoes. His anonymous questioner wants him to account for his movements during a recent visit to Novi Sad.

> Did it take you two hours to walk from Station Street to Louis Barthou Street?
> Yes. I dropped in to see the priest.
> What did you want from the priest?
> Certificates from the baptismal records for members of my family.
> How much did you pay him for them?
> The price of tax stamps.
> We will check your statements.
> Two pengő for each certificate.
> Did you go into the church?
> No.
> So the priest gave you the certificates?
> Yes.
> Did he give them to you in his rooms? Yes or no?
> Yes.
> Through whom did you get in touch with him?
> Through the parish.
> Had you known him before?
> No.
> Who sent you to him?
> There was a young secretary at the parish office, I don't remember his name; he sent me to the priest. This secretary was extremely cautious. He told me there had been many requests of this kind lately, that lots of people were trying to get false papers for family members. I assured him that I was not one of those, and what I wanted was perfectly legal. Then he directed me to the priest.

To fit this incident within the scheme of his novel, Kiš locates it in March 1942. In fact, Kiš's certificate bears the date 31 August 1940. (Under "confession", Eduard was identified as "Mosaic" and Milica as "Eastern Orthodox".) His father had obtained the documents long before he fled to Hungary with the family in February 1942—indeed, well before the Axis powers invaded Yugoslavia in 1941.

This saved my life.

As promulgated in May 1939, the Hungarian Second Jewish Law defined a Jew as "one who himself, or at least one of his parents, or at least two of his grandparents were at the time of entry into force of the present Law members of the Jewish religious community, or have been such prior to the entry into force of the Law". That final, catch-all clause ("or have been such") snared Danilo and Danica Kiš. For their father was the Jewish son of Jewish parents, and his change of surname had not altered his confessional and legal identity. He had never converted to Christianity.

However, the law set out certain exemptions, one of which was agonisingly relevant to the Kiš family. It stated that persons born of parents who had married before 1 January 1939 would *not* be regarded as Jews provided that *only* one parent and *not more* than two grandparents were Jewish, and *also* provided that:

1. both parents were at the time of the marriage already members of a Christian church and continued to be members of the same church, or
2. by virtue of an agreement . . . the person concerned follows the religion of the Christian parent, and that the parent who at the time of the marriage was of the Jewish religion, was converted prior to 1 January 1939 . . .
3. the person concerned was born Christian, or was converted to the Christian faith before the completion of his or her seventh year of age, and the Jewish parent became Christian prior to 1 January 1939.

If Eduard Kiš had converted at any point prior to 1 January 1939, his children would not have counted as Jewish under this law.

Regardless of the children's status in law, their certificates from the Orthodox Church may still have given vital protection on that day in May 1944 when the Hungarian gendarmes rode into Kerkabarabás like the Horsemen of the Apocalypse. Danilo never tried to quote or invent the words that may have passed that day between his parents and the gendarmes, perhaps with the mayor assisting. (In *Garden, Ashes*, the gendarmes are not even mentioned: Eduard is borne away on a cart, soliloquising dementedly "in the face of the world", as if yielding to a force so immense that it can dispense with human agents.) Perhaps the gendarmes accepted the parents' desperate assurances 77 that both children were Christian, especially if local people nodded in agreement. For his part, Kiš had no doubt that the certificate saved his life in Novi Sad in 1942 and again when the Hungarian gendarmes took his father away in 1944.

In his *Crowds and Power*, Elias Canetti—another Jewish Central European with Balkan origins—wrote that

> transformation for flight, that is, in order to escape an enemy, is universal, being found in myths and fairy stories all over the world. . . . One creature is pursuing another, the distance between them diminishing all the time until, at the very moment when the quarry is about to be seized, it escapes by transforming itself into something different. The hunt continues, or rather, starts afresh.

Stories of such transformation may lie at the root of literature. Kiš's baptism—a simple ceremony and piece of paper—turned him into a metaphor of himself: his own double. Without altering in appearance or substance, he was now somebody else. Surely this experience underlay Kiš's faith in the fabulous power of language and instilled a sense that he had incurred a debt which could be paid in only one way. Fifty years after the priest poured water over his head, Kiš the unbeliever wrote his last will and testament, stating his wish to be buried in Belgrade according to the rites of the Orthodox Church.

I lived until my thirteenth year in my father's native region of Hungary, to which we fled in 1942 after the Novi Sad massacre.

On 25 March 1941, Yugoslavia's hapless government signed the Tripartite Pact and joined the Axis. Two days later, a group of army officers, incited by British agents, mounted a bloodless and hugely popular coup. Kiš told an interviewer in 1986 that, as a six-year-old at primary school, he had waved a Yugoslav flag and chanted "*Bolje rat nego pakt!*" (Better war than the Pact), with his schoolmates in Novi Sad on that day. He was fascinated by the "assonant rhyme" of the chant, even though its "mysterious meaning went over my head".[24]

Regent Prince Paul, who supported the Pact, was ousted in favour of King Peter, just seventeen, who opposed it. Hitler issued orders "to destroy Yugoslavia as a nation". When Germany invited Hungary to join the imminent invasion, Regent Horthy seized the chance to "liberate Southern Hungary", meaning the extensive territories which had been awarded to the new Yugoslav state after the First World War. Horthy's government promptly disowned the treaty of "eternal friendship" which had been agreed with Yugoslavia a few months earlier. This vengeful opportunism was supported even by the pro-Western faction in parliament. The Hungarian press launched a propaganda campaign against Yugoslavia.

German troops massed on the border on 2 April. The Blitzkrieg was unleashed four days later, with seven Panzer divisions and a thousand aircraft to smash Yugoslav defences and raze much of Belgrade. On 11 April, Hungarian troops followed the Germans, kissing the ground when they marched into Vojvodina.

Further south, inside Serbia proper, the German command began to segregate the Jewish population at the end of May, filtering Jews out of public employment, ordering them to wear yellow stars, and introducing forced labour. Over the summer, Jews were rounded up and put in concentration camps. Others were murdered in sealed vans,

24 Kiš may truly have noticed, and remembered forty-five years later, that "every barbershop window displayed a portrait of young King Peter in three-quarter profile, as on postage stamps", and he may have brandished a flag with other children, but he had no schoolmates because he had not started school. As Sava Babić points out, Danilo would have entered primary school only in autumn 1941. His school records confirm this. Perhaps Kiš meant to say 'playmates', or perhaps it was a false memory, inspired by a wish to tie his biography to that iconic anti-fascist moment which was not pro-communist, although Tito's regime later claimed it for its own pre-history. Every citizen of postwar Yugoslavia knew that chant and its mythic meaning: valiant rebellion against evil authority, whatever the odds.

79

asphyxiated with exhaust fumes. By August 1942, the Germans could declare that Belgrade was the first major city in Europe to be free of Jews.

In December 1941, when Hungary insanely declared war on Britain, the United States, and the USSR, it annexed the portion of Yugoslavia which it had occupied. Jews in this territory were subject to beatings and extortion but not, at this stage, to massacre or deportation. Partisan attacks on the Hungarian occupiers, late in 1941, may have been supported by the Germans, in order to sharpen Hungarian hatred of Serbs. Whatever the truth about this, the reprisals were terrible. Spiralling violence around an internment camp led to the involvement of Hungarian army units under General Feketehalmi-Czeydner, who used the utmost severity to punish local partisans and also to convince the Germans that Hungary deserved to get more of the Vojvodina. He raised 'home guards' from local ethnic Hungarian communities and went on the attack. Men, women, and children were massacred, and their bodies thrown in the Tisza river. By mid-January, some two thousand people had been killed. The government then gave Czeydner permission to extend the "purge" to Novi Sad, capital of the Vojvodina, "while stipulating that no 'superfluous' or 'exaggerated' measures should be taken."

Troops and gendarmes entered Novi Sad on 20 January—at the very hour, it so happened, when fifteen members of the Nazi elite met in a lakeside villa at Wannsee, on the outskirts of Berlin, to plan "the final solution of the Jewish question". Novi Sad was sealed off, communications with the outside world were cut or forbidden, and Czeydner announced that the military was taking over for three days "to clean up". Gendarmes and police were warned not to show weakness. Posters instructed civilians to stay off the streets. Householders were instructed to shutter their windows or draw the curtains. The next day, with the temperature sinking to –30° Celsius, the occupying forces went from door to door, checking papers.[25] Some 7,000 suspects were rounded up for interrogation. Fewer than one hundred were detained; of these, fifteen to twenty were shot and their bodies dumped in the frozen Danube.

On 22 January, perhaps in reprisal after shots were fired at them, the military took hostages, most of them Jewish and many of them wealthy. Czeydner wanted to see more bodies. Although no one was killed by those futile shots, which may have been staged by the gendarme commander, they started to execute the hostages. Groups were executed at street corners, in an Orthodox cemetery, and inside a stadium. The worst brutality took place on a beach beside the Danube, at the city's edge. Here, according to one historian, the slaughter "was carried through with unbelievable brutality." Victims were marched to the beach, forced to strip, and then shot in fours. The corpses were pushed into holes that had been blasted through the ice. "The naked bodies, some of them

---

25 According to the novelist Aleksandar Tišma (1924–2003), who was partly Jewish on his mother's side, gendarme patrols were the most brutal. Tišma and his family were saved by a Hungarian neighbour, who spoke up for them when soldiers burst into their flat. Tišma's novel about the massacre in Novi Sad, *The Book about Blam,* was published in 1972, the same year as *Hourglass.*

mutilated, were found when the ice melted, weeks later." When the killing was stopped by order from Budapest, late on 23 January, at least 879 people had died in Novi Sad, including 550 Jews (from a pre-war Jewish population of 3,600). The "pacification" in the Vojvodina had cost some 3,300 civilian lives, including as many as 1,500 Jews. The episode sent shock waves through Hungary which brought down the pro-Nazi government in March.

The new prime minister evaded German demands to eradicate the Jews, and Hungary became "a haven for Jews, to which even refugees from Poland and Slovakia could sometimes still escape." (By March 1944, when this government fell, Hungary had taken in some 300,000 Jewish refugees.) In this new climate, Horthy reluctantly agreed to investigate the Novi Sad massacre. As the official who led the inquiry was a secret member of Hungary's fascist movement, the Arrow Cross Party, its outcome was not in doubt. The massacred Jews and Serbs were branded collectively as "partisans", the army officers were exonerated, and Horthy dismissed all charges. Czeydner blamed the gendarmes for any excesses.

Even amid the accumulating horrors of war, the massacre was not forgotten. In December 1943, when the tide had turned against the Axis and the government wanted to improve Hungary's standing with the Allies, the inquiry was reopened. The officers were tried, found guilty, and eight of them received heavy prison sentences. Four of them, including Czeydner, fled to Vienna where the Gestapo took them in. When Germany occupied Hungary a few months later, Hitler insisted on the guilty men's reinstatement. Captured at the end of the war, Czeydner and several other senior officers with similar records were sentenced to death in Hungary and then again in Novi Sad, where they were executed in November 1946.

When the Soviet Red Army and Tito's forces liberated Vojvodina in October 1944, revenge against the native Hungarian and German minorities was swift. A local partisan newspaper signalled what was about to befall the at the end of October. "Although we destroyed the occupying German and Hungarian hordes and drove them back to the west, we have not yet eradicated the roots of the poisonous weeds planted by them. . . . The people feel that determined, energetic steps are needed to ensure the Yugoslav [i.e. Slavic] character of Vojvodina." The massacre of thousands of Hungarians was shrouded in silence until Tito's Yugoslavia disintegrated. Accounts by survivors are as harrowing as those from Novi Sad in 1942.

Eduard Kis and his family remained in Novi Sad under Hungarian occupation, changing addresses more than once: "my father was following the logic of his financial ruin", after the failure of several ventures into business. He did his best to conceal his Jewish identity and was, anyway, too old to be drafted into the labour brigades.

Eduard lived quietly until January 1942 when, according to an account that Kiš gave in 1986, the family was "torn from sleep one night by a volley of shots fired under our window. My mother turned on a light, but turned it off again immediately and took me out of bed in the dark. I knew I wasn't dreaming or having a nightmare: my mother was trembling." Eduard was taken away by a patrol; the children were left with their mother. They survived the massacre "by a miracle", Kiš recalled.

According to Danica, speaking nearly fifty years after the event, "We were sitting on a sofa or divan. Our mother put a Hungarian magazine in our hands. Police came to the door and asked 'What are the children doing?' We replied in Hungarian, 'We're reading!'" Their father would have taught them this phrase, parrot-fashion, as the children had not yet learned Hungarian.

Kiš's account differs slightly: it was their father who put the magazine in their hands, the first patrol comprised soldiers and police, and it was a second patrol—of police—that took Eduard away. His account shows the literary imagination at work: "The magazine featured pictures from the Eastern front—a Hungarian soldier being welcomed by Ukrainian peasants with icons and bread and salt, a girl with blond braids embracing a young tank driver, houses in flames, the brutal landscape of the Russian steppe." One page showed a picture of a tank in the snow: "It's been hit by a shell and looks like a man punched in the solar plexus." As the police search the house, Eduard handed over his papers for inspection. A police patrol returned an hour later and led him away.

Kiš claimed their house was not daubed with a yellow star because Eduard had not told the landlady that he was Jewish. ("How disappointed she must have been a week later when she saw a Star of David on his chest.") Historical accounts of the massacre do not mention yellow stars on buildings; besides, Eduard's Jewishness would have been discovered when his papers were checked, so his children, who were Jewish under Hungarian law, could have been seized at that point. Their survival was probably due to carelessness on the patrollers' part, the careful *tableau vivant* with the magazine, the unforeseen order to halt the massacre, and perhaps also to the children's certificates of baptism.

Survivors of the killing beside the Danube recalled that many victims begged their captors to shoot them because the cold was unbearable. One survivor was Eduard Kis. According to his son, the hole in the ice had become jammed with corpses, forcing the killers to pause, when the order came to stop. He came to believe that his father never recovered from this experience.

"I saw death very close up, and I was afraid," Kiš remembered. "At the time I was completely cut off from time and space. I had no idea what day, what year, what century it was. I was like a trembling puppy." Forty years later, he dated the beginning of his "conscious life" to this trauma. That experience of helpless fear in the face of inexplicable mortal danger turned out to be formative: proof, once and for all, that history was the realm of coercion and violence.

The following month, Eduard led his family to his birthplace in south-western Hungary. The winter's journey from Novi Sad to the village is evoked in *Garden, Ashes*:

Very early one morning, my mother jolted me awake and told me in an excited whisper to get dressed. Our few remaining things had already been packed in trunks. . . . We changed sleighs outside gloomy barns, hastily, warming ourselves with hot tea and cognac, and falling into a deep sleep in the sleigh, clinging together as the sleigh-bells wove a lyrical echo around our slumber and our flight. My father tried to make the coachmen hurry, tempting them shamefully with cognac and bribes, talking hurriedly and panting, as if somebody was chasing him. . . . We travelled for days through a snowy wasteland, blank as the ocean, losing all sense of direction. My father, however, steered our ship with a sure hand, gazing up at the starry sky, calling instructions to the frightened coachmen. Now and then he pulled a star chart out of his inside pocket and spread it across his knees, just as he used to consult his railway timetable when we were on a train. . . . From time to time we halt and my father hammers on gates like a dethroned Russian prince. I don't have the strength or will to ask anything, all I can feel is how my eyelids are glued by sleep and weariness, and how I'm trembling with a sort of fear that I'm not used to yet, a fear of unknown places and people, a fear of closed gates. I hear the sleigh-bells fade into the distance, accompanied by dogs' barking. My father keeps hammering on the gate, compelled by some inner zeal or stubborn conviction. Keys jangle on the other side and my father speaks his name plangently, as one who utters the names of the prophets. The bolt moves—"Wait a moment, we can't do it any faster, we weren't expecting you at this time of night"—then unknown faces materialise in front of us, the faces of sleepwalkers, faces dragged up from the depths of winter's sleep. They take me by the hand and kiss me with dry lips that smell of some dark residue. They lead us into murky rooms where they light the lamps and speak in sleepy voices, low and hoarse. A legion of relatives parade before me, unknown and remote, grown-ups with dark curly hair, freckled, with noses like snail shells, and I kiss them one after the other, unable to make sense of anything that's happening.

Eduard's sister gave the newcomers a two-room shack to live in, behind the Kon family house. While Milica sewed and knitted for the villagers, the children went to school or earned pennies by minding the cattle for farmers. Dani, as he was known in the village, also cleaned henhouses: a revolting job. Eduard roamed the village and nearby countryside, at odds with all and sundry; often drunk, carousing with gypsies, sleeping off his hangovers under hedgerows and haystacks, accusing the relatives of slights that were probably real, like his anguish, and also imaginary.

{SECOND INTERLUDE}

Garden, Ashes (1965)

On late summer mornings my mother came silently into the room, carrying a tray. The tray had already begun to lose its thin coating of nickel. Around the edge, where the flat surface curves up to form a raised rim, traces of bygone splendour were still visible in the flaky patches of nickel, looking like tinfoil rubbed flat under a fingernail. The narrow, level rim ends in an oval trough that curls downward and is dented and misshapen. Tiny swellings—a necklace of little metallic grapes—decorate the upper edge of the rim. Anyone holding the tray (most often my mother) was bound to feel at least three or four of these hemispherical bumps under their thumb-tips, like Braille letters. Ringlike layers of grease had collected just there, around those swellings: barely visible, like shadows cast by tiny cupolas. These small rings, the colour of fingernail dirt, were made of coffee grounds, cod-liver oil, honey, and sherbet. Thin crescents on the smooth, shiny surface show where glassware had just been taken away. Without opening my eyes, I knew from the crystal chime of teaspoons on glass that my mother had set down the tray for a moment and was moving decisively toward the window, to open the dark curtain. Then the room lit up with the dazzling light of morning, and I would shut my eyes tight as the light played from yellow to blue to red.

Intimate and playful, pointillist in method, minutely focused yet lavish: from its first lines, *Garden, Ashes* sounds like nothing Kiš had written before. He leads us from the initial simple statement to the entranced, forensic account of the tray, with its sudden shifts of focus and its allegory of decline.

The glory of *Garden, Ashes* comes from the use of adult craft to evoke a child's experience and imagination. Kiš gives us a hybrid narrator who blends the expressive power of an accomplished artist with the limited understanding—but unlimited imagination, or intuition—of a young person. The boy invests the decorative beading on the worn tray with significance; the adult recreates this meaning for readers, drawing on literary resources beyond the boy's awareness.

We enjoy the descriptive detail, but we also interpret it, like Braille. When (Turkish) sherbet segues to (Islamic) crescents, we notice the delicate linking of Ottoman motifs, always resonant in Serbia, without being sure if the man or the boy is responsible; for a precocious boy might make the connection intuitively. When, a few pages later, the narrator sees a group of young *Volksdeutscher*, ethnic Germans, setting off for a weekend's camping, attired in lederhosen and carrying "splendid scout knives, with rosewood handles, tucked into their belts", the image is fraught with omens; for this scene is precisely dated: it is late in the year 1940, a few months before Germany invaded Yugoslavia. The boy might have noticed the hale *Volksdeutscher*; he would not have registered that the knife handles were rosewood. Again, when we learn that "a gentleman in a bowler hat, presumably representing the Banovina, gave a speech that my mother found witty and touching", the historical information has to come from the author, while the intent observation of the mother's response can only belong to the son.[26]

Kiš was always searching for ways to tell stories reflexively, so that a book's style became a vital dimension of the reader's experience. In *Garden, Ashes* he found, for the first time, a solution. (*The Garret* had revealed haphazard elements of possible solutions.) He said that "within a chapter, even within the same phrase, you will find two points of view: a reality as seen by a child, and as commented on by the man writing the book". Analysing this oscillation or double focus, Alexandre Prstojević suggests that *récit* and *commentaire* are interwoven so completely that the text produces "*un effet de simultanéité*: le lecteur a l'impression qu'il saisit toute la richesse de l'oeuvre au fil même de sa lecture." This is well said; the effect of simultaneity is essential to the book's dappled, gem-like opulence. In *Garden, Ashes*, Kiš learned to write polyphonic sentences; polyphonic structure would follow, in *Hourglass*.

He loses no time in thematising the doubled awareness that his mix of *récit* and *commentaire* produces. In the first of the book's twelve chapters, Andi's mother mentions that his uncle, her brother, has died. Although Andi has never met this uncle, he then dwells obsessively upon death. "I stood petrified, thinking that one day I too would die. At the same time I was horror-stricken to realise that my mother would also die." This new and shocking foreknowledge of mortality means that Andi has crossed a threshold—the one that leads to Rilke's *Doppelbereich*, the 'double realm' of which we all become subjects.

This painful realization becomes a key to self-consciousness and self-knowledge:

> I couldn't imagine how my hand would die one day, how my eyes would die. Inspecting my hand, I surprised this thought on my palm, connected to my body, indivisible from it. Astonished and fearful, I realised then that I was a boy named Andreas Sam, called Andi by my doting mother, that I was the only one with that particular name, that nose, that taste of honey and cod-liver oil in his mouth, the only one in the world whose uncle had died of tuberculosis the previous day, the only boy with a sister named Ana and a father named Eduard Sam, the only one in the world who

---

26 In 1929, the Kingdom of Yugoslavia was divided into provinces called banovinas. Vojvodina was in the Danube Banovina, with its capital at Novi Sad, where *Garden, Ashes* begins.

was thinking at that particular moment that he was the only boy named Andreas Sam, whom his mother was fond of calling Andi.

His terror grows as bedtime approaches: "When I thought of death, and it came to mind as soon as darkness enveloped the room, the thought unwound like a bolt of black silk thrown from a third-floor window."[27] Worst of all, darkness and sleep bring the anticipation of his mother's death, funeral, and burial "beneath beds of roses".

He decides that the best thing is to catch "the angel of sleep" as it descends. If he can seize its wings, he will understand it and so render it harmless. In some obscure way, this will train him for the "great struggle with death". Of course he fails: consciousness cannot catch itself unawares. But this hardly matters, for Andi has caught the habit of self-analysis, and he relishes the process. *Garden, Ashes* is in this sense anti-Wordsworthian, anti-romantic, with no nostalgia for childish unawareness.

Only at the end of the book will Andi discover a remedy for his nightmares. His sudden awareness of death provides the book's first drama and establishes two things: his sensitive and thoughtful nature, as befits a future artist; and his mother's role as a unique source of love, who knows instinctively how to comfort and encourage him. *Garden, Ashes* goes on to tell the twin stories of how Andi's imagination survives and even thrives, while his father Eduard struggles with his fate, succumbs, and disappears. They are locked together by Andi's fascination with his elusive parent, whose eccentricity provides vital stimulus.

More than anything, it is Eduard's *Yugoslav National and International Travel Guide* (see chapter 22), with its limitless horizons, which lifts Andi to rapt, comic heights:

Once he had secured sufficient capital to allow his research to begin, my father supplied himself with new maps and books. Late one evening, in a flight of inspiration and illumination, he put down on paper the first sentence, meant for some sort of preface or instructions for use. This glorious thought, this ingenious question, came to him like the voice out of the burning bush to Moses, without warning. And this one sentence, this great and fateful question, transposed to a higher, metaphysical plane, would soon ravish my father with its meaning and its enigma, which he resolved to answer: *How can one travel to Nicaragua?*

---

27 The Bosnian-American writer Aleksandar Hemon marvels at this sentence: "Every time I read this passage I hear the fluttering of the silk—the sound of death. The thought has been materialized: the black silk roll is the objective correlative of a death thought, evanescent and evasive though it may be. But Kiš knows that to achieve this, the writing has to be absolutely precise."

At 21, Palmotićeva Street, Belgrade, 1965, the year *Garden, Ashes* was published

The lyrical wonderment is all Andi's, while the ironic style belongs to the narrator. In his son's eyes, Eduard is a giant whose head is wreathed in cigarette smoke.

The chapters reflect the motion of the hybrid narrator's mind, which, not being 'adult', does not follow a pre-planned course. Instead, it alights on one thing, then another, by a leap of association, usually sensory, triggered by a colour, a smell, or an image, evoking—and celebrating—the unbiddable play of consciousness. The sensuous vividness of the writing led one critic to commend Kiš's "magical memories of a Holocaust childhood". It is odd praise, but accurate. The result is a series of tableaux, showing Andi's life at home; his father's mysterious comings and goings, and frantic work on his *Travel Guide*; the family's flight from Novi Sad to Hungary (neither of them named in the text); Andi's life in the village, including school and church; his pubescent love for schoolmate Julia; his reflections on memory, sin and the Bible; his ignorance of the adult political world, which exposes by contrast the barbarism of that world: "The Reverend Father explains that my wish to become an altar boy cannot be met under the present difficult circumstances, the way things stand *today*." The narrative inhabits Andi's emotions and preoccupations; other people and events appear through that prism.

Andi's vision of Eduard intensifies in the village, because he can "no longer hide". The boy still sees his father in mythic terms, monitoring his drunken ways and conjuring them in resplendent prose:

> He subsisted on wild mushrooms, sorrel, wild apples, and birds' eggs that he plucked from their nests with the crook of his cane. And in the summertime, we would come across him unexpectedly in the fields, his black derby emerging from the fiery wheat, his glasses flashing in the sun. He moved through the fields like a sleepwalker, lost in thought, waving his cane high in the air, following his star, which he would lose amid the sunflowers only to find it again at the edge of the field—on his greasy black frock coat.

Andi feels that the yellow star on his father's coat is of fateful importance, but he does not know why.

Then, in chapter eight, the perspectives alter. The narrator announces that "this account is becoming more and more the story of my father, the story of the brilliant Eduard Sam. . . . It overshadows the self-centred stories about my mother, my sister and myself, the seasons and landscapes." This is the adult Andi, and he recounts conversations with his father, ending with Eduard's testamentary confession:

> My role as a victim, which I have been playing more or less successfully all my life—we all act out our lives, our destinies, after all—that role is gradually coming to an end. You must remember this once and for all, young

fellow; you cannot play the role of a victim all your life without becoming one in the end. As you see, there is nothing to be done about it now. I shall have to do my best to play the part with dignity right to the end. The forgiveness you will give me shall be my redemption.

The moment of Eduard's removal is easily missed, because Andi's emotional focus on his father never diminishes. He mistakes complete strangers for his absent father, imagines how his parents first met (see chapter 19), and wrestles with the tormented legacy that Eduard has bequeathed. This wrestling continues up to the time of writing: at the end of chapter eight, Andi describes the most recent vision of his father, acting as provocatively as ever, taunting his son with a reference to a painful episode "over twenty years" earlier. "WHO IS THIS MAN AND WHAT DOES HE WANT FROM ME?" cries Andi—which could be any troubled son about any difficult father.

The imagination that young Andi uses to keep unbearable facts at bay is nurtured by his mother within secure boundaries that only she can set (see chapter 21). Maria's intensity is overbearing in its way, and Andi needs another influence to qualify and counteract it. This is provided by books: not high literature, but "novels of adventure, crime and heroism". Where the Bible had burdened and branded his imagination with the conviction of sin (see chapter 18), fiction releases it by training him to tell fantasy apart from reality, "to control my dreams, channel them in a particular direction". At this point Andi's story becomes one of liberation, rising toward the mock-heroic emergence of his first poem (see chapter 20). Novels save him by flooding him with fiction, which reveals that more than one thing at a time can be true. As Kiš quipped to an interviewer, "I wanted to show someone saving himself from annihilation—with lies."

Kiš wrote *Garden, Ashes* in Strasbourg (see chapter 31), mainly at night, "in spurts" as he said, completing two or three drafts, seven hundred or eight hundred pages in all. His friend Georges Krygier remembers him grumbling about how difficult the writing was, and it is easy to believe that the labour of weaving this tissue of irony and ecstasy took the author by surprise. (He had composed *The Garret* and *Psalm 44* swiftly and easily.)

He had set himself a challenge that was both intimate and profound, involving a re-examination of his traumatic past and its creation in a novel. At the heart of this endeavour was the figure of his father. When an interviewer asked him about resemblances between the two Eduards, Kiš said: "Why, they are one and the same. Except that my father was much greater and much more lost." Indeed, all four members of the Sam family were like their originals: "I am convinced that it is me, that it's my father, my mother, my sister—that they are us as we should have been," if history had not trampled them down.

Studies of Kiš's generation of Holocaust survivors illuminate the reconstructive and reparative ambition of *Garden, Ashes*. Susan Rubin Suleiman argues that survivors between the ages of four and ten were "old enough to remember but too young to understand". Hence, they shared an experience of "premature bewilderment and helplessness". Over time, this generation discovered the need "to acknowledge their childhood traumas, often denied in their desire for 'normalcy' after the war, and to transmit their memories of that time to subsequent generations." She also observes that "there is a privileged place for the *literary* in the narratives of (child) survivors". Looking at the works of this generation, she says "The fact that some of these works are called memoirs where others are called novels is not pertinent, if one considers them as essentially autobiographical in nature."

Thinking about families that survived the Holocaust in whole or part, Eva Hoffman observes that "there was almost always the reparative urge on the children's part, an urge to help, a shared mourning." The children sense the inward meanings of calamity, "and then have to work their way outwards towards the facts and the worldly shape of events." *Garden, Ashes* is like this: it catches the inward meaning of calamity and is filled with the reparative urge. (Late in the book, Andi cries out: "I don't want to curse God, I don't want to complain about life.") Hoffman cites Freud's theory that mourning becomes melancholia or depression if we do not know what we have lost. *Garden, Ashes* and *Hourglass* are attempts to discover what the lost object is, the first in relation to the author and the second in relation to itself and the world, keeping melancholia at bay with the renewing power of art.

Comparing *Garden, Ashes* with other fictions about the Holocaust, from a child's perspective, Kiš's book stands out for its truth to that frame of reference. The Israeli author Aharon Appelfeld, born in 1932 in the Ukraine, published *The Age of Wonders* in 1978. "Many years ago", runs the first sentence, "Mother and I took the night train home from the quiet, little-known retreat where we had spent the summer." Appelfeld's evocation of childhood emotion, especially of complex feelings about his parents, is delicate and skilled. Yet his account is saturated with retrospective knowledge—allusions and clues that are not thematised within a child's consciousness—including documentary sentences such as this: "Passengers were requested to bring their passports, identity cards, or any other identifying documents with them." Where does that come from? The steady perspective is an extraordinary achievement in human terms, but Appelfeld tells instead of showing.

Perhaps the novel closest to *Garden, Ashes*—even its sequel or sibling—is *Fatelessness* (1975) by the Hungarian Imre Kertész (b. 1929), who survived Auschwitz and Buchenwald. Kertész's narrator is several years older than Andi and less at the mercy of his own innocence. Watchful but robust, dismayed by nothing, György Köves is embarrassed by his family's air of tragedy when the deportations from Budapest gather pace; for nothing in his reading of the situation warrants such gloom. He stays fairly buoyant on the train: "The sliding door was closed on us, with something being hammered onto it on the outside, then there was some signalling, a whistle, busy railwaymen, a lurch, and—we were off. We boys made ourselves comfortable in the rear third of the wagon, which we took over as soon as we boarded." Once in Auschwitz, the evidence of horror does not sweep away György's resources of reasonableness and hope. In the report or statement that forms the narrative, he clings to phatic phrases that make his experience manageable: at any rate, naturally, needless to say, by and large, that's for sure, not surprisingly, as luck would have it. His teenage blitheness wears very thin, yet it never disappears. "For even there, next to the chimneys, in the intervals between torments, there was something that resembled happiness."

Jerzy Kosinski, two years older than Kiš, caused a stir with *The Painted Bird*, also published in 1965. Kosinski painted his atrocities in thick, coarse lines, with a pornographic focus on violence and violation—rather like Kiš's Yugoslav contemporary, Miodrag Bulatović. The child's eye becomes an alibi for simplified and sadistic descriptions of horror: something Kiš would see as unworthy of an artist.

His own inspirations had nothing to do with war or atrocity. He told Velimir Visković, a Croatian critic, that Marcel Proust had been important, and the first line is almost a homage to the opening of *À la recherche du temps perdu*.[28] And he hugely admired Miroslav Krleža's memoir, *Childhood in Zagreb in 1902–1903*.

Perhaps a third author exerted a helpful negative influence as Kiš grappled with his sprawling manuscript. This was Isidore Ducasse, the self-styled Comte de Lautréamont, whose delirious *Songs of Maldoror* (1869) would become the bible of the Surrealists. Kiš and his wife Mirjana Miočinović translated Lautréamont in Strasbourg, and one pictures them absorbed in those "dark and poison-drenched pages", whose "toxic emanations" might, the author warned dramatically, "saturate [the reader's] soul like sugar dissolving in water." Did the madness of Maldoror help Kiš to frame the very different lunacy of Eduard Sam? Did Lautréamont's extravagance encourage him to persist with his own eccentric, anti-realist project? Whatever the answers, the illustration of Maria's sewing machine in *Garden, Ashes* plainly alludes to Lautréamont's most famous simile, when someone is said to be "as beautiful as the fortuitous encounter upon a dissecting table of a sewing-machine and

---

28 Compare Aleksandar Hemon's very different tribute to Proust at the start of his story, "Imitation of Life": "For a long time I used to go to bed early, but then my parents finally bought their first TV set." As a member of the punk generation, Hemon is no captive of the veneration for Europe's literary heritage that came naturally to Kiš and his Central European contemporaries (see chapter 4).

an umbrella!" In Kiš's text, the sewing machine ceases to be an image of incongruity and is restored as a sign of maternal industry and devotion.

As an editor of the magazine *Vidici* (see chapter 30), Kiš had helped Filip David, Mirko Kovač, and Borislav Pekić to publish their first stories. The four young writers became close friends and formed what David calls "an informal group" who met to discuss their work. Kiš set a strict condition: they should not be lobbyists, by trying to get good notices for each other's books and suchlike. When he returned from Strasbourg, he read the manuscript of *Garden, Ashes* to these friends, who were dazzled. So were the critics, when the book was published. The setting of fascist brutality ensured a positive reaction even from reviewers who might have balked at its strangeness.

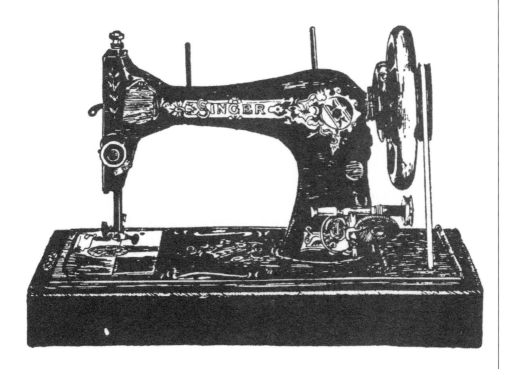

I worked as a servant for rich peasants, and in school
I listened to the catechism and Catholic Bible study.

Kerkabarabás (population: 303) lies low in the south-west corner of Hungary, amid terrain that drains southwards to the sleek waters of the grey-green river Mura. Slovenia is half an hour away, Croatia a little farther. The towns are sleepy. Deciduous forest, telegraph poles, and bulbous, russet-coloured church spires break the horizon. The road from the border lifts and falls, and then falls again past brick farms where storks' nests spill over the chimney stacks. Traffic noise does not penetrate far into the woods and fields.

Arriving in the village one wet summer Sunday, near the end of the last century, we rolled along puddled roads, past low houses with peeling window frames, mossy roof tiles and ragged orchards. Pipes were being laid to connect the village to the gas mains. In the bar, a quartet of men rocked on their heels. When we explained our purpose, one man spread his arms and grinned: "My friend Dani!" This was István Molnár, whose father Sándor had, as mayor in 1947, signed Milica's papers confirming that she and Eduard had been married; that "because of his Jewish nationality", Eduard was taken away to Germany, where "they had killed him"; that he had not collaborated with "the occupier"; that she had not remarried or broken the law. (These documents were essential to establish her right to a Yugoslav pension.)

István introduced us to several neighbours, and their collective memories poured out. Dani liked animals. A stray dog called Dingo followed him everywhere. István was five or six years older than Dani, but they milked the cows together. Milica knitted jumpers for the Molnár children and sewed curtains for their mother, who paid her with food. Eduard was tall and thin; he had a fine singing voice. They all lived in a sort of shed behind the Kon house, which included a shop with a little bar. They sold everything in that shop: groceries, yeast, petrol.

(The family shop is evoked in *Garden, Ashes* by convex-lensed fragments:

a dark, low-ceilinged room smelling of petrol, soap, chicory and camomile tea. Large blue and red enamel signs flash their slogans, pithy and pointed, on behalf of *Franck* chicory. On the other flap of the door, a campaign of dazzling promises is underway for *Schmoll* shoe polish. Pinned to the wall with a tack, next to a maxim in the best French style about healthy, radiant teeth, to which *Kalodont* brings a porcelain sheen while filling the mouth with the freshness and tang of wild strawberries, a scrap of corrugated paper torn from a grocery bag bears a Pythian, prophetic utterance from my aunt Nettie, in indelible pencil: "From the Monday following Sunday 11 Feb. 1942 sugar will cost 200 pengő per kg. loose and 230 pengő in cubes."

In *Hourglass*, the shop is described very differently by E.S., burning with dislike of his nephew who manages the business and of the village where fate has trapped him:

Nothing in the world would make him enlarge or modernise his shop, or stock anything more than the standard articles—paraffin, sugar, shoe polish (two colours), shoelaces (two dozen), candles, flypaper, cheap sweets, etc. He thinks that supplying anything else, such as fine soap or cologne or even electric belts could make the peasants and the authorities suspicious. Apart from that, he's afraid the peasants would denounce him as a modernist and pornographer, destroying the patriarchal way of life. . . . I said toilet soap, when actually it's common household soap made from animal waste. He bought it from a peasant just in case someone should want soap, someone from the city, or an officer, or a random passer-by. I'm inclined to think, though, that he only got that smelly soap so he could sell it to me. I can't see anyone else in the village buying soap.)

Eduard had a good pension, he used to be a chief inspector on the railways, but the family was very poor. Milica was very nice, refined, well accepted in the village, although

she came from Yugoslavia and the village was Catholic with only one Jewish family. Every village had a Jewish family. István's uncle had huge drinking binges with Eduard; then they'd sleep it off under a haystack. Eduard drank a lot and didn't treat his wife well. She was very beautiful, and he was jealous. He was all right with the children but not with her.

How, I asked, did the village feel about this Jewish family?—We had no problems. They had been here several generations, they were part of the village. They gave us credit when we had no money. They put up a marquee in the garden and hosted parties. People were closer then than they are now. There are two gypsy families here now. After the father was taken away in 1944, the family was left with nothing at all.

How were they taken away?—In the middle of the night. Probably by the Germans. They took them all away, and they all died. One aunt survived; she's in Budapest. She said she remembered seeing Mengele. Dani worked as a cowherd. When we saw German troop carriers, we chased them down the road: we'd never seen their like! The mother knitted day and night. The children went barefoot because they had no money for shoes. We took them jam and things, and invited them for meals. How beautiful the children were! Black hair and blue eyes! Children came specially to see the beautiful Jewish girl. Before 1944, no one bothered them.

Dani was in primary school for four years, here in the village. It's been knocked down now. The secondary school was a mile or two away in Zalabaksa.—Was he unhappy at school?—No! He was happy. He fitted in. The teacher was very strict; she caned the pupils. She realised Dani had a talent for writing. He wasn't interested in religious studies or mathematics. He was always talking, always performing, surrounded by other kids. Then he was in secondary school for a year, until the family went away.

Can you show us the Kon house?—No, it has been knocked down. It stood empty for thirty years; then someone wanted the land, the council let it be demolished, and a new house was built.

Another neighbour joined the conversation.—Oh, I remember them, of course I do. The father used to cover the yellow star on his brown jacket with his hand, so people couldn't see it.—She imitated Eduard's futile attempt at concealment, which only served to draw attention.

Dani was handsome but his sister was *beautiful*. The father was taken away because he was Jewish. Then they had a difficult life. People helped them when they could, gave them bread out of pity, but it was wartime and nobody had much. The father was a clever man, and Dani was clever too. He did very well.—Yoy, how beautiful the girl was, what was her name, Danica, yes: black hair, white complexion, blue eyes.—Like her mother. Dani was like his father. A lively boy, a scamp.—We'd give them milk and potatoes in exchange for errands.—The mother was a very good woman, always knitting and sewing.—The father was always walking in the woods and taking photographs, so people wondered if he was a spy. His lungs were bad.—He didn't bother anybody, he had a friendly word for everyone, a delightful man. I can't say anything bad about them.— They took the Jews because Hitler ordered it.—Pity they didn't take more gypsies, because there are going to be more of them than of us Hungarians.—When we read Dani's obituary in the newspaper, the villagers gathered together and we were proud that this famous man had come from our village.

We took photographs of Kiš's old schoolmates, bade them a grateful farewell, and went to see the site of the Kon property. The smartest house in the village now stood on this plot, at a corner in the road. Two storeys, with a clipped gable roof and a dormer facing the road. Gauze curtains stirred behind double-glazed windows, ajar, between stained wood shutters. There was a small marquee in the front garden. The doorbell broke the surrounding silence, but nobody came. Time filtered through our fingers like sand. Following the road around the corner, the back of the property came into view: half an acre of lumpy ground, "undulating" just as Kiš wrote in *Hourglass*, with—of all things—a pile of old timbers on or very near the spot where the converted stable had once stood.

(Here is the description from *Garden, Ashes*: ". . . our new home, 'servants' quarters' from the feudal age, empty and dilapidated, dating from those far-off mythical times when my paternal grandfather Maks kept a four-horse carriage and servants. There are two gloomy, low rooms with floors of compacted clay which thaws out every spring, lending an air of false fertility, but in fact utterly barren, incapable of sprouting so much as a weed. The roof-beams ooze resin blackened and blended with soot, which hangs precariously in the air for a long time, swelling and glistening like drops of clotted black blood.")

For a moment, I thought these timbers had to be the remains of their hut. This was impossible, for the hut was demolished soon after Kiš's visit in the mid-1960s, his only return to Kerkabarabás after 1947. Years after that visit, he wrote a description of the hut, as though nothing but bare facts could communicate his undimmed loathing, or limn the dimensions of so much misery:

From the outside:

The hut is screened on one side by a manor house, on the other by a wooden stable, and in front by low beech trees. It is made of mud with a roof of darkened bricks that are broken or shearing apart, here and there. The entrance is so low that adults can only enter by bending from the waist. A window, half a metre square, looks towards the trees about ten metres away. This window opens outward. On the other side, facing the "garden", with the latrines and a bit of neglected waste ground, overgrown with weeds, a little round window is built directly into the wall. This window is partly broken. The opening is plugged with rags.

From the inside:

A thin mud wall divides the interior. The bigger space is 2 × 2 metres, the smaller, 2 × 1. The former is "the bedroom"; the latter, "the kitchen". The walls are tinted with an ochre wash, obtained by dissolving clay in tepid water. Under the influence of damp and sunlight, this layer has bubbled or cracked like fish

scales or the faded oil paintings of old masters. The floor is likewise of compacted clay that is several centimetres lower than the ground outside. In sultry weather the clay stinks of urine. (There used to be a stable on this spot.)

There are two wooden beds in the bigger space, and two cupboards stand some 10 centimetres from the wall. A mat is laid diagonally across the floor from the entrance to the kitchen. An enamel stove stands in a corner of the kitchen, with two or three pots hanging from large screws and a wooden chest that serves as a couch and a larder. Rotting, damp pine cones are heaped beside the stove. There is thick smoke in the kitchen, so thick that people sitting on the chest or the low wooden stools can hardly see each other. Voices float through the smoke as if through water.

"An alarm clock used to hang from this screw," I tell the man who drove me here from Budapest. "A drunken Russian soldier took it in 1945."

"They'll put a plaque up," the man says ironically as we step outside. "It will say THE YUGOSLAV WRITER D.K. LIVED HERE FROM 1942 TO 1947."

"Luckily the house is going to be pulled down," I say.

"Pity," says the man who drove me from Budapest. "If I had a camera, I'd take a photo."

By the time he wrote this, probably in 1983, Kiš knew that nowhere else he had lived since 1947, or might live in the future, could matter as much to him.

Leaving the village, as the roadside poles and wires lifted and dipped at the edge of my vision, I realised that Kiš would have seen this same sight when he visited the village as an adult; and that it produced the beautiful metaphor in the epilogue to *Early Sorrows* (see the third interlude).

Someone had mentioned that Eduard's forebears were buried in a Jewish graveyard not far from the village. We spent hours following hints, pushing through dripping undergrowth, deciphering worn headstones in roadside cemeteries. Not a Kon, Kohn, Kiss, or Kis did we find. Reaching the outskirts of Zalaegerszeg, we looked for the synagogue, at the heart of the Second World War ghetto where Eduard Kis was taken in 1944. The streets were clean and empty. The temple itself had been made over as a concert hall and exhibition space, lobster pink on the outside, antiseptic inside, with rows of interlocking chairs. Our miniature quest petered out here. What was the point? The legions of amnesia were invincible: state-sponsored, cunningly disguised as honourable commemorators. Years later, a poem by Wisława Szymborska conciliated that experience in my memory, by explaining why oblivion and honour need not be antithetical. "The End and the Beginning" speaks about the needful evanescence of traumatic memory, after wars.

> . . . Those who knew
> what was going on here
> must give way to
> those who know little.
> And less than little.
> And finally as little as nothing.

———

Kiš was enrolled at the village primary school as "Kiss, Dániel". Birthplace: "Szabadka, Hungary". Confession: "Orthodox" (as per his baptism certificate). He spent four years there, followed by a year at the secondary school in the next village. He and Danica sometimes had to share a single pair of shoes; in harsh weather, they went to school on alternate days. She remembers her little brother as the best pupil in his class, excelling in every subject. She also remembers that their teacher picked on them because they were Jewish. According to Kiš, this teacher was a fascist sympathiser who nevertheless showed them real kindness. She recognised how unusual Kiš was. One of the essays she set was called "What I want to be when I grow up." Danilo, age 10 or 11, thought it would be pretentious to say writer and dangerous to say poet (asking for jeers from the village boys). "So," he remembered, "I said 'some kind of intellectual work'. The teacher said 'What do you mean?' She was not surprised."

This teacher made sure Danica and Danilo were included in religious education. Catechism class, with Catholic instruction in question-and-answer form, was a novelty. According to Danica, there were no religious practices at home except their mother's nightly prayers for her children, which they too learned by heart. Milica also kept a little picture of the Virgin among her few possessions.

In *Garden, Ashes,* Andi's experience of persecution and escape to the village convince him that the family is being punished for its sins. He himself must be guilty of something—but what? His encounter with the Old Testament stories is momentous because they seem to answer that question. Desperate to make sense of his situation, he wants to be an altar server in the village church. But he is barred, as Dani was in real life, from confirmation and First Communion, so prevented from shriving "the frightful burden" of his sins. Unable to see the Church, wielding its intimate and penetrating authority, as anything but all-powerful, Andi logically suspects that his father's troubles are created by the village congregation, whose agents spy on poor distracted Eduard as he wanders the countryside.

Long afterwards, Kiš described his inside-outside position as a would-be Catholic in the village:

> All the lyrical pathos of the Catholic Church—the servers in satin and lace ringing handbells and carrying on a solemn, Latin dialogue with the village priest (the *plébános*), the congregation chanting, the harmonium (played by the schoolmistress) exalting the soul to Heaven—seemed to me no more than a pretext for penitence and torment, and when the schoolmistress (clearly wishing to secure the indulgence of the village fascists for us) appointed me chief carol singer and I went from house to house with my schoolmates dressed in floppy linen peasant trousers and vest, with the hat and whip of a *csikós* [Magyar horseman] and carrying the manger with cloth-and-wood figures of the newborn babe and the Three Magi, I was still sick at heart, because even as I stood singing "Shepherds, arise" on the village doorsteps, I knew I was only there thanks to the schoolmistress.

In Andi's state of mind, the *Shorter School Bible* becomes "the quintessence of all miracles, all myths and legends, great deeds and terrors." As a source of moral myths, it both oppresses and feeds Dani's imagination. The engraved illustrations turn him into "a witness, as if I were in some sort of transcendental time machine, attending the events themselves."

One story haunts him more than any other: "I experienced the Biblical drama of the Flood as my own personal drama." Will he perish or be saved like Noah and his family? He imagines both outcomes by turns: "I was loafing on Noah's ark and drowning in the sea with the sinners." But he knows in his depths that there would be no place for him in the ark:

> so I imagined myself trembling in my mother's lap, wrapped in a soaking blanket, or on the roof of some house with the only handful of survivors, all too aware that this was our last refuge, as the rain poured down without let, Biblically. I'm

consumed by the flames of repentance along with the others on the roof, as on a coral reef in the middle of the sea, while the swollen corpses of animals and people float around us, and the bodies of newborn infants glimmer like fish beside the wrinkled, hairy bodies of old people. And that man wrapped in a caftan, with a mad gleam in his eye and hands upraised to heaven, that's my father, the sinful prophet and false apostle. And as the water rises centimetre by centimetre, remorselessly, turning everything into an immense fluid blank, Noah's ark floats in the inky distance like some enormous fruit that will sprout people and beasts and plants, a great laboratory sailing away full of human and animal sperm,[29] specimens of all species with Latin labels, as in a pharmacy, young onions and potato tubers, apples packed in wooden boxes like a market stall, oranges and lemons each secreting a grain of light and eternity, caged birds that will soon sow the air with the tiny seeds of their chirruping and grace the vacant deserts of the sky with the panache of their flight.

(Andi's imagination heals itself through the exercise of its irrepressible power until it soars like those birds, turning a vision of doom into one of recovery. Noah, selecting specimens to save species, is a figure of the artist labouring to refine and condense, the better to communicate universality.)

When his father and other relatives are herded away to the ghetto in Zalaegerszeg, with as many of their possessions as they can fit onto a cart, Andi sees "the descendants of Noah, in all their innocence, going off to their deaths as the Pharaohs went into the silence of their magnificent pyramids, bearing all their earthly goods." Even the farm animals sense "the approach of a grand, apocalyptic deluge."

The Noah story is woven into the texture of *Hourglass*, too, in ominous tropes that rise to the surface of E.S.'s besieged mind. The wallpaper in his hut is decorated with sleighs which, "endlessly repeated, . . . reduce themselves to a single sleigh": "old fashioned, with high curved runners that make it look like an ark." Meditating on the potato, he expresses a conviction "that it will survive us; that it will survive the great cataclysm. When the dove returns with the olive branch in its beak, when the ark touches dry land again, its keel will scrape up a clump of tubers from the ravaged, exhausted, flooded, long-suffering earth, on some new Ararat." Like Andi in *Garden, Ashes*, E.S. knows that he is doomed but dreams of escape. Dozing in a horse-drawn cab, he finds himself

swimming in deep water, in total darkness, but throughout his dream he knew for sure that he was saved, like Noah, and that all those who had been with him only a short time before had been drowned, that he alone had survived the catastrophe. And in his dream this knowledge filled him with vague pride, for he

---

29 In the epic of Gilgamesh, the boat is loaded "with all the seed of living things, all of them". In the Bible (King James version), God tells Noah how "to keep seed alive upon the face of all the earth".

owed his salvation not only to God's mercy but also to his own merit, his ability to cope with difficult situations in life.

In his peroration, E.S.'s mind settles on the tropes that had caught Andi's imagination in *Garden, Ashes*, and inhabits them—literally. The ark is his body; then it becomes the novel we are finishing; then it is both body and book:

Let my body be my ark and my death a long floating on the waves of eternity. A nothing amid nothingness. What defence have I against nothingness but this ark in which I have tried to gather everything that was dear to me, people, birds, beasts and plants, everything that I carry in my eye and in my heart, in the triple-decked ark of my body and soul. Like the pharaohs in the majestic peace of their tombs, I wanted to have all those things with me in death, I wanted everything to be as it was before; . . . I have wanted and still want to depart this life with specimens of people, flora and fauna, to lodge them all in my heart as in an ark, to shut them up behind my eyelids when they close for the last time.

———————

When the Mesopotamian source of the Flood myth was discovered, historians assumed the original event must have been caused by the Tigris and Euphrates rivers, bursting their banks. Recent research claims instead that Mediterranean waters burst into the Black Sea basin some 7,600 years ago. "Only half a mile across at its narrowest point in the Bosporus valley, with the ocean's limitless power behind it, the salt water roared through the strait at speeds greater than fifty miles an hour, crashing through unabated, radiating a thunderous din and vibration that could probably have been heard and felt around the entire rim of the Black Sea."

The peoples who had flourished beside the vast freshwater lake scattered towards Western Europe or Mesopotamia, where memories of the deluge were "reinforced by the frequent if irregular floods", and passed eventually into the Akkadian epic of Atrahasis and the Gilgamesh myths of Sumeria. "Each year that the floods came was probably the occasion to retell the story of that ancient time when the Great Flood destroyed all people but one single family from whom all were descended." Echoes lingered in "ancient Hebraic writings" and in the Deucalion flood myth, which may have passed to the Greeks from the Phoenicians. The Old Testament version sharpens the moral motive, as corrupt humanity is swept away by an outraged deity. This vengeful morality fastened on young Danilo's imagination; but the boy survived and grew into an author of whom it may be said, as the first tablet from Nineveh says of Gilgamesh, that

He found out what was secret and uncovered what was hidden,
He brought back a tale of times before the Flood.

The 'troubling dissimilarity' that Freud calls
Heimlichkeit was to be my basic literary and
metaphysical stimulus;

*D*issimilarity was Kiš's favourite word to explain his multiple, unresolved identities.[30] He described it as a birthmark, not to be expunged by migration or
the passage of time. And he associated it bluntly with sickness; the return to
Yugoslavia in 1947—"to *my own home*", as he emphasised—had not "cured" him.

On the other hand, "the 'shameful stamp' of dissimilarity" was "the detonator of
imagination". Without the "ambiguity of my origins," he said in 1986, "without the
'troubling dissimilarity' that comes with Jewishness, and the hardships of my wartime
childhood, I would certainly not have become a writer."

The strange word crops up again when Kiš describes his fascination with "the dissimilarity of things". This was an aesthetic counterpart of the author's own syndrome. In
expressing the dissimilarity of things, Kiš sought literary equivalents of his condition, images to objectify his differentness, make it communicable, clarify it and so, perhaps, reduce
it with the help of metaphors, which discover similarity inside unlikeness. This was the
personal pressure behind a handful of plotless poems that Kiš wrote in the 1960s, such as:

Still Life with Fish

X-ray image of a candle: ribs.
A candlestick: cathedral of silver.

On porcelain, shivering, a bloody piece of liver.
Of salted wounds sturgeon expire.

Lemon yellow, fragrant skin.
White plate's hiatus. Knife's sheen.

Like liquid rubber—oozing cheese.
Reddish apple   Biblical peace.

The room-double blinks in the mirror.
Candle flame gathers in the moth.

---

30 At a pinch, "differentness" would do for Kiš's word "*različnost*".

With a cold and painterly relish for the grotesque, these poems were exercises in meta-phorical and assonant ingenuity, framing the world's incoherence and his own.

He never published "Still Life with Fish", but it stayed with him. Years later, argu-ing that modern writers should "preserve the disintegrated condition of the world" by itemising its contents in arbitrary combinations, Kiš said: "In the old days, the writers like the painters painted a 'still life with fish', but next to the fish they just put a lemon, and even a knife for cutting the lemon, but these things were all *arranged in advance*, like the peeling stage-set in a theatre, or a village photographer's backdrops. Modern writers (and painters) don't believe in the order of things and objects," for they know "the world in its entirety and everything in it, every *object*, is 'still life', and there is no hierarchy of values whatsoever in it, a fish and a knife are worth as much as a sewing machine and an operating table. Everything consists in the relationships, oppositions and parallels."

Poems like "Still Life with Fish" were a dead-end, and he knew it. Lyric poetry was too monologic and ahistorical to sustain his interest, and too rarefied: he needed the har-ness of story-telling and the friction of irony to stir the full creative effort.

———

The standard English title of Sigmund Freud's famous essay, *Das Unheimliche* (1919), is "The Uncanny". There isn't a better translation, though it lacks the ambiva-lence that intrigued Freud. For 'uncanny' is not pregnant with 'canny', as *heimlich* sits inside *unheimlich*. The first edition of the *Oxford English Dictionary* hit the Freudian mark only in a subset of its fifth meaning: "mysterious, weird, uncomfortably strange or unfamiliar (Common from c. 1850)".

Of the translations mooted in Croatian and Serbian, none catches the element of discomfort that can be aroused by the suddenly encountered strangeness of something that has been familiar. Perhaps he encountered Freud's concept in a paper by the French feminist thinker Hélène Cixous. "Fiction and Its Phantoms: A Reading of Freud's *Das Unheimliche* (The 'Uncanny')" is a title that would have appealed.[31] She also provided an alternative translation of *Unheimliche*—"disquieting strangeness"—that could easily be the origin of Kiš's Serbo-Croatian version, "*uznemirujuća različnost*". Be this as it may, Kiš is certainly alluding to Freud's notion that we call the uncanny. And his slip, omitting the negative prefix *Un-*, is oddly appropriate, because Freud's argument hinges on the bonds that twin *Unheimlichkeit* with its semantic opposite, *Heimlichkeit*. The word that means uncanniness is itself uncanny: it contains its own opposite and double.

Freud begins by stating that the *unheimlich* belongs "to all that is terrible—all that arouses dread and creeping horror." Although it is "not always used in a clearly defin-able sense, . . . we may expect that it implies some intrinsic quality". His purpose is to identify "this peculiar quality", and he sets about this by considering the semantics of

---

31 Remembering "those mysterious disappeared people, who form the essence of my literature . . ."

uncanniness. *Unheimlich* must, he reasons, mean the opposite of its antonym *heimlich*, which means familiar, native or homely. Yet there is more to the uncanny than novelty and unfamiliarity. An extra ingredient is involved, a crucial paradox; for the uncanny, he says, by way of an initial definition, "is that class of the terrifying which leads back to something long known to us, once very familiar."

Seeking the origins of this paradox, he glances at comparable terms in other languages. These provide no clues; indeed, they lack that extra ingredient altogether. So Freud returns to the German dictionaries. Examining *heimlich* in more detail, he notices that one sense of the word is "concealed, kept from sight, withheld from others". A twist is provided by the philosopher Friedrich Schelling: "'*Unheimlich*' is the name for everything that ought to have remained . . . hidden and secret and has become visible."

This gives Freud his breakthrough: he sees that *heimlich* "belongs to two sets of ideas . . . that which is familiar and congenial, and that which is concealed and kept out of sight." Delving into this ambiguity, he finds support in the dictionary of the brothers Jacob and Wilhelm Grimm—philologists as well as folklorists—who had traced the morphing reversal in their fourth sense of *heimlich*: "From the idea of 'homelike', belonging to the house, the further idea is developed of something withdrawn from the eyes of others, something concealed, secret . . .". It turns up again in their ninth sense: "The notion of something hidden and dangerous . . . is still further developed, so that '*heimlich*' comes to have the meaning usually ascribed to '*unheimlich*'."

Freud now clinches his definition: *heimlich* is "a word the meaning of which develops towards an ambivalence, until it finally coincides with its opposite, *unheimlich*. In some way or other, *unheimlich* is a kind of *heimlich*." He then considers some instances of uncanniness from literature and life. There is a long and subsequently much-discussed examination of a story by E. T. A. Hoffmann, "The Sandman" (1815), about a student's obsession with a beautiful doll. This leads Freud via the castration complex to the theme of *doubles* as a motif or figure of the uncanny. He approves the argument of a fellow psychoanalyst, Otto Rank, that the idea of the double has undergone an "astonishing evolution". In our childhood, and also in the childhood of *Homo sapiens*, it was an insurance against destruction, a denial of the power of death; "probably the immortal soul was the first 'double' of the body." This is the doubling of Freud's "primary narcissism", the phase of "unbounded self-love".

As with *Heimlichkeit* itself, the idea of the double then absorbs its antithesis: it slowly turns into the "ego-criticising faculty" that is offended by our narcissism. By this process, the double incorporates "the function of observing and criticising the self and exercising a censorship within the mind, and this we become aware of as our 'conscience'." The double is a projected figure or trope of self-observation. In this way, "from having been an assurance of immortality, he [the double] becomes the ghastly harbinger of death."

The element of uncanniness derives, in Freud's reckoning, from "the circumstance of the double being a creation dating back to a very early mental stage, long since left behind, and one, no doubt, in which it wore a more friendly aspect." The uncanniness of the double originates in its combined but antithetical associations with both the warm phase of primary narcissism, and the subsequent, overwhelming hostility and persecution of the "ego-criticising faculty".

Settling himself on the couch, Freud explains that the uncanny in his own experience was associated with "a recurrence of the same situations, things and events", "a factor of involuntary repetition" rooted in infantile psychology. This leads him to "postulate the principle of a repetition-compulsion in the unconscious mind . . . a principle powerful enough to overrule the pleasure-principle, lending to certain aspects of the mind their daemonic character". The repetition-compulsion stems from efforts at repression that fail and hence recur. This generates "morbid anxiety" that is tantamount to the uncanny, a variant that Freud defines as "something familiar and old-established in the mind which has become alienated from it only by the process of repression." Without repression, primitive feelings do not recur "in the shape of an uncanny effect."

The strong association between superstition and the uncanny may have the same cause. Belief in the significance of coincidences, for example, betrays resentment at the defeat of the principle that Freud calls "omnipotence of thoughts" by "the inexorable laws of reality". This is how the uncanny involves us in "the old, animistic conception of the universe, which was characterised by the idea that the world was peopled with the spirits of human beings, and by the narcissistic overestimation of subjective mental processes". Animism, magic, and sorcery are among the "factors" that "turn something frightening into something uncanny".

On this view, modern citizens should have outgrown the susceptibility to uncanniness. In the final part of his paper, Freud tries to explain why, on the contrary, we remain a prey to it. Unable to go further in psychoanalysing the uncanny, he reflects on the powerful association between uncanniness and death. Again, primitive feelings are in play. "Since practically all of us still think as savages do on this topic, it is no matter of surprise that the primitive fear of the dead is still so strong within us and always ready to come to the surface." Repression takes the form of our "educated" refusal "to believe, officially at any rate, that the dead can become visible as spirits". Death is something we are all aware of and want—most of us—not to think about; oblique reminders, in unexpected contexts, trouble us. Freud ends with a shrugging admission that the subject cannot be concluded:

> Concerning the factors of silence, solitude, and darkness, we can only say that they are actually elements in the production of the infantile anxiety from which the majority of human beings have never become quite free. This problem has been discussed from a psychoanalytic point of view elsewhere.

This was heady stuff, appealing more to literary critics and cultural commentators than to analysts, not only because Freud admitted that literature provided more uncanny effects than life. The immense growth since the 1960s of academic interest in identity and difference led to the rediscovery of Freud's paper; to its application to disparate fields (gender, ethnicity, post-colonialism); and eventually to its deconstruction by critics who demonstrated—redundantly perhaps—that the uncanny had defied Freud's methodical clarification, dancing beyond his grasp as uncontainably as any repressed primitive feeling. Cixous wondered if Freud's text was "less a discourse than a strange theoretical novel". His pen had run away with him, she suggested, leading him to trespass outside his own doctrine.

Accepting Freud's linkage of the uncanny with thoughts of mortality and repressed fear of death, Cixous went further: death is always the inadmissible subject. The effect of uncanniness is "reverberation" rather than "emergence": it hints at a presence that cannot be represented. And death is par excellence that which cannot be represented. The beautiful doll in Hoffmann's story evokes uncanniness because its imitation of life is a metonym of death. If death could be represented, the uncanny would be drained of its power; it might even vanish as a category of feeling. It would certainly lose its potent literary resonance, because literature thrives on indirectness, suggestion, and evocation. "As an impossible representation," Cixous wrote with sibylline eloquence, "death is that which mimes, by this very impossibility, the reality of death. . . . only the dead know the secret of death. Death will recognise us, but we shall not recognise it."

———

Kiš never volunteered further thoughts on the uncanny, and no interviewer took the hint dropped here. This is curious because the uncanny, and particularly the motif of the double, had marked his work since 1959, when he wrote the third of his essays or prose-poems inspired by Joyce's *Ulysses* (see chapter 8):

Noah's Ark (From Mr Poppy's notebook)

Rooms are oases in the grey wastes of a dubious world, havens of tranquillity, shells of security, warm wombs of sleep, places for bold encounters with ourselves, our *alter ego*, our Double who also feels safe and serene here (in the room), which is why he takes a bow, bare and sharp-toothed. For he it is who creates what we usually call the 'atmosphere', the 'homely warmth' and so on, and the Biedermeier[32] mouldings and all the amenities—the washbasins and pots of jam, drinks cabinet and crystalware, silverware and polished surfaces, electric switches and light music on the radio, gramophone records, family portraits, and prints (or originals) of the Maja Desnuda and a kitschy Venus—all these things are

---

32 In northern Yugoslavia as elsewhere in central Europe, the nineteenth-century Germanic décor known as Biedermeier was a byword for conventional bourgeois taste.

immaterial to the powerful Double when he finds himself alone before you and safe from the world locked in with a complicated Wertheim lock,[33] which only appears to be a significant factor in this process of facing up to yourself. That solid Wertheim lock may prove to be as vain and deceitful as the whole gilded and polished Biedermeier lie, for you cannot escape from yourself, cannot lock yourself out. Serenity is born in the complex mechanism of the heart, which is simple at the same time; the Double who emerges when he's left alone with you, as mighty as great-steel,[34] as huge as can be, never mind all the locks and alarms, can be found in one of those quarters called ventricles and auricles, sealed behind a Wertheim lock. Tranquillity's home is one of these reddish purple chambers, bright portraits of all the loved ones and warm impressionist canvases are hanging there, glowing like music from an imaginary museum of memories. A Platonic world of ideas hides in these red rooms, source of shreds of imagination, images that will take concrete shape as imperfect and semi-perfect things and objects (mere distant reflections of those perfect models that drowse in the warm quarters of the heart), things imperfect compared to the model: the radio, the portrait in oils, the book case, the set of Chinese porcelain, the ashtray of seashells . . .

But nothing changes if you swap this pompous externalisation of ideas for the modesty of a cast-iron bedstead, a van Gogh reproduction cut out of a magazine, a plain glass tumbler, two or three books from a lending library, a picture of your girlfriend in a plain frame.—It is not just a question of amenities.

What matters is daring to stay alone with yourself. With your Double.

---

33 Made in Austria since 1852, Wertheim locks were known as the finest brand available in Yugoslavia. (There is another Wertheim safe in *Hourglass*.)

34 This simile ("*silni kao bašcelik*") alludes to one of the best-known villains in Serbian folklore, the mighty Baš Celik ("great steel" or "big steel"). The story goes like this. An old king has three sons and three daughters. Before he dies, he tells his sons to give his daughters to the first comers. The youngest prince insists on respecting their father's wish, and the girls are taken away by ominous suitors. After the brothers hear nothing from their sisters, they set out in search of them. They survive adventures with dragons, serpents, and man-eating giants. The youngest prince saves a princess, whom he marries. Before he goes travelling one day, the king (his father-in-law) entrusts nine keys to this prince. The first eight chambers hold treasure, he says, and then warns him not to enter the ninth on any account. The prince of course disobeys, and in the ninth chamber he finds Baš Celik, in steel chains up to his knees, both arms manacled to the elbows, unable to move an inch. "Bring me a drink of water from the pump," Baš Celik pleads, "and I will grant you an extra life." The prince fills a pitcher (encrusted with gems) and gives it to Baš Celik. "Give me another drink and I shall grant you another life," he says. Again the prince complies. Baš Celik promises the prince a third life if he will just sprinkle water on his head. But this liberates Baš Celik, who bounds away like lightning, seizes the princess, spreads his wings and flies off. The king urges the prince not to follow: it would mean certain death; he will find him another wife instead. Again the prince disobeys and sets out to rescue his princess. On the way he meets the Dragon King who warns him to go no further: even with his army of 7,000 dragons, he himself could not defeat Baš Celik. The Falcon King and the Eagle King tell him the same. The valiant prince will not be dissuaded. He finds and fights Baš Celik, who quickly rids him of his spare lives. "Go home now and don't lose the life God gave you," he thunders. The three animal kings rush to his support with their armies, but in vain. Resolved to try cunning instead of force, they discover that the villain's courage is hidden in a bird inside the heart of a fox on a distant mountain. When they catch the bird and kill it, Baš Celik dies. The prince takes back his wife and home they go.—This minuscule allusion to folklore is one of very few in Kiš's work. It opens like a loophole on to a hinterland of pre-modern archetypes.

No-one would ever choose to leave their warm room, just as no-one chose to leave their mother's womb. Which is exactly the problem. If—due to some cruel but heroic destiny—you have to leave the warm hearth of family tranquillity, the children's room with portraits on the wall that serve as guardian angels—how to go back and start all over again? Change the portraits on the wall, start protecting instead of being protected. Take on the part of demiurge and orchestrator of a world that lies halfway between the microcosm and the macrocosm.

A room is not a piece of philistine equipment, it is a psychological factor, the completion of a personality. You have to grow accustomed to a room as you have to grow accustomed to life. It is hardest for those who have not grown accustomed to walls and mirrors, those who know how to be alone only in a crowd. For even someone who has been expelled from the warm room of childhood often isn't able—due to a confluence of fateful circumstances, objective and subjective—or allowed to return to a different cell, which more often than not is less warm than the others, which are heated by flames from the hearth of memory.

Here starts the odyssey of a man without a room. All walls and all things are less lovely, less perfect than those that came before, or in dreams. The room becomes a hell with concave and convex mirrors that always throw back a fake-objective mask of an unshaven face, with black circles under his eyes and eyes clouded with sleeplessness or drink.

Then the flight begins. Anything not to stay alone with yourself as you really are, or aren't. You cannot leave the clamour of the world, indeed you seek it out, for the silence of solitude is hell, hell—that is you yourself alone.

The rooms of childhood (if they ever existed) were warmed with warm words and kindness. Try then, friend, to carry the smile of friendship, embraces, a woman's warm eyes between the bare walls of the room—something will remain against solitude, words and smiles will remain. The dank staleness will vanish, smoke will drift gaily from the chimney top.

The phantom grimacing in the mirror will disappear too. The encounter with yourself, with your Double, will bring only the joy of recognition. As happens with scents. And with colours.

———

Rain on the windowpane, evening rain beating down, and wind—on *that* side—while you lie down with a cigarette and a book, safe behind a Wertheim lock, which is now just a symbol of your warm peace of mind. And outside the rain beating crazily beyond the tightly shut Venetian blinds, which are the sensitive keys of a harpsichord drummed by the rain's long fingers, and the wind plays accompaniment on the strings of the branches. The room becomes a hollow seashell booming softly, bearing you like Noah's ark over the flood that spreads

devastation, you are an onlooker, an eyewitness and a participant in this apocalyptic destruction that will cleanse everything from the face of the earth, but
for this one night you can live in the beauty of the destruction of the world, for
birds are singing in your ark, seeds are preserved there for the great awakening,
for tomorrow, seeds from which will sprout—with the dawn—a new world. . . .

So, which is it: did you leave your little room because you've made a habit
of getting drenched, or because you don't know which you like more: rain on the
windowpane or rain on your hair?

Some of Kiš's most distinctive concerns and procedures are broached for the first
time in this odd, impassioned text whose only allusion to Joyce is the word "odyssey".
Setting out as a pastiche moral critique of bourgeois complacency, an ironic Freudian
take on the biblical warning against the traps of Mammon, it switches into a meditation
on the uncanny and on exile—not the forcible displacement suffered by millions in mid-
century Europe, including Kiš and his family, but the expulsion from childhood that
growing up entails. The "warmth" of childhood cannot be recreated in later life, try as we
might, though it may, with luck, be echoed in new affections.

The text veers into the uplifting rhetoric of self-help manuals before settling finally
into *literature*, perhaps a sort of love letter, which figures the sum of our remembered
experience as an ark we carry around, or that carries us, through the splendid wreckage
of our days: a cabinet of personal curiosities, but also our store of fertile and unsinkable
possibilities. Everyone is his or her own ark, harbouring customised versions (doubles) of
the world and its contents.

In aesthetic terms, the "amenities" listed with ironic disdain are the kind of lumber
that crowds the interiors in naturalist fiction: lifeless matter that has not been transposed
by technique, merely named. As we live our lives, remembrance casts a unique aura of
association around objects and spaces which, lacking it, are "philistine equipment". We
are expelled from childhood trailing cords of memory: umbilical cords, if memory really
can supply primal nourishment and lasting illumination. "For Kiš," as his friend Predrag
Čudić remarked, "there was no such thing as invention; there was only the search for
what has been lost; everything else is night and fog."

A poem written in Strasbourg, in 1963, while he worked on *Garden, Ashes*, anticipates the taste of desolation to come, the retrospective staleness of experience that still lies
ahead, and future dependence on dwindling supplies from his personal ark:

I've drawn from love, like everyone else,
all my infinite, inimitable Selves,

but the rain will catch me on the way,
rain that'll stop every mouth one day.

A day when the zest of crazy youth
reaches an empty (empty) dune,

and nowhere shelter, no more discovering,
only what's drawn from your own past being.

———————

Literature worthy of the name should rival this power to "recreate life out of life", in Joyce's phrase. Evocative, lyrical forms of expression could not achieve this vital transposition, for they had been bled white by the entrepreneurs of kitsch art and mass culture. The recreation of life out of life means the generation of *unlikeness*, related to its genitor but different from it as children are to parents. The way to achieve this was with modernist techniques for confounding expectations, not confirming them. In later years, Kiš cited Viktor Shklovsky's "*ostranenie*," or defamiliarisation, as the keystone of his thinking. But this was only a fancy word for something simple: the moment when an object changes meaning so completely that it might be a different thing—when it becomes its own double.

The brawny, enigmatic Double in Kiš's text seems at first like a cousin of the nineteenth-century *Doppelgänger*, the physical doubles invented by Edgar Allan Poe, Fyodor Dostoevsky, Oscar Wilde, and Robert Louis Stevenson: a figure of regression, of civilisation brushed against the grain, allegorising the repressed conflict of ego and id in a divided self, perhaps a figure of death.

Instead, he turns out to be the process and product of thought itself. It is the idea of myself that becomes present to me when I am not performing in the theatre created by other people's company. ("Think you're escaping and run into yourself," muses Joyce's Bloom. "Longest way round is the shortest way home.") This Double's strength is not that of the elemental id: it is the unstoppable energy of the mind reflecting on its situation, experiences, desires—and on its own reflections; ramifying like screensaver pipelines. Literature is its home; which is why Kiš defined literature as a parallel life, a second life.

Unstoppable, that is, until life itself stops. In his story, "The Mirror of the Unknown", Kiš's chronicle of deaths foreseen, two doomed sisters "make believe they are dozing, but each is absorbed in her own thoughts." As the fertile home of doubling, such silent thought proves that imagination is about its vital business, weaving with a noiseless shuttle. Elsewhere, at that moment, a third sister "brings the mirror up to her face, but for a moment she does not see anything." For a process that is identical with life, suspension is fatal. The empty mirror signals the end of doubling, which augurs death—the imminent murder of the girl's father and sisters.[35]

———————

35 The Polish critic Stanisław Barańczak writes that Kiš's is an art of mirrors, echoes, and shadows; of correspondences and symmetries which reveal the hidden meaning of the universe. The mirrors in Kiš's writing are, he suggests, haunted by the multiple reflections of the face of human suffering. This particular story might also be read as a comment on attempts to 'explain' the Holocaust. When the murderers in the story are caught along with their bloodstained loot, they admit their guilt and ask for a priest to hear their confession: a request as senseless as the crime. A remark of Hannah Arendt provides an appropriate gloss: "evil is never 'radical', it is only extreme, and possesses neither depth nor any demonic dimension."

Kiš's Double in the "warm room" is a projection, animated by remembrance and imagination. It creates the homely warmth because it *is* the power of remembrance, and our love of cosiness harks back to childhood. The final section of the text ("Rain on the windowpane . . .") falls into place as a revelation of doubling fulfilled in metaphor, hence literature: the slats of the blind are harpsichord keys, the branches outside double as strings, the room as an ark.

When this integration is lacking, our doubles become dangerous. Just as doubling can be enrichment, addition, and ambiguity, it can also be subtraction, splitting, and psychosis. Consider Kiš's much-reprinted polemic against the self-righteous bigotry of nationalism (see chapter 22): "The nationalist fears no one, 'no one but God'. Yet his is a God made to measure, his double sitting at the next table, his own brother, every bit as impotent as himself". The double has warped into bad authority, intrusive, deformed by *ideology*, a word Kiš always used with animus, as a synonym of false consciousness.[36]

Or his swipe at local feuds over language: "the philological jousts between Zagreb and Belgrade, each of which has its 'sweet mother tongue' down on index cards, so alike in structure, so different in aroma, queen bees ready at any moment to stab each other with their poisoned stings, each convinced of the authenticity and purity of her particular healing nectar."[37] Again, lack of reflection unleashes stupidity and evil: the two sides in the language war cannot even see that each is the other's double, a cannibal projection of its insecurity. (See also chapter 31.)

Kiš's intuitions, pointing to a psychological theory of false consciousness, can be given a wider historical reading, beyond the deadly antinomies of Balkan nationalism. The critic Geoffrey Hartman traced "poetics after the Holocaust" to the Romantic poets, specifically to William Wordsworth's image of "a barrier . . . that from humanity divorced / Humanity, splitting the race of man / In twain, yet leaving the same outward form." In Hartman's rather portentous gloss, Wordsworth was describing "an ominous breach in the human, one that opens the possibility of deceptive look-alikes, and, since the human form is not radically affected, drives a wedge between outward appearance and inner reality." Whether this breach opens the way to pluralist compassion or aggressive hatred may depend on many things, not least on our aptitude for insight into the ways of our own imaginations. If we fail to understand the doubling process, we leave ourselves at its mercy. Embattled nationalists do not recognise their fantasies about identity *as* fantasies. Incapable of reflecting truthfully on the private sources of their values or convictions, they impose them compulsively on others. One reason why Kiš despised nationalism is its laziness: nationalists live out a particularly noxious version of the unexamined life.

---

36 Or this, from an essay on self-censorship (1985): "The subject of self-censorship is the writer's double, a double who leans over his shoulder and interferes with the text *in statu nascendi,* keeping him from making an ideological misstep."

37 As well as meaning 'queen bee', *matica* refers to the Serbian and Croatian cultural academies, *Matica srpska* and *Matica hrvatska,* which, as self-appointed guardians of national identity, patrol their respective linguistic boundaries. It is a measure of Kiš's resolve to stay above nationalist disputes that this was almost his only published comment on Serbian-Croatian rivalry—the cause to which entire literary careers, and many thousands of lives, have been sacrificed.

Hartman hints that the Holocaust was the most consistent political exploitation of this breach which, in literary terms, had been felt by the Romantics and then mapped by novelists in the nineteenth century—Dostoevsky, Stevenson, and so on. The enormities of the twentieth century were perpetrated by souls whose blindness to their own disintegration drove them to invent enemy doubles and seek their extermination. Twentieth-century art traced this breakdown in a literature of cognitive or imaginative doubling. Borges is the great rueful ironist and magus. More recently, John M. Coetzee has drawn novel after novel from the doubling power of the imagination.

Reality is one; images or versions of it are infinite. Magritte's famous painting of a pipe above the caption "*Ceci n'est pas une pipe*" is a clever joke, but false to the experience of aesthetic enchantment, which says, "The image in the painting is indeed a pipe, but it is not the same pipe as the one that the artist was copying or imagining when he painted it." Nor are we helped much by observing that one pipe is real while the other is a representation; for this observation is too reflective, too coolly intellectual, at least when the enchantment is strong. It is the nature of that experience to blur and multiply our sense of reality.

Style should embody self-knowledge. The process of perception needs to be caught and rendered in the artwork—not substituting for story but as the price of not recycling formulas from bygone times. Art which pretends its contents are identical with reality is false (by denying representation), deceptive (by promising impossible kinds of certainty), and banal (because anachronistic). The same is true of poetry that expresses an uncomplicated lyric voice, "gazing at its own narcissistic likeness, its own heart."

Doubling is, then, entailed by the dynamics of perception. The psychotherapist Adam Phillips observes that "everyone we meet invents us, whether we like it or not." My perception of you is not yours of yourself; it doubles you. If I deny this, I efface your reality with my version of it. Politicians do this all the time; so do lovers and artists, even as their passions and works provide our strongest evidence that they are mistaken. Writing performs the trick twice: the 'you' in my description of you is your double, not the real you; but also, the 'I' that writes about you, and lingers as a presence in my own text, is not identical with the I living in the world. Arthur Rimbaud's *Je est un autre* was a sober ontological remark.

Kiš called this the "magical and self-fertilising transformation that creates a process of simultaneous separation and unification between the *I* in the novel and the real *I*, for the *I* of the person who writes about himself and the *I* that does the writing both *are not* and *are* the same person." This goes beyond Proust's remark that "a book is the product of a *self other* than the self we manifest in our habits, our social life, our vices", or Aleksandr Solzhenitsyn—another hero—saying his books were written by "a twin"; or Roland Barthes declaring that "Who *speaks* is not who *writes*, and who *writes* is not who *is*." For Kiš, the writer's I and the writing I are not fixed in distinct doubleness or counterposition; they merge and separate like the braided channels of a single stream.

You double my words—or their meaning—by reading them. This is not to deny that an original object is more real, in some sense, than its doubles. But the uniqueness of that primary object is available only to itself, perhaps also to its creator, except when art manages to communicate it to others. For Kiš, communication of this kind was occult, alchemical, worthy of veneration. Since the romantic age, art has achieved this alchemy not by claiming to be the first in its field, pristine, untouched by previous endeavours, but rather by recognising those endeavours, absorbing and glancing off them, finding paths through or around them. Which points eventually to Adorno's anti-Romantic insight: "It was by way of imitation, not by avoiding it, that art achieved its autonomy; in it, art acquired the means to its freedom."

These transformations fascinated Kiš. In pedagogic mood he framed them, as when he writes that "The room becomes a hollow seashell booming softly . . .", or in his paean to telegraph poles at the end of *Early Sorrows*: "All you have to do is put your ear to the pole; though it is no longer a pole, now it is a harp." Writing at full pitch, however, he let language do the work of doubling, as in the sentence already quoted from *Garden, Ashes*, about Eduard Sam's compulsive wandering: "He moved through the fields like a sleepwalker, lost in thought, waving his cane high in the air, following his star, which he would lose amid the sunflowers, only to find it again at the edge of the field on his greasy black frock coat." The yellow star patched onto Eduard's coat fades in and out of his consciousness, merging into its double: the star of his destiny.

The star reappears when Andi-Dani imagines his troubled father's first glimpse of his mother, in a café. Drink, love's hireling wisp of a double, warms Eduard up for the real unfamiliar thing, with its healing integrative power.

> Mr Sam was sitting up stiff and straight, feeling as if his body were someone else's, until a warm wave of alcohol swept over him, making him feel closer to his own organs. This warm rumbling in his intestines, this invisible sun that lit him up from inside, restored his personality, and he once again saw his fingers on the table as part of *his own* hand, *his own* body, he had regained his integrity, his body reconstituted and stretched out to its true size, unfragmented, from the tips of his toes to the last hair on his head. . . . He ascribed this fantastic surge of strength to alcohol alone, yet at the same time he felt a shudder akin to fear: some unknown force was welling up inside him. . . . For an instant he glimpsed his body in its wholeness, dressed and naked at the same time, he felt the hardness of his toenails as if his socks were silken gloves, he felt his skin, white and freckled like a trout, he felt his ashen hair, which, freshly cut, crept under his rigid collar and scratched tinily against the edge when he turned his head. In one single glance of satisfaction and fresh courage, he saw that everything was there, just as it once was: the big sharp shoulder blades that made him seem a little hunched, the bony joints of his wrists and fingers, everything, absolutely everything, as if none of it had ever been estranged from him, as if he had never hated any of it. . . . That same evening, Eduard Sam noticed a woman among the company at the next table: an extraordinarily beautiful woman. And he an-

nounced quite lucidly, as if wanting to preserve this unexpected integrity of mind and body (which he rightly associated with the presence of that woman), 'Gentlemen, _____

_____

_____.' The intense silence that fell upon the table for a moment marked the fateful encounter of two creatures, two stars.

The star is also present in *Early Sorrows*, as we saw, and in *Hourglass*, where its transformation is laconic and unsettling: "The man has draped his coat over his shoulders. He has a large yellow flower in his left-hand buttonhole." Other memorable transformations are woven into *Hourglass*, as when E.S.'s spade turns up "a red brick, as red and moist as a chunk of fresh beef". (E.S. experiences life as bestial, his own flesh with its red freckles and hairs is "human meat".) E.S.'s room is a boat, dashed by the waves of night. The wick in his oil lamp is "as white and sluggish as a sated tapeworm". (The wick has been guzzling the oil, trying to extinguish the lamp before E.S. can finish his letter.) The lamp's flame is a star, and the reader's eye is a moth. A column of cigarette ash is toothpaste, a catkin, a worm fossil, the ruined column of time, hence "transience itself".

These dynamics of perception are most intense in the closed arena of what Kiš called the family circus. The summit of his art, in this sense, may be "The Game", a story in *Early Sorrows*, where Eduard spies through a keyhole on little Andreas as he plays at being a feather merchant, trying to sell feathers to the image of Mona Lisa and the portraits of his grandparents on the wall. Andi does not know why he likes this game or why it feels naughty—or that he is doubling his Jewish ancestors. This is the uncanniness of *Unheimlichkeit* at full pitch, drawing on the belief "that children are reincarnations of the souls of parents or of ancestors." The draughty keyhole is a tunnel through time and space to the spirit world of the ancestors.

Ultimately, *doubling* is a synonym for figurative language—similes, metaphors, the whole tribe of tropes. His superstitious awe at the transformative power of language grew out of childhood experience. Tapping such power, an artist could be "the double of the Demiurge". In some ways, his sense of language was shamanist, like the traditional Bushman, whose presentiments could turn his body into "the body of his father, of his wife, of an ostrich and of a springbok"; or the Asaba people of Nigeria, who believe that "everyone is considered to be created in duplicate"; or the Sicilian folk belief that "every material thing has an impalpable image or double, which can be detached, and can penetrate other bodies."

Language usurps the world in our imaginations. The heroic lucidity of Kiš's explications of literary modernism—offered against the realist inertia of his Yugoslav milieu— could not dispel this mystery. Nor did he want it to. Exposing the mysticism around literature would isolate its authentic mystery, which spread over the act of writing itself. In 1982, he wrote an appreciation of M. C. Escher's famous drawing of several ants or a single ant crawling along a Möbius band, a strip of paper twisted once and glued together so that it has a single surface and a single edge. The Möbius band is a solid instance of the uncanny, and Escher's functional style, as if to illustrate a textbook, would have appealed strongly to Kiš's taste for *expert plainness*—the taste that led him to extol cookery books over novels (see chapter 23). Perhaps it appealed, too, as a metaphor of Kiš's ideal continuity between life and literature. The writer brings material from that "Platonic world of ideas", the private inwardness of memory, into the light of communicative form with only a ribbon of ink trailing from the nib onto paper: a trail quite as uncanny as any Möbius band, and hardly less so if the nib is a plastic cartridge and the words become pixels, pulsing on a screen.

When Freud wrote that an uncanny effect "is often and easily produced when the distinction between imagination and reality is effaced, as when something that we have hitherto regarded as imaginary appears before us as reality", he might have been defining Kiš's mature ambition: to persuade readers that fiction could be as salient and compelling as reality, without shrugging off its status *as* fiction. To achieve this, Kiš used real people, documents, and other non-literary sources. Doubling was what he was did with himself and his family when he transposed them in books. Eduard Kiš became Eduard Sam or E.S., Milica became Maria, his sister Danica became Ana, while he became Andi. Fictional Andi both is and is not historical Dani. We can neither escape the similarity nor turn it into identity.

He also paid the closest attention to questions of knowledge, perspective, and credibility in fiction. When he and Mirjana visited Spain in 1964 with their friend Wladimir Krysinski, they went to the Prado museum in Madrid. Kiš stood for a long time in front of *Las Meninas*, Velázquez's astonishing depiction of the royal children and the artist himself, which puts the spectator in the position that the king and queen must be occupying, outside the painting, as onlookers. Some time later, he told Krysinski what he admired about the painting: "the dialectics of interdependent points of view". What does a narrator seem or claim to know about the story he is in? What does the author seem or claim to know about the characters and their situations? How credible are these claims? Where does the reader stand in relation to all this?

These matters absorbed him as much as any avant-garde prose writers in the 1960s and 1970s—Beckett, Georges Perec, the *nouveau romanciers*—and never more than in *Hourglass*. The most conventional version of doubling occurs in Chapter 53, where E.S. describes the "feeling of being abandoned by myself, this perception of myself through the eyes of another, this confrontation with myself as a stranger":

> on one side E.S., fifty-three years old, married, father of two, who thinks, smokes, works, writes, shaves with a safety razor; and on the other side, next to him, or rather inside him, somewhere in the centre of his brain, as though asleep or half asleep, another E.S., who is and is not I, because while the first E.S. is shaving

with the precise movements of an untrembling hand, the second, shrunk to the size of an embryo, is doing something entirely different, engaged in unknown and dangerous occupations, and sometimes, just for an instant, I catch him in these forbidden, secret activities, catch him *in flagrante*, doing something different, something utterly incomprehensible to me, for it is absolutely unrelated not only to shaving or tying a tie or eating but also to my ideas and thought processes: he is someone else!

This is doubling as psychosis, anguished disconnection. Summoning his fragile rationality, E.S. manages a series of truer definitions of "the other man, who is and is not I . . . this other self, who is connected with me like a Siamese twin by the backbone, the brain, and the sympathetic nervous system . . . this twin brother of mine, this I and not-I of mine, actually thinks with my brain, steals the thoughts of my brain . . . this other self pursues me, turning up unexpectedly inside me while I am shaving in front of the cracked mirror". Just when E.S. feels that everything is safe at home, "my other self turns up inside me; anguished and trembling, he escapes my brain, because something terrible has just happened to him, a disastrous thought has inflamed his brain, the thought of death, an intense, merciless thought . . ." This is Dr Jekyll's confession as revised by a Hungarian Jew in 1942, perhaps after reading Freud on the uncanny: "from having been an assurance of immortality, he [the double] becomes the ghastly harbinger of death".

Coming halfway through the novel, this chapter has—ironically, given that its subject is E.S.'s "pitiful split self"—a stabilising and even reassuring function. By proving that E.S. has an impressive insight into his condition, it gives us (at last) a yardstick for measuring his actions and words. Punch-drunk from Kiš's riddling assaults on our need for narrative coherence, readers can catch their breath before re-entering the maze.

Kiš's finest achievement of uncanny effects is the seventh chapter of *Hourglass*. It starts with the simplest of statements: "The man is sitting on a boulder by the roadside." The boulder is described in minute detail before "The man turns around." He examines the scene behind him: more rocks, plants, the road winding out of sight on a far mountainside. The description spreads beyond this field of vision to take in the sea, which stretches in front of the seated man. "Along the curving, broken line dividing land and sea, there are deep fjords and bays, with jagged mountain peaks between them." We are told about "schematic clusters of houses" on the horizon, a tall chimney-stack emitting "a black thread of smoke", fiery sunlight reflected on factory windows, and a jetty with a stone lighthouse at the end. After two pages of such description, including ominous detail (wormwood sprouting through cracks on the road, evoking the Book of Revelations; that chimney, portending the Shoah; that fiery sun), the silence of the scene grows audible. Then comes the doubling: "There are bollards on both sides of the jetty. The man is sitting on one of them, not far from the middle of the pier, his face turned toward the sea." Nothing suggests this is not the same man who is (was?) sitting on the boulder, except that the man on the boulder cannot be in two places at once—or can he? The question is implied, but what follows is another forensic description: this time, of a solitary boat moored at the jetty: "The outside is painted black and the spaces between the boards are caulked with shiny black tar that blisters like coagulated blood." This segues to a description of the shadow cast on the seabed by the boat, through calm water.

Then, for the first time since the man turned around on his boulder, there is movement: "Suddenly the shadow of the boat begins to tremble, disintegrate, and disappear." Another vessel is approaching the jetty "in a narrow curve". Instead of showing us the second boat, Kiš catalogues the detritus that swills around the jetty, set in motion by the bow wave. The last two items in the list carry an extra weight:

> . . . a king of diamonds, dog-eared and creased down the middle but still in one piece, his two symmetrical faces clearly distinguishable; a picture postcard showing in the foreground the blue sea and the jetty with lighthouse, alongside the jetty a fishing cutter tied to a stone bollard, while another boat approaches, cutting through the water in a gentle arc; in the background, behind green palms, little white houses with red roofs; in the far distance, high mountains with a narrow road twining around them; and, overhead, a blue sky with two or three pink clouds in it. Somewhere near the middle of the jetty, a man is sitting on a bollard. The man is slightly stooped. He is wearing a straw hat tilted back, and between his knees he is holding a cane, or possibly a fishing rod. Ten meters away from him, there is a woman with a five or six year-old boy and a little girl who is somewhat older. All are looking toward the horizon, at the sunset no doubt. They are in the centre of a curve, in the place where the road widens into a kind of observation terrace. . . . The woman also looks toward the man who is sitting on the stone a little farther down. But he doesn't seem to notice the others. He is looking into the distance, at the sunset, no doubt.

It is impossible to understand what is happening without careful rereading, pencil in hand. We will learn in chapter 32 that E.S. had seen a photograph of a seaside scene identical in some particulars to the scene in chapter 7. The photograph was displayed in the carriage of a train carrying E.S. to Novi Sad, two weeks or so before the 'present tense' events in chapter 7. In chapter 35, E.S. reaches Novi Sad, where he notices an old family photograph of his family beside the sea in August 1939. Again, some particulars are identical with chapter 7. Later in the same chapter (35), with the memory of this holiday photo in his mind, he is reminded of the sunset flaring in factory windows in Kotor, Montenegro, by the sea.

Now we see that chapter 7 began as a remembrance: writing the letter to his sister, E.S. mentions "two Montenegrin villages". These words remind him of the photographs of Montenegro that he recently saw in the train and in Novi Sad. He is interpreting the photographs, which fuse in a dreamlike scene that is laden with dread. This is how our minds work, superimposing scenes and people, dodging unwelcome meanings while dwelling on them compulsively.

Cetinje, August 1939: the family's only
visit to Montenegro. Danilo squints at
the camera, Danica curtseys, Milica
and Risto Dragićević smile at their
sister Draginja, but Eduard looks
anxious. He would be hospitalized with
a psychiatric disorder in the following
month.

As the novel moves to its close, there is one further allusion to E.S.'s memory of
stopping by the sea in Montenegro with his wife and children. In the early hours of the
morning, worn out by writing the letter that forms the matrix of the novel, E.S. gazes
absently at a colour lithograph on the wall of his hovel. It shows the allegorical Ages of
Man, and in E.S.'s mind this trite tableau of the Garden of Eden evokes the familiar
"curving, broken line dividing land and sea (in the background), deep bays and fjords,
with jagged mountain peaks between them."[38]

Kiš conveys a mind under unbearable stress, haunted by memories of a scene redolent of lost happiness and therefore of hopelessness, almost overborne with dread. The
folk-belief that seeing one's own double portends death may be in play; and the two
boats, one with tar like blood (the effect of sunset, but the simile reveals what E.S. can
not admit), the other audible but out of sight, are felt as emblems of fate.[39] We are led
by steps to the insight that E.S. himself suppresses: gazing at the sunset, he gazes at the
prospect of his own death, the "impossible representation".

---

38 We know this was the Bay of Kotor in Montenegro, a "magical place" for Kiš, by virtue of its elemental
beauty and its association with his father, because he says so in a late essay ("A and B"); see chapter 24. His sister
Danica lived there with her husband and children; Kiš stayed with them every summer.

39 Kiš once said that Kafka—whose heroes cannot do the only thing they want to do and must undergo the
very thing they try to avoid—had helped him in writing *Hourglass*. There is an echo here of Kafka's tale, "The
Hunter Gracchus". Mysteriously prevented from either living or dying, Gracchus wanders the seas in a rudderless
boat, "driven by the wind that blows in the nethermost region of death". It is a "clumsy old craft, relatively low
and very broad, as filthy as if it has been swamped with bilge water," which "glided silently into the little harbour,
as if borne over the water."

His poetics of doubling look like an invitation to postmodern relativism, reducing the real to another ludic fiction or figment. But Kiš never extends that invitation; on the contrary, he won't let us forget that doubling thrives only in the imagination and counts for nothing in the face of violence. What's more, although he never wrote about the ethics of dialogue, his work associates naturally with Western moral philosophers from the Greeks, for whom thinking was "a soundless solitary dialogue", to Immanuel Kant, for whom thinking was "talking with oneself . . . hence also inwardly listening", and Hannah Arendt, who defined "this duality of myself with myself" as that which "makes thinking a true activity, in which I am both the one who asks and the one who answers." Dialogism in Kiš's practice, especially in *Hourglass* and *A Tomb for Boris Davidovich*, dramatizes the expression of conscience in this highest sense: the "voice within" which stopped Socrates from doing wrong to save his own life.

———

His visions of the uncanny are not always dark. In 1973, he wrote a note for a catalogue by Safet Zec, a Bosnian artist renowned for pictures of windows, often with double frames, peeling paint, worn lace curtains, and geraniums on the sill. Typically, Kiš avoids the obvious: rather than imagine the room that we glimpse through Zec's window, he imagines what his double might see, standing in that non-existent interior, looking through that non-existent window in our direction—but he no more sees us than we see him. Unlike E.S., this nameless man is not trapped by history; he can opt out of his uncanny experience of serial doubling. For this courtly vision touched with paranoia is, in the end, a harmless dream.

A Window is a Window is a Window is a Window

A man stands before a window, looking out, and touches with his eyes and then his fingers, timidly, the green frame and the casement, the bronze handle and the screws that fasten the lace curtain. Now he sees nothing but sky and some white clouds on the other side, or perhaps there's a violet sunset, he doesn't know, for the time being he simply touches the solid forms of the casement and the frame with his gaze and perhaps with his hand, and wonders if he should push the patterned lace aside or reach for the bronze hasp and see what lies on the other side. Moved by some strange anxiety, he sees his hand stretch towards the hasp and open the window wide with an ominous creak of dry hinges. Then the man looks through the window, and there is the dawn, an aquamarine sky with white clouds, pots of geraniums and creepers, and green gardens as far as the eye can see. Just then the light changes above the scene, suddenly and only for a moment, and at that moment he glimpses, through dense overgrowth, a window so much like the one he's standing beside now that he turns around to look for the mirror where he can find the reflection of this scene and this window, but there is only an open window behind him, geranium blooms and the leathery leaves of the creepers, no mirror anywhere. With the forced smile of a man familiar with nightmares, he approaches the second window, so turning his back on the first one, but when he leans out, he sees only that the daylight has changed, the clouds have moved a little way, otherwise everything is just as it was before, as if in a mirror, and he turns around once again: still no mirror to be seen, and windows multiplying out of sight in both directions. Panicking, the man leans through the casement and catches sight of a green garden, down in the depths before him, illumined by the morning sun, acacias and creepers in bloom, and in the middle of the deserted garden, silent except for the rustle of leathery plants, a plaster Pomona stands and casts her green shadow on the grass. When the sound of a hunting horn reaches him from somewhere in the distance, the man jumps over the low sill and runs towards the sound, but the sound retreats before him.[40] Hurrying towards the sound, breathless, soaked with dew, the searcher reaches a wall with a window in it. The window is wide open, and he leans forward to see into the room: down in the depths below, a green garden in the dense chill of afternoon, the sun doesn't penetrate the greenery, only a plaster Pomona in the middle of the garden, in the twilight, casting her shadow on the damp lawn. The beholder jumps through the window and lies back on the damp grass.

He watches white clouds passing overhead.

---

40 As the writing of others echoes in Kiš's work, so the word 'echo' itself recurs there. From the last page of *Garden, Ashes*: "Our father's ghost hovered in the woods. Did we not hear him blowing his nose into a scrap of newspaper only a few minutes ago, while the woods reverberated with a triple echo?" And indeed, when the father anticipates his end, on the last page of *Hourglass,* the word tolls three times: "Or perhaps—if all else is drowned in the great flood—my madness and my dream will remain like a northern light and a distant echo. Perhaps someone will see that light or hear that distant echo, the shadow of a sound that was once, and will grasp the meaning of that light, that echo." A shadow is surely cast, here, by Hamlet's father's ghost, which "faded on the crowing of the cock" that "is the trumpet to the morn". (Whether Kiš knew T. S. Eliot's *Four Quartets,* with its "familiar compound ghost" which "faded on the blowing of the horn", is not known.)

Moja je majka čitala romane do svoje dvadesete godine, kada
je shvatila, ne bez žaljenja, da su romani "izmišljotina" i odbacila
ih jednom zauvek. Ta njena averzija prema "pustim izmišljotinama"
prisutna je latentno i u meni, ~~xxxxxxxxxxxxxxxxxxxxxxxxxxxxx~~
~~xxxxxxxxxxxxxxxxxxxxxxxxxxxxxxxxxxxxxx~~

Godine 1947, posredstvom Crvenog krsta repatrirani smo na
Cetinje, gde je živeo moj ujak, poznati istoričar, biograf i komen-
tator Njegoša. Odmah po dolasku polagao sam ispit za likovnu školu.
U ispitnoj komisiji bili su Petar Lubarda i Milo Milunović. Voltere-
~~gipsani odlivak~~ Hudonova ~~portretne statue~~, Nemicu
va bista koju smo crtali/ličila mi je na jednu starue koju sam po-
navao u Novom Sadu; tako sam ga i nacrtao. Ipak sam bio primljen,
valjda zbog drugih mojih radova. Trebalo je da sačekam godinu-dve
kako bih mogao imati potrebnu gimnazijsku spremu. Za to vreme ~~sam~~
                sam ipak
~~sam~~ odlučio da završim maturu.

Dve godine sam učio violinu u muzičkoj školi, gde mi je pre-
              ne samo zbog izgleda nego i zat
davao Simonuti stariji, koga smo zvali "Paganini", jer je obožavao
tremola. Upravo kada sam bio stigao do druge pozicije, muzička se
škola odselila u Kotor. Tada sam nastavio da sviram bez nota, cigan-
                                         igrankama
sku muziku i madjarske romanse, a na školskim ~~xxxxxx~~ tango i
inglis-valcere.

U gimnaziji sam nastavio da pišem pesme i da prevodim madjarske, ruske i francuske pesnike, u prvom redu radi stilske i jezič-
ke vežbe: spremao sam se za pesnika i izučavao ~~sam~~ književni zanat.
Ruski su nam predavali beli oficiri, emigranti iz dvadesetih godina,
koji su, zamenjujući odsutne profesore, držali s jednakom spremom ~~x~~
~~znanja~~ predmete kao što su matematika, fizika, hemija, francuski,
latinski.

Posle mature upisao sam se na Beogradski univerzitet, gde sam
diplomirao kao prvi student na novootvorenoj katedri za Uporednu knji
ževnost.

{THIRD INTERLUDE}

Early Sorrows (1969)

Early Sorrows collects seventeen brief stories about Kiš's childhood. There is an obscure chronology, as the stories move from Novi Sad to Kerkabarabás and end with the departure to Montenegro. As in *Garden, Ashes*, the family are Eduard, Maria, Anna, and Andreas (Andi) Sam. The stories are flanked by poetic essays that serve as prologue and epilogue. The prologue begins thus:

> In autumn, when the winds come up, the leaves of the horse chestnut tree fall helter-skelter, stalk first. Then the sound: like a bird rapping the ground with its beak. But the nut falls without a breath of wind, on its own, as stars fall—headlong. Then hits the earth with a muffled scream. It does not hatch like a bird from the egg, gradually, but bursts its prickly shell at once, whitish-blue inside, and out pop mischievous, dark half-breeds with glistening cheeks, like a laughing Negro. Some of the pods contain twins, though they're not hard to tell apart: one has a blaze on its forehead, like a horse. So the mother will always know it—by the star on its brow.[41]

After this talk of half-breeds and stars, Andreas appears, as on cue: "The boy gathers the horse chestnuts hiding in holes in the law and stuffs them in his cheeks. His mouth fills with sticky bitterness. The boy smiles. You have to climb the tree, choose a cluster, and wait. Don't let the angel of sleep deceive you."

The first story is a monologue, as if spoken by the adult Andreas, trying to find the house in Novi Sad where he had lived before the war.

> Excuse me, sir, can you tell me the way to Horse Chestnut Street? You don't remember? But it's got to be here somewhere, I don't recall the names myself any more but I know for a fact it's somewhere here. What's that? You're saying there aren't any streets lined with horse chestnut trees anywhere here? Oh but there must be, sir. Memories can't possibly play so false.

---

41 Emblems of childhood, horse chestnuts kept their meaning for Kiš. Several were found in his writing case after his death, with the pens and pencils.

The trees have disappeared, the street names have been changed (as happens after political convulsions in Central Europe). Eventually the narrator realises the house has gone. "There's an apple tree where the head of my bed used to be. A gnarled and knotty tree, and barren. . . . the place where my mother's Singer sewing machine stood is a bed of roses."

This scene segues to the story that follows. "The Game" starts with a man peering through a keyhole, "thinking *That's not him, that's not Andreas.*" Ignoring the discomfort of bending over, and the cold draft that blows from the room "as if along a corridor", he "did not budge". For his son has turned into his father: "there stands Max Ahasuerus, feather merchant, proffering his wares nimbly, Jewishly." His trance breaks when he touches the lock with his spectacles. "*I'll have to show this to Maria*, he thought maliciously, without realising what he was thinking or that it was malicious. *I've got to show Max Ahasuerus, the feather merchant, to Maria.* He did not know why, but he needed to hurt her." He wants his wife to see that her "blue-eyed boy" has become the spitting image of his Jewish grandfather.

Cut to the boy, alone in the cold room, playing his "harmless" and nameless game, which involves pretending to be a merchant selling feathers from a pillow to the cheap print of *Mona Lisa* and the portraits of his grandparents on the wall. Smitten by Mona Lisa, he thinks "*This is no job for me. I'd give this woman all my stuff for her beautiful eyes and her smile, and my business would go under. Well, let it,* he thinks, his eyes shining softly. *Let it, I'd give her everything so she could sleep in a soft bed.*" He speaks aloud to the print, offering his feathers as a gift. "You have paid already with your smile, Madame." At once he feels ashamed of his "callow gallantry and self-betrayal, because if someone is even playing at business, you have to try and sell your goods for the best price and not bankrupt yourself for a smile."

On the other side of the keyhole, the (still unnamed) man is transfixed by the sight of "his late father. It was not a ghost. It was Max Ahasuerus, goose-feather merchant, in person. He had come from somewhere far away." Finally he turns to his wife. "'Maria,' he says softly, 'guess who's in the bedroom? Look for yourself! But softly now.'" Turning from her position at the stove, she "can see the pupils narrowing behind his glasses." When he tells her his late father is in the room, her hands tremble. She goes into the room, making the boy jump, telling him the room is too cold for playing in and to put the pillow down. Instead, he tries to draw her into the game: "Can I interest you in some nice swan feathers?" She does not respond. "The smile fades from the boy's face (yes, he knew it, he sensed it, there was something bad about the game)." His mother tears the pillow from his hands.

That evening, Andi's mother invents a bedtime story about a king who marries a gypsy girl. After she has borne him a son and heir, the king has the girl killed, "because if it got out that she was the boy's mother, the boy would lose the throne. So he never knew who his mother was. Luckily he looked like his father, and no one could see even a hint of gypsy blood in the colour of his skin." Here the boy interrupts: "I don't understand." His mother regrets having begun the story and doesn't know how to end it. One day, she says, the king looks into his son's room to see if he has gone to sleep. He finds the child standing in front of a picture of his mother, holding a pillow, and begging. "Like one driven mad, the king rushed into the room and seized his son. What are you doing, prince? he cried. Begging, father, said the prince. I'm tired of all my other games, and the horses, and the falcons, so now I'm playing being a beggar." Believing Andi has fallen asleep, she tiptoes away. But a question comes out of the darkness: "Did he kill his son too?" She turns back to stroke the child. "No," she whispers, "no, he didn't."

The next story, "The Pogrom", is related from Andi's childish point of view, but with an adult's comprehension. The boy is swept along in a crowd looting a warehouse; presumably this is Novi Sad in January 1942, and the victim is Jewish. The boy sees what is happening and records it unblinkingly. He realises the frenzied crowd is stealing things, yet cannot grasp the reason for the violence, which he experiences as a natural disaster.

> Suddenly I heard a crash of glass which flared like a bolt of lightning over the crowd, and then, like a distant echo, the splitting of boards and finally a sigh of satisfaction when the door gave way under pressure. I didn't budge from the entrance to the warehouse, hanging on to coattails and women's skirts, pushed this way and that, always getting back again, stubbornly crawling through the forest of legs, driven by fear, convinced that my best protection from these people was here at the heart of danger, knowing that I mustn't lose the secure shelter of their rage, mustn't be separated from the manifold crowd even for a moment, or they would seize and trample me underfoot.

Witnessing an incomprehensible scene, Andi sees surreal fragments:

> candles bundled together in blue paper and rattling like dry bones, apples falling with a dull sound only to be ground underfoot the same moment, like being chewed up. . . . One woman was biting into a bolt of silk she had pulled out from under her coat. . . . I watched a roll of flowered chintz winding stubbornly around legs and heads in the crowd, like strips of crêpe-paper on New Year's Eve. The colourful chintz started tightening dangerously, women began screaming. But this only increased the crowd's agitation . . .

A woman thrusts a tin of spaghetti into Andi's hands. He stands there, not knowing what to do, "lacking the courage to throw it away or take it home. I looked in horror at Mr Anton, the tax inspector, who was standing on a barrel throwing confetti in the air."

Without the curt title, readers would be challenged to understand what happens in the story, which catches beautifully Kiš's view that, as he once told a French interviewer, "*l'homme ne vit pas l'Histoire, il vit dans l'histoire*." History with a capital H is recognized in hindsight, not experienced at the time, least of all by children.

A collection at the level of these first stories would be breath-taking. Sadly, the dozen stories that follow "The Game" and "The Pogrom" are pallid things. They evoke incidents and motifs from his Hungarian boyhood: gathering chestnuts, wetting the bed, his first erotic feelings for a girl, losing a neighbour's cow, picking vermin off his skin after cleaning a henhouse, mushrooming with his mother and sister in the woods, memories of a touring circus and his father, watching soldiers' horses dying in a stable near his home. A couple of episodes are reprised from *Garden, Ashes*.[42] As in the other book, some of the names—Molnár, Berki—belong to real people in Kerkabarabás. There are striking passages, and the sensuousness of the writing has been rightly praised. A long paragraph about Eduard Sam, in "The Meadow, in Autumn", is worthy of *Garden, Ashes*. Yet the stories are too often marred by abrupt, sentimental resolutions. Kiš seems to have mislaid his usual defences against pathos. "Serenade for Ana", for example, ends like this:

> Tell me, Ana, did I make it all up?
> (The flowers and the fragrances.)

The swoon that closes the story about the soldiers' horses feels mawkish:

> The soldiers loaded the carcasses onto a sleigh and took them to the horse cemetery. The sleigh was drawn by a horse that would clearly end up there too before long, and was followed by a boy sick at heart, Andi by name, and a dog whose name was Dingo.

Poise is partly recovered in the longest story, "From a Velvet Album", set at the end of the war, when two of Andi's relatives return from concentration camp. The boy wonders if his mother even wants his father back, and only realises that she has forgiven his impossible ways when he sees her flinch on the doorstep,

> clearly expecting to discover our father at home, to find his whole family there, reconciled at last by the shared sufferings and Calvary of their

---

42 He finished writing *Early Sorrows* in 1965, the year that *Garden, Ashes* was published. He once said the stories centred on "images" that "could not be worked into" the other book.

entire tribe. But the only one we found was Aunt Rebecca, and the way she looked did not bode well. At first sight we were too shocked to say a word. Lord, how changed she was! There was no trace of her luxuriant hair, her black chignon was burned away, the curls fringing her brow were scorched, as if by flames.

The aunt makes it clear that Eduard is no more. "My father—dead! In any case, I completely refused to believe in his death. I was certain Aunt Rebecca was not telling the truth. . . . The whole thing struck me as a hoax—Aunt Rebecca's desire to write off my father as painlessly as possible, by slowly shaking her head." Andi then describes the impression made by "the only other member of my family to return" (from Auschwitz, not named). This was Uncle Andrej, "he too scorched by a strange sun, an infernal light that gave his skin a sickly dank hue—the fatal brand of a black sun."[43]

A dozen years after the book's publication, Kiš wrote a new story and added it to the collection "as a kind of lyrical epilogue". Called "The Aeolian Harp", it is unlike anything else in the book. It begins in the dry, half-mocking voice that was his hallmark from *Hourglass* (1972) to the end of his life.

The harp is the instrument that more than any other combines the mediaeval formulae of the beautiful (*perfectio prima*) and the useful (*perfectio secunda*), as such pleasing to the eye, which means satisfying the rules of formal harmony while, above all, fulfilling its basic purpose: to yield a pleasing sound.

I had a harp when I was nine. It consisted of a telegraph pole and six pairs of electric wires connected to porcelain insulators that looked like an incomplete tea service. (I had damaged one of them with my catapult before discovering the musical function of this Chinese porcelain.)

As Kiš describes how the harp's strings are "tuned" by the porcelain "buttons", and held up by poles of tarred fir trunks, an allegory unfolds. The story is a mysterious paean to primitive telecommunication,[44] suggesting in the deftest way that literary forms are universal.

When the poles are connected by wires and topped not by green branches but by a Chinese tea set . . ., they begin to sing and pluck their strings.

---

43 Except for *Psalm 44*, this is the only piece of 'Holocaust writing' in Kiš's works. The echo of Paul Celan's most celebrated poem, the "*Todesfuge*" (published in 1948), is probably coincidental.
44 Is this also a private tribute to his maternal grandfather, Jakov Dragićević, who helped to build the telegraph network across the mountains of Montenegro before the First World War?

All you have to do is put your ear to the pole; though it is no longer a pole, now it is a harp.

Inexperienced readers (who have never put their ears to a wooden telegraph pole) may think wind is also needed. Not at all. The ideal time for a harp like this is a hot day in July . . . when the wood is so dry and resonant it sounds hollow.

Without naming Andi, the story homes in to the particular.

I almost forgot: the ideal place for a harp like this is along an ancient road. The one I am describing lay along the old post road, which dates back to the times when Pannonia was being settled by the Romans. Thanks to this, the harp's mast can, like an antenna, pick up sounds from ancient times; melodies reach it from past and future. . . .

Now all that is left to do is turn and check that the Imperial highway is deserted, there's no one in the wheat fields, no one in the ditch, no one on the horizon.

The emptiness measures the scale of the Holocaust, but it is also timeless. The countryside around Kerkabarabás is like that today: arable fields framed by drain-

The road from Kerkabarabás, complete with "Aeolian harps"

age ditches and straight roads, the horizontal lines broken by brakes of trees, low buildings—and telegraph poles. Safe from prying eyes that might suspect him of listening for Allied planes, the boy puts his ear to the telegraph pole and

> recognises *the sound of time*, because the sounds reach him from the depths of time and history as if from a quasar, from far off stars. (The smell of melting pitch is only a stimulant, like burning herbs, sandalwood or incense in a temple or church.)
>
> And here is what the harp sings into his ear while he listens with eyes shut: that he will soon stop herding cattle for Mr Molnár, his father will never return, he will leave the hut with the earthen floor, he will finally go to his grandfather's in Montenegro; that he will have new books; he will have 1500 pencils, 200 fountain pens, and 5000 books; that his mother will die soon, he will meet a girl he will love forever, he will travel, he will see oceans and cities; that he will investigate his murky past by probing into far-off history and biblical times; that he will write a story about an Aeolian harp of telegraph poles and electric wires.

This promise of escape sounds the only note of joy in the book. The harp's promise to the listening boy is reported by the author who was that boy and writes these words.[45] This circular motion resolves the knot of different tenses, synchronising writer and reader in a perennial present. It also ends the book in Kiš's favourite way: highlighting the illusions that fiction sets in play, and deleting them.

Probably the story was inspired by the memory of the telegraph poles linking Kerkabarabás and nearby Zalabaksa, which Kiš would have seen on his return visit to the village in the 1960s. Yet, alongside its intimacy, the scene feels archetypal, intertextual: an exalted double effect that Kiš loved to aim for.

As Boris Pilnyak was a favourite author, he probably knew the story called "Snow", where the wires of a telegraph post "hummed ceaselessly in the room somewhere in a corner of the ceiling—a monotonous, barely audible sound, like a snow storm". As a film-goer in Belgrade, he may have seen *Pather Panchali*, Satyajit Ray's 1955 film, with its scene where little Apu and his sister press their ears to the electricity pylons in a field, fascinated by the humming wires. And he would have read a poem by Dezső Kosztolányi (1885–1936), a Hungarian writer whom he much admired, about the poet's youthful yearning to escape from Szabadka (Subotica), his and Kiš's birthplace.

---

45 Kiš had mentioned the telegraph wires in *Hourglass*, without metamorphosing them into harp strings. In that wintry fiction about a deadened world, the wires are silent, "weighed down by snow".

. . . How I want to leave, go far away,
Where the railway twists,
And a red and green lamp beckoning burns,
There, I spread my arms, trackwards.
And look at the engine, and the wire on the poles,
There's joy, there's the world, perhaps.
But I stay here and struggle and stamp,
Like prisoners in the prison yard.

The unevenness of *Early Sorrows* is unique in Kiš's work. The success of "The Game" seems inseparable from its juxtaposition of several viewpoints. Andi's impulse to play the game is matched by the father's blind glee at hurting his wife and the wife's compulsion to punish Andi through the cruel twists in her bedtime story. Both adults are absorbed in their 'ethnic', or genetic, reading of the boy's game—a reading that reflects the anguish caused by fascist persecution of the Jews, but also something beyond this: the (Jewish) man's resentment of the (Christian) woman's fear that their child will take after his troubled, unhappy father.

Trapped in their mutual torment, they see Andi as a puppet of his Jewish genes, never wondering what he himself makes of what he is doing. Play, they forget, is play: questing, experimental. Kiš shows what they miss when he evokes Andi's shame. Whatever his reasons for playing the game, they are not ethnic or racial.

The strength of "The Pogrom" lies in the completeness of its childish vision of the political world. Swept along helplessly but also willingly, the narrator sees the pieces of the jigsaw while he misses the whole design. The result is a tableau of absurd images: objects are animated, while people act inhumanly. The purity of Andi's account illumines the adults' madness.

What then goes amiss in most of the stories? The problem is not that young Andi is shown maltreated and suffering, or feeling sorry for himself. It is that Kiš is swayed by pity for his younger self. This was humanly understandable but artistically demeaning. In terms of technique, this weakness was aggravated by a feature of the stories that the critic Ivana Vuletić has explored with finesse. The first-person narratives are deliberately shorn of the complexity and irony which are Kiš's usual defences against the inundation of "lyricism". By subordinating other points of view so thoroughly to Andi's, none of the stories after "The Game" and "The Pogrom" can dramatise the encounter between the child's consciousness and the corrupted adult world.

More problematic still is how the third-person narratives are first-person narratives in all but name; they do not use the wider scope that a third-person frame makes available. If Andi's consciousness was richer than Kiš allows it to be, this might not matter. But Kiš leaches much of the interest out of Andi by imposing what Vuletić calls a willed or false simplicity. The frost-sharp perceptions in "The Pogrom" are hardly to be found later in the book, which is more often faux-naïf than truly naïve.

These flaws confirm that the ironic poise of his other "family" books—*Garden, Ashes* and *Hourglass*—was hard won. ("There was a very small, unfulfilled, beaten child inside that big man," recalls his friend Gabi Gleichmann. "It was there all the time.") Had his return to Kerkabarabás released the self-pity that undermined these stories? It seems possible that memory was a more truthful muse before he returned to the scene. And for anyone who finds the sentimentality hard to swallow, Kiš's subtitle, "For Children and Sensitive Readers", holds a hint of special pleading, as if he sensed that his book fell short.

A final reflection: visiting Kerkabarabás in 1998, I met villagers who had been Dani's schoolmates. They were small-holding farmers, unaware of what Kiš had written. I was baffled by the contrast between their memories of a carefree boy and the mournful picture of a victimised child that emerges from *Early Sorrows*. There is no need to reconcile the two views. Writing this chapter, however, I discovered the ground where such reconciliation could occur. For the best stories do acknowledge the resilience of a real child and refuse to revise him into a harrowed miniature adult burdened with tragic knowledge.

in my ninth year I wrote my first poems, in Hungarian: one was about hunger, the other was a love poem *par excellence.*

Precocity and dramatic antithesis create another *coup de théâtre*. If he was seven when he began to learn Hungarian, was Danilo really writing verses a year or so later? Possibly, but the account of this moment at the end of *Garden, Ashes* carries more conviction: touching and richly absurd, a pastiche annunciation.

One autumn evening (if the reader allows us to isolate this event), one ordinary evening when I was eleven years old,[46] Euterpe, the Muse of lyric poetry, burst into our house without preparation or forewarning, with no heavenly portents—but with wonderful simplicity. It was the only big event of that season, the only light in the torpor of that murky autumn. I was lying on the wooden chest in the kitchen with a blanket pulled over my head, desperately willing myself to sleep through the autumnal tedium and master my hunger with stoical meditations on the future and on love. Hunger begets refinement, refinement begets love, love begets poetry. This extremely vague idea about love and the future turned into a glittering map of the world outlined in bold colours (a supplement to my father's timetable), into something unattainable, into despair. To travel! To love! Oh Africa, oh Asia, oh horizons, oh life of mine! I clenched my eyes tight shut, until they hurt, and grey reality clashed with the fires of fantasy beneath my eyelids and blazed there in a reddish glow, then shimmered in yellow, blue and violet. The heavens opened for a moment, the fanfares rang out, and I glimpsed bare-bottomed cherubs, their wings vibrating like houseflies' as they fluttered around the radiant red hub of paradise. But this only lasted a trice. The next instant, I fell headlong into an abyss, and this was no dream. Some kind of wonderful, universal rhythm fluttered inside me, and words came out of my mouth like a medium uttering Hebrew. The words really were in some strange language, full of some unknown sonority. Only after the first wave of feverish excitement was spent did I give any thought to their meaning, and then I discovered that the

---

46 He confirmed to an interviewer in 1985 that he had started writing poetry thirty-nine years before, that is, in 1946, when he was eleven.

words below the billowing surface of music and rhythm were quite ordinary, like the gondoliers' songs my father used to sing. Only too aware as I am of how impossible it would be to translate those verses faithfully, I beseech the reader to note the elements which they contain and of which they are comprised, so they can serve as proof that those verses truly once existed. Here it is, then, the whole of this lyrical fantasy-ballad, this authentic masterpiece of inspiration, consisting of the following few words arranged in an ideal order, never to be repeated: *coral reef, instant, eternity, leaf,* and one wholly incomprehensible and mysterious word: *plumaseria.*

Beside myself with fear, I sat hunched on the chest for a while, then told my mother in a voice cracking with excitement: "I have written a poem."

Twenty years after Kiš's death, the writer Miljenko Jergović (b. 1966) said that his own generation, "the first post-Party, post-Partisan generation" in Yugoslavia, avid for "any word or image that called the faith of our fathers into question", was bewitched by Kiš. For them, he was above all "a *tender* writer, a voice that was heard with a private, lyrical ear, even when he was writing about concentration camps. . . . We loved him, and were obliged to him, in a way that was unrepeatable and could not have involved any other writer."

There really is a French word *plumasserie*, by the way, and it means the craft of working with feathers, as ornaments or fashion. As such it forms another link in the chain of Kiš's paternal ancestry, leading back to the goose-feather merchants from Alsace. And the phrase "a love poem *par excellence*" will recur in the last story in his last book, closing the circle.

From my mother I inherited a propensity for telling
tales with a mixture of fact and legend; from my
father—pathos and irony.

A
fter pen/sword and hunger/love, here are mother/father, fact/legend, pathos/
irony. Kiš's writing fledged in this nest of dissimilarities.

Milica's trick of blending fact and legend is beautifully caught in *Garden,
Ashes*. After Eduard Sam's disappearance, mother and son spend evenings together in the
benighted village. Maria Sam tells Andi stories about her homeland, turning history into
myth to cheer herself up and, in the process, imbuing him with her nostalgia:

> Then, in a long lyrical monologue, she would tell me the story of her childhood,
> spent amidst fig and orange trees, an idealised childhood like those in Biblical
> stories, because there, as in the Bible, golden-fleeced sheep grazed and donkeys
> brayed, and the fig was the chosen fruit. My mother tried to counter the fairy
> tales told by the autumn rains with a legend of her own, fixed in space and
> time: as proof, she would bring me a map of the world (on a scale of 1:500,000,
> found among my father's possessions) and point with the tip of her knitting
> needle to her Arcadia, this sun-drenched Eldorado of her idealised childhood,
> this illuminated Mount of Olives, this 'black mountain', this Montenegro.
> Above all, she wanted to diminish the rain's power and liberate me from the
> spell in which it held me with its triplets and quatrains. So my mother lit up the
> landscape of her childhood with eternal sunshine and bright summer colours,
> setting it in a cultivated piece of land, an oasis among mountain ranges and
> fields of boulders. Carried away by her own storytelling and mythmaking, she
> always reverted to our genealogy and, not without a touch of pride, she would
> discover our ancestors in the distant and clouded history of the Middle Ages,
> among medieval lords and ladies of the court, linking them with the rulers and
> princes of the republics of Ragusa and Venice as well as with Albanian heroes
> and usurpers. The family tree, which shone in the pale glow of the oil lamp like
> the illustrations on medieval parchments radiant with gilt lettering, included
> on its more remote branches knights, ladies-in-waiting, and renowned seafarers
> who sailed from one end of the world to the other, from Kotor and Constanti-
> nople to China and Japan.

This vision has a touching silliness and fairy-tale warmth quite unlike the writing about Eduard. Valiant Montenegro, eclipsed by a knitting needle! Never again did he write about his mother—or her homeland—with this comic pathos.

They listen to the tale told by the rain "in long rhythmical lines without a break . . . a long epic-lyrical poem like Omer and Merima, a poem about the witches that lie in ambush behind the chimney, waiting to pounce, about a nymph passing by all in white, veiled, lit by lightning-bolts, and a brave hero who rescues her at the last moment, about a lake with swans, about gypsies brandishing their knives and picking blood-stained gold coins out of the mud." Thanks to Maria-Milica, the boy has learned to convert the dreary rain into motifs from folk ballads.[47] Andi or Dani grew up to be an author who would not write about brave heroes and cosy villains, but who never forgot what it meant to believe in such things and carried the wonder of that belief into his books.

Milica Dragićević (r.) with her sisters Milosava (l.) and Draginja. Cetinje, 1921

---

47 Surely it is the same "evening rain beating down" that features in Kiš's sketch about Mr Poppy and the Double (chapter 19).

Milica had another motive for telling Dani about Montenegro. Worried that he was turning into a Hungarian village boy, she wanted to teach him *her* culture and language. She recited the epic poems that she had absorbed, growing up in Cetinje. Hundreds of these poems were collected by the pioneering folklorists of the nineteenth century, who discovered that the common people had transmitted these decasyllabic verses down the generations. Many of the poems related tales about the battle of Kosovo in 1389, when the medieval Serbian empire succumbed to Ottoman power. Nineteenth-century politicians and artists turned the "Kosovo cycle" into a nationalist cult which endures to the present.

Late in life, speaking to a French audience, Kiš extolled Yugoslav folk poetry in conventional patriotic terms as encapsulating "our history, our ethnography, our psychology, our language and speech", the very source of "our culture". As a writer, however, he was unmoved by the obvious legacy of epic poems. Their settings and motifs—monasteries, villages, falcons, riddles, wise peasants, valiant heroes, maidens, battles, blessings, curses, and incantations—were not for him.

Consider the poem alluded to above, "The Death of Omer and Merima":

Two young people fell in love so sweetly:
Omer his name, the maiden's—Merima,
In springtime with the flowers flowering,
Hyacinths, carnations, richly blooming,
Someone ever watchful, watching, saw them:
Omer's mother, watchful, spoke to Omer:
'Darling Omer, O youthful lad, my son,
you should not love the maiden Merima!
Let mother find you fairer love to wed—
Beautiful Fatima'. . .

Omer obeys his mother but refuses to betray his "dear heart", Merima. Fatima wisely understands. Death is Omer's only exit, as it then becomes Merima's when she sees his corpse. Omer's mother sheds useless tears. Fatima survives.

Nothing could be farther than this from Kiš's exigent poetics. Yet he absorbed these legends, and they left their mark. As a boy in Montenegro, he "dreamed of collecting folk poetry like Vuk Karadžić". This fascination did not last, but his love of story-telling—what he called "the pleasure of narration", which tugged against his love of experiment and kept the juices flowing through his most formal constructions—grew from that inoculation by oral literature.

This mark is found above all on his last book, *The Encyclopaedia of the Dead*. For the point of legends is not to be original, but to be well told and memorable, so that they bring tears to our eyes or make the hair bristle on our neck—Kiš's notion of the proper aim of literature, as he told Stanko Cerović. When his mother's memory failed, she improvised in ways that prefigure his own fondness as a writer for working variations on borrowed themes. Linking these improvisations to the craft that kept the family from starvation, he paid homage in *Early Sorrows*:

> Without realising it, my mother had created her own knitting machine: a narrow groove had dug itself into the tender pulp of each index finger as if the soft yarn flowing along it were the sharp metal wire of an instrument. Long, white pages of angora knitting were spun like fairy tales from that set of a dozen needles, a magical script; when you blew on the downy surface to smooth it a little, you saw wondrous patterns like those on oriental rugs. The secret of her skill was very simple: she never repeated herself. If Mrs Fanika wanted the same jersey as Miss Maria, my mother accepted the commission without a murmur and then, without even trying to explain herself to the trivial vanity of the village belles, she worked a new variation into the theme, identical only at a glance, altering both the script and the motifs, creating a new style entirely, which seemed to resemble its predecessor, but only enough to reveal the master's hand: her personal and inimitable seal.

Never repeating himself would become a point of honour for her son. "I can't write at all without two conditions," he said, "a subject that excites me, obsesses me, that I've got to get off my chest, and the appropriate form, a form I haven't used before. . . . I like starting from scratch each time."

{FOURTH INTERLUDE}

Hourglass (1972)

ESTRAGON: All the dead voices.
VLADIMIR: They make a noise like wings.
ESTRAGON: Like leaves.
VLADIMIR: Like sand.

—Samuel Beckett, *Waiting for Godot*

1. The difference between a story and novel, Kiš believed, is that a novel cannot be told.

2. Late in 1967, he recovered a letter from his father to one of his aunts. He had brought the letter to Yugoslavia twenty years earlier, with Eduard's other surviving papers. (Presumably the letter was never delivered.) He mislaid it in the early 1960s, and thought it was lost. Its reappearance proved to be momentous. For this letter, dated April 1942, was, Kiš would say later, the sole authentic evidence of the world that he had written about in *Garden, Ashes*. Unlike his father's other papers, it was not a printed, official document. He gazed upon it "as if it were an opening in the Great Pyramid or a scroll from the Dead Sea".

3. What, though, was he to make of its contents? The letter was a long, anguished screed to Eduard's sister Olga, who would also be killed in Auschwitz in 1944, dense with references to people, places, and events that Kiš could barely recognise, looming out of his father's minuscule script. There was even a reference to himself, the seven-year-old Danilo. "I simply did not have the information to interpret the letter—the allusions in it, the personalities—so most of it was an enigma, a secret. I had to decode it," he said.

4. As the letter fermented in his imagination, Kiš put aside something he had been working on—a scriptural pastiche called *The Legend of the Sleepers*. Gradually, his efforts to construe the letter took literary form. As always, he wrote in furious bouts, destroying more than he kept. By summer 1970, he had done "300 or 400 pages, two or three versions, none of them finished, always starting over again". A year later, he told a friend that the novel was still "pushing ahead millimetre by millimetre". Early in 1972, struggling to complete it, he rented a room in a mountain resort in Slovenia. Mirko Kovač, his companion on the trip, marvelled at his absorption in reducing "at least a thousand pages" of typescript to the compact novel that he submitted to the publisher Prosveta and

appeared at the end of the year. All in all, Kiš reckoned—not without pride—that he had used 8 kilos of paper in drafts and false starts. Of the two or three thousand pages, he "kept fewer than 300—those that achieved the grace of form!"

5. He had already decided on a title. His friend Miroslav Karaulac remembers when Kiš called to ask what he understood by the word *peščanik*. Karaulac, stumped for a tidy answer, fetched a dictionary and read out the entry, with its three distinct meanings: a structure of sand and cement; a sand quarry or pit; an hourglass. Kiš listened, and said "Every word of that is balm for the soul."[48]

6. The novel comprises sixty-seven numbered sections under six headings: Prologue, Travel Scenes, Notes of a Madman, Criminal Investigation, A Witness Interrogated, and Letter, or Table of Contents. The Prologue opens with a complex descriptive statement:

> The flickering shadows dissolve the outlines of things and break up the surfaces of the cube, the walls and ceiling move to and fro to the rhythm of the jagged flame, which by turns flares up and dies down as though about to go out.

This continues for several pages, offering no enticement, warning us to take nothing for granted and use our senses well. When stable, recognisable shapes emerge from the welter of shifting impressions they are simple. A man, alone in a room at night, lit by a single lamp, sits at a table. The floor is of bare clay. Wintry weather batters the window.

7. The narrator—an eye and a disembodied, somewhat didactic voice—wants us to register the illusions that are created by the swaying flame, as it is magnified by the lamp chimney and multiplied by the concave reflecting mirror behind the flame. The first three chapters are Kiš's most elaborate vision of the emergence of form from formlessness (see chapter 7). Objects blend with their shadows. Recovering from the lamp's dazzle, the eye notes other objects in the room: a stove, a chest, a school satchel. On the desk, a pile of writing paper, a newspaper, a magazine, a book. Finally, we are told about cigarette smoke that "somehow finds its way to the lamp and pours, bluish, through the chimney." We will remember this when we read about the tall chimney-stack in Montenegro

---

48 Was the choice of title influenced by a favourite writer, Bruno Schulz, whose story "Sanatorium under the Sign of the Hourglass" tells of the narrator's visit to a sanatorium whose director reactivates time past?—" 'Is my father alive?' I asked, staring anxiously into his calm face. 'Yes, of course,' he answered. 'That is, within the limits imposed by the situation,' he added."

with its "black thread of smoke".[49] Plot and metaphor are interwoven with the density of poetry.

8. Kiš inserts an illustration of a Rubin vase: an ambiguous image which can be seen as a vase or as two human faces in profile, facing each other. Or, almost, as an hourglass or a lamp chimney.

9. This opening is allegorical and painterly, a *tableau nocturne*: a canvas of Plato's cave. But it is not timeless or placeless. The author-artist's commentary, with its pedantic shearing of reality from semblance ("lateral shadows of uncertain origin"), its lordly control and arch solemnity: these all announce something austere and Francophile, a postwar "antinovel". We can admire the defiance while wondering how many readers let the book drop from their hand.

10. With Travel Scenes (I), the narrator makes way for the nameless man at the desk. We learn about his inner life ("Something tells him that the people in the adjoining room are asleep"). Increasingly, the perceptions and uncertainties are transferred from the godlike narrator-educator to the nameless man. He is writing a letter, and wants to finish it before "the finger's breadth of oil" in the lamp runs out. So "he hastens to start writing again, to continue what he has begun and win his race with darkness." After pages of nuanced qualifications, the stark urgency strikes home.

---

49 We may also remember "the narrow chimney / of the crematorium", from Kiš's early poem about his father (see chapter 2).

11. As the man's consciousness filters into the story, focalisation shifts between external (the narrator) and internal (the nameless man). At first reading, we cannot tell one from the other, for the voice and visual exactness are unvarying, in the present tense.

12. In the fifth chapter, we enter fully the man's mind. He lies in bed, gazing at the wallpaper with its pattern of horse-drawn sleighs. Then—in one of these shifts—the narration tells us about a woman alighting from a sleigh. She closely resembles a woman who had appeared unexplained in chapter four, climbs out of a sleigh and pushes a letter through the door of the nameless man's dwelling. This near-duplicate scene either spirits us into a tale of the supernatural, or draws us into the mirror-halls of memory.

13. The scenes that follow have the edgeless and magnified intensity of dream. The man is seen outside his dwelling, the spectator of a dismal feast in a nearby house; then he sits on a stone beside a harbour (as discussed in chapter 19). Unexplained duplications—as of the woman and the sleigh—recur. The man appears twice beside the harbour. The lamp chimney and the unfinished letter from the first pages of the novel are glimpsed among the refuse swilling around the bow of a boat entering the harbour. (These motifs stitch the narrative together.) The refuse is itemised in Kiš's most desolate inventory: ". . . bloated cigarette butts, a dead fish, crusts of bread, a dead rat, a box of matches. . .".

14. This is drama of the purest kind; the mind, remembering, reorders what the eyes once saw. It does not think 'now I will remember sitting on the stone by that harbour, then I will remember how I moved closer to the water and watched that boat coming in.' It sees these things headlong, in streams of association. When our minds circle around a problem, they do not begin each revolution by restating the terms of the issue. They focus on obsessive notions or images. Memory and imagination edit each other ceaselessly, beyond our bidding. The man remembers and therefore imagines; Kiš's task is to make us see the process without explaining (which would compromise his poetics) or losing the reader.

15. After some twenty pages, the novel's narrative voice feels fully alienated, almost mechanical. Relief comes with a new rubric: Notes of a Madman is a first-person narrative that is evidently related by the nameless man. It is startling to hear his voice, which offers brilliant, disjointed flights of fancy and imagination, rising to "the heaven of pure abstraction" before plummeting to the geological depths below his feet. When he writes that "the thought of *Montenegrin villages* would not have come" if his wife "had not been sleeping in the next room", a superhu-

man reader may recall the "schematic clusters of houses" that could be seen from the harbour.

16. Criminal Investigation (I) marks another narrative departure. It starts with a question: "Did E.S. postdate his letter?" The man now has initials, if not a name. The answer begins: "After the name of his village he wrote the next day's date." So it goes on, like a catechism: questions and answers build a mosaic about E.S., from a mildly wayward youth to his present plight. The order of information follows no visible logic, but the reader is used to this. What's new is the dialogue, which allows a reader to relax for the first time and enjoy two things: the hints of a double-act, where each question (posed by whom?) sets up the answer; and the naturalistic detail, which overflows, as in a traditional novel. This formal pleasure granted to the reader contrasts with E.S.'s situation, which emerges as desperate: he is beset by poverty, dogs,[50] hunger, and anti-Semitic suspicion.

17. Notes of a Madman (II) lists meals that E.S. enjoyed long ago in Yugoslavia, Hungary, and Trieste, then continues with a blissful fantasy about one of those meals: paella valenciana, imagined as the deposit of a trawler's net, hoisted dripping from the Mediterranean seabed. This passage also recalls—and counterpoints—the grim geological vision of Pannonia. These themes and developments loom out of the fog like cairns.

18. The Notes reflect on paella and potatoes, then Jews, pigs, Mohammed, Isaac Newton, gravity and faeces, menstruation, blood, pregnancy, goose feathers, the massacre in Novi Sad, cigarette ash, the passage of time, "weeping children who understand nothing", "the terrible clamour of history", and finally Marie Antoinette facing the revolutionary rabble in all her "snow-white" radiance and self-deceit. The transitions are unexplained but the sequence feels obscurely meaningful in ways that E.S. cannot bring himself to address.

19. Criminal Investigation (II) returns us to the letter. The questions refer to "the letter writer" and "the draft manuscript". The draft betrays a shaky hand, due to the motion of the train in which it was composed. Four photographs are displayed in the train's first-class compartment. The first sets the scene for what has to be E.S.'s train journey to Novi Sad and for the whole novel: "a Pannonian landscape. A snow-covered plain as far as the eye can see." The second shows a city panorama with

---

50 Leopold Bloom's list of the "attendant indignities" of destitution and penury includes "the latration of illegitimate unlicensed vagabond dogs".

a cathedral (it is Novi Sad, unnamed). The third shows a jetty with a boat moored to a stone bollard "while on the other side an identical boat approaches the jetty". It is the Travel Scene from forty pages earlier. Last, another city panorama with cathedral, or the same city as in the second photograph, from a different angle. The narrator provides more information about this image than a traveller could possibly see—perhaps investing it with remembered detail from an experience of his own.

20. The questioner wants to know more about E.S.'s journey. He was expelled from the first class carriage when the "young blond" conductor saw the yellow star on his chest. We find out what he noticed and felt about fellow passengers, the contents of his briefcase, and that the station is a threatening place, patrolled by the military, infested by secret agents. We learn of his emotions as a cab bears him away from the danger zone, and of his dream when he dozes. We follow the reunion with Gavanski, his old "and in a manner of speaking, only" friend, as they drink, play chess, and discuss the political situation "in an undertone". We read the list of their common acquaintances, and their fates: a catalogue of human folly, wretchedness, and gallows humour. We know what E.S. conceals from Gavanski, and vice-versa. And we are privy to E.S.'s terrifying nightmare about bone-thieves as he sleeps fitfully on Gavanski's couch.

21. The Q & A then focuses on the removal of E.S.'s goods from Novi Sad. There is another ekphrastic sequence, this time involving "a cardboard box full of family photographs". Information about E.S.'s wife and children comes in the form of captions or annotations. Phrases from earlier chapters recur, such as the "deep fjords and bays with jagged mountain peaks behind them", from the harbour scene. A monumental statue, glimpsed in a photograph in the train, reappears in one of the family photographs.[51] When E.S. describes an impossible photo of himself picking through the photos, we know it is an image of his self-reflection.

22. A pattern is emerging from the fragmentary mosaic; the motifs link backward and forward, dramatizing the memory of E.S., or his imagination. Or not so much a pattern as a chemical reaction in our head, which reveals the novel as an object with a fourth dimension, haunted by time, until it feels like a hologram of something intricate turning

---

51 It is a sculpture by Ivan Meštrović, erected in 1939. (See chapter 33 for a comparison of Meštrović and Kiš as Yugoslav artists.)

on its axis, or some other paradoxical thing: a tesseract, say, or a Klein bottle, or a Möbius strip.

23. E.S.'s lucky escape from the house, moments before its collapse, occupies twenty-five virtuosic pages about E.S.'s paranoid interpretations, philosophical speculations, and burlesque conjectures. Realising that he is unharmed, his imagination spins out the alternative scenario of his death. We get a newspaper report on the fatal accident; the post mortem report; a list of people who sent telegrams of condolence; his preference for an ecumenical funeral service; the shabby behaviour of his detested relatives, a mock-heroic oration by a fellow railway inspector, and the putative reactions of "certain famous men" to the news of his demise—Kafka, Karl Marx, Freud, and Proust. (Jews and Jewishness lie always near the surface of his mind, associated with guilt, conspiracy, and death.)

24. Notes of a Madman (III) provide further angry recriminations against his relatives, thoughts on global over-population, premonitions of divine punishment ("All will suffer alike, and more than anyone else we the chosen people"), and Midrashic dicta that seem chosen to rebuke and dismay those same relatives. Travel Scenes (II) reverts to the objectivist style. E.S. digs up the clay floor of the hut. By a seamless association, this activity reminds E.S. of an experience with a labour brigade, the units that Jews in fascist Hungary were forced to join. Here it is: E.S. has wrapped his hands in rags to protect them against the rough work and the cold. The knotted rags work loose; unless he can fix them, he will be beaten by the guards. Blinded by the mud on his glasses, he hesitates. "Suddenly two hands as muddy as his own, but free from bandages, appear just in front of his glasses, in the small space framed by his cramped fingers." This is a fellow victim, one Ofner, who ties E.S.'s rags. Before he can finish, the two men are cudgelled to the ground by their guards. This experience is the moral fulcrum of the novel, and Kiš will return to it from different angles. Ofner's charity measures the hatred with which the book often brims over. (E.S. has since heard that Ofner is dead.)

25. In another instalment of Notes of a Madman, E.S. analyses his psychic disintegration. "What terrifies me (knowledge brings no consolation) and adds to my inner trembling", he concludes, "is the consciousness that my madness is in reality lucidity, and that what I need if I am to recover—for this constant trembling is unbearable—is precisely madness, lunacy, forgetfulness; only lunacy can save me, only madness can make me well."

26. Now comes the fourth and last of the book's narrative strands. A Witness Interrogated also has a question-and-answer format, but unlike the Criminal Investigation, it is a pastiche inquisition. A nameless interrogator asks E.S. to describe and explain his recent actions and to supply further detail. His limitless authority to probe is shown by the arbitrariness of his demands. Highly intelligent and suspicious, seemingly armed with a file on E.S., he wants to trap his victim into contradicting himself or confessing to being a spy or saboteur. E.S. rises to the challenge with sharp wits and total recall, producing fantastically precise descriptions, for example of a ceramic figurine that belongs to the son of a friend, and the contents of a shop in Novi Sad. The exaggeration has the air of a cat and mouse game, and not less than everything is at stake.

27. The reader seizes on the naturalism of this dialogue and the suspense it generates, and the story rips along. Hitherto mysterious details, hints, and barely explained images find their clarification. We learn more about the family quarrel that burdens E.S. and that after spending the night in Novi Sad with Gavanski, he had visited the Orthodox Church to obtain certificates of baptism for his children (see chapter 15). He had then tried to sort out his railway pension. ("Half of a Jew's life," Joseph Roth observed in the 1930s, "is consumed by the futile battle with papers.") We learn more about the labour brigades and the collapsing house in Novi Sad. Eventually, after fifty pages, E.S. begins to flag:

> Did you ever see anyone fiddling with the padlock on the cellar door?
> No.
> Describe the padlock.
> I'm tired.
> Describe the padlock.
> I don't remember it.
> I repeat: describe the padlock.

This bullying interrogator is the omniscient narrator of realist fiction, acting for his age-old clients—you and me, the consumers, brooking no denial, craving information about people who don't exist.

28. Criminal Investigation (III) includes E.S.'s ludicrous fantasies of a windfall that would solve his money worries at a stroke and of violent revenge on his ungenerous siblings. This leads to a summary of "the short novel that E.S. was planning to write in 1932" for "therapeutic purposes", on the advice of his doctor. Apparently the novel "treats the protagonist's recent and often

incredible experiences with ironic detachment". We get a brief review which banally summarises *Hourglass* itself:

> After a shattering experience (the carnage in Novi Sad), E.S., an extremely sensitive and somewhat disturbed individual, is unable to cope with the commonplace situations of bourgeois life. The action of the novel occurs in the space of a single night, from late evening until dawn. In this short time he relives some of the most important episodes in his life thus far, both recent and remote, and comes to certain conclusions. His war with the world is in reality a war with death, a struggle with death, whose approach he senses.

29. A Witness Interrogated (II) adds more mosaic tiles about the labour brigades, his sister Netty, the origins of the siblings' feud, the move from Novi Sad, and various doomed acquaintances, most of them Jewish, though that word is not used. E.S.'s answers are dauntless, mocking the insatiable interrogator with solemn minutiae. There is a sly mastery about his performance, at odds with the persecution and brutality that form the substance of his statements.

30. With the unread pages dwindling, loose ends are tied up, as experiences are revisited and memories remembered for the last time. A final journey (to Budapest and back), last reflections (on drunkenness) and erotic reveries (apropos of "a lady in black, leaning her lovely head against the high plush backrest"); a final glimpse of Pannonia by night; a final ekphrasis (that lithograph of the Ages of Man). In the last Notes of a Madman, E.S. foresees his and his siblings' fate, then draws up his will and testament. The final pages are magnificent; E.S rises to a grandeur beyond irony as he gives instructions for his cremation (ashes to be strewn upon the Danube from a railway bridge), and sets down the principle behind his actions, in words that say much about the novel we are finishing:

> If nothing else survives, perhaps my material herbarium or my notes or my letters will live on, and what are they but condensed, materialised idea; materialised life: a paltry, pathetic human victory over immense, eternal, divine nothingness. Or perhaps—if all else is drowned in the great flood—my madness and my dream will remain like a northern light and a distant echo. . . . Perhaps it will be my son who will one day publish my notes and my herbarium of Pannonian plants (unfinished and incomplete, like all things human). But anything that survives death is a paltry, trivial victory over the eternity of nothingness—a proof of human greatness and Yahweh's mercy. *Non omnis moriar.*

(By this point, we hardly know for sure which is the son and which the father. The faux-naïf tales of *Early Sorrows* dissolved into the miniature Proustian flow of *Garden, Ashes*, which now becomes the "frozen music" of *Hourglass*. Seen whole, the three panels of Kiš's "triptych", as he called these books, seem to narrate a single life: as if the child of the first book has grown into the man who prepares to die.)

31. The last chapter is called Letter, of Table of Contents. Datelined "Kerkabarabás, 5 April 1942", it combines a rambling litany of complaints about the writer's alleged ill treatment by his sister and nephew, with a chronicle of recent activities. Signed "Your loving brother, Eduard", it ends with a postscript: "It is better to be among the persecuted than among the persecutors." Peevish and vivid, the letter sounds like the Notes of a Madman, though less literary. I was unsure of its status until I read Nadine Gordimer's review of *Hourglass*: "It is an *actual* letter, written by Kiš's father two years before he was killed in Auschwitz." The novel is a vast coiled commentary on Eduard Kiš's letter. A man writes a letter, and as he writes, the events recounted and the emotions shaping it move in his mind and memory. The novel's convolutions disguise and disclose a simple plot, with a plea at its heart for humane generosity in the face of oppression. That's what *Hourglass* is, though not all it is—just as the greater labyrinth of Joyce's *Ulysses* both is, and is more than, the tale of a Dubliner's day with a plea at its core for the transcendence of hatred.

32. Knowing this, we match statements and images in the letter to passages in the novel.[52] Eduard's grumble that his sister Netty begrudges him "a few frozen potatoes" has its counterpart in E.S.'s "Treatise on the Potato". His sarcastic reference to "your sister Marie Antoinette" is elaborated. His mention of "some policemen" checking his papers gives the cue for A Witness Interrogated. And so on.

33. "The letter was necessary," Kiš said, because "it provides a framework for literary fantasy. The framework given by this document, this actual letter, does not allow me to take liberties with my fantasy, and turn the bloody reality of the massacre in Novi Sad, the fate of Central European Jewry, into some sort of sheer psychological fabrication." He always insisted on the authenticity of the letter as a found object, and critics have taken him at his word. However, when Mirjana Miočinović pub-

---

52 Bernard-Henri Lévy, Kiš's publisher and friend in Paris, remembers how Kiš praised "work that has the courage to reveal how it came into being. Great is that which flaunts and celebrates what others are ashamed of."

lished the full text of Eduard's letter in 2001, it became clear that Kiš had adapted the document to his purposes, omitting certain passages, compressing others, moving paragraphs around, and adding words and images, such as the reference to Marie Antoinette, the phrase "fate is a dog" (which gives the cue for E.S.'s frightening confrontation with the hungry dogs), and keywords such as *hourglass*, *Pannonian*, and *bourgeois*. The real significance of the letter is that it gave Kiš permission to overcome his innate resistance to sustained fabrication, for the purpose of "correcting" History's injustice to his obliterated father.[53]

34. Kiš also added the Talmudic postscript, from a maxim of Rabbi Abbahu of Caesarea, found in the Bava Kamma tractate.[54] This unmistakably Jewish reference links to precepts in other religions and philosophies, particularly the Socratic and Kantian moral tradition (see chapter 19). Socrates proposed that it is better to be wronged than to do wrong. Why so? Because, in Hannah Arendt's gloss, "you can remain the friend of the sufferer; who would want to be the friend of and have to live together with a murderer? Not even another murderer. . . . while I am alive I must be able to live with myself." By doing wrong, I harm what Arendt called the "silent dialogue between me and myself". In *Hourglass*, this dialogue is far from silent; E.S.'s capacity to sustain it, despite everything, measures his humanity.

35. The postscript earns its place in the novel as a final reminder of the moment when E.S. was helped by a fellow Jewish member of the labour brigade. The implication is that his helper, Ofner, acted as a free man despite the coercion and barbarity surrounding him: what Joyce's Bloom calls "force, hatred, history, all that."

36. Kiš liked to say that literature is freedom. His novel's ultimate purpose is to release E.S. from slavery to the murderous fate which history had reserved for Eduard Kiš. While E.S. could not escape that fate, he could be granted the rich human significance which had been denied to E.K. Within the enchanted space of a novel, the father could be restored to centrality within the world which had extinguished him in the most cursory way.

37. But the laws of literature are inescapable: this human significance could not be borrowed from the pathetic facts of Eduard Kiš's life; it had to

---

53 As he told an interviewer in 1985, "I believe that literature must correct History: History is general, literature concrete; History is manifold, literature individual. . . . Literature corrects the indifference of historical data by replacing History's lack of specificity with a specific individual."

54 The maxim continues: ". . . for there are none among the birds more persecuted than turtle-doves and pigeons, and the Scriptures declare them worthy of the altar."

be won by means of art. Consciousness had to be created by craft. Kiš, so prone to self-doubt, knew that, in *Hourglass*, he had succeeded. We know this because of his triumphal tone in interviews after its publication (to journalists who were so mystified by the book that they had nothing interesting to say or ask). And because of a remark that he scribbled in the margins of a book on his shelf.

38. In an essay, once famous, about liberty in the novel, Jean-Paul Sartre discussed a scene in *Beauchamp's Career* (1876) by George Meredith, where the hero and his beloved Renée meet, talk, misunderstand each other, and part—for ever.

> Beauchamp had time to say "Believe in me." Even that was false to his own hearing, and in a struggle with the painful impression of insincerity which was denied and scorned by his impulse to fling his arms around her and have her his for ever, he found himself deferentially accepting her brief directions concerning her boxes at the hotel. . . . She gave him her hand. He bowed over her fingers. "Until tomorrow, madame." "Adieu!" said Renée.

Sartre, at his most winning, comments: "When they meet, *anything* is possible between them. The future does not yet exist. . . . up to the very end, even when I begin to fear that they may break up, I still feel that *it may all still work out*. The reason is that they are free. Their final separation will be of their own making. *Beauchamp's Career* is a novel!" Kiš scored this passage heavily in his volume of Sartre's essays, and scrawled across the bottom of the page:

E.S.—he is free!

What sort of freedom can E.S. be said to possess? The liberal philosopher, Isaiah Berlin, once reflected on the Nazi practice of telling Jews bound for the death camps that they were travelling to a better place. "Why does this deception, which may in fact have diminished the anguish of the victims, arouse a really unutterable kind of horror in us?" asked Berlin. "Surely because we cannot bear the thought of human beings denied their last rights—of knowing the truth, of acting with at least the freedom of the condemned, of being able to face their destruction with fear or courage, according to their temperaments, but at least as human beings." Freedom of consciousness, the sovereignty of the inner realm, what law calls the *forum internum*: with this final freedom of the condemned, E.S. has been richly endowed. *Hourglass* is a novel!

39. The book's architecture is one of the consummate inventions of modern fiction. The only analogue that comes to mind is Vladimir Nabokov's *Pale Fire* (1962), which Mary McCarthy praised as "a Jack-in-the-box, a Fabergé gem, a clockwork toy, a chess problem, an infernal machine, a trap to catch reviewers, . . . a do-it-yourself kit." *Hourglass* is those things too. It fulfils Kiš's credo as a modernist, which he had spelled out when reviewing a Yugoslav experimental novel in 1960. He noted that novel's grim achievements: "no masquerade of plot, no hero, not even any psychology. . . . The ideal of the nouveau roman has at last been attained. . . . It offers a wonderfully futile example of art for art's sake, the bitter triumph of technocracy. Form finally split from (human) content, conventions vanquished at long last . . . an event in the dehumanisation of literature." This outcome, Kiš decided, was "disastrous", and it moved him to an avowal:

> As an admirer of all adventures of the spirit and rebellions of the mind and heart, I am full of admiration for anyone who despises the sentence "The Marquise went out at five o'clock",[55] yet I am convinced that there is more art and more life in that sentence than in a muffled crunch of sand with no human footprints or human voice. As an admirer of experiments and suffering, faithful to the idea of rebelling against convention, I draw the line at stammering, even if I am obliged to start my own novel with the sentence: "This morning I found human footprints in the sand."

40. Valid literary experiment convinces the reader of its necessity. In *Hourglass*, a man tries to save himself and his family in particular circumstances. This is the backdrop against which E.S. struggles to transport his furniture, get his hands on vital documents, and preserve his sanity.

41. The objectivist style of the Prologue and Travel Scenes renders a consciousness that is alienated from its surroundings and divided against itself. In Notes of a Madman, the narrative thread is buried deep. E.S.'s mind is clouded by suspicions and presentiments, and part-suppressed rage. He suffers from paranoid delusions, but almost never mentions the persecution hanging over his head. Kiš shows how the intolerability

---

55 According to André Breton, this was Paul Valéry's model of the conventional fictional utterance *par excellence.*

of this threat affects his knowledge of it. E.S.'s fears are displaced into apocalyptic visions, for example of the global threat posed by overpopulation (as if that were a danger in central Europe in the 1940s). The bare inventory of common acquaintances has, after all, a traditional Tolstoyan purpose: the portrayal of an entire society at a certain moment, like a geological cross-section.

42. The catechistic mode of the Criminal Investigation makes a comedy of omniscient narration; for the answers are always a foregone conclusion. In historical terms, this procedure exposes the charade of legal authority in a tyrannical regime. For what crime is being investigated? Is it the crime of his guilty (because Jewish) existence? In truth, it is the investigation that is criminal.

43. This contrasts with the tireless inquisition in the Witness Interrogated sections, where the questions are in deadly earnest. As Guy Scarpetta, the book's best critic, observes, narrative revelations delivered through replies to questions differ from those yielded through free indirect style or dialogue. The mere dynamics of interrogation imply a potential for violence.[56]

44. The cubist method in the book, relating the same episodes from different points of view, is a staunchly modernist means to a traditional end: psychological characterisation. (By contrast with *Ulysses*, where Joyce used this technique in the Wandering Rocks episode to convey stasis and futility.) E.S.'s pre-war visit to Montenegro, the mysterious collapse of the rented quarters in Novi Sad, the visit to Gavanski, the brain of Dr Freud on the pavement (see chapters 23 and 28), and above all the incident when the labour brigade is clearing rubble: these scenes haunt E.S.'s mind.

45. "I tried to replace the monotony of a given style with polyphony, a formal polyphony," Kiš explained. "Hence the use of the most varied literary devices—lyrical and essayistic, ironic and tragi-serious, philosophical and parodic." A traditional novel catches multiple perspectives by imitating the points of view of multiple characters or buttressing the story with subplots. Kiš, instead, grounds multiplicity in language. Raymond Queneau's *Exercises in Style* was an influence, spinning variations out of an ur-text (see chapter 28), showing how Eduard Kiš's let-

---

56 Kiš's detractors during the *Boris Davidovich* affair accused him of having plagiarised Robert Pinget's novel *L'Inquisitoire* (1963). This 400-page inquiry into the disappearance of a secretary, involving over 2,000 questions and answers, left this reader, at least, feeling like a guinea-pig. The contrast between Pinget's effect of numbing triviality and Kiš's creation of suspense and significance could hardly be more marked.

ter could become a "generative device". The reason why novels cannot be told is that simultaneity cannot be paraphrased. The experience of reading *Hourglass* is one of wonderment that so many things can happen at once, forging such close and ample connections.

46. But why this complexity at all, if the final purpose is the revelation of something simple?—Because simplicity that has not been distilled from its opposite is usually banal. Because complex forms are beautiful when they create harmony. Because Kiš wanted to make a book which brewed the "barely transparent darkness" that he found in *Ulysses*. For the double pleasure of mystifying, then enlightening the reader. For the private glory of making something radically new. Above all, to make us see: the novelist's defining task. As the facts of the persecution of the Jews blind the imagination with their scale, and the human situation in the novel is so extreme, the mode of representation needed to be extreme, and extremely cunning, if readers were to recreate the situation of E.S. for themselves.

47. Perhaps there was also a biographical pressure behind Kiš's devotion to experiment. Eva Hoffman has written about "the kind of prohibition on the very quality of coherence" that she felt, in relation to her parents' wartime experiences as Polish Jews. "To make a sequential narrative of what happened would have been to make indecently rational what had been obscenely irrational. It would have been to normalise through familiar form an utterly aberrant context." We glean almost as much information about E.S. as we would be given by a traditional novel, but in ways that make us wonder about its source. It is a question of authority. An orphan novel which constructs a missing father, killed in the Holocaust, is doubly obliged to reject omniscience. In this sense, the difficulty of *Hourglass* is historical—and historically necessary.

48. *Hourglass* merits a place in debates about the alleged impossibility or immorality of encompassing the Holocaust in art—debates that Kiš forbore to join, except for one reply to an interviewer. "I feel the issue is not so much moral as literary," he said, "or even stylistic: how to speak of such things without lapsing into banality. . . . How can you be ironic in the face of so tragic a subject?" If literature shies from this enormity, it is not because of metaphysics—unique evil that defies representation—but because literature lacks resources to treat the matter without cliché and anachronism. The sense of infinity that the Holocaust induces cannot be transposed into literature except by epitomising it within a single human fate; but how to epitomise victimhood without

sanctifying or abstracting that single fate, and dehumanising it in the process? Kiš's reply makes us work for the cathartic clarification. For the artful plurality of information about a single life is the opposite of artless (banal) information about many lives, trading on the rightful pathos which so easily usurps our imagination. The opposite, and also the most we can hope for.

49. Even after that catharsis, a mystery remains. The shape of *Hourglass* both as a narrative and as an object is not an hourglass, in which the sands of E.S.'s life trickle away, or a Rubin vase, in which father and son, author and character, interrogator and interrogee face each other. It is a circle or sphere. The last chapter (Table of Contents) loops back to the first. Kiš shows time telescoping in a mind under stress, turning memory into the presentiment of doom. E.S. says of himself that he has "come full circle. My return to the village is just that, a return to my beginnings, to the earth, the final state of the great circle that every living creature describes in its headlong race from birth to death, where the two ends meet."

50. How does the novel's egg-like completeness become an opening into history? How can a novel obsessed with technique, committed to a concept of literature as, in Calvino's words, "a combinatorial game that pursues the possibilities inherent in its own material," also be acclaimed as "the most convincing account we have of the Jewish experience in the Second World War"? Roland Barthes has an answer: "it is precisely when the author's work becomes its own end that it regains a mediating character: the author conceives of literature as an end, the world restores it to him as a means." Of course this explains nothing; it eloquently restates the paradox. Kiš did the same when he assured an interviewer that *Hourglass* was flawless, "there are no cracks in it", only to add that "the *whole* of *Hourglass* is a crack, and this crack is the 'strait gate' through which you enter the book, this crack is its very 'perfection', its closedness, its untimeliness, its hybridity."

51. The reviews ranged from respectful to glowing, as usual, though perplexity lay close beneath the compliments.[57] Early in 1973, *Hourglass* won Yugoslavia's foremost prize for fiction. But Kiš wanted his book to be read, not only praised, and he tried to present it in reassuring terms—which were still fairly alarming: he called it an anthropological novel, a meta-novel (but never a Holocaust novel).

---

57 It took Serbian criticism thirty years to catch up with *Hourglass:* the first critic to plumb its construction (not always convincingly) was Dragan Bošković in 2004.

52. Despite these efforts, he was soon referring to *Hourglass* as an unread book. The nouveau roman was, he had once suggested, the fictional equivalent of twelve-tone music; *Hourglass*, borrowing from the same repertory of techniques, could hardly be popular. Yet he wondered if he had muted the emotion too much, and worried that younger readers would miss the historical references. He also wondered if he had made a mistake by putting the Letter at the end of the book. Inevitably, it became a novelist's novel. The much-translated Serbian writer David Albahari (b. 1948), then finishing his first collection of stories, was bowled over. "What mimetic power, what metamorphic strength! It is no longer a single voice speaking but a multitude of voices, simultaneous, different, contradictory. Behind all this, however, what I heard was silence."

53. It is likely that the reviewers were relieved to be able to praise a politically irreproachable—because safely "anti-fascist"—work by a local star. For *Hourglass* was published at the end of 1972: a delicate moment in Belgrade. In 1969, the Serbian communist party had come under the leadership of an intelligent, broad-minded group that wanted to modernise the economy. By seeking to strengthen the role of elected

With Koča Popović on the terrace of the Hotel Argentina, Dubrovnik, 1985

bodies in policy-making, and openly warning against the danger to Yugoslavia posed by nationalist currents in Serbia, these self-styled "revolutionary democrats" alarmed conservative officials and intellectuals. Meanwhile, a reform movement in neighbouring Croatia was also led by the communist party in that republic, urged on by students and intellectuals.

54. After Tito cracked down on the Croatian Spring at the end of 1971, a showdown with Serbia's modernisers was inevitable. Following several days of talks with the impenitent Serbs in September 1972, Tito called on the Serbian communist party to strengthen its unity and renew the struggle against "petty bourgeois psychology", "bureaucratic centralism", and "opportunists and careerists". The message was unmistakable; rather than wait to be dismissed, the modernisers resigned. Ritually accused in the press of being anti-Titoist, techno-managerialist, Sovietophobic, opportunist, and elitist, and even of being "a Trojan horse of the class enemy within the League of Communists", the disgraced leaders vanished from public life. In effect, they had been defeated by what one of them, Latinka Perović, who became a distinguished historian, called "a broad coalition of Stalinists and nationalists". Likeminded leaders in Slovenia and Macedonia were also ousted or forced to resign.

55. A collateral victim of the purge was Koča Popović (1908–1992). As a pre-war surrealist poet who joined the communist party and fought in Spain, then played a leading part in the partisan victory, Popović cut an exceptional figure in the circle around Tito. Although by the late 1960s he was a generation older than the Serbian party leaders, he supported their pro-Western ideas. Seeing their removal as a palace *coup*, and final proof that liberalising reforms could not prevail against the entrenched self-interest of a communist bureaucracy, Popović resigned from the Yugoslav presidency. Even Tito felt the loss as ominous. "Do you really have to go?" he asked plaintively at their last meeting.

56. These events cleared the way for what Popović would call the "incorrigible opportunists and cynical power-seekers" to take over the communist party while vowing eternal loyalty to Tito and his ideology. Yugoslavia's counter-reformation culminated in a new constitution, adopted in 1974, which extended the devolution of authority to the republics while it reinforced the monopoly power of the communist party in each republic. This lit a fuse that eventually blew up Yugoslavia.

57. Although Kiš never commented publicly on the political scene and placed no hope in any communist grouping, he would have agreed with Latinka Perović that the choice facing Serbia was

either "Europeanisation" or "the ethnic state", with her critique of centralism, and her contention that Yugoslavia was inherently a *liberal* conception, because "it assumed that life embraced numerous differences: historical, confessional, linguistic, cultural, economic, civilisational. Each of the peoples who entered into the Yugoslav state expected, and had, to find its own vital interest within that state."

58. The artistic legacy of Serbia's experiment with liberal reform was itself experimental: above all, Kiš's novel and several films of Dušan Makavejev, culminating in *WR: Mysteries of the Organism* (1971). As he brought *Hourglass* to completion, Kiš became a spokesman for pluralism and against nationalism in the field of culture (see chapter 22). In a polemical essay, "For Pluralism" (1972), he attacked Yugoslav literary criticism as "traditionalist, positivist, sociological", still bolstered by Soviet "critical realism".

> The richness, freedom and maturity of a culture emerge precisely in its pluralism, just as the richness of a fictional tradition emerges in the pluralism of its fictional realities and procedures. Until this pluralism has been achieved in criticism and literature, and as long as a single view of the world and of art continues to be proclaimed as canonical (whether by critics or the administration [i.e., political authorities] makes no difference), and hence exclusively important and meaningful, a culture cannot grasp its own elementary freedom. In this sense, *hic et nunc*, to write differently—which is to say, outside and despite the canons and orders of the day as these are dictated by ruling groups (both critics and the so-called political subculture, which are usually one and the same)—means to struggle for the moral and political freedom of a culture.

And it was not without significance for my relationship to literature that my father was the author of an international railway timetable: an entire cosmopolitan and literary legacy in itself.

"Eduard M. Kiš, Senior Inspector of Railways" was editor-in-chief of the *Yugoslav National and International Travel Guide* for 1938–1939 (Novi Sad, 148 pages), which lists the train, bus, ferry, and aeroplane services throughout the kingdom and to neighbouring countries.

When Milica took the children to Montenegro in 1947, Danilo stowed his father's copy of the *Guide* among the possessions that he refused to leave behind. As his sense of a literary vocation grew, Eduard's solitary publication acquired totemic importance. The fact that the *Guide* was a compilation of names and numbers, adorned with advertisements ("Triumph Metals—Sarajevo", "Brenier & Co. Carpets, Novi Sad"), remote from anything that would normally count as literature, only increased the son's pleasure in his father's authorship, for it forged a fanciful link with the experimental writing that he admired while it validated his love of inventories and proper names. The inspector was an undiscovered modernist, and his *Guide* was "a rubbish bin of cities writ large . . . a sort of Kabbalah".

Kiš the elder had bequeathed a family tradition in letters—as Danilo genuinely felt, turning adversity to account, however wryly he expressed it; and he proved the connection by putting the *Guide* into his own work. It makes its debut in an essay about Paris in 1959. It then features in *The Garret*, unnamed, among the precious books that the narrator preserves under a bell-jar in his squalid room. In *Garden, Ashes*, it takes centre stage in Andreas Sam's imagination as it veers between ecstatic fascination with his father and shame at his failures. Andreas sees Eduard Sam wrestle with his "masterpiece" like any creative artist. When eventually published, it is promptly "put on the Index by the new order (for its liberal and revolutionary ideas)." This fate was inevitable, given "the significance and magnitude of my father's undertaking", which began with research into tourist information and grew into a quest for the farthest horizons of human knowledge:

the questions to which he sought answers began to carry him afield both in depth and in breadth, and he assembled an enormous inventory of literature in the most diverse disciplines, in almost all European languages, and the lexicons came to be replaced by alchemical, anthropological, anthroposophical, archae-

161

ological, astrological, astronomical, Darwinist, Deistical, dialectical, dichoto-
mistic, dietetical, diluvial, dipsomaniac, diplomatic, dualistic, dynamic, exact,
exorcistic . . .

and so on for two pages, ending with "vulcanological, Zionistical, zoogeographical, zoo-
graphical and zoological studies."[58] Andi's epic mystification of a humble timetable reflects his hunger for paternal glory (in which he, too, might bathe).

But Kiš's parody serves a further purpose. His list of "diverse disciplines" aspires to
something absurdly unattainable: *totality*, a concept that triggered a landmark debate in
the middle of the last century, where ideology, philosophy, and aesthetics clashed. The
young Kiš took an interest in this debate through the work of György Lukács (1885–
1971), the Hungarian Marxist philosopher. In the course of many books, Lukács marked
out an emphatic pro-realist position, which led him to condemn much modernist writing
in withering political terms as retrograde, "static", and devoid of historical understanding. Writers such as Joyce, Lukács charged, had forsaken the realist mission to capture the
whole of social life in their work. For Lukács, *Ulysses* was a monument of dead subjectiv-
ity; its teeming surface concealed no human or social depths. For Joyce had fallen into allegory, Lukács's bugbear, contemptible because of its claim to transhistorical timelessness.

When *The Meaning of Contemporary Realism* appeared in Serbo-Croatian translation in 1960, Kiš reviewed it. Lukács had, he said, identified a genuine aesthetic problem:
the disappearance of realist styles that could embrace the whole of contemporary life.
However, this problem reflects the disintegration of the world, or of our experience of
the world (which comes to the same thing). The avant-garde realises this; as such, it has
the merit of not refusing to accept the evidence of its senses.

Lukács's attacks on "avant-garde decadence" were the outcome of *political* despair,
while his angry dogmatism reflected the impossibility of salvaging realism from the fatal
embrace of "socialist realism", the propagandist style promoted by the Soviet Union. The
avant-garde, Kiš concluded, "has sought and traced in art a compensation for that which
it could not find in life. To write despairing books still means something more than howling with the wolves. It is still a cry for humankind."

In sum, he agreed with Lukács's diagnosis of the loss of totality in the modern
world and shared his nostalgia for an inclusive humanist culture. He even agreed that the
literature of Flaubert and his successors was "decadent". But, unlike Lukács, he knew that
humanist totality was lost beyond recovery and could not be resurrected by any political
or aesthetic creed. He saw no alternative to self-scrutinising modernism for anyone who
wanted his or her writing to speak truthfully.

If he sympathised with Lukács's narrative, it was not for the other man's reasons but from a sense of loss, based in childhood experience. And the lost realm is

---

58 Kiš's inspiration may have been Rabelais's parody of (Germanic) erudition: ". . . to know the truth more fully
by Pyromancy, Aëromancy, Hydromancy or Lecomancy . . . by Catoptromancy . . . Cosinomancy", and so on.

individual, not social: for our only totality is childhood, gone before we know what it is. In Lukács's opinion, "the broad masses can learn nothing from avant-garde literature, for its view of reality is so subjective, confused and disfigured". Maybe so, Kiš would reply; there is nothing to be done about that; reality is what it is. Urging writers to abandon the avant-garde, regardless of its truth-telling power, is childish and dogmatic. Nineteenth-century realism was defunct and could not be willed back to life.

Kiš soon stopped worrying about realism and Lukács, but his appetite for lists and place-names never waned. In the early 1960s, around the time that he abandoned lyric poetry, he wrote—in *Garden, Ashes*—the first of the inventories that became his signature. These lists of persons, places, images, epithets, names, or objects hold an intense appeal. They are more wistful (like Proust's roll call of Norman towns) than euphoric (like Whitman's hymns to "free range and diversity"), and seem romantic or even naïve beside the name-checking catalogues that sprawl across post-modernist fiction, signifying anomic, commodity-stunned affluence.

In Kiš's hands the inventory is a wonderfully suggestive form, adaptable to narrative needs; sometimes comic, more often nostalgic; artificial jungles of metaphor; arks of objects redeemed from oblivion; compact anthologies of dissimilarity; fragments of a godless creation; shortcuts to a reader's imagination. They are sources of verbal largesse in his fiction, places where he relaxed, unbound by the duty to grow stories from objects. These feasts of naming, rich with implied description, are generous in their economy.

In Budapest in 1966, he wrote a pure inventory, freewheeling, unindebted to narrative. He made no attempt to publish it, yet it mattered to him: long afterwards, he said that he had once written "a poem that was nothing more than a detailed list of the contents of a rubbish tip: the summary of an entire world, the simplest of all summaries. . . ."

Rubbish Dump

Human and animal debris: nail parings, locks of hair
Women's hair that crackled under the comb's static electricity
Mica flakes of callus shaved with a razor
Dark brown lichens of wounds
Hairs from legs   noses   ears
Fragrant moss from women's armpits
Fish skulls
Spread fans of the tails
Double-edged combs of fish spines
Scalded chicken heads
Black damp feathers
Crooked chicken legs of waxy scales,
Animal bones with the marrow sucked out

Green giblets tied in a knot
Fishbones, tubed, like specimen needles,
Double balloons of fish bladders
Apple scraps
Plumstones   peachstones   melon pips
Cherrystones like vitamins
Crumpled carbon paper, coded
Rotten fruit whose flesh worms eat like human flesh
Chewed pipestems of cherry wood   rubber-tree   wood amber
Blue razor-blades   blue   razor-blade   wrappers, tram   tickets, labels
Paper lacework of tickertape ribbon
Empty golden lipstick-holders like cartridge cases . . .

Like an endless periodic table of substance and simile, the inventory rolls on. Its
momentum eventually fades during a serial naming of roses—each different, all the
same—that becomes an incantation. Applying the brakes with care, Kiš halts the jugger-
naut with a genial reminder that this is only language, words that could be other words,
words that lie stiff on the page without the fire of a human situation.

Clusters of lilac that disintegrate magnificently
    like a smoker's excised lung
Rags   elastic   collars
Oilcloth   muslin kerchiefs   silk
Roses
roses that suit a rubbish dump as beautifully as they suit a poem
roses starting to reek like people
roses that flies alight on
roses wrapped in thin rustling paper by salesgirls' moist hands
roses kept in crystal vases like goldfish
roses with their water changed like the compress on a patient's head
roses bound with wire like criminals
roses with joints like ungulates' joints
roses with leaves that look so artificial
roses that woke me at 3.30 a.m. so I wouldn't
    forget them tomorrow

Totality, Kiš implies, is available only for dead and finished things. The poem ends ex-
pansively, opening away from the dump towards an encounter, love, newness. Perhaps
totality can never be aggregated but known only in the present tense, a state of being, as
the poet experiences his anticipation of the next day's encounter. It is the ultimate rebuttal of Lukács.

Hourglass can be read as a compilation of inventories large and small, epic, tragic and tragicomic, from the garbage washing against a quay to the mourners who would have sent condolences had E.S. perished when his house collapsed. From famous individuals to whom E.S. might have written a letter such as he wrote to his sister Olga, to the infinite "companions of death", starting with porters, firemen, gravediggers, and undertakers and then continuing through 117 other sorts of people before ending in a shrug with "everyone else". From the disgusting offal under the butcher's counter to its antithesis: a paella valenciana, its contents blissfully itemised in a dream of the warm south. From the contents of E.S's briefcase to the list of his and Mr Gavanski's common acquaintances, noting their for-the-most-part wretched ends. From the reasons why E.S. likes dreams (which include "their faculty of transforming unknown places, people and landscapes into known ones, and vice versa") to his fantasies of salvation by the Allies. From the description of photographs belonging to E.S. to the numerous purported benefits of drunkenness. These lists achieve an extraordinary range of effects; the paragraph about the briefcase manages to comprise biography (E.S.'s weakness for drink), psychology (insight into a mind at the end of its tether), history (items such as celluloid collars, from a past era), ethnography (Serbian, Hungarian, and German brand names mingle naturally), comedy (produced by incongruity), queasiness (excess of detail), but also euphoria—what Guy Scarpetta calls "a liberated imagination" expressing itself through "exuberance of information".

After *Hourglass*, Kiš's fictional inventories evolved towards highly condensed epitomes, often with a biographical narrative. They still, as a critic said, "strive to (re)construct a (lost) totality", though the totality in question is now a life in history, such as Karl Taube's origins in the provinces:

> born in 1899 in Esztergom, Hungary. Despite the meagre data about his earliest years, the provincial bleakness of central European towns at the turn of the century emerges clearly from the depths of time: grey, one-storey houses with back yards that the sun in its slow course divides with a clear line of demarcation into quarters of murderous light and damp, mouldy shade like darkness; rows of acacia trees which in springtime exude the aroma of childhood sickness, like thick cough syrups and lozenges; the cold, baroque gleam of the pharmacy glittering with the Gothic of white porcelain vessels; the gloomy high school with its paved yard (green, peeling benches, broken swings like gallows, whitewashed wooden lavatories); the municipal building painted Maria Theresa yellow, the colour of dead leaves and the autumn roses from ballads played at dusk by the gypsy band in the garden of the Grand Hotel.

Or consider Kiš's vision of an Irish revolutionary in the Spanish Civil War:

> I see Verschoyle retreating from Malaga on foot, in the leather coat he took from a dead Falangist (the coat concealing only the thin, naked body and a silver

cross on a leather string); I see him charging toward a bayonet, borne along by his own war cry as if by the wings of the exterminating angel; I see him in a shouting match with anarchists, whose black flag is raised on the bare hills near Guadalajara, and who are ready to die a noble, senseless death; I see him under the red-hot sky beside a cemetery near Bilbao, listening to lectures in which, as at the Creation, life and death, heaven and earth, freedom and tyranny are fixed within boundaries.

Or the nameless narrator of the last story in *The Encyclopaedia of the Dead*, remembering the letters from her lover, letters which she has destroyed in a jealous passion:

> I still recall descriptions of a rose, of a sunrise, variations on the theme of bedbugs, speculations on the probability of life after death. I remember the description of a tree, a simile in which the cicadas beneath a hotel window in the Crimea chirp like wristwatches being wound,[59] the etymology of a name, of a city, the interpretation of a nightmare.

Here and elsewhere, a reader feels what Georges Perec praised as "the ineffable joys of enumeration". Kiš was fascinated by the power of inventories to make our imagination resonate and sing by releasing associations, seducing it into activity (what is the logic of this list, how are these objects linked?). Items in an inventory imply their own narrative, and a writer is hard put to rival the pleasure of letting that narrative hatch in a reader's imagination. Beyond this, he believed that inventories were metaphysically honest about the human situation in a godless world.

Kiš's lists are not virtuosic, like Italo Calvino's, nor are they like the "rather too perfectly astonishing" inventories of Borges. They are not luminous and lightweight catalogues of quasi-normal phenomena, like Perec's; or hyper-animated, like those of Bruno Schulz. They are melancholy and lyrical, merging historical violence with intimate history; their true precursors are to be found in Isaac Babel's stories.[60] A Portuguese critic, Leyla Perrone-Moisés, reminds us that Kiš's inventories are imaginary, whatever their inspiration. "And images that are invented by poets can withstand time and destruction better than things that depend on inventories." This is true; but Perec, another master inventorist, also spoke truly when he said the "work of writing is always done in relation to something that no longer exists, which may be fixed for a moment in writing, like a trace, but which has vanished." Kiš's inventories are elegiac and hopeful, reliquaries that radiate energy.

---

59 See chapter 24: "the chirring of the cicadas (like a million wristwatches ticking)".
60 As here: "A notebook and fragments of Piłsudski's proclamations lay beside the corpse. In the Pole's notebook were notes of minor expenses, the order of the shows at the Kraków theatre and the birthday of a woman named Maria-Luisa."

A few months before his death, he jotted this final insight in the back of—as it happens—Perec's memoir *W, or the Memory of Childhood*: "I have only just understood the significance ('function') of lists in my writing: after harsh, condensed sentences, lists are relaxation, *anarchy*."

———

Cosmopolitan is an important word for Kiš, bound up with travel and the wider perspectives that travel reveals: horizons seen for the first time and old sights seen anew. As a student, he argued that cosmopolitanism was the primary attribute of the contemporary novel, and he admired Endre Ady and Béla Bartók for managing to combine "cosmopolitan and autochthonous, European and Hungarian" elements in their art. Much later, he acclaimed Borges as cosmopolitan. His father earned this epithet because his humble timetable was, after all, both national and international.

"Fatherland" and "cosmopolitanism" are paired in the list of imponderable questions to which the narrator of *The Garret* seeks answers. Spelled out, the question was this: can cosmopolitanism be reconciled with a secure national identity? Perhaps the closest that Kiš came to an answer was a passage in the charming account of his first trip to Paris, written in September 1959, a few weeks before he began to write *The Garret*. He describes his mood of anticipation some months earlier, as he waited for a pre-dawn flight to Belgrade, and links the happiness of that homecoming to the next departure.

> For I had already soared above Belgrade the previous evening, as in a dream, seeing the city as if by miracle in the jewellery and pearls of its illumination, which from a bird's eye view looked seductive and almost unattainable. Strewn with ashes, penitent, and swelling with the tranquil joy of return, high in the pure air, some thousand metres from the ground, I shed my dappled, conceited cosmopolitan plumage in a trice and landed at Belgrade airport as at my home port.
>
> With this feeling, that I had indeed found my home port once and for all, it was easy to set out on a journey.

Beneath the irony, the implication was stark: Kiš could be either cosmopolitan or at home in Belgrade, but not cosmopolitan in Belgrade. In the realm of imagination, the tension between his self-identification as cosmopolitan and his public Yugoslav identity was exhilarating: he could shed the plumage without pain and grow it back when he chose. In practical terms, though, identity was a stony, earthbound thing and cosmopolitanism was shadowed with ambiguity and danger. He once described himself as "marked with shameful 'cosmopolitanism', which has a specific meaning in East Europe." This was an allusion to his Jewishness and to communist propaganda, which tied cosmopolitanism to its opposite: 'bourgeois nationalism'. (Shostakovich was accused of composing "cosmopolitan" music.) In the USSR, during the anti-Semitic campaign of the late 1940s and early 1950s, cut short only by Stalin's death, the term "rootless cosmopolitan" became a murderous euphemism for Jewish.

Cosmopolitanism was Stalinist code for what a recent critic called "a form of malicious though illusory detachment from one's class or economic status", to which Jews were supposedly prone. At the same time, it was despised by a different Marxist tradition for not being national enough. The Italian Antonio Gramsci contrasted "cosmopolitan" unfavourably with "organic" intellectuals, who emanated from the "people-nation". Elsewhere on the political spectrum, an older tradition of liberal thought—dating from the nineteenth century, the age of nationalism—deprecated cosmopolitanism in proleptic Soviet terms as sterile, rootless, and by extension unprincipled. A contemporary subset of this liberalism suspects cosmopolitans of crypto-colonialism, pursuing not "a free circulation around the globe but, instead, the imposition outward of a major power's values and influence, a nationalism writ large."

Adding this hostility from the left and centre to the automatic loathing expressed by nationalists, the foes of cosmopolitanism were legion. Why, then, did Kiš not leave the word alone inside its rings of fire? Because its positive value mattered too much; and because—as we saw in chapter 13—he was drawn to dangerous words like a jester or scapegoat.

On three occasions as a writer, Kiš attacked the nationalist foe head-on. In *A Tomb for Boris Davidovich*, he mocked the macho conception of creative power that dominated Belgrade's literary world; and then, as a sequel, he analysed his critics' errors and clichés with exhaustive, crushing precision in *The Anatomy Lesson*. Years before that, however, in 1973, he launched an extraordinary assault on (literary) nationalism in a long interview with journalist Boro Krivokapić. As the text is available elsewhere, let an excerpt give its jaunty, scorching flavour:

> The nationalist typically knows no foreign language (or regional variant of his own), no foreign cultures (they do not concern him), but if as an intellectual he does have access to another language and thus to the cultural heritage of another nation, great or small, he uses it only to draw comparisons—invidious comparisons, naturally. Kitsch and folklore—folk kitsch, if you prefer—are nothing if not nationalism in disguise, a fertile soil for nationalist ideology. The upsurge of interest in folklore both here and abroad is due less to anthropology than to nationalism. Insisting on the famous *couleur locale* is likewise, outside an artistic context (in the service of artistic truth), covert nationalism. Above all, nationalism is negation: a negative spiritual category, because it thrives on denial and by denial. We are not what they are. We are the positive pole, they the negative. Our values, national, nationalist, have no function except in relation to the nationalism of those others: we *are* nationalist, but they are even more so. We slit throats (when we must) but so do they, and even more; we are drunkards, they are alcoholics; our history is

valid only *in relation* to theirs; our language is pure only *in relation* to theirs. Nationalism thrives on relativism. It admits no universal values—aesthetic, ethical, etc. And because its only values are relative, it is a reactionary ideology. All that matters is to be better than my brother or half-brother, the rest are no concern of mine.

The timing of Kiš's broadside caused some surprise. In 1973, political nationalism was banned in Yugoslavia. Kiš seemed to be aligning himself with communist repression. In fact, he was eyeing a different target. For he saw signs that nationalism—"the last ideology and demagogy addressed to *the people*", as he called it—was dangerously powerful in the culture at large.

He was glad when the interview became "notorious" in Belgrade. Literary gossip is inherently elusive, but in this case we have evidence in the form of a letter from the writer Dragoslav Mihailović. Mihailović (b. 1930) spent fifteen months as a political prisoner in the early 1950s. By the early 1970s, he had earned a reputation as one of Serbia's more interesting novelists, addressing controversial themes. He and Kiš were on good terms until an explosive quarrel in spring 1974, when they met in a café in Bordeaux. Mihailović promptly penned a blow-by-blow account to their mutual friend, the writer Borislav Pekić.

The fact that Kiš and Pekić were intimates weighs on Mihailović, who cannot be sure where the other man's loyalty lies. He starts by remarking how unpleasant it had become to meet Kiš in recent years and on how he expected Kiš to have gossiped against him to Pekić. (He hadn't.) When they met in Bordeaux, Kiš soon mentioned his interview about nationalism. He had heard that Mihailović objected to it and asked for his frank opinion. Mihailović confirmed that he disliked the interview, because it treated literature in a political way and played into the hands of communist authorities who were always looking for ammunition to use against free-thinking writers such as Kiš's friends Mirko Kovač and Pekić, as well as Mihailović himself. Moreover, Kiš's comments about *couleur locale* had targeted him almost explicitly. Given that Mihailović had recently published a series of stories that had "exploited local colour and provincial language to the maximum", whom else could Kiš have had in mind? Kiš said no, he had other writers in mind, "powerful" writers who were "true products of communist society". In that case, countered Mihailović, why did Kiš not attack Oskar Davičo? (Davičo was a politically influential novelist who—as Mihailović may have known—had helped Kiš to find a publisher for his first book.) At this, Kiš banged the table: "Why Davičo? Because he's Jewish?! You are a communist, nationalist and anti-Semite!" As the people at the next table shrank away, Mihailović smiled: "Not because he's Jewish, but because he is the number one literary communist. You say you're anti-communist. Well then, attack him!" According to Mihailović, Kiš fell silent and then said: "His turn will come."—"But I don't think he really believed it himself," Mihailović glossed.

He told Kiš that nobody has the right to turn *private paranoia* ("That's what I said!") into a *general literary principle*. However, when he added conciliatingly that there was no need for them to quarrel, Kiš disagreed. "I sincerely wonder whether his mind is all right," Mihailović concluded—anticipating the allegations that Kiš's opponents would level a few years later in the court case over *A Tomb for Boris Davidovich*. After jeering at Kiš as "a French intellectual", Mihailović described the end of their evening "at two o'clock in the morning: we were both drunk and embraced again, but I'm not sure it meant anything real."

According to Mirjana, the quarrel also left Kiš shaken. However, as far as we know, he did not write about it privately. He continued to praise Mihailović publicly and urged his publisher in Paris to have one of his novels translated.

This encounter reveals something important about Kiš and Yugoslav literary life. While Mihailović's account reads convincingly enough, we cannot be certain who said what. It is a matter of record, however, that Kiš was later attacked by powerful figures in Belgrade for his internationalism, whereas Mihailović became a vociferous advocate of Serbian nationalist opinions, for example about the "suicidal stupidity" of Serbia's historical support for the idea of Yugoslavia and about the wars of the 1990s as the result of other Yugoslav nations' refusal to "live with us". A recent study named Mihailović among the writers who were most "actively engaged in promoting Serbian nationalism and pro-war discourse while arguing for the impossibility of a multiethnic Yugoslavia."

Kiš had a sixth sense for detecting nationalism and an uncanny ability to provoke nationalists, even at a time—the early 1970s—when nationalism was buried deep beneath the ruling ideology and, apparently, presented no threat to anybody. In 1971 and 1972, as we saw, Tito and his apparatus had suppressed reform movements in Croatia and Serbia, which orthodox communists saw as threatening Yugoslavia's stability.

This is why Kiš's polemic in 1973 looked to some like blaming the victim. However, *cultural* nationalism was not merely tolerated by the system: from the 1960s onward, it was actively encouraged within certain limits.[61] The weakening of communism during the 1980s went hand in hand with the strengthening of nationalist ideas and sentiments. More than this: the weakening, as Andrew Wachtel has shown, was accelerated and shaped by these ideologies, which then filled the vacuum. The educational system, journalism and the mass media, popular culture, and also high culture: these were increasingly given over to republican-based organisations which claimed legitimacy by defining themselves against the federal order. The abandonment of Yugoslav nation-building policies in culture and education led to the demarcation of ethno-nationalist cultural zones, breeding rivalry among the leaders of the various republics.

Unlike the Yugoslav state, Kiš was consistent in his anti-nationalism, as also in his anti-communism. He shunned left and right alike; this was extremely unusual. Accord-

---

61 The wittiest analysis of this paradoxical, and eventually tragic policy is to be found in the essays of Dubravka Ugrešić [2003].

ing to Oto Tolnai, an ethnic Hungarian writer from Vojvodina: "Danilo was practically the only Serbian writer who held back equally from leftist ideology, Marxists, Bolsheviks, and from rightists, nationalists." In this, he was the antithesis of Serbia's most famous postwar novelist, Dobrica Ćosić (b. 1921), who flipped from ardent communism to equally ardent nationalism while penning would-be Tolstoyan epics about Serbia's martyrdom in the twentieth century. During the late 1980s and early 1990s, Ćosić lent invaluable dignity and prestige to the war-mongering policies of Slobodan Milošević.

Near the end of his life, Kiš began to write a long satirical poem that mocked Ćosić's phase as a sycophantic Titoist. An anecdote from an earlier time suggests that Kiš had always understood Ćosić's ominous importance. He was walking through Belgrade with his friend Tolnai when they paused at a kiosk for cigarettes and a newspaper. Kiš was flicking through the paper when he stopped in his tracks, leaning into the pages of his newspaper until he almost lost his balance. Then he stood up straight, tossed the paper into a nearby bin and said, "Dobrica has opened the Serb national question." This would have been in May 1968, when Ćosić caused a stir by criticising non-Serb nationalism in a speech to the central committee of the Serbian communist party. (By strict convention, communists criticised only the nationalism of their own nation.) It proved to be a turning point for Ćosić, who in due course became known as the "spiritual father of the nation". Kiš knew all about fake fatherhood and its political dangers: the stories in *A Tomb for Boris Davidovich* circle like planets around a dark sun, named only as the "Father of the People".

My mother read novels until her twentieth year, when she realised, not without regret, that novels are 'made up' and rejected them once and for all. This aversion to 'sheer fabrication' is latent in me as well.

The first sentence tells a story: a fable with a strong moral. The second sentence plants that moral in the soil of Kiš's own writing.

Did Milica really experience this disenchantment around 1922? It hardly matters, for Kiš's purpose is to show that disenchantment with the literature of pure imagination is part of growing up. If Milica's discovery and response are somehow comic (with Montenegrin naivety and vehemence as the butt), they also form part of her legacy. If Danilo had followed a different calling, this trait might not matter; but he became a writer of fiction, a teller of tales, so it was fundamental.

Kiš liked to express this "aversion" and did so, often. It is a pity that none of his interviewers pressed for an explanation. For "sheer fabrication" is hardly a self-evident category. Fiction is written out of a writer's experience, which includes the experience of literature. Novels are shaped by previous novels, more or less. Traces of the non-fictional world smuggle their way aboard the most imaginative and lyrical flights of story-telling. François Rabelais, Miguel Cervantes, Lawrence Sterne, Daniel Defoe, Honoré de Balzac, Leo Tolstoy, Proust, Joyce, Ivo Andrić: who would claim that they produced sheer fabrications?

Kiš set up this straw man to justify his own poetics of fiction, involving invented commentary on real non-fictional documents and the imitation of such documents. These techniques had become virtually unavoidable, Kiš believed, for writers who wanted to convince their readers what they were reading was *true*. "All that matters is convincing the reader," he would say, "conveying the illusion of truth." And: "Making your readers believe in the truth of your story, believe that what they are reading actually happened— this is the chief goal of every work of literature. Any means to that end is acceptable as long as it works."

If the transient conviction of truth was the essential joy of reading, writers had better provide it. And simpler methods of doing so were, Kiš believed, obsolete. "Unfortunately the modern novel is quite unable to speak about the world or other people," he pronounced in 1965. "Nobody believes it any longer. If you as a writer want to take somebody in [i.e., deceive somebody], you can only do it by talking about yourself, by lying about yourself." On this argument, novelists can only convince us by drawing minutely on their experience, transforming it with the resources of literature so that readers **173** are led to identify so intensely with the fictional character that they forget the act of reading and suspend their disbelief.

He was, as we have seen, fascinated by the doubling power of the imagination to create endless representations of singular reality; and by the way that imagination strains against intellect, yearning to believe in the truth of something fictitious. When this yearning is satisfied, fiction is free to cast its spell and by the same token to delude us in ways that would be boring if solemn or prolonged, and that may even be fateful. (He wrote a story about *The Protocols of the Elders of Zion*, worst of all modern novels.)

Kiš's theory of conviction hinges on two assumptions: that readers are sophisticated and hungry for "the illusion of truth"; and that writers achieve their best—most convincing—work by focusing on material closest to themselves. Obviously Kiš himself was such a reader and writer, even if he never wrote at length about the person who was closest to him in his childhood. In *Garden, Ashes*, the character of Maria takes on some colour of her own only after Eduard's disappearance. At that time, he still hoped his mother would become "the heroine of a future book".

From Kiš's perspective, well written fiction convinces us of its truth while it refuses to let us relax in that illusion. This cannot even be attempted if the imagination is not free to invest a fictional character with attributes that convince in *literary* terms. Kiš enjoyed this freedom with his father but not with his mother. By spurning fiction as something unworthy, Milica in effect forbade her son to write about her. This prohibition was imposed when Danilo was still a boy, and her early death sealed its authority. The loving saviour of her children was also a bitterly disappointed wife and widow. Her deathbed entreaties to Danilo to disown his Jewish legacy were, at some level, a final attempt to possess the boy completely, wresting him from the shade of his crazy irresponsible fantasist of a father.

For Danilo to reinvent his mother in fiction would have constituted a betrayal: an unimaginable act for an adoring son who had—as he told Stanko Cerović—inherited his mother's somewhat oppressive moralism. For him to write fiction at all, in the face of Milica's undying disapproval, verged on a contradiction. This helps to account for the triple-distilled compactness and metaphorical density of his prose, unlike anything else in the language, and his horror of kitsch as the negation of art—a vortex of banality, automatism, and formless feeling. Ascetic and self-scrutinising perfection of style was a tribute that had to be paid for breaking the maternal veto.

It was also a foundation of his achievement. For parental legacies are rarely simple, and Milica herself was not hostile to fiction in the form of traditional stories. After Eduard disappeared, she helped her children to pass the dreary evenings by relating folk stories and epic ballads from Montenegro. These stories filled the desolate hut where they lived, and filled the village, and filled Danilo's world with their reassuring spell. Perhaps, too, this maternal stricture against fabrication illuminates Kiš's impulse to pay ambiguous tribute to his modernist masters—Proust, Joyce, Queneau, Borges—in the form of ethical revisions, "counter-books" (in Borges's term) which bridge the gap between literary experiment and historical enormity: between Combray and Kerkabarabás, Leopold Bloom and Eduard Sam—glittering exercises in style, on one hand, and despairing exertions to survive, on the other.

Kiš's most dogged critic complained that he wanted the prestige of documentary truth without the responsibility of being truthful. But the literary functions of true and invented facts are indistinguishable, as long as they are plausible.[62] And Kiš never denied he was writing fiction or claimed to write history.

Consider the detail about the Jewish physician in *Hourglass*, whose brain is blown out of his skull and lies in the snow at a street corner. As an image of atrocity, it is dreadful and surreal. Critics have simply assumed that there was really a doctor called Maksim Freud who was murdered in Novi Sad. But there wasn't. According to the archives, the victims included one Maksim Frajd or Freud, a hotelier or an industrialist. Was Kiš lying? No; the vocation of physician was important for literary reasons, sharpening the contrast between healing the body and destroying it. If we want to learn facts about the historical victims in Novi Sad, we should consult archives, not novels. A writer's accuracy in fabricating information is a source of our enjoyment and a gauge of his or her artistry. As a scholar of documentary fiction puts it, "The finer the line distinguishing fact from fiction, the keener the *frisson* of readerly pleasure becomes."

When Karlo Štajner faulted the accuracy of certain details in *A Tomb for Boris Davidovich*, Kiš was not troubled, because he believed the errors were plausible enough to serve his purpose. He described the basis of *Boris Davidovich* as "facts in literary form", or—a striking term—"narrative facts". He could have said the same of this *Birth Certificate*, where he mistakes the birthplace of Joyce's hero Bloom, bungles the name of a Habsburg emperor, misquotes Freud, wrongly claims that his father was underage when his name was Magyarised, writes *tremolo* instead of *vibrato*, and misnames the university department where he studied.

Do these things matter? Only if we demand juridical accuracy from literature. For Kiš, the illusion of truth was best achieved by using techniques, styles, and modes of address from non-fiction. The key word is *document*, meaning fictional texts that imitate non-fictional forms and allusions in a fictional text to other texts that may or may not be genuine. While these methods of winning credibility date back two thousand years, their modern master is Borges, of whom Kiš remarked that his complex narrative methods aimed at something simple: to make us believe "that *it was really like that* (more or less), because, see here, we've got the documents, books and confessions, the ancient tomes, that are all needed to grant the legitimacy of conviction to our obsessions and fantasies." The polyphonic ingenuity of *Hourglass* serves the same goal.

---

62 The point was made with professorial gravitas by Michael Riffaterre in his study of *Fictional Truth:* "Metalanguage remains the same whether it rests on an actual referentiality or is an image of referentiality. There is no formal difference between a metalinguistic reading of a text about accepted facts and that of a text whose contents are a figment of the author's imagination."

His attitude to documents was respectful, and even fearful; for they radiate a power that can nourish literature but may also burn it up.

He translated hundreds of poems from French, Russian, and Hungarian into Serbo-Croatian, but only two from English, a language he never mastered. One of these English poems was by Dennis Enright (1920–2002), a distinguished poet and critic. In old age, and under sentence by cancer, Enright kept a commonplace book. One entry began: "Once again I pull out a large old envelope marked 'Important Papers', containing my will, birth certificate, marriage certificate, national insurance and health service numbers. . . ." With extinction looming, Enright turns to the truly fundamental texts. We all have them: some letters, diplomas, the hymn-sheet from a funeral service, diaries. Written with the same words that we use casually and urgently every day, in all settings.

Kiš wanted his books to be worthy of being read with the same kind of attention that we bring to such documents. To be, in other words, as serious as our lives. Or as a cookery book. He once copied out some samples of good and bad writing, perhaps for teaching purposes. The good prose began thus: "Take seven or eight onions, a parsnip, a carrot, a celeriac, chop them up, add black peppercorns and a bayleaf. Put everything in a large saucepan, add water, cover and simmer." The bad prose came from a lauded Yugoslav novel: "Then, before our terrified eyes, he spun on the spot like a top and began to run off again. We watched him, not moving. In fact, he made off so fast that we could no longer quell the impression that he was being helped by some invisible and mysterious force—something beyond any reality that we could comprehend." What the first passage had and the second lacked, Kiš said, was "substance" or "subject-matter". Documents always have it; fiction too often does not.

His faith in documents drew on a modernist view that fiction's traditional means of holding our attention, the resources inherited from the nineteenth century French and Russian realists above all, had been overtaken by events. The crimes of Europe's 30-year convulsion (1914–1945), followed by the shadow-boxing of the Cold War, as well as other processes of scientific discovery, social atomisation, and intercourse among cultures, had stripped the realist tapestry of enchantment, leaving it threadbare. The original sins of the realist novel, he argued, were "psychological motivation"—accounting for human behaviour with a predetermined interpretative key—and the "divine or godlike point-of-view". For the technique of omniscient narrative was played out, time-expired: exposed as a childish illusion; radically untrue to contemporary experience.

What were those writers to do who felt the bleak exhilaration of this loss, sharing what Samuel Beckett called "a vision and sense of a time-honoured conception of humanity in ruins, and perhaps even an inkling of the terms in which our condition is to be thought again"? The American poet Wallace Stevens had summarised one possibility: "In the presence of extraordinary reality, consciousness takes the place of imagination." Artistic achievement had to be gauged by the expression of contemporary states of mind rather than the invention of scenarios and rounded characters. This was the avenue taken by Joyce, Woolf, Proust, Hermann Broch, and others. By the late 1970s, Susan Sontag, well attuned to the *Zeitgeist*, believed that for "more and more readers", credibility had fled from "fine writing" into the "raw record—edited or unedited talk into tape recorders; fragments or the integral texts of sub-literary documents (court records, letters, diaries, psychiatric case histories, etc.)."

Kiš's distinction was that he wanted fine writing *and* credibility. Pure invention was not interesting. We can all make things up all day long; what's the point? Don't adults need more? When the *New Yorker* magazine suggested that he might wish to change the end of "The Encyclopaedia of the Dead", so that the narrative would not be revealed as a dream, he was indignant. "I don't write so-called fantastic tales. "I am a realistic writer." Dreams are real, after all. ("Whereof we cannot dream," he once quipped, adapting Wittgenstein, "thereof we must be silent.") He would never insult his readers by assuming they could be induced to believe in the impossible Encyclopaedia or humiliate himself by the attempt. On this point of principle, he was quite ready to sacrifice the *New Yorker*'s immense fee of $3,000.

We read novels to escape the incompleteness of our knowledge of the real world; we want the god-like omniscience of realist fiction *because* it is not lifelike. To be credible and interesting, however, this omniscience should imitate our sense of being in the real world. We want fiction that sets our local confusions and limited knowledge within structures that are completely controlled. Our escapist instinct is satisfied by craftsmanship that delivers an unlifelike coherence.

Kiš could be implacable about literal accuracy and respectful discretion. Certain friends remember his stern dislike of gossip as another way in which he stood apart from the Belgrade milieu. For talk among writers can be ruthless, vying to make the sharpest crack about each other or absent friends, lovers, and rivals. Where everybody lives cheek by jowl, votaries of a language like a secret society, little is sacrosanct.

Kiš was all of a whole, and his revulsion from gossip was rooted in veneration for the printed word. Mirko Kovač remembers his tolerance of chatter about himself, because he could retaliate. When such things were published, however, his attitude hardened. And if he thought the published information was misleading or false, he would fight for a correction or retraction.

In 1983, Kovač published an excerpt from his forthcoming book in a Belgrade journal. An autobiographical novel, it featured a description of Kiš (under his own name) carousing in bars, playing the guitar till his fingertips bled (to impress a girl "with the sweetest lips I've ever touched"), and so forth. According to Kovač, Kiš was furious: "Isn't there anything else to be said about me, am I really so pathetic that I get put into my friend's novel as a layabout and boozer, a busker in the street?" Kovač protested that he had not treated himself any differently. "That's not the same," Kiš fired back. "The narrative *I* is always fictional. The story-teller enjoys humiliating himself, that's why he's a writer. You know this very well and you can always say 'see how I'm fucking around with myself'. But when you do it to someone else, then you really *are* fucking them around.

And I won't let anyone fuck me around, not even a close friend. Whatever's written becomes true in a new way, it always cancels out the original. And if there's anything I can do with my fists or my pen to stop being put in print as a drunken slob, then I'll do it." Realising their friendship was at stake, Kovač swore that he had meant no harm and told his publisher to delete the passage.

A few years later, Kovač tried again; he read to Kiš from a manuscript memoir with more friendly anecdotes about Kiš's antics in bars. Again, he got short shrift. "Talent isn't enough," Kiš warned. "Only a bastard exploits private information. You must always beware of doing something that you might not be able to forgive yourself later. What you've written here can only pass when I'm dead. Any kind of rubbish can be published about dead writers."

In 1947 we were repatriated by the Red Cross to Cetinje where lived my uncle, a well-known historian and a biographer of and commentator on Njegoš.

After the Axis crushed Yugoslavia in April 1941, Montenegro came under Italian occupation. Partisan resistance was fierce, and the fighting was bloody. As many as 50,000 Montenegrins died in the war: one in eight of its population. When Italy capitulated in September 1943, German units transferred from Serbia, Albania, and Herzegovina. Wehrmacht tanks rolled into Cetinje under smatterings of Italian small-arms fire. Even so, before the Italians could withdraw, the partisans managed to disarm six of their eight divisions. "The other two went over to the partisans to fight against the Germans."

By October, Tito's partisans controlled two-thirds of the tiny country, though not Cetinje, where the Germans delegated authority to the Chetniks and other anti-partisan forces, which proved more vicious than the Italians. When liberation came in November 1944, scores were settled with real or suspected collaborators who had not fled with the last German units. "The same day they entered Cetinje," a witness remembers, "the Partisans went around houses with a list and picked up 25 people, and shot them." Peace brought humiliation when Cetinje lost its status as Montenegro's capital. (That honour was transferred to Titograd, as the city of Podgorica was now called.) Without industry or a railway, high in its barren mountains, Cetinje became a shadow of itself.

After the war, Milica tried to contact her family in Cetinje. Early in 1947, nearly three years after Eduard's disappearance, one of her postcards reached Jakov Dragićević, who had assumed that his daughter and grandchildren were dead. He sent his son Risto to bring them home.

Leaving Hungary in early September, the family travelled to Belgrade, where they spent a month or six weeks with Milica's sister Draginja and her children. Danilo's cousins noticed that he spoke very little Serbian, whereas his Hungarian appeared to be excellent. He also sang beautifully in Hungarian.

While Milica put her documents in order, a new organisation of communist states was founded at Stalin's proposal, with headquarters in Belgrade. This was the Communist Information Bureau, known as the Cominform. Its formation followed Stalin's withdrawal from the Marshall Plan, which Tito loyally imitated, and then for good measure he ordered the United Nations relief agency to pull out of Yugoslavia. A few weeks later, the press acclaimed the thirtieth anniversary of Russia's October Revolution with **179** frenzied joy, "more noisily than in Moscow", according to one of Tito's closest advisors. Stalinist fervour was at its height and anti-Western xenophobia was officially encouraged.

The family moved to Cetinje in time for the new school year. For Milica, it was a homecoming; for the children, a fresh start, "starting a new life in a second language", as one of Kiš's Hungarian friends from Subotica would put it. This experience underlay his acute sensitivity to language's power of doubling (see chapter 19).

Milica's brother Risto Dragićević (1901–1980) was a teacher who had studied theology in Poland. After the war, with theology banned from school curricula, he had to find new employment. In 1949 he became the director of the royal museum in Cetinje after the previous incumbent was arrested as a suspected Soviet sympathiser. Risto was also a writer and scholar. He contributed to *Republika*, one of the rare non-communist periodicals that were allowed to publish in the postwar period. His pseudonym was 'Semper Idem', and when he sent young Danilo out to buy the newspapers, he showed him how to fold the *Republika* between the officially-approved newspapers so that nobody would see it as he walked home. His historical essays on Montenegro's greatest son, Prince-Bishop Petar Petrović Njegoš, were admired for their rigour; on the basis of evidence, he securely established certain long-contested biographical data and disproved certain legends, such as the fond pan-Slavic rumour that Njegoš had witnessed the funeral of Pushkin.

In Montenegro's riven political landscape, Risto belonged in the pro-Serbian camp, which saw Serbs and Montenegrins as one people. Even so, he wrote a scrupulous monograph about the Serbian campaign of black propaganda against Montenegro before the First World War. It was probably his reputation for incorruptible integrity that gained him the museum directorship—a position that would usually have been reserved for a dutiful communist.

This integrity was reflected in his propriety and orderliness, at variance with the Montenegrin male stereotype. He took a small glass of wine with lunch and another with supper. Somebody was looking for Risto one summer and was told that he could be found at the seaside with his family: the only man on the beach in a shirt and tie. He tipped his hat to acquaintances, including children. Nobody called him "comrade", the standard term of address in that era; he was always "Mr Risto".

His generosity to Milica was the more noteworthy, as 1947 was the year when he married. The first of his three children was born in 1948, so sharing a small house with several relatives was a significant gesture. Everyone depended on his income, and there was nothing to spare. Food was rationed and scarce. In Belgrade, Kiš's cousins ate bread and dripping for breakfast and supper, with bean broth at lunchtime. The situation was no better in Montenegro.

The children held their uncle in deep respect. He treated Milica's children "as if we were his own", Danica remembered half a century later. And Danilo discovered Risto's private library, which inoculated him against the communist teaching of literature at school. Risto's reference books came to fascinate him, one in particular: "*Le Petit Larousse*

Illustré, 1923 edition, with its prints and colour plates and its motto '*Je sème à tout vent*' [I sow the four winds], planted the seed of a dangerous curiosity in me." Risto's veneration for documentary evidence was a trait that Danilo would come to share.

Kiš wrote only once about Dragićević family life. Evoking the Orthodox celebration of Christmas in 1947, the year of their salvation and homecoming, he conveyed an atmosphere where communism could make no inroads:

> I, as "man of the house", carried in the Yule log across the floor strewn with straw, and my aunt blessed me with sugar and walnuts, and crossed herself and bowed low, uttering the enchanted words of the blessing, the magic formula in Old [Church] Slavonic: *Da priidet carstvije Tvoje* (Thy Kingdom come)—adding her own made-up charm against sorcery and the foul fiend: "*Anatemate na te, ćorilo!*", Anathema-upon-you! . . . with the sugar crunching under our feet, the candle flames flickering, and the lamp crackling beneath the icon of the Archangel Michael, our glorious saint and protector, or rather the pagan tutelary god, our *domovoi* [house spirit, in Russian], covered with soot, gilt and fly droppings, we toasted the occasion with brandy and wine: *Hristos se rodi—vaistinu se rodi. . . .* Christ is born, verily he is born.

He never wrote about Risto by name, though he paid a splendid tribute in *Garden, Ashes*:

> my uncles,[63] worldly people in the best sense, men who spoke foreign languages and travelled around Europe tearing down old myths in the name of new European and world myths, and one of whom, the best pupil in his class, had been invited to luncheon with the King of Serbia, and following this luncheon betrayed his European principles by dropping in at the Café Dardanelles to order a plate of good Serbian beans that cost 25 para (bread included).

Njegoš was Rade Petrović (1813–1851), the *Vladika* or Prince-Bishop Petar II Petrović-Njegoš: a giant straddling the history of Montenegro, casting a shadow that reaches to the present. Two metres tall, strikingly handsome, he ruled a country that measured some 30 by 60 kilometres, with fifty or one hundred thousand inhabitants. Njegoš believed that, if the Montenegrins—destitute clans in a backward corner of Europe— were to have any chance against the Ottoman Empire, they had to change their ways. So he struggled to unify the clans, to win or coerce their acceptance of rudimentary institu-

---

63 The other uncle was Luka Dragićević, a schoolteacher who taught German language in Macedonia. He died in 1941, in unknown circumstances.

tions, including taxation and policing. He built schools and roads, ended blood feuds between the clans, and tried to stop the custom of exhibiting Turkish heads on poles.

These reforms pushed against the grain of martial values, and resistance was strong. "One may expect anything from such a people," Njegoš wrote gloomily. "Woe unto him who is their ruler." Savage measures were sometimes needed; according to Marko Miljanov, Kiš's famous ancestor, Njegoš put no fewer than eighty-three of his opponents to death.

Meanwhile he travelled to Venice, Vienna, and Russia, seeking money and aid against the Ottomans. He was ailing from tuberculosis before his last journey and dying when he reached the coast below Mount Lovćen for the last time, in August 1851. "He could not stay on a horse, and yet he did not wish to be carried on a stretcher, like a corpse," writes a biographer. "So something had to be done: they attached an armchair to the poles of a stretcher, he sat in it, and they bore him sitting thus to Cetinje. Such a mode of travel was inconvenient and more tiring than had he been lying down. But he wished to remain upright—to watch and to meditate as he watched." Njegoš died regretting that he had "done nothing notable", and he was buried on top of Lovćen, according to his wish.

Few today know about Njegoš's feats as a moderniser. His fame rests on his status as the language's greatest poet. Above all, he is the author of *The Mountain Wreath* (1847), a verse drama about an incident in Montenegrin history. The plot concerns an alleged massacre of "renegades"—local converts to Islam—under Danilo Petrović in 1702. In point of historical fact, the renegades may have been expelled, not killed. In mythic terms, the clans amputated their unsound limb in order to be whole.

Metropolitan Danilo is troubled; how can he rouse his people from inertia, make them fight for their freedom? How can he stop more of them from easing their lot by converting to Islam? The chieftains do not share their leader's uncertainty; they call on him to destroy the renegades, "*da čistimo zemlju od nekrsti*" (so that we can cleanse the land of infidels). Danilo hesitates, not from squeamishness but for fear of the effects that such evil (a mass killing) would unleash. A chorus, meanwhile, links Danilo's dilemma to the fateful moment in Serbian history—rather, the mythic version of Serbian history that had been transmitted orally for centuries in folk poems—when divisions among the Serbs led to defeat at Kosovo in 1389. Drawing on the legend that survivors had found refuge in Montenegro, Njegoš depicts the task facing Danilo as the restitution of something lost centuries before, in Kosovo. He tries to negotiate with the renegades, who suggest a compromise: they can share the land between them. The Christians reject this: "We would like to, Turks, but it cannot be!" After other bloodthirsty interventions, notably by an octogenarian abbot, Danilo accedes to the massacre, hailing the "heroic liberty" that it brings.

In Njegoš's handling, Danilo faces a moral predicament from the world of Greek tragedy. The massacre is a sacrificial sin committed for the sake of the future. He takes the burden of this crime on his shoulders so that Montenegro—and Serbia—will grow strong. Although he never orders the slaughter, the play is in no doubt that Danilo is right to approve it. It is this endorsement of massacre that makes *The Mountain Wreath* so troubling. Imagine *Macbeth* recast as a drama of Scottish nation-building: the murders of King Duncan, Banquo and their followers are dreadful but necessary; the usurper's misgivings melt away; he dies, a martyr to national liberty, or survives, haloed with glory. Or *King Lear* rewritten to vindicate Goneril, Regan, and Edmund as freedom fighters against patriarchal wilfulness. Or *Othello* as a tale of Iago's heroic revenge upon the alien Moor. . . .

What makes *The Mountain Wreath* a blazing masterpiece is Njegoš's writing. Densely vernacular, proverbial, sinewy, occasionally lyrical, humorous: his decasyllabic lines convey many moods and tones. The work has shortcomings as theatrical drama but not as a work of poetic genius. Yet these qualities have been almost marginal to its cultural status. For *The Mountain Wreath* became the most ideologised work in the language. The first appropriation was by the nation-building intellectuals who strove for a unified South Slav state. Jovan Skerlić (see chapter 12) hailed *The Mountain Wreath* as expressing "the whole Serb race" and its "national spirit". This cult was transferred to the young terrorists who conspired to assassinate Franz Ferdinand in Sarajevo in 1914.

In the new Kingdom of Serbs, Croats, and Slovenes, the cult was lavishly promoted; the reburial of Njegoš's remains in 1925 was attended by King Aleksandar, who praised the *vladika* as a poet "whose words, planted in the souls of all our millions, sprouted through the generations like the words of our oral poetry." Ivo Andrić acclaimed Njegoš as "the complete expression of our fundamental, deepest collective sentiment". School children memorised reams of his poetry. Commentators extolled his political and cultural importance, avoiding the ticklish fact that his slaughtered "Turks" were not Turks at all but Islamicised Slavs. During the Second World War, suitable passages were recited to Montenegrin partisans in Tito's army. "Though most of them were illiterate, they all knew *The Mountain Wreath* more or less by heart," one of them has recalled.

In communist Yugoslavia, *The Mountain Wreath* retained its pre-eminence, but no longer as a symbol of Serbian or Serb-Montenegrin militancy. Now it was acclaimed as a Montenegrin masterpiece and even as a proleptic example of socialist realism, Stalin's favoured school of literature. The centenary in 1947 was seized as a chance to unveil Njegoš in his new guise as—in the words of another enthusiast—a "dialectical" champion of "the ordinary working man", who saw the destructive influence of Western capitalism percolating into Montenegro and penned *The Mountain Wreath* as an epic song of "national and social liberation, liberation of the peasantry from their Turkish feudal masters". If Njegoš was a pioneer of the class war, then Danilo and his clan chieftains could be recast as forerunners of the partisan armies that fought the German divisions across Yugoslavia's forests and mountains.

The moral toxicity of Njegoš's drama should have proved awkward in a communist federation premised on national equality ("brotherhood and unity", in the Titoist slogan). But the toxin was not analysed, nor were antidotes developed. Instead, it was ignored. Sanitary excerpts were included in school textbooks and taught as though *The Mountain Wreath* were healthily uplifting. For Serb nationalists, however, be they from Serbia, Montenegro, or Bosnia and Herzegovina, *The Mountain Wreath* expressed a permanent call to arms. The call was most seductive when the oppressors were, or could be represented as, Muslim renegades. This, tragically, was the situation that occurred in Bosnia and Herzegovina when Yugoslavia disintegrated. Danilo's cry of "Let there be what cannot be!", which had inspired Yugoslav unitarists to struggle against the Ottoman and Habsburg empires, became a watchword for Serb nationalists who dreamed of Yugoslavia's negation in the form of a Greater Serbian state "cleansed" of ethnic rivals.

Njegoš was not the only writer whose work and reputation were misused during Yugoslavia's terminal crisis; Ivo Andrić was another. Serb and Croat nationalists ransacked their libraries for seeming endorsements of their prejudices. Kiš's friend, the Dubrovnik poet Milan Milišić, appalled by this fashion, wrote a squib:

(Nation)

Drunk
on profound misunderstanding
of their dead poets
flaunting the darkness in their cellar

The misuse of Njegoš mattered most because his name could be brandished like a weapon and there was genuine darkness in his work. When the Montenegrin government was subverted by pro-Serbian elements in 1988, the protesters carried banners with lines from Njegoš, cursing the "bosses" who had poisoned "the Serb tribe" with "the bitter seed of schism". And when Bosnian Serb leader Radovan Karadžić boasted in 1991 that he was ready to "sacrifice this entire generation if it means that future generations will live better", he evoked Danilo's prediction that "On the grave flowers will grow/ For a distant future generation", appealing to the violent irrationalism that claimed Njegoš as its emblem.

When Montenegrin forces poured into southern Croatia in autumn 1991, burning and plundering as they advanced on Dubrovnik, a British journalist saw "an unshaven soldier passing out immaculate four-colour posters of Njegoš. His colleagues were distributing them around any sign, tree or house-front they could find." When the Serb wartime leader in Herzegovina, a truck driver called Božidar Vučurević, denounced the corruption and rottenness of Dubrovnik, as he liked to do in front of journalists, he was echoing a famous passage in *The Mountain Wreath* where one of Danilo's chieftains (comically) contrasts Venice—spoiled, perfidious—with the natural vigour and health of Montenegro. After the war, when more than 100,000 Bosnians had been killed and their country lay in ruins, Karadžić told a sympathetic interviewer that "when the war began [in 1992], Njegoš was on my mind all the time because things were happening just as he had predicted. I knew *The Mountain Wreath*, his great epic poem, by heart." Little wonder that Croatian historians, trying to counter Serb propaganda in the early 1990s, accused *The Mountain Wreath* of being "a true breviary of interethnic hatred", practically a warrant for genocide. Or that middle-aged Bosnian Muslims, asked today about their encounter with Njegoš at school in Yugoslavia, marvel sadly or bitterly at their gullible acceptance of the view that he was 'merely' a great poet.

As Joyce is the only other writer named in this *Birth Certificate*, we might expect that Njegoš mattered to Kiš. He would certainly have heard a good deal about him in Cetinje, not only from uncle Risto. The centenary of *The Mountain Wreath* in 1947 was followed four years later by the centenary commemoration of the poet's death, which naturally—after Tito's expulsion from the Soviet bloc—focused on his effort to liberate Montenegro from Russia's oppressive tutelage.

In fact, Kiš's references to Njegoš are very scarce. At the end of *A Tomb for Boris Davidovich*, the (fictional) Russian poet A. A. Darmolatov is glimpsed in Cetinje at those centenary celebrations for *The Mountain Wreath*, "fragments of which, it seems, he was translating":

> Although well on in years, ungainly and clumsy, he stepped lightly over the red silk ribbon separating Njegoš's giant chair, which looked like the throne of a god, from the poets and mortals.

Njegoš is remote, colossal, and eclipsed by his status as an icon of pan-Slavic, pro-Soviet brotherhood. The other reference comes in *The Anatomy Lesson*, where Kiš argues that the Serbian romantic notion of literary originality boiled down to writers claiming that they have been influenced purely by "reading Njegoš, our folk poetry, and listening to their grandmothers' tales".

While these references confirm Kiš's scepticism about Njegoš's convenience for local nationalists and Stalinists who needed a dead genius to call their own, they by no means justify a recent French critic's claim that Kiš "mocked" the grandiloquence of Njegoš's poetry. Rather, they suggest an indifference to the poetic reality beneath the ideological carapace. Probably the ironclad clichés around Njegoš deterred Kiš from engaging with him. He may well, like the contemporary Montenegrin poet Jevrem Brković, have reckoned that the works of Njegoš and Marko Miljanov were "not so much books to be read as some kind of tedious household Bibles to be memorised."

This indifference feels like a loss, for Kiš could—one imagines—have written a marvellous story about the uses and abuses of Njegoš's work during the twentieth century. That story would have partnered "The Book of Kings and Fools", his fictionalised essay about the *Protocols of the Elders of Zion*. It might have begun with an account of Njegoš growing up in the shadow of Mount Lovćen, above the Adriatic, tending cattle (as Kiš had done in wartime Hungary), before he was appointed to succeed his uncle as

"as clouds / piled landward from the sea beyond": on the summit of Mount Lovćen. Photo by Nataša Perović.

ruler, fated to be an outsider among Montenegro's chieftains; and to play the part of a Christian leader. For "Njegoš's pessimism was cosmic, metaphysical, not Christian", as Dvorniković noted.

This sense of loss is sharpened by knowing what happened when Kiš eventually encountered the 'real' Njegoš who lived and wrote before the political abuses of his work. His friend Stanko Cerović—a Montenegrin writer living in Paris—was a passionate advocate of Njegoš's genius; after Kiš's death, he wrote a study of his work, reclaiming him from nationalist intellectuals. One evening in the early 1980s, when Stanko realised that Kiš did not know Njegoš's "Testament", he read it aloud to him.

> Thanks be to Thee, O Lord, for deigning to bring me to a crest of this Thy world,[64] and for having been pleased to nourish me in the rays of this, Thy wondrous sun.
>
> Thanks be to Thee, O Lord, for having favoured me above millions in soul and body. Since the days of my childhood, as often as Thine unattainable majesty has moved me to hymns, hymns of divine rapture and awe before Thy great beauty, so often have I beheld in horror and bewailed man's wretched lot.

---

64 This "crest" was surely Mount Lovćen.

Thy word has created all from nothing, to Thy law are all things subject. Man is mortal and must die. With hope I come before Thy sacred altar, whose radiant glory I glimpsed even from the crest which my mortal steps have measured. I go calmly at Thy call, either to abide in eternal sleep beneath Thy countenance, or to glorify Thee eternally in deathless choirs.

Kiš was thrilled by this sublime, half-pagan valediction to the world, which Njegoš wrote in a single draft.[65] "He was dismayed that he had never known of it before," Stanko says. "He shouted about Yugoslav education, denouncing our stupid critics and writers who should have made sure that a text like this was taught throughout the country." As often when he fell in love with a piece of writing, he wanted to translate it. In this case, he tried to versify it in French, to bring out the rhythm. But he soon gave up, telling Stanko that Njegoš's heroic ethos could not be rendered in contemporary French.

By this point, he was defeatist about Montenegro from a literary point of view. For he had wanted to write something extended about his mother's homeland since the mid-1960s, without managing more than the exquisite passage in *Garden, Ashes* (see chapter 21). He told Boško Mijanović in Cetinje that he meant to spend some time in the archives, researching a historical topic for a novel, perhaps related to the period before the First World War, when the capital was crowded with embassies to the court of King Nikola. After the scandal over *Boris Davidovich*, however, he told friends that he could not write a novel on that theme, because his detractors would accuse him of imitating Ivo Andrić's classic *Travnik Chronicle* (1945), which drew on French diplomatic records of Bosnia.

In 1982, he told an interviewer: "I owe myself a book about my Cetinje years. . . . Some sort of book, a novel—this exists in me. Whether and when I will write it, I don't know. It's a technical question. It is difficult to encompass this material. I hope I'll write it some time." He mentioned this to friends in Montenegro; others, too, guessed that it was on his mind. Why then could he not—as he told Marko Špadijer, a friend in Podgorica—"find the key"? One reason may have been his block in writing about his mother (see chapter 23). Another, which he suggested himself, was that Montenegro was "a petrified world, and very difficult for literature".

Montenegro was shaped by the struggle for survival against the Ottoman Empire. Its patriarchal clan structures, cult of martial heroism, droning oral poetry, ferocious traditionalism (with what he called its "cruel moral climate"), backwardness, and poverty could not stir Kiš's creative imagination, compassion for victims of terror, or love of fiction that avowed "the inherent *presence of culture* by way of allusion, reminiscence or ref-

---

65 Was Kiš moved by the analogies and contrasts between Njegoš's text and the testamentary passage at the end of *Hourglass,* where the unbelieving E.S. anticipates his end?—"I wish to go to my death with dignity, as befits the great moment after which all dignity and majesty cease. Let my body be my ark and my death a long floating on the waves of eternity."

erence to the whole European heritage". Defining himself, in effect, against the petrified world of Montenegro,[66] Kiš could not become what he had some credentials to be: the fictional chronicler and ironic interpreter of Balkan heroic culture for our time—of that culture's twilight, final flare of partisan glory in the Second World War, then posthumous recycling as coercive stereotype and pastiche.

The only way he succeeded in writing about Montenegro was by evoking his mother's wartime nostalgia for the lost land of her childhood. Yet his idea of a novel about the embassies in Cetinje was excellent; it could have let him write about Montenegro through foreign eyes. On a smaller scale, he also thought of writing a story centred on the spectacular road that zigzags up the mountain range from Kotor to the village of Njeguši, where Njegoš was born and raised, below Mount Lovčen. It is the road that connects the wilderness of Montenegro to the Adriatic, Venice, and the world. He discussed this idea with Stanko Cerović, who doubts that the story would have featured Njegoš directly, though it might have been coloured by Njegoš's sense of the fateful "dissimilarity" between these two worlds, linked by the zigzagging road: the one that Njegoš followed on his last return home, in 1851, and that Kiš mentioned in *Hourglass* ("a white road descending in ribbons cut out of the rock").

Although that story did not get written, Kiš did complete—around 1983—a short text which features the road from Kotor.

(The magical place)

> Set off from Kotor (*Kotor se trouve dans la région de la Zeta, en Yougoslavie, dans le golfe de Cattaro, une embouchure de la mer Adriatique*) at about 5 o'clock in the afternoon. Follow the steeply twisting road for an hour or so, then park the car somewhere and wait.
>
> It should be a clear day, but with some white clouds in the west, looking like a herd of white elephants.
>
> Then: absorb the view of sea, mountains and sky.
>
> After that—the sky, mountains and sea.
>
> You need to know for certain that your father came by this same way, taking a motor bus or a taxi from Kotor, and to be convinced that he saw this scene for himself: the sun in the west cutting into the clouds that look like white elephants, the high mountains that fade into the haze, the inky dark blueness of the sea in the bay, the town at the foot of the mountain, the white ship putting ashore at the pier, the soap factory belching smoke from its chimney, its huge windows ablaze like sheets of flame.
>
> And you need to pay attention to the chirring of the cicadas (like a million wristwatches ticking), because otherwise it is easily forgotten, just as you can

---

66 In *Garden, Ashes,* the childhood home is described tellingly as "our patriarchal petrifaction".

miss the scent of the shaggy wormwood by the roadside, because it is perpetual.

Then you need to forget everything else and contemplate the meeting of elements—air, earth, water—from this godlike perspective.

If you fulfil all the conditions, a sensation of eternity will stir within you—what Koestler called "the oceanic feeling".[67]

P.S. A friend of mine, a photo-journalist, had permission from the captain of a Soviet cruiser anchored off Kotor to take some pictures. Back on shore, he took more pictures of the cruiser against the backdrop of the bay. When he developed the film, it was black as pitch.

The apprehension of eternity, "the oceanic feeling", leaves nothing except red, black or green blots on a roll of film, quite apart from the technology of scrambling, insofar as any of the senses was missing when the shutter clicked: hearing, smell or sight.

My father contemplated this very scene in 1939 (five years before he disappeared in Auschwitz), as did Mr. Sigmund Freud in 1898, before he dreamed his well-known dream about the three Fates.

Kiš never tried to publish this text, so we do not know if it was a sketch for something more substantial. It feels complete but slight, like an attempt to break new ground that loses heart. For these unsettling details—chimney, wormwood, factory windows aflame—have unsettled us before: in *Hourglass*. The first part of the text simply glosses chapter seven of that novel, as if Kiš's imagination were still entranced by his highest achievement. Perhaps he could not write otherwise about Montenegro because his creativity was so interwoven with the figure of his father, whose experience had barely intersected with Milica's homeland. (That visit in 1939 was Eduard's only one.) The anti-communist flavour in the postscript belongs to Kiš's last phase, after *The Anatomy Lesson*. But there is no fresh literary opening here. To name "the oceanic feeling" is by no means to re-create it.

Compare, by contrast, Njegoš's expression of lofty, lordly ravishment in *The Mountain Wreath*, where one of Danilo's chieftains evokes the panoramic view from the peak of Lovćen, then soars even higher:

I whiled away my summers here on Lovćen,
scaling these topmost heights and crags
to watch a hundred times as clouds
piled landward from the sea beyond

---

67 Koestler took this phrase from Freud (*Civilization and Its Discontents*), who owed it to Romain Rolland. The "*presence of culture*" again, as a miniature palimpsest.

to mantle this great range from end to end:
chasing here, there, yonder, far and wide,
with lightning bolts and the mighty crash
and rumbling boom of dreadful thunder.
A hundred times I've lingered here,
basking in the sun, myself at peace,
seen lightning and thunder far below,
heard thunderbolts split the sky in twain,
watched as frightful hailstorms
lashed from the barren clouds beneath my feet.
But here's a wonder that I've never seen:
can you, by our faith, see now
how much there is of sea and shore, of
lowly Bosnia and Herzegovina,
Albania stretching to the sea?
How much, too, of our own Montenegro?
The clouds do burden all these lands alike,
the thunder's roar can all around be heard,
beneath us everywhere the lightning flares,
but we alone are warmed through by the sun. . . .

Njegoš's chieftain can be sure of group acclaim for this sublime vision. In *Hourglass*, Kiš describes E.S.'s escape from a collapsing building and then asks what image flashes in his mind. E.S.'s answer evokes that visit to Montenegro which has been on his mind:

The fiery reflection of the sun on the glass front of the soap factory in Kotor in 1939, and a cloud seen from celestial heights above the bay.

The difference between the two writers and their epochs is epitomised here: on one side, those anthropomorphised clouds that serve Njegoš as décor or choral extras in his warrior's declamation; on the other side, Kiš's solitary cloud that may be a memory or a figment: a metonym for E.S.'s utter isolation.

Immediately after we arrived, I took the art-school entrance examination. (The admissions committee included Petar Lubarda and Milo Milunović.) The bust of Voltaire we were asked to draw—a plaster cast of Houdon's statue—reminded me of an old German woman I had known in Novi Sad, and that is how I drew him. I was accepted nonetheless, probably on the basis of other work.

With partisan soldiers flocking home after the war, accommodation in Cetinje was hard to find. When Lubarda and Milunović—famous names both—took their initiative for an art school to the mayor, all he could offer was the first floor of the town's primary school, built before the war and now under-subscribed. The rooms were large and light enough to serve. Montenegro's first School of Fine Arts opened in 1946. Lubarda was appointed director, and Milunović was one of the four teachers on his staff.

Danica enrolled at the school in November 1947, weeks after the family arrived in Cetinje. During the second year—within a few months of Kiš's examination—the school transferred to Herceg Novi, on the coast of Montenegro. Danica followed; a few years later, she married one of her teachers. Kiš was left to care for their mother when she was dying of cancer.

An American scholar says "we can't know" who the nameless old woman in Novi Sad was. But surely she is Fräulein Weiss from *Garden, Ashes*, the "old German woman who sells boiled sweets", glimpsed at a street corner under a load of cardboard boxes. "Age and illness have turned her face into a dark puddle. Wrinkles radiate from around her mouth, which has shifted to the centre of her face, like the wound in Christ's hand. All the channels of her wrinkles pour, starlike, towards that gaping sore." If this child-frightening vision seems remote from Jean-Antoine Houdon's famous bust of a smiling Voltaire (1778), the difference confirms that creativity is "heated by flames from the hearth of memory" (see chapter 19). The self-deprecating estimate in the last sentence feels like a reflex or superstition: as if any success may be poisoned by hubris and demands the compensation of a self-censuring gesture.

The old woman reminds us of multiethnic Vojvodina, Kiš's birthplace, with its patchwork of nationalities; and of ethnic cleansing in the aftermath of the Second World War, when, as a historian writes, "Yugoslavia's half-million-strong German community was annihilated: more than 10 per cent were murdered, while the rest were displaced or expelled from their homeland." By 1947, when Kiš returned to Yugoslavia, the German minority had been almost eliminated.

If Montenegro is "very difficult for literature", as Kiš believed, it has been easier for painting. Montenegrins made a disproportionate contribution to the fine arts in Yugoslavia. Petar Lubarda (1907–1974) and Milo Milunović (1897–1967), both born in Cetinje, were the most distinguished painters of the generation that came to maturity between the world wars. Lubarda trained in Paris, while Milunović studied in Florence, and they were saturated in European traditions; at the same time, both were Montenegrin as well as Yugoslav patriots.

In the 1940s, Lubarda's life took on the shape of a Montenegrin allegory, when his family was split by lethal political pressures. He spent the war interned in German and Italian prison camps. As he made his way back to Belgrade in 1945, his father, who had been an officer in the pre-war royal Yugoslav army, was put to death by the new regime; the circumstances are obscure, but he may have collaborated with the Italian occupiers of Montenegro. One of his brothers disappeared during the war, and another relative died in an accident while fleeing Cetinje with the last German troops.

These tragedies did not undermine Petar Lubarda's heartfelt anti-fascism, expressed in images of suffering humanity, burned-out villages and scenes of reconstruction. He joined the communist party, according to Milovan Đilas, in pursuit of "fairness and justice, and the chance to participate in a cultural renaissance." Nevertheless, the new regime was suspicious of cosmopolitan "formalists", especially when they had dubious family pedigrees. Lubarda may have been despatched to Cetinje along with Milunović so they could prove their political reliability by educating a new generation. One of his admirers argues that he was saddled with the directorship so that he would have less time for experimental painting. Be this as it may, Lubarda resisted official pressure to teach Soviet-style socialist realism, even though his own style at this time was compatible with that orthodoxy. But he was his own man; by 1950, he had forged a monumental language for depicting Montenegro's mountainous interior and motifs from folklore, including the Kosovo legends. His exhibition in Belgrade in May 1951 is credited with marking the end of socialist realism in Yugoslavia. Đilas wrote that he turned the stone of Montenegro—the unyielding "petrified world" that repelled Kiš—into art: "And he found stone in everything—in the human form and beneath it, in that sky which is snagged on the crags and crests, and in the air charged with a violent storm waiting in ambush behind the clouds." Eventually Lubarda won much favour among Yugoslavia's political elite.

Milunović too was on good terms with the new regime; for a few years after the war he became "a pure socialist realist artist", painting revolutionary allegories (such as "Birth of the New Yugoslavia", 1947/1948) and the inevitable portrait of Marshal Tito with sombre mien. Like Lubarda, he went on to chart his own course, spending much time on the Montenegrin coast, rendering marine motifs: fish, lobsters, olive trees on rocky shorelines.

A decade later, Kiš compared the two painters in a short essay. After praising the "wealth of associations" that are stirred by Milunović's "Mediterranean impressionism" and contrasting his maritime horizons with the plunging verticals of Lubarda, Kiš lists the antitheses: white sails versus eagle's talons, doves cooing versus ravens croaking, sunlit seas and southerly winds versus gnarled crags under "twilit, epic illumination". Yet he warns against missing the tragic element in Milunović's canvases, where the sun often reveals a black cavern or caged birds singing mournfully beside open sea. The future author of *Garden, Ashes* was drawn more to Milunović's indirect emotion than to Lubarda's grandeur.

By naming these men here, Kiš links himself to the best achievements of Yugoslav academic painting. He also hints at something that his friends had always known: he preferred the company of painters to that of writers. He found their talk less political, ideological, and pretentious. By 1983, the scandal over *Boris Davidovich* had strengthened this preference. This may explain why no Yugoslav writers except Njegoš are mentioned in the *Birth Certificate*.

Nor, however, does he name the Yugoslav artist who meant most to him. This was Leonid Šejka (1932–1970), by all accounts one of the strangest men of his time. The son of a White Ukrainian officer, Šejka was "a gentle, peaceable and tolerant man", according to a contemporary; slight in stature, with "large watery eyes", drawn to extremes in art and other experience. Intellectually omnivorous, convinced that artists had to be visionary and experimental, redeem the world's ills, restore wholeness and reveal purity amid corruption, Šejka investigated mystical traditions and dabbled in the occult (demonology, numerology). His paintings were intended to be objects about representation, not only representations. Fascinated by labyrinths, by Borges's Aleph,[68] *trompe-l'oeil*, false perspectives, visual feints, and dimensional riddles, playing—like Magritte—with the plane of the canvas, Šejka had a strong mathematical interest in perspective and proportion. He worked Renaissance motifs into canvases redolent of a postwar wasteland, from Bosch to the early Venetians (especially Carpaccio's animals) and the Flemish masters (the geometric interiors of Vermeer and de Hoogh).

Like Kiš, he had a strong explicatory drive. The "function of contemporary painting" might lie, Šejka argued, in "arranging and classifying all categories of the real", and thereby "truly integrating the whole heritage of the modern age". In this spirit, he painted a series about the rubbish dump: assemblages of disjecta, discarded manufactures, modern detritus, industrial-age middens. There was an aesthetic of rubble and rubbish dump in 1960s Yugoslavia, as elsewhere in Europe. It was most intense in Belgrade, and Šejka's work exemplified it. Kiš's poem, "Rubbish Dump" (see chapter 22), was certainly inspired by Šejka. The dump is where all roads end, a terminus with no centre or focus. It is monstrously itself, yet rife with all things. Lifeless, but pregnant with metaphor. It was, in more than one sense, the end of modern art. Šejka's rubbish dumps yielded to 'warehouses': less rebarbative, more playful anthologies of unlike objects. Meret Oppenheim, of the legendary fur-lined teacup and saucer, was thrilled by these canvases.

---

68 In Borges's story, the Aleph is "a small iridescent sphere . . . two or three centimetres in diameter, but universal space was contained inside it, with no diminution in size."

Kiš loved the painter as a friend and admired him as a sage as well an artist and a fellow outsider. He revered his experimental energy and learned from his attention to narrative positioning and the exactness of his allusions. The two men spent much time in Belgrade cafés with a guitar, singing Hungarian and French songs, Russian prison-camp songs and the ballads of Bulat Okudzhava, discussing art and Soviet totalitarianism, a vividly argumentative and high-spirited duo. "He was stoical, with a strange cheerfulness towards life and himself and the world—despite a very unhappy life," Kiš recalled. "He painted in deepest poverty, in impossible circumstances, in wretched little rooms." Šejka "rescued me from the ideologised language used by the literary journals. I was also writing theoretical texts, but from *outside* those ideological frameworks."

A few hours before his death from a brain tumour at just thirty-eight, Šejka wrote in a testamentary message that if he had a second chance, he would paint in the way "that offers most joy, like the old masters, [even] at the price of not being original." He ended with the statement: "Painting is a form of prayer." In a grieving tribute, Kiš honoured Šejka's "striving for totality", trying to synthesise classicism and modernity. According to Mirjana Miočinović, this was the only obituary for Šejka in any Yugoslav newspaper. He never lost his importance for Kiš; Pascale Delpech, his partner in the last decade of his life, recalls how often he talked about Šejka. One of his last stories mentions him as "the self-styled 'classifier'", telling a tale about the Soviet Union, "solitary, ill and Russian", but aware that the tale was illuminated by "the same mysterious light that glows from his paintings."

Šejka was the most distinguished member of *Mediala*, a grouping of artists in Belgrade. Kiš was close to these artists for a time; he was even introduced to others as

With Leonid Šejka, and the back of Bulat Okudzhava's head. Belgrade, 1967

a member. "I preferred the company of painters to that of writers in the Fifties," he explained. "The writers were clannish. I didn't join the literary in-fighting. I felt much better among the members of the 'underground' Mediala." Except for the "Rubbish Dump" poem, it is hard now to see much common ground, for the Mediala painters specialised in lavish images of ugliness and irrationalism. Šejka's esoteric inventions were not typical products of the group, which favoured images of decay in a lurid palette, phosphorescent nightmares from a zone demarcated by Hieronymus Bosch, Matthias Grünewald, and Salvador Dalí.

The success of Mediala's shock tactics depended on the oppressive orthodoxy of communist uplift and renewal, favouring realist depictions of a "positive" kind. In that context, it has been said, the Mediala offered "the only alternative to the governing nomenklatura in the late Fifties and the Sixties", and its gloomy repertory was felt by some as valuable and truthful, where now it seems a black joke that took itself too seriously.

Kiš respected the Mediala's *non serviam*, its surly negation of Yugoslav optimism; and he enjoyed the company of the artists themselves, whose Bohemian eccentricities rivalled Šejka's. Did he, one wonders, notice a paradox about the Mediala? Although the artists gave the lie to official rhetoric, their contempt for what one of them called modernism's "graveyard of dead styles and aborted -isms" betrayed a naïve dogmatism of their own. Kiš's sense of the interaction between past and present was finer than that.

By the early 1970s, the most talented members of Mediala were dead (Šejka) or living in Paris (Dado Đurić, Vladimir Veličković). As nationalism waxed in Serbia during the 1980s, the dark ferment of Mediala became toxic. Occultism became Serbian Orthodox religiosity and even anti-Semitism; painterly interest in folk motifs hardened into national bigotry. Not in every case, to be sure, but such were the trends among some vocal former members, whose avant-garde vitality aged into vicious reaction. What Kiš made of this dismal decline, he did not say in public.

Thinking about Kiš's respect for the avant-garde, and about a question that his friends pondered in the 1990s—what would he have said about the war that destroyed Yugoslavia?—I'm convinced he would have admired a work by the performance artist Marina Abramović, herself half Montenegrin. Given in Venice in 1997, "Balkan Baroque" involved Abramović squatting on a heap of animal bones—the femurs and tibias of cattle, fresh from the slaughterhouse, blotched with blood and fibres of meat. She scrubbed the bones with a big brush for hours at a time, crooning as she worked amid the summer heat and stench, while the audience tried not to gag. She explained that the idea originated in her "tremendous feeling of shame" over the recent war in her homeland. The Montenegrin minister of culture tried to block Abramović's performance at the Biennale, in vain: it won the Golden Lion. Even the stills are unforgettable. Perhaps "Balkan Baroque" was a definitive comment on ethnic cleansing: an undertaking of prodigious stamina and selflessness, a woman's symbolic assumption of responsibility, mourning a disaster created by men who refused to be responsible, and a vindication of the avant-garde—proving its power to unmask ideology with more than verbal eloquence.

"Balkan Baroque," XLVII Biennale, Venice, June 1997. © Marina Abramović. Courtesy Sean Kelly Gallery, New York.

I had to wait a year or two in order to get the
necessary academic qualifications. Meanwhile I
decided to finish secondary school after all.

Founded in 1880, the Gymnasium in Cetinje was Montenegro's oldest secondary school. Kiš enrolled as a third-year pupil just as the school transferred from the Prince's Palace to a new building on the Street of Montenegrin Heroes. "There were excellent teachers, including White Russians," he told an interviewer. "I'm still proud of it."

Two and a half years after the war, conditions were still very hard. The class had forty-five pupils; most were, like Kiš, about twelve and a half years old; some were much older; a few were eighteen—youths who had missed school because of the war. There was hardly space for them all in the classroom. He was enrolled as Kis, perhaps because his mother or uncle wanted to show respect for his father's memory. Whatever the reason, the surname emphasised the boy's "troubling dissimilarity", which led to bullying. "Magyar! Magyar!" was the playground taunt until Danilo lashed out at his persecutors, and won. It was a turning point. The sense of liberation from fear was something he never forgot. His friend Gabi Gleichmann, the son of Hungarian Jews, sees this incident as marking Kiš's break with the stoical passivity that he absorbed through his father. (In *Garden, Ashes*, Eduard says that you fool an enemy by lying down like a dog.) "There's no amount of pain that a Jew cannot outlive. Servility as the way to survive: that's the style," Gleichmann explains. "In Montenegro, where the whole approach is the *opposite* of Hungarian Jewish, this didn't work. So, once, at school, he beat up his tormentors, which earned him the respect of all."

Life was hard in other ways as well. Pupils were hungry most of the time; Pavle Đonović, one of the lifelong friends Kiš made at the Gymnasium, believes their average weight was no more than 40 kilograms (6.3 stones). Thin as rails, with hair cropped to the scalp every fortnight, "we looked more like prisoners than teenagers". They were also subject to an informal curfew and punished if seen in public by their teachers after 8 o'clock.

At the end of the year, pupils had to pass exams in six subjects (three arts, three sciences) before they could advance to the upper school. Although Danilo was a very good student, he failed history. Instead of retaking the exam in late summer, he decided to take a year out. He moved to Belgrade and stayed with his aunt, Draginja Malović, until the following June. He later said that he spent the time reading, immersing himself in books, and improving his Serbo-Croatian.

Đonović said that their teachers were outstanding, and not much "interested in politics". Boško Mijanović, another lifelong friend, agrees. One of the teachers, Zorka Vukčević, recalled much later how Kiš had held everyone spellbound with an account of his years in Hungary and how this changed his standing in the class. He impressed with his singing as well as his speaking voice, and his fists. He serenaded pretty classmates from the street below their windows, accompanying himself on a battered violin: "probably his sole inheritance from his father", Đonović guessed.

Another teacher, Branko Šaranović, set up reading groups and a debating club at school and organised literary events in the town, which he encouraged pupils to attend. There was a lot of culture in Cetinje, most of it coloured a deep communist red. In October 1949, the Cultural-Educational League of the People's Republic of Montenegro mounted a festival of choirs (from trades unions and youth groups), theatre companies, folklore societies, orchestras, and soloists. The virtues of "revolutionary folklore" were promoted as the best way of teaching the masses how to build a happy socialist future.

Kiš and Đonović whiled away much time in the town library during Cetinje's grim autumns and winters, when the town was either awash with rain or snowbound. As a copyright library, it had the biggest holdings in Yugoslavia after Belgrade and Rijeka. Kiš discovered the works of Miroslav Krleža. They also managed to get their hands on Miloš Crnjanski's books, even though the author (1893–1977) was in political odium with the regime and banned from the school syllabus.

The senior class of Cetinje gymnasium on a visit to Dubrovnik, 1954

A few months after Kiš began at the Gymnasium, the Yugoslav regime was shaken to its core. Irked by the Yugoslavs' lack of automatic deference to Moscow, Stalin had withdrawn his advisers and accused the Yugoslav leaders of being "intoxicated with their successes, which are not so very great." Instead of prostrating themselves, the Yugoslavs insisted that they were "tenaciously building socialism and remaining true to the Soviet Union". Expulsion from the Cominform (the Soviet-led front of European communist states) came in June 1948, with an open appeal to "healthy members of the CPY [Communist Party of Yugoslavia]" to make their leaders change their ways or remove them.

The regime responded by redoubling its dedication to the Soviet model while clamping down on anybody who gave any hint of heeding Stalin's appeal. Instead of relenting, Cominform pressure on Yugoslavia intensified. In 1949, Tito announced that Yugoslavia would defend itself if attacked; the United States and Britain promised support. Suspected pro-Soviet sympathisers were sent, with no judicial process and often on the flimsiest pretexts, to a prison island in the northern Adriatic called Goli otok, 'Bare Island' (see chapter 33).

Raised in a culture that prized epic consistency and pan-Slavic loyalty, many Montenegrin communists could not accept that Mother Russia, cradle of communism, leader in the anti-fascist struggle, might be wrong. One of them summed up their confusion: "I do not know what all this is about, but I know that Russia is great and Stalin is mighty." Some 9 per cent of known 'Cominformists' were Montenegrins, who formed just over 2 per cent of Yugoslavia's population (of 15.7 million). The party organisations in a number of large towns—including Cetinje—supported the Cominform. Tito's secret police was deployed in strength to suppress pro-Soviet guerrilla operations. The brutality of this suppression troubled loyal Montenegrin comrades.

"I will shake my little finger and there will be no more Tito," Stalin boasted. When the Yugoslav regime did not buckle, he tried the method that had silenced Trotsky. After Stalin's death, a note from Tito was reportedly found among his papers: "Stalin. Stop sending assassins to murder me. We have already caught five, one with a bomb, another with a rifle. . . . If this doesn't stop, I will send one man to Moscow and there will be no need to send another." The Yugoslavs endured, and their endurance became another myth of socialist Yugoslavia, merging with the myths around partisan victory. The initial panicky reaction of 1948–1949 was written out of the story.

As a schoolboy in Cetinje, Kiš would have absorbed the climate of fear created by the Cominform crisis—a climate that older Montenegrins remember to this day. As members of the Communist Party youth organisation, he and his friends took part in organised discussions and reading groups. They read *Borba*, the federal newspaper that was the party mouthpiece. Everyone noticed when neighbours disappeared for two or three years. And Kiš would have known how his uncle Risto had come to be appointed as director of the museum.

Meanwhile, Kiš and his sister faced a personal tragedy. Not long after bringing her children to the haven of Cetinje, Milica fell ill. It turned out to be cancer of the spine. Danilo was given exceptional permission to sleep at her hospital bedside, which became his second home until her death three years later in 1951. Before the advent of palliative techniques, patients in Milica's terminal condition had to endure excruciating torment, with no hope of improvement. At one point, she begged Danilo to bring her a pair of scissors, so she could put an end to it all. He refused, just as he had—on his mother's instruction—refused his father's identical plea twelve years before in the psychiatric hospital at Kovin. "History was repeating itself."

Kiš wrote only once about this experience: in a brief essay, in French, the year before he died. "The worst thing was, she suffered so much that her death felt like a relief," he recalled. "Like the end of a dreadful existence that she had taken upon herself in an effort to spare her children as much as she could. Just as she must have felt my father's disappearance as a sort of liberation, in spite of the monstrosity of it." The experience had destroyed his belief in God. "This is how I reasoned: if someone like my mother has to suffer so much and so long, this is proof that there is no God," he said. "That was my starting point, and it's still as far as I've got." The refusal of reconciliation in that remark was defiant, as it was in a savage remark to Gabi Gleichmann; he had, he said, spent three years caring for his mother while she "rotted away".

He told friends that he could not write about her because the truth about her suffering was too terrible for irony; and irony was the key to fiction. He had witnessed her suffering so closely that imagination had no room for play. Yet, even when a mother does not undergo Milica's extreme wretchedness, such reticence may not be unusual for a literary son. In verses about his own mother, the English poet William Empson wrote: "Stars how much further from me fill my night, / Strange that she too should be inaccessible, / Who shares my sun."

Kiš's father, by contrast, was remote and enigmatic even before he "disappeared" in Auschwitz, so his fate could only be imagined. Where Milica's mute suffering, compliant and self-sacrificial, rebuked the playfulness of fiction, Eduard's life could be re-created as a vagrant spirit, a Wandering Jew, blessed and cursed with a yearning for unattainable liberty.

For two years I learned violin at the music school, where I was taught by Simonuti Senior, whom we called 'Paganini' not only for his appearance but because he loved tremolos. Just when I reached the second position, the music school moved to Kotor. I went on playing by ear—Gypsy music, Hungarian romances, and the tango and 'English' waltzes at school dances.

The music school had opened in 1932, the first of its kind in Montenegro. It reopened in 1947, just a year after the School of Fine Arts. The school choir and orchestra gave their debut concert on 21 December that year, celebrating the sixty-eighth birthday of J. V. Stalin.

Kiš applied to learn an instrument, and the teachers "decided that I had an 'ear'. When they asked which instrument I wanted to learn, I could not choose between piano and violin." Impelled—as he came to see much later—by an obscure urge to find some connection with his father through music, he opted for the violin. His teacher was Stevo Simonuti (1891–1973), a building contractor by trade, of remote Italian ancestry, and an excellent amateur musician who taught flute and violin. He and Kiš grew fond of each other, as Stevo's son Tripo remembers. (Tripo also points out that Kiš should have written *vibrato*, not *tremolo*, in the *Birth Certificate*.) For his part, Kiš remembered Simonuti as "a wonderful old gentleman" and himself as "a very good pupil."

When the school moved to Kotor in 1951, Kiš could not follow, so he took up the guitar instead. For the rest of his life he played guitar in company, whether of friends or strangers, usually to accompany himself, singing in Serbo-Croatian, Hungarian, Russian, and French in a memorable baritone voice. As a student, he earned drinking money by busking in the cafés of Belgrade. Central Europeans of his generation learned many songs in childhood and youth, and Kiš knew them by the dozen: Gypsy ballads, concentration camp songs from Auschwitz, folk songs, Ottoman love songs, Magyar romances, French chansons. Pascale Delpech remembers that Kiš was always singing, "always and everywhere, at home, in other people's homes, in cafés". Classical music, on the other hand, was not part of daily life; there was no radio or gramophone in his home.

Much could be said about the musical structure of his books. The artist Radomir Reljić went further; the very shape of Kiš's life and work was, he told me, like a *ricercar*— a Renaissance or Baroque term for polyphonic instrumental music whose themes develop through repetition.

When I asked Kiš's friends about his relationship to the songs that he played and sang, they said that he loved their ardour and pathos. He, who rewrote his books until he had planed away the direct emotion, was free of that compulsion when he sang, as also when he talked. Literature was too important for conversation anyway; much better to wallow sociably in the colourful sentiments of traditional song. Yet there was a connection between singing and writing. For Kiš wanted his work to carry an indirect emotional charge such as songs communicate directly.

His vulnerability to this kind of emotional assault was familiar to close friends. Miroslav Karaulac was with him in a Belgrade café in the 1970s when a gypsy singer with a zither sang a famous Hungarian song about lost love. Kiš, visibly disturbed, jumped up and demanded how the singer knew that song. "What do you mean?" said the singer. "I sang it for you every night in Skadarlija twenty years ago."[69]

This sensitivity to the tides of feeling that songs can release says much about his own temperament—and his determination to bar those tides from his own writing. It was an aspect of Kiš that is caught in a short memoir by the playwright Vida Ognjenović:

Gloomy Sunday

On a sluggish Sunday afternoon towards the end of June, some time in the mid Seventies, Kiš, Mirko Kovač and I were sitting in my rented flat in Takovska Street. It was sweltering, one of those days when Belgrade wilts and dies like a deserted barracks, and the steaming asphalt swells like wet moss under the wheels of passing traffic.

We had the usual 'office beverages', as Kiš called coffee and mineral water, as well as some red wine, but none of it was refreshing. The cloying afternoon heat had sapped us and our little party dragged on listlessly, not at all like our usual rowdy reunions. We did not feel like staying in the room, but we lacked the energy to go outside. Even our conversation was lethargic and desultory.

Kiš kept interrupting us. He was in a strange mood, melancholic and prickly at the same time. He jumped up in the middle of a conversation to shut the window because of the smoke and smell from a barbecue on a nearby balcony, only to rush over and throw it wide open a moment later because of the broiling heat. He moved aimlessly around the room, humming some Hungarian song as he leafed through the newspapers and glanced at some of the books.

I asked Mirko to come into the kitchen and open a fresh bottle of chilled mineral water, so that I could ask him what was going on. Mirko was evasive, he wasn't sure, it was just a touch of nerves because of the heat, but eventually he

---

69 Skadarlija is the cobbled Ottoman quarter in central Belgrade with many cafés and restaurants.

admitted that he thought Danilo's bad mood was due to a lovers' tiff. Nothing major, he added, a passing thing. But he would not let me tease him. Don't make anything of it, he warned, sounding serious, this isn't the time to pull his leg, which I found odd, because in such situations we were always merciless, usually with Danilo's full participation; but I took heed.

When we went back into the room, Danilo was finishing a cigarette, blowing smoke out of the window. Then he carried on humming the same Hungarian song and we sat there quietly, not wanting to disturb him.

Do you know what I'm singing?, he asked suddenly, slowing down, articulating every word clearly, to make it easier for me to recognize: *Álmokat keregtő vasárnap délelőtt, bánatom hintaja, nélküled visszajőt.* No I don't, I don't think I've ever heard it, I said, not as far as I remember. Listen, this has to ring a bell, he insisted, repeating the words and then the melody several times: *Szomorú vasárnap száz fehér virággal vártalak kedvesem templomi imavál,* then the refrain: *Szomorú vasárnap . . .*

It's something about a white flower and a Sunday, I said, because I did understand a few words, such as *fehér*, meaning white, *virággal*, blossoms, and *vasárnap*, Sunday, but I honestly don't know the song. He tried to remember some of the other verses, line by line, spinning out the lovely melody, and I kept trying to recognise it, and failing.

It's Rezső Seress, he announced in the end like a teacher, pausing for the name to register. Surely now you know who I'm talking about. It's his famous song, "Gloomy Sunday". Now do you know? No, I didn't. I can't believe you don't know who Rezső Seress is, or his song. Never heard of it, I said. Nor had Mirko.[70]

Rezső Seress was a really big star, a songwriting genius, Danilo explained excitedly, lighting another cigarette. He performed in a small café in Pest called *Kispipa*, mostly his own songs. They say the cream of Europe came to that dive as if it were a shrine, even the Shah of Persia. There was so little room that even celebrated musicians had to stand if they wanted to hear him. He was completely self-taught, he never spent a day in school. They say he composed by whistling. He drew the keys on the kitchen table, ran his hands over them and whistled. Europe went mad about the song. In fact, sometime in the mid-Thirties, the whole world was crazy about the melancholy of Pest and the song "Gloomy Sunday". The song was banned for a time on the ground that it made people suicidal, because suicide notes quoted lines from the song. And you know what? The song was secretly played in cafés, but only at the request of the despairing rich and influential. They say that during the war, officers in Pest requested the song by using certain code words and special signs.

---

70 Several recordings of "Gloomy Sunday" can be accessed online. A list of recordings is available at http://www.phespirit.info/gloomysunday/recordings.htm.

Can you imagine the perversity of it?, he suddenly cheered up and began waving his arms around, you request the song but it's got to be sung in a whisper and the entire orchestra has to play pianissimo, you catch just the barely audible gist of the melody; if a patrol suddenly came in, it was agreed that they would immediately bang out something lively. Then, humming the song, he abruptly switched from the sorrowful tune to a fast *czardas*. Mirko and I applauded.

It's strange how on the eve of the Second World War, Rezső Seress and his song unwittingly foretold the catastrophe to come, the suicide of European liberalism, Danilo went on, flicking his lighter to ignite another cigarette, whereas all the poor little café entertainer wanted was to express love's despair. He was only one and a half metres tall, poor, sensitive, a brilliant lunatic. He was unbelievably popular. That's why it's so hard to believe you never heard of him.

Do you think Rezső Seress is still alive?, I asked. No, no, I think he committed suicide, Kiš said, he killed himself, and not so long ago either.[71] He managed to survive the war as a Jew, that much I know; his fans and friends hid him in Pest, but I seem to recall he was purged by the communists for bourgeois sentimentalism. I think one of those Hungarian writers told me that later, while you were still singing your young communist songs about renewal and reconstruction, he jumped out of the window of his Pest flat in despair, because he wasn't performing any more. He earned big money before the war, but as he didn't dare to leave Pest and his little *Kispipa* café, he was dying of hunger because not a cent could be brought into Hungary from abroad after the war.

And so, on one of his gloomy Sundays, he skipped out of the window, Kiš added, then took a sip of wine, complaining that it had almost boiled over, but it would be bad taste to talk about Rezső Seress with a drink as insipid as mineral water.

---

71 Seress committed suicide on 11 January 1968. According to the obituary in the *New York Times* (14 January 1968), he "complained that the success of 'Gloomy Sunday' actually increased his unhappiness, because he knew he would never be able to write a second hit."

At the secondary school I continued to write poetry.
I also translated Hungarian, Russian, and French poets,
primarily as stylistic and linguistic exercises:
I was training to be a poet, learning the craft
of literature.

Kiš was fond of saying that he trained to be a writer long before he became one. "Even in Cetinje, I was beginning to prepare for the craft of writing." The notion that literature is a skill to train for, like woodwork or musicianship, belonged to his anti-romantic outlook. Translation was a valuable part of the apprenticeship, as many writers have found. For Kiš, however, it was more: he translated throughout his writing life, as naturally as he breathed. Unusually again, his translations are woven into the fabric of his own work.

Poetry was another stage in the apprenticeship. He talked about himself as a failed poet, partly as a comic turn (the fiasco of my juvenilia, etc.) when interviewers pressed him on the importance of poetry in his life; and partly because it implied that growing up meant leaving poetry for something more suited to man's estate. Near the end of his life, he said it openly: "I kept myself for something harder—prose. That's much harder work."

Yet poetry was always central. He and his schoolmates absorbed Bogdan Popović's famous old anthology of Serbian poetry—the same Popović who had founded comparative literary studies in Belgrade before the war. "The poetic energy of young people—that youthful energy that we spent in learning poetry by heart—now goes into pop music." There was a lot of poetry around; Belgrade poets were invited to Cetinje to read their work before the literary society. In his final year or two at school, his own poems were accepted by magazines (see chapter 2). The few poems he wrote as a student plotted his growing awareness of language. He kept writing poetry in Strasbourg, where Wladimir Krysinski remembers his passionate recitals of Tin Ujević, Charles Baudelaire, Aleksandr Blok, and Rimbaud. His last as well as his first published work was a poem. Increasingly, he wanted to write prose as concentrated and elliptical as poetry, with minimal connective tissue, where narration is borne by metaphor, and character or voice are sustained by the patterning of images.

Although he wrote occasional poems until the mid-1960s, and returned to verse at the end of his life, his poetic energies from Strasbourg onwards were channelled into translation. Translating poetry was an appetite, an addiction, a mode of possession—and of being possessed. He came to think it was also a valve to release lyrical emotion that otherwise might vitiate his prose. With his anti-symbolist sense of language and poetry, he had no time for the idea that poetry is what's lost in translation. A poem is a semantic **205** event, not a record of transcendent experience, and semantics are translatable; but the music too can be communicated, given patience and skill. Of course a translation cannot *be* the original in another language, but this truism cannot count as a defeat, because nothing can be anything else.

In all, he translated more than 10,000 lines of verse from Hungarian, French, and Russian, as well as several novels and plays, and quantities of non-fiction. According to the poet Predrag Čudić, his translations are unequalled in the language except by Stanislav Vinaver.[72] Sava Babić, another bilingual writer and translator from Subotica, believes Kiš's achievements in this field are so prodigious that he was "not a single translator but several translators simultaneously." His versions of Endre Ady (1877–1919), the Hungarian lyric poet, are, Babić says, perhaps the only ones that let readers of Serbo-Croatian know how great a poet Ady was.

As a young man, Kiš was fascinated by Ady, whose genius combined decadent lyrical poetry with political invective that raged against Hungarian backwardness. Ady's lyrical verse "poisoned me with yearning", he wrote in 1959, "the same kind from which he died". (Ady was killed by syphilis.) Thirty years later, at the end of his life, he told an interviewer that Ady had "castrated" him "as a poet" when he was twenty years old: "madly in love like every other young idiot, I started writing poetry", only to find that Ady had already described every facet of his every emotion. "I thought, what is there left for me to write?" His first translations of Ady were published in 1955, and he continued to work on him for decades.

To suggest the quality of his translations, consider "New Year's Greeting" by Marina Tsvetaeva (1892–1941), written in February 1927 as an elegy or lamentation for Rainer Maria Rilke, who had died a few weeks earlier. Here are the poem's first lines in Russian, followed by Joseph Brodsky's English crib,[73] then Kiš's Serbo-Croatian version (dating from 1969), and finally a distinguished English translation.

> S Novym godom—svetom—kraem—krovom!
> Pervoe pis'mo tebe na novom
> —Nedorozumenie, chto zlachnom—
> (Zlachnom—zhvachnom) meste zychnom, meste zvuchnom
> Kak Eolova pustaya bashnya.

> Happy New Year—World/Light—Edge/Realm—Haven!
> The first letter to you in your new
> —Mistaken as lush/green—

---

72 Vinaver (1891–1955) is known to English readers as "Constantine", Rebecca West's ebullient guide around pre-war Yugoslavia, in *Black Lamb and Grey Falcon* (1941). Kiš admired Vinaver's modernist irreverence and adored his translation of Rabelais.

73 The crib—and more in this discussion—comes from Joseph Brodsky's wonderful essay on Tsvetaeva's poem.

(Lush [suggests] ruminant) clamorous, sonorous place
Like Aeolus's empty tower.

Srećna ti Nova—i dan—i kraj—pod novom krovom!
I prvo pismo tebi na novom
—Nesporazum je da je rodnom—
(Rodnom—plodnom) mestu zvučnom, mestu zvonkom,
Kao Eolova kula prazna i strašna.

Happy New Year—new sphere—horizon—haven!
This is my first letter to your new address,
—notorious region, misunderstood, unsettled—,
as clamorous and empty as the Aeolian tower

While Kiš keeps strict faith with Tsvetaeva's rhymes, enjambments, and sound patterns, if not quite with her metre, his liberties with her sense are daring but also loyal; evolutions more than liberties. Her *zlachny*, meaning green or lush, becomes *rodni*, meaning native. Thus, Tsvetaeva's parenthetic assonance (*Zlachnom—zhvachnom*: green / lush—ruminant), fleeting and playful, is rendered as (*Rodnom—plodnom*: native—fertile / fruitful), bringing to the fore an association of birthplace with creativity: death has silenced Rilke by exiling him from earth. The Serbo-Croatian *kraj* means end (and, as a euphemism, death) as well as limit or territory. Its pairing here with *dan* (day, dawn, daylight) suggests first and last things, birth and death. This linkage is echoed by the third line, where Kiš's "native" narrows the error down, almost pitilessly, to the (religious) illusion that in our end is our beginning. And, having once exposed this, he insists—being Kiš—on acknowledging the price of its loss: the empty tower is *strašna*, terrible, something Tsvetaeva neither says nor implies.

Feinstein's first line lifts splendidly, replicating some of Tsvetaeva's internal rhymes and energy. The second line lapses, however, in ways that confirm how shared Slavonic structures ease Kiš's task in ways not available in English. As if resigned to failure, Feinstein opts for prose: one's spirit sinks at "This is", and "address" feels too precise for the grave or afterlife of immortality which are now Rilke's "place" (*mesto*). Another disappointment follows: Feinstein does not try to catch the sidelong clarification in the third line. Instead, she calls this place or territory "notorious . . . misunderstood, unsettled": the first and third epithets are Feinstein's inventions, while the second is transferred from that missing digression in line three. Lacking the euphoric serial assonance that links Tsvetaeva's (and Kiš's) third and fourth lines, she can name only the surging, toppling "clamour" of the Russian and Serbo-Croatian.

More than anyone else, Elaine Feinstein has made Tsvetaeva known in English. The gulf between her version and the original measures the difficulty (impossibility?) of her endeavour—and, by contrast, Kiš's achievement. What he does dozens of times for Tsvetaeva, he also did for Nikolay Gumilev, Osip Mandelstam, Anna Akhmatova,

Sergei Yesenin, and others. Čudić says that Kiš's translations from Russian "opened up a new poetic continent for us". He performed the same service for Hungarian and French poetry, bringing not only particular verses or authors but entire poetic traditions into his own language.[74]

The connection with Hungarian language and literature was closest of all, for obvious reasons. He had many friends in Budapest, including the novelist György Konrád, who called Kiš "one of us": a Hungarian writer, for all intents and purposes. Near the end of his life, he wondered if his translations from Hungarian had not nourished his writing all along. He was right. The account of his first, ecstatic visit to Paris, in 1959, was wholly coloured by Ady, "that foreigner with 'barbarous pronunciation', that infatuated nomad who sang the praises of Paris from his nostalgic nomad's perspective—sang as, I still maintain, no other foreigner has done." Twenty-odd years later, one of his last stories, "Man without a Country", was saturated in Kiš's lifelong engagement with Ady, "this poet" who "had a monument and streets to his name, he had generations of devotees and his own myth, he had his admirers who praised him to the skies and extolled his verse and language as epitomising the national spirit, and he had mortal enemies who saw him as a traitor to the popular ideal who had sold himself to the Germans and the Jews".

Another example of nourishing influence was "The grave of Attila József" by Ferenc Juhász (b. 1928). This magnificent inventory-poem laments the fate of Hungary's greatest poet since Ady, who spent much of his life (1905–1937) in dire poverty, isolation, and ill health before suicide ended his suffering. The poem starts: "Rose of imagination, thought's narcissus, mind chrysanthemum, lily of nothing, / fermenting, raving, heavy-mouthed, piled blind flowers with teeth of scent. . .", and then addresses the poet's bones with brutal vividness, accusing posterity of failing to honour József even in death.

When it appeared in 1963, the poem sent shock waves through Hungary's cultural circles. Kiš, a dependable supporter of "tasteless" innovation, joined Juhász's defenders, though he did not agree that he was a surrealist. (Lautréamont, that surrealist before the fact, whom Kiš had recently translated with Mirjana, was, he thought, Juhász's true ancestor.) Piling image upon image in rhapsodic and outlandish sequences, naming dozens of flora and fauna as he elaborates his denunciation, Juhász had created, Kiš said, "an entire living organic world, an entire life, which can be counterposed to the inventory of the graveyard and the vanity of human transience." The jamming together of these antitheses was bound to appeal. Garden, ashes. But Kiš went further: Juhász had accomplished nothing less than "a complete stock list of Hungarian 'dead capitalism', a terrible and triumphal posthumous procession, the *reliquiae reliquiarum* of bygone wealth and vanity, a complete inventory of bygone feudal Hungary, an eerie exhumation of a dead class, the whole Austro-Hungarian world."

Juhász's poem probably inspired Kiš's own inventory-epic, "Rubbish Dump" (see chapter 19). I suggest also that his metaphorical flights on the subject of Attila József's

---

74 Honourable mention should be made of *The Muses' Bordello* (1972), his anthology of French erotic poetry, which broke new ground in Yugoslavia's oddly prim literary scene.

skull were in Kiš's mind a few years later, when he settled on his central image of atrocity in *Hourglass*: the brain of a distinguished Jewish physician, Dr Freud, lying on a snowy pavement in Novi Sad. Here is Juhász: "the light skull's broken bubble of bone", "your skull washed in my blood, freed from its sinews". And here is Kiš: "the brain of Dr Freud . . . an intelligence torn from its cranial husk as a mollusc is torn from its emerald shell . . . preserved and protected in nature's incubator". The connection would look convincing even if the name of Freud had not occurred in Juhász's poem, as it does: "gutted Rose rooted in Freud's heart".

The last Hungarian poetry he translated was by György Petri, which meant more to him in the 1980s than any work in his own language. Petri (1943–2000) was one of Hungary's few genuine dissident writers. His work, circulated in samizdat, was gleefully uncompromising in the face of what he called "the stylistic, cultural and other *diktats* that they wanted to impose on us". His political satires were scabrous and scathing. The sheer vehemence of his contempt squeezes incredulous humour out of grim situations. "*Poetry as ugly as reality*", was Kiš's approving judgement. "Yet Petri's poetry is not a poetry of protest: it makes no claims, bears no message, wreaks no revenge; what it wants to be—and what it is—is a snapshot of the wasteland that is Hungary." Sex in his poetry is a matter of "unrelieved barrenness and despair", according to one partly admiring critic. "His poetry feeds off disgust and anger, whether for the state or himself. Petri is obsessed with getting at the heart of things, where inevitably he finds desolation. He cannot help himself. Poetic notions of beauty or the ideal are obscene and ridiculous to him." When Petri snarled "All that can save us now, all that can save, / is absolute distrust", Kiš in his last phase would have nodded in despair.

His single most important translation, in terms of influence on his own work as well as its reach in Yugoslavia, was from the third of his languages. In *Exercises du style* (1947), inspired by Johann Bach's *The Art of Fugue*, Raymond Queneau found ninety-nine ways of telling a pointless anecdote about two men on a bus. His book found a cult following and became the foundation for the *Ouvroir de Littérature Potentielle* (OULIPO, the Workshop for Potential Literature).

Kiš admired these almost infinite variations on a slight theme, pulling rabbits out of a literary hat, as a masterpiece of parody. During his time in Strasbourg, he translated Queneau's "combinatorial art" into his own language. The result is a superb performance, conveying Queneau's repertoire of voices by imitating a range of Serbian and Montenegrin styles and jargons—those variants of Serbo-Croatian which he knew from experience. When two young Croatian writers asked permission to 'Zagrebify' a selection of his *Exercises* for the stage, he gave it. The show was a success and toured Yugoslavia. It has been a staple of the theatre in Croatia since 1968.

Kiš was always proud of his *Stilske vežbe*, but his estimation of Queneau's original altered in one respect. He understood that Queneau's choice of a trivial subject was essential if nothing was to distract from his technical wizardry. By 1986, however, he felt that Queneau should have taken a theme more worthy of his virtuosity. "The *Exercises du style* would have lost nothing in technical interest, while gaining in substance." This echoes his strictures on Borges for promising a *Universal History of Infamy* but delivering facetious chronicles of low life in Buenos Aires. Just as his best critique of Borges was a creative tribute—*A Tomb for Boris Davidovich*—so his best critique of Queneau was the novel *Hourglass*, where the combinatorial technique is applied to matters of life and death.

Postscript

During the war in Croatia (1991–1995), I watched a performance of the Croatian version of Kiš's *Stilske vežbe* in Zagreb. The actor was Pero Kvrgić, who had made this role his own over many years; the audience were mostly pupils on a school outing. One of the exercises impersonated the accent and gestures of a Serb policeman. Policing had provided a career for generations of Serbs from the impoverished provinces of Croatia. Slow, dull-witted, officious when not malevolent, the stock figure of the Serb policeman—always ready with his truncheon to uphold an unjust political order—had been viewed with exasperation at best, loathing at worst, by generations of Croats, long before the violence created by Yugoslavia's disintegration led them to be lionised by one side in the conflict and demonised by the other. The children in the audience had been raised, like their parents before them, to suspect and hate Serb policemen. Yet they loved this segment of the play, eyes shining with mirth as the diminutive Kvrgić huffed and strutted. In partnership with Queneau and Kiš, he was showing how art can "correct" the barbarism of politics and history: creating an image of the deadly cliché, revealing its other dimensions, opening the windows of our eyes to the breadth of the world.

We were taught Russian by White Army officers, émigrés
from the Twenties who substituted for absent teachers
and were equally at home with mathematics, physics,
chemistry, French and Latin.

After the German old woman in Novi Sad, Kiš gives us Russian exiles in Cetinje:
another minority, framed by another enormity. What with the Hungarians and
Montenegrins, the Jews, the Turkish brute, and the music teacher of Italian extraction, Yugoslavia emerges by hints in this *Birth Certificate* not as the South Slavic
homeland, forged in heroic unity, but as a tidal zone where conquerors clash and blend
with their victims, turn and turn about; or as a sump of nations, where history's latecom-
ers and *disjecta membra* vie for dismal primacy or mere survival.

The first refugees from Russia's civil war appeared in Yugoslavia at the end of 1919.
Eventually the government in Belgrade accepted some 40,000 refugees from the new
Bolshevik state. The majority settled in Serbia and Montenegro, aware of the historic
links between their lands and the bond of Eastern Orthodox faith. Tsarist Russia had de-
clared war in 1914 on Serbia's account; Regent Aleksandar was schooled in St Petersburg;
Montenegro's links with Russia were venerable and legendary; and there were blood ties
among Russian, Serbian, and Montenegrin royalty. Serbia and then Yugoslavia supported
the anti-Bolshevik side in the civil war that dragged on until 1923, by which time the
Holy Synod of the Russian Orthodox Church Abroad was established near Belgrade.
Yugoslavia did not recognise the Soviet Union until June 1940, well after the start of the
Second World War.

By this point, the number of émigrés in Yugoslavia had stabilised at 20,500. As
one of them recorded: "Russians moved to Serbia, unhampered by quotas, visas, restrictions, passports or anything similar. A friendly country let the Russians in, not feeling
constrained by the formalities that existed upon entry into other countries in Europe
or America." They were known as White Russians, in recognition of their links and
sympathy with the White forces that had fought the Red Army. Many were not ethnic
Russians, however, but Ukrainians, Byelorussians, or another nationality. Often better
educated than their hosts, they made a rich contribution to Yugoslav culture, education,
and science. (The next generation included at least two of Kiš's friends: Leonid Šejka and
Predrag Matvejević.)

Refugees arrived in Montenegro by ship from the Black Sea, landing at the little
port of Tivat, in the Bay of Kotor. Cetinje, historic seat of the old kingdom, was the main
attraction. By the late 1930s, there was "a sizeable group of Russian émigré families",   **211**

according to Bato Tomašević (b. 1929), who grew up among them. The White Russians were horrified by the spread of communism among younger Yugoslavs in the late 1930s. As the Allies gained the upper hand in the Second World War, they dreaded the prospect of Red liberation. When Soviet forces joined Tito's partisans to take Belgrade at the end of 1944, the bishop of the Russian Orthodox church in Belgrade hurriedly took down the military standards of Imperial Russia that hung from the vaulted ceiling and packed them off to New York. At the back of the church, the tombstone of General Pyotr Wrangel, commander-in-chief of White forces in Crimea, who had organised the mass evacuation in 1920, was concealed behind a painting.

By 1945, only 7,000 White Russians were left in the new Yugoslavia. Stalin's Red Army took no part in the liberation of Montenegro, so Cetinje's Russians—those who had survived the general carnage—did not flee. Kiš's teachers included Pavle Lyvov, who taught French and Russian, and Panteleimon Bugaj, a geodetic engineer who had served as a major in the Imperial army and now taught mathematics. Bugaj, who died in 1952, wanted to be buried in his uniform. According to Pavle Đonović, the Russian teachers were "true intellectuals" who, as lifelong anti-communists, were not cowed by the new regime. Many of the town's physicians, engineers, and architects were also Russian. The doctors' abilities, far in advance of their Yugoslav colleagues', won a high reputation for the hospital in Cetinje.

By praising his White Russian teachers, Kiš delivered a mild anti-communist snub. More to the point, he was paying respect to the resilience of political exiles who refused to be capsized by history. Then there was the terrible magnetism of Russia. For Kiš was immune to Serbian and Montenegrin empathy with mystic Russia's sufferings and greatness. Saturated in Russian literature, he was appalled by the unbroken pageant of cruelty in Russian history. (This emotion is formative in *A Tomb for Boris Davidovich* and in "Red Stamps with Lenin's Head".) He admired the journals of the Marquis de Custine (1790–1857), a French diplomat who recorded his fascination with Russia's threatening backwardness and Asiatic vastness in a book that was printed in huge numbers and translated into all the major European languages. And he would have agreed with Tito's ambassador to Moscow during the 1948 crisis, who said "There's no human consideration there, no mercy."

As a student in Belgrade, Kiš came to know a White Russian couple. He and Boško Mijanović lodged with Nikolai and Maria Aleksinski in a flaking tenement near the city centre. Nikolai had been wounded in the First World War, then joined the White forces, retreated through the Crimea, and took ship to Yugoslavia, where he became a forestry engineer.[75] Boško remembers how close Nikolai and Danilo became; the old man was

---

75 The infinite archives of the Internet hold images of a magazine called the *Croatian Forestry Journal* (*Hrvatski šumarski list*). The issue for February 1941 mentions (on p. 44) "Eng. Aleksinski Nikola, attached to the 8th group, Unit for Management of State Forests, Ministry for Forests and Mines in Belgrade." Available at http://www.sumari.hr/sumlist/194102.pdf.

well read, and they discussed books as well as life. Although Nikolai was deaf, they found a way to communicate; and they both liked to play the guitar. Maria did not take to Kiš, however; she complained that he encouraged Nikolai to drink too much. After he moved out, in 1959, he stayed in touch. In the early 1980s, he wrote a story about this triangular relationship.

The Lute and the Scars

Although I had sworn never to set foot there again, one evening, after two years away from Belgrade, I dropped in at the Writers' Club. I had already had ample occasion to discover how unpleasant the company of writers can be, fraught as it is with quarrels, envy and abuse. But I was also aware that this kind of abstract wrangling, of *escrime littéraire* [literary fencing], bitter and barren, is part of the literary craft, like writing book reviews or checking proofs. And I was mindful of Chekhov's advice to a young writer, when he urged him to abandon the provinces and mingle with the literary set in the big city, so that by getting to know writers, he would judge them with less idealism.

It was a warm early autumn evening and people were still dining outside in the garden. You could hear the hubbub of voices, the clatter of cutlery, the bursts of women's laughter. As I walked in, I glanced around at the guests and discovered, not without surprise, that nothing had changed in my two years away; everybody was sitting at their old tables, looking as if they were finishing the same bottle of wine they had ordered the last time I was here. Except that the women had become a little heavier and the men had turned grey at the temples and grown bellies. The circles under their eyes were darker, their voices huskier from all the drink and cigarettes. As I turned away from the garden, there was only one table left in my field of vision, the one under the gnarled tree, closest to the front door. Sitting there were two middle-age men whom I did not know, and a woman with a round face, dyed blond hair and small sparkling eyes. She smiled up.

"Don't you recognise me?"

I shook my head.

"Anyutka," she says. "We met at Mr. Nikola's once upon a time."

Then I remembered.

"Don't spit in the well you drink from," I said under my breath. "How are you?"

"I'm married," she says. "This is my husband."

She looked like an old shaggy dog. She kept smoothing back the hair that fell over her eyes, and when she tossed her head flirtatiously, the sagging skin quivered on her cheeks. She was one of those women who do not know how to grow old, so add the grotesque mask of false youth to the sorrow of passing time.

It was easy to work out her age. She had been thirty-nine when we slept together; I, twenty-three. That was about fifteen years ago. "I could be your mother," she had said. "Almost." I was living near the Danube railway station. She insisted on my using the formal *Vi* when we talked. "*That* does not give you the right to be familiar with me and say *ti*," she said; then she rolled her eyes and pretended to be gripped by passion. In the morning I walked her to the tram stop and told her we would not see each other again. She replied with the saying: "Don't spit in the well you drink from." She was right. A week later I was back: "I've been thinking about you, Anyutka." In the morning I woke up with my head on her motherly breast.

She was working at the time as a Russian tour guide and dabbling in the black market. She managed to sell me Bulgarian rosewater (a tiny ampoule in a wooden holder shaped like a salt shaker), a portrait of Pushkin in copper bas-relief on a plinth of Caspian marble, Blok's selected works in three volumes (Moscow, 1958). I knew these were all presents from her tour groups. . . .

Leaning across the table to the two men, she said something softly, shaking her head. I watched the fatal effect of time on her face.

I ordered a bottle of wine for her table and, finishing my soup, got up to leave. It was about three o'clock in the morning. As I pass by, she grabs my sleeve.

"You weren't at Mr. Nikola's funeral," she says. "You must have been abroad again."

"Yes, I was."

"There were only four of us at the cemetery. He died in his sleep. They found him a week later. I don't think he suffered. Here's my business card. Call me."

I heard her voice as if from afar. I remember shaking hands with the two men at the table, one of whom was her husband. I went up Francuska Street to Republic Square and then towards the Moskva Hotel. The shop windows in the passage by the *Star* cinema were still lit; dust had embedded itself in the fabric of the buttons, changing their colour; dead flies littered the bottom of the glass panes, like an aquarium gone dry.[76] It was a purplish early dawn, with the distant promise of sunrise. As I walked along the passage I heard the shrill ring of an alarm clock; a light bulb went on in one of the windows above a courtyard.

---

76 Kiš's fancy was often caught by house-flies, swarming on the meat that Eduard carries in his hat, sucking up the juice of acacia and milkweed, or dropping from the air, "drunk on their own flight and the late summer warmth" (*Garden, Ashes*). In *Hourglass,* E.S. imagines himself as a fly, then a flyspeck. In *Boris Davidovich,* gulag inmates place bets on which lump of sugar a wandering fly will choose. In *Garden, Ashes,* Dani daydreams of cherubs with wings fluttering like flies. Late in life, Kiš noticed a prose-poem by the Belgian poet Géo Norge (1898–1990) in *Le nouvel observateur,* and promptly translated it into his own language: "The fly is a swallow of the salon. It takes delight in sport, in taunts, in flaunting its cunning. A domestic creature, it knows when you are watching, it flits flips and buzzes around with childlike joy. When it commits suicide, it prefers a glass of milk for the deed. What a sublime death! I could not live on this earth without flies."

The doorway at the end of the courtyard was boarded up with rotting planks; lined up in front of it were rusty rubbish bins. A cat leaped out from between the bins and shot right past me. I peered between the rotten boards: it was dark inside, and reeked of urine; I thought I could hear rats squealing. I went back out into the street. It was first light. Turning into Balkanska Street, I saw a warehouse through the iron fence. The wall separating it from the house where I used to live had collapsed; the windows of the house had been pulled out and the roof had caved in. Inside the warehouse, next to some huge spools of cable, a lorry was piled high with bricks and debris. Suddenly I heard a bird chirping and I looked to see where the sound was coming from. A tall ailanthus tree leaned over the courtyard, its leaves still green and fluttering, distressed more by the hint of sunrise than by the breeze. I remembered: "You can cut it down, but a shoot will spring up somewhere else. It will push its way through the stone or concrete."[77]

In my last years at the university, I found lodgings in the city centre—every student's dream, especially if you came from the provinces. Along with a certain social status, it brought the privilege of being able to stay out late in cafés without fear of missing the last bus and having to wait until early morning, frozen to the marrow in winter (an experience I knew only too well). The building was down a passageway with access from both ends. Following the passageway—with its display windows of leather goods, nylon stocking repairs, fountain pens and covered buttons—you reached a courtyard paved with flagstones. At the far end of the courtyard, on the left, was a doorway with crumbling brick steps leading down to Balkanska Street. It was an old tenement, on the ground floor, with a Turkish oriel, plaster flaking off the walls, warped window frames and a rickety wooden door. The landlords were an elderly Russian couple, childless, immigrants from the Twenties. They rented out the room for a sum that met part of their electricity and water bills; in other words, next to nothing. It was this Anyutka, the tourist guide, who told me about them. I had met her in *Skadarlija* where she handed over a group of Russian writers for me to escort to an official dinner at the Writers' Club.

I slept on a soldier's iron cot; the other bed, against the wall on the opposite side of the room, was occupied by Mr. Nikola. Maria Nikolaevna slept in the other smaller room, which doubled as a kitchen.

---

77 The poet Ibrahim Hadžić, who got to know Kiš in the early 1980s, when this story was written, remembers a soliloquy in a café about an ailanthus that had forced its way between the paving stones in one of Belgrade's old suburbs. "Danilo marvelled at that tree's tenacity. Where did its roots find nourishment and water, how did it withstand the gales and frost when it was doomed all along, in advance?" Hadžić felt at the time that a literary metaphor was taking shape.

Since I was out most of the time—in the library during the day and the Writers' Club at night—I was quite satisfied with my new accommodation; it meant an almost free bed in the centre of town; I had use of the bathroom with hot water; my landlords made no difficulties about coming home late.

Maria Nikolaevna was an ailing, rather sarcastic woman with a puffy face, one side of which had been disfigured by burns. Her arms had been burned too; the shrivelled skin pulled at the muscles and tendons; her fingers were like claws. Maria Nikolaevna seldom came into the "men's room". She would knock, poke her head around the door and utter some rebuke which admitted no reply. "I know you've got nothing but that guitar, so there's no point in lying." Or: "Somebody was sick in the bathroom last night. I trust it wasn't Nyikola. Next time, do a better job of cleaning it up. Good night." Or: "The bathroom was full of smoke yesterday. You weren't at home. Which means Nyikola has taken up smoking. It's all your bad influence." Very sternly: "He's started drinking with you too. He *never* used to drink before. You've turned him into a bohemian."

Nikolai Aleksinski was an old man with a straight back, short grey hair and laughing blue eyes. He was as deaf as a post but this had no effect on his humour and good spirits. He rose early, took a cold shower both summer and winter (when you heard "ooh, ooh, ooh", and "aah, aah, aah" from the bathroom), and fasted once a week—every Friday—for his health; on that day he drank nothing but spring water which he brought from somewhere by the demijohn. But this had nothing in common with the almost indecent attempt to elude death that is so typical of old people; rather it was a sort of spiritual, military discipline, combined with hedonism. I learned how to speak to him by using my hands. This involved making signs like the old Russian Cyrillic alphabet, with symbolic abbreviations: touching my hair meant the first letter of a word or the word itself: *v* as in *volosi*. Touching my tooth meant *z,* as in *zub*; clenched fists were *d* as in *druzhbá,* and so on. It was enough to show him the first few signs; as soon as he got the beginning of a word, he would complete it aloud, looking you straight in the eye.

I show him an open thumb and index finger (*s*), then press the tips together (*o*) and touch my hair with them (*v*).

"Soviet," he says.

I sign: *l, i, t* . . .

"Literature," he says, completing the word. "Soviet literature is still young," he adds, "like young grass. You have to wait for it to grow."

I say (using my fingers): "They keep trampling on that grass."

"Nobody can stop the grass growing," he says. "You see that tree of heaven in the yard? It pushed its way up through the concrete. Take a look."

I say: "You . . ."

"You can cut it down," he reads my mind, "but a shoot will spring up somewhere else. It will push its way through the stone or concrete."

I ask: "Did you know Prince Zhevakhov?"

He looks at me in surprise: "Where did you rake up that name?"

I reply: "I read his book on Nilus."[78]

He waves a hand dismissively.

"Zhevakhov was living in Novi Sad until not so long ago," I say. "Russian émigrés had their headquarters in Sremska Mitrovica."

"Zhevakhov was a hapless fellow. His mind went completely in the end. He even saw ghosts. Don't you have anything smarter to do than fuss over mad Prince Zhevakhov?"

"I'm collecting people's memories of him," I say. "When he wrote about Nilus, he discussed the *Protocols of the Elders of Zion*. What did he look like, this Zhevakhov?"

"As a young man, he was tall and handsome. The last time I saw him was just before the war. He was still wearing his old-fashioned pince-nez and the Order of St. Nicholas pinned on his threadbare jacket."

I give him my first book, in manuscript. (It would not be published for another three or four years.)

"You carry on like the Serapion Brotherhood," he says. "One picks up the same sort of programme. Your reality is poetical."[79]

I tell him that a poetic reality is reality too.

"Reality is like the grass and the soil," he says. "Reality is the grass that grows and the feet that trample it."

I tell him that this, too, is a poetic image. A metaphor.

"An image, perhaps," he says. "Let's have another glass. This cherry brandy is home-made. Some friends brought it."

"A writer should see life in the round," he goes on. "Announce the great theme of dying—so that people become less proud, less selfish, less wicked—but also give meaning to life. Art is the balance between these two conflicting ideas. When a man leaves this world, a writer above all, it is his duty—you'll say I'm rambling like an old codger—not to leave *works* behind him, *works* can be anything, but rather to leave a little goodness, a little learning. Every written word is like the creation of the world." He pauses. "Do you hear that? The birds are singing already. Let's go to sleep. We'll upset Maria Nikolaevna if we go on like this until dawn. She has had a hard life. Very hard."

---

78 Zhevakhov and Nilus appear in "The Book of Kings and Fools", in *The Encyclopaedia of the Dead*.

79 These Russian writers declared in 1922 that art was sovereign, independent of politics and history. Opposing the "widespread regimentation, registration, and barrack-room regulations" that were imposed on artists in the Soviet Union, the Serapion Brotherhood demanded "but one thing: that a work of art be original and real, and that it live its own peculiar life".

I never dared to ask him about the fire that left those terrible scars on her body. Just as I never found out anything about his own life. I merely heard, from the woman who had recommended me to them and sent me to their flat, that Maria Nikolaevna had been "injured in a fire when she was escaping from Russia", Nikolai Aleksinski had come to Belgrade via Constantinople and he was a forest engineer (a profession that I later gave to the fictional hero of one of my stories, in memory of Nikolai Aleksinski who already looked to me like a work of fiction).[80] Although I spent many a night talking with this old man of cheerful disposition and good heart, I never heard a single confessional word from him. I thought that if I confided in him myself, I would put him in my debt, so to speak, and one day he would open up. But in spite of everything I told him about myself, I never heard him say a single thing about his former life.

I say: "What . . . should . . . I . . . do? I . . . love . . . two . . . women."

His face suddenly assumes a look of sincere concern: his eyes, his encouraging smile, tell me that the sorrows of my love life have touched his heart.

"Love is a terribly serious thing. Don't hurt either of them. And don't be rash. For your sake. And theirs."

I say: "You met one of them . . . I introduced her to you a month ago."

"Clytemnaestra," he says. "A proper Clytemnaestra. She's capable of doing harm. To herself or to you. Love is a terrible thing. What can I tell you? In love one cannot learn from the experience of others. Every encounter between a man and a woman begins as if it were the first in the history of the world. As if there had not been billions of such encounters since Adam and Eve. And yet, you see, love is not a transferable experience. It brings great woe, and great blessings. God willed it thus. Just one more, then I'm putting the bottle away. Otherwise Maria Nikolaevna will be angry. So be careful. Do not hurt anybody. Love's wounds cut deepest in the soul. And don't let literature be a substitute for love. Literature, too, is dangerous. Nothing can replace life."

Sometimes I asked him to play me something on his lute. If he was in a good mood, he said: "Tune it for me. You know how to do it now."

I would tune the lute and he would begin to play. He knew some *lieder* and gypsy romances by heart. Certain melodies smouldered in his extinct hearing like a distant memory; he would make strange noises, like grunting.

"I think the sound is good today," he says.

I nod agreement.

"That's because it's cloudy outside," he says. "The lute is dry. This weather is good for it. Is it tuned properly?"

---

80 This is Arkady Ippolitovich Belogortsev, also in "The Book of Kings and Fools".

Leaning over the instrument as if trying to hear it, he plays a few chords. Then he looks me straight in the eye.

"A-minor," I say.

"It's cloudy outside. The humidity is good for it."

I came back to see him for years, long after I had moved out. Whenever there was a problem, whenever I needed some advice, it was to him that I turned. I knew he followed all my writing in the magazines, and also reviews of my books.

"Talent is a curse," he would say. "Pushkin died for his talent. Nothing is envied more than a God-given talent. Talents are rare; mediocrities are numbered by the million. It's an eternal struggle. And don't bury yourself entirely in books. You should travel. Listen to people. And listen to your inner voice. Maria Nikolaevna is waiting for you. Don't hold it against her if she scolds you sometimes. She is ill. And unhappy."

Maria Nikolaevna sits by the window with a frayed woollen shawl around her shoulders. The window looks onto the dark courtyard and the crumbling wall that rings it.

"I read in the papers that the theatre where you work is going to Russia," she says. "Are you going with them?"

"Yes," I say, "we are going on tour for about a fortnight."

"Yes, that's what the papers say. Would you be able to do us a favour?"

"With pleasure."

"Here, I wrote down these two addresses for you, both in Moscow. The first is my sister's: Valeria Mikhailovna Shchukina. The other, Maria, like me, Yermolaevna Shishkova, is her best friend. She used to be mine too. The last letter I received from them was in January 1956. So, nine years ago.[81] It's possible that they are still alive, or at least one of them is. I suppose somebody would have told me if they had died. Just in case, here is another name: Karaeva, Natalia Viktorovna. She's the youngest. Let me write that address down for you as well. If you don't find the first two, she could tell you what happened to them. Would you do that for us?"

On our second day in Moscow I managed to bribe the stern female guard on our floor. In front of the hotel was a disabled man in a long threadbare army coat, leaning on a crutch; he held out his greasy cap to passers-by. I dropped a few coins in. He thanked me as if he were reciting a passage from Dostoevsky.

---

81 This places the story in 1965, three years before Kiš's only visit to Russia, in 1968.

As soon as I turned the corner, I found the taxi rank I had noticed the day before, during our official tour of the city. The taxi took me to a large apartment building with a dark entrance and long cold corridors.

I went over to some little girls who were playing by the entrance. They looked at me in surprise and ran off without a word. Eventually a woman appeared and I read out the names on my piece of paper.

"I don't know them," she said.

"Who can I ask?"

"I don't know. Lots of people live here."

I did not want to give up. Finding myself inside the building, I managed to work out the meaning of the numbers and abbreviations in the addresses I had been given: they were the entryways, floors, wings of the building, and apartments. Eventually, having decoded the message on the paper, I knocked on one of the doors. After a long silence, I heard a woman say: "Who is it?"

"I'm looking for Valeria Mikhailovna Shchukina."

"She doesn't live here."

The voice comes from right behind the door; I know the woman is watching me through the peep hole.

"Do you know where I could find her?"

"You a foreigner?"

"Yes. A foreigner."

I hear the door unlocking. The woman pokes her head out:

"Let me see."

I give her the piece of paper. "Do you know any of these three women?" She shakes her head.

"We've only been living here for three years. Ask down there, at the end of the corridor, the last door on the right. Ivanovna. Varya Ivanovna Strakhovska. She might know."

She hands back the paper; I hear her lock the door again.

I knock slowly, tentatively. Nobody answers. All at once I know there is nobody behind this door, so I press down the handle and push it open. The room is five metres by five. A naked light bulb dangles from the ceiling. In the corner is a large stove, the sort they put in factory canteens. I realize that I'm in the shared kitchen for this wing of the building. As if I have stepped into a secret hideaway, I leave quickly, shutting the door behind me. Evidently, my inspection has not gone unnoticed.

"What are you doing here? Who are you?"

The woman is swaddled in a big woollen shawl; her hair is pinned back tight behind her head. She wears stiff army boots.

"Excuse me," I say, holding out the piece of paper with the addresses as if it were an official document. "I was told that Varya Ivanovna Strakhovska lives here."

"Are you a relative?"

"So to speak."

"A foreigner?"

"A foreigner."

"Varya Ivanovna is very sick. It's her heart. Wait here."

She knocks at the door across from the shared kitchen, disappears for a moment, then returns.

"She says she doesn't have anybody abroad. Or anywhere else."

"I am a friend of Maria Nikolaevna Aleksinska. Tell her that. She'll know."

The woman went back in, without knocking. This time she stays inside longer. Finally she reappears.

"You can come in for a moment. I'm responsible for this building. You should have given notice of your visit. Follow me."

The room is like a prison cell. Bare walls. A bed against the wall; a wooden stool next to the bed, with a glass of water and a bottle of pills. Lying on the flat pillow is a pale, thin woman, covered up to her throat by an army blanket with scorch marks on it.

"I am Varya Ivanovna Strakhovska. I know who you are. You're asking about Natalia Viktorovna Karaeva. She died two years ago, in this very bed. She was a friend of Maria Yermolaevna's who died four years ago. No, five. I knew Maria Nikolaevna Aleksinska myself. And her children. They died in the fire. I'm glad to hear she's still alive. Her sister Valeria Mikhailovna Shchukina was the first to die, about eight years ago. Now it's my turn. I've told you everything I know, now please leave me alone. Memories are no longer for me, nor is talk. I'm preparing for death. There are no more encounters for me in this world."

"Forgive me, but I'd like to be able to tell Maria Nikolaevna something more about her sister. About all of them."

"What is there to say. There are lives that never deserved to be lived. We lived as if we were dead. Good-bye."

She shut her eyes to show there would be no more words. At that moment the door opens. "Well, you found her alive," says the woman with her hair pinned back. "Now get out before I call the police."

For months after the tour, I put off going to see my old landlords. Then one day, passing the *Star* cinema, I called by. Nikolai Aleksinski was reading Berdyaev. I described my impressions of the tour, the visits to Novodevichy cemetery and Lenin's mausoleum. He pours me a cherry brandy.

Then Maria Nikolaevna appears in the doorway.

"Pardon me," she says, "I don't want to stop you *having a binge*. I just wanted to see how our traveller is doing. Is he still unlucky in love?"

"We're talking about Moscow," I say. "And Leningrad."

"Ah," she says, "what could you see in fifteen days? Nothing."

"I saw Dostoevsky's tomb," I say. "And Blok's."

"You see," says Maria Nikolaevna, gesticulating as she turned to the old man, "I told you he would forget to look for my sister. All he did in Russia was drink vodka with actresses. He's a bohemian."

"I couldn't get away from the group," I say. "It's not so easy in Russia." (Then I translate this into sign language.)

"I knew as much," she says and goes away.

"Never mind," says Nikolai Aleksinski. "Better to sit and drink with actresses than wander around Moscow. It's better this way. For *her* not to find out anything."

I saw that he knew very well I had kept my word.

"Let's have one more," he says. "Then I'll have to put the bottle away. Maria Nikolaevna is very ill."

{FIFTH INTERLUDE}

A Tomb for Boris Davidovich (1976)

The story that I am about to tell, a story born in doubt and perplexity, has only the misfortune (some say fortune) of being true: it was recorded by the hands of honourable people and reliable witnesses. But to be true in the way its author dreams of, it would have to be told in Romanian, Hungarian, Ukrainian or Yiddish; or rather, in a mixture of all these languages. Then, by the logic of chance and of murky, profound, unconscious events, a Russian word or two would flash in the consciousness of the story-teller, now something tender like *teljatina*, now hard like *kindjal*. If, then, the story-teller could attain the unattainable and terrifying moment of Babylonian confusion, the humble pleading and terrible cursing of Hanna Krzyzewska would be heard in Romanian, Polish and Ukrainian by turns (as if the matter of her death were only the consequence of some great and fatal misunderstanding), and just before the final spasm and stillness her raving would turn into a prayer for the dead, uttered in Hebrew, the language of being and dying.

So begins the first of seven stories that make up Kiš's best-known book. The story tells of young Miksha, apprenticed to a Jewish tailor somewhere in easternmost Czechoslovakia (a Habsburg territory now in Romania and Ukraine). When a polecat steals the tailor's hens, he turns to his apprentice for help. Miksha traps the polecat, nails it by the nostrils to a door-post, and skins it alive. Reb Mendel is aghast and sends him packing with a curse. Miksha cannot understand. When the other tailors learn of Reb Mendel's curse, he cannot find work. His peasant anti-Semitism flares up: he vows revenge on "the Talmudists". Recruited to a revolutionary organisation, he murders a fellow member who has been identified as a traitor by the leader of the cell. Miksha flees to the USSR and becomes "an excellent slaughterhouse worker". But his victim was innocent: the real traitor was the cell leader. When Czechoslovakia requests Miksha's extradition, Soviet Intelligence arrests and tortures him. Glimpsing an image of Stalin in the interrogator's office, he experiences a "sudden rapture of faith" and confesses first to the murder and then to anti-Soviet crimes that he never committed. Miksha dies in a prison camp in 1941.

The protagonist of the second story, "The Sow That Eats Her Farrow",[82] is a young Irishman for whom his native Dublin is a "black marsh in which the stench

---

82 The title alludes to Stephen's famous utterance in Joyce's *Portrait of the Artist:* "Ireland is the old sow that eats her farrow." Some Yugoslav readers might have heard an echo of Tito's (false) boast during the 1948 crisis: "Our revolution does not devour its children!"

and injustice are more heavily oppressive than anywhere else." He goes to sea, but jumps ship in Marseilles. It is 1935. The next year, he turns up in Spain fighting for the Republicans. After Verschoyle warns his battalion commander that Soviet agents are trying to usurp leading positions in the Republican army, he is tricked into boarding a Soviet vessel. During the voyage, two strangers enter his cabin. "The three men spoke of justice, of freedom, of the proletariat, of the goals of the Revolution, vehemently trying to prove their beliefs, as if they had purposely chosen this semi-dark cabin of a ship in international waters as the only possible objective and neutral terrain for this terrible game of argument, passion, persuasion and fanaticism." But the interrogation does not go according to plan: in Leningrad, all three men are arrested. The two interrogators are last seen in a prison camp hospital, "half blind and wasted with scurvy". Verschoyle is murdered after trying to escape from a camp in Karaganda in 1945. "His frozen, naked corpse, bound with wire and hung upside down, was displayed in front of the camp's entrance as a warning to all those who dream of the impossible."

The third story tells of a deception practised on a distinguished French socialist, Edouard Herriot. To allay his concern that priests are being persecuted in the Soviet Union, a service is staged in a church. The brewery equipment housed in the Church of St Sophia is swiftly disguised. The obligatory portrait of the "Father of the People" (Stalin, never mentioned in the book except as a ship's name) is removed, and the frescoes and altar are uncovered. Emergency restoration is carried out by prison labour. The official charged with orchestrating the performance is one Chelyustnikov, who acts the part of a bearded, paunchy priest. Other comrades and their wives dress as worshippers. Security agents in civilian clothes "spontaneously" recognise and welcome the V.I.P. at the railway station. The charade succeeds. Chelyustnikov is decorated and promoted, but four years later is arrested on charges of political sabotage and supporting the Trotskyists in Spain. Despite torture, he resists until his wife and child are threatened. Sentenced to ten years, he turns informer in prison and is rehabilitated in 1958. As a tourist, he visits the late French V.I.P.'s memorial library in Lyons in 1963.

The characters at the centre of the fourth story, "The Magical Circulation of Cards", are Karl Taube (alias Kiril Beitz), doctor and revolutionary, and Kostik Korshunidze, a Georgian arch-criminal. Taube is a child of the provinces (see chapter 22) who moves to Budapest, then Vienna. "Disillusioned by the slow rate of revolutionary ferment", he goes to Berlin where, in 1935, he "forecast all the horrors of Dachau". Called to Moscow by the Comintern, he spends idle months walking the city streets "as if under a spell".

Taube is arrested in November 1936. His death sentence is commuted to twenty years' hard labour, and he practises medicine in the camp. When a criminal inmate called Segidulin mutilates his hand to escape work in the mines, Taube saves two of his fingers. Segidulin, enraged, vows to cut his throat. When he defeats Kostik at cards, Segidulin orders the Georgian to murder Taube. Kostik's first chance to pay his humiliating debt to Segidulin comes after eight years, when both he and Taube are free men. Tracing the rehabilitated doctor to the hospital where he now works, Kostik beats him to death with a crowbar.

The title story tells about a man whose name is missing from "the 246 authorised biographies and autobiographies of great men and participants in the Revolution". Politicised by tales of peasant uprisings and precocious reading, the young B. D. Novsky takes menial jobs while organising strikes and demonstrations. He graduates to a terrorist group, learning to make bombs and smuggling guns and explosives into Russia. He escapes "twice from prison and once from a labour camp." Fleeing to Paris, "we find him in the Russian library on the Avenue des Gobelins, and in the Musée Guimet, where he studied the philosophy of history and religion; and in the evening, in La Rotonde in Montparnasse with a glass of beer". Arrested after the outbreak of war in August 1914, Novsky escapes or is expelled to Germany. Converted to Bolshevism, he joins the civil war against the Whites. "The terrifying explosions in the south-west sector of the front, occurring suddenly and mysteriously, leaving a slaughterhouse behind them, bore Novsky's stamp just as a manuscript bears the stamp of a great writer."

Amid the tumult, he falls in love. "My only passion", he writes to Zinaida, "has been this arduous, rapturous and mysterious calling of revolutionary. . . . Forgive me, Zina, and carry me in your heart; it will hurt like a kidney stone." They wed on a torpedo boat anchored in Kronstadt harbour. However,

> it is impossible to establish the exact chronology of Novsky's life during the civil war years and those immediately following. It is known that in 1920 he fought against the rebellious and despotic emirs in Turkestan, and subjugated them with their own weapons of cunning and cruelty; that during the sweltering summer of 1921, recorded in the annals for the invasion of malarial mosquitoes and horseflies that swarmed down to suck the people's blood, he was tasked with liquidating the bandits in the Tambov region, which led to the sabre or knife wound that gave his face the cruel stamp of heroism.

Novsky is arrested in Kazakhstan in 1930. His interrogator is one Fedukin, who "extracted confessions in line with the deepest principles of depth psychology without knowing that such a thing existed." Their epic duel begins. Novsky's determination to preserve the integrity of his life-story as a revolutionary lends him strength: he refuses to admit to imaginary anti-Soviet offences. But his nemesis finds a way to break his will: Novsky is confronted with a young prisoner who is shot on the spot when he, Novsky, again refuses to "confess". The procedure is repeated the following day. Despite realising that his cherished biography is tainted by every new murder "committed in his name", Novsky holds out—until one of these doomed prisoners whispers "Boris Davidovich, don't let the sons of bitches get you!"

Fedukin collaborates with Novsky on his confession, "each trying to incorporate into it some of his own passion, his own beliefs, his own outlook". Novsky seems to get the upper hand in shaping the text—"pure fiction", as they both know—when Fedukin springs a trap. New confessions wrung from other prisoners implicate Novsky in further greedy betrayals of the Revolution. Eventually prosecutor and victim reach terms: Novsky is jailed briefly, then exiled, but his name is not "dragged through the mud". Arrested again "during the terrible winter of 1937" and sent to a camp in Norilsk, he manages to escape. Guards track him to an ironworks. As they approach, Novsky leaps into the furnace and "rose like a wisp of smoke, deaf to their commands, defiant, free from Alsatian dogs, from cold, from heat, from punishment, and from remorse." Deprived of all else, he can still choose his death. He is then erased from official history, as if he had never lived.

The sixth story, "Dogs and Books", is a reworked document from the Inquisition, held in the Vatican library. It tells of the forced conversion of Jews in southern France, in the fourteenth century, at the hands of a movement of Catholic fanatics known as the *Pastoureaux*. Two Jews are caught and given the choice of conversion or death. After converting, they consult a learned Jew in Toulouse, one Baruch David Neumann. Given the nature of their conversion, may they revert to their own faith? Neumann seeks guidance from local clerics, who reply that conversion against a person's will is illicit. The two Jews duly return "to the faith of Moses". But the following week, hordes of *Pastoureaux* are brought to Toulouse, where they inflame a local mob and pour into the Jewish quarter. Neumann is seized and given the same choice. "Witnessing the blind fury of this mob and seeing them kill before my eyes those Jews who refused to be converted (some out of conviction, others from that pride which can sometimes be perilous), I answered that I would rather be converted than killed, since, *in spite of everything*, the temporary anguish of existence is worth more than the ultimate void of nothingness."

When Neumann tries to delay the brutal rites of conversion, two young Jews are killed before his eyes. The priests escorting him say, "Your delay is killing those who believed in your teachings and followed your example." He converts and is led back to his plundered home. "The killing and looting of the Jews lasted well into the night; the town was lit by flames, the dogs were howling on all sides." Captured and interrogated by another mob, Neumann denies he is a Jew, then angers them with questions of his own.

And they shouted "Arrest him! His words reek of doubt and disbelief!" So they bound my wrists and led me away. I also asked them, "Is your power over people such that you can dispose of their freedom?" And they said "We are Christ's soldiers, and have final authority to separate the diseased from the healthy, the infidel from the faithful." Then I told them that faith was born of doubt and I told them that doubt was my faith, and that I was a Jew, because I hoped they would not kill me with my hands bound.

Bored by his elusive words, the mob vents its random fury on another captive. Neumann journeys to the town of Pamiers, where Jews enjoy relative security. But the bishop of Pamiers learns of his conversion and reversion, and has him arrested "and thrown into the dungeon". Under pressure of His Excellency's "boundless patience in bringing the said Baruch to the Truth", he again denies his Jewish faith. Yet his doubts remain and cannot be silenced: he sways again. He probably died under torture in 1337. In an Afterword, Kiš explains that he came across this narrative just after finishing the story about Novsky. The parallels left him with "a feeling of miraculous illumination" (see chapter 7).

The seventh and final story is "The Short Biography of A. A. Darmolatov (1892–1968)". Darmolatov is a (fictitious) Russian poet, a lesser star in the constellation of Akhmatova, Gumilev, Tsvetayeva, and Mandelstam. Like Kiš's other protagonists, he arrives in a city already half-politicised by adolescence in the provinces. While he studies medicine in St Petersburg, his first poems are published in reviews. "It is not my intention here to concern myself closely with the qualities of Darmolatov's poetry", writes Kiš primly, before cataloguing some of the "empirical (poetic) facts" in his work that, "like old postcards or photographs in a shabby album, testify as much to his travels, ecstasies and passions as to literary fashion". It is one of his best inventories, wicked about Darmolatov's hackneyed motifs, yet thrilling:

the agreeable effect of the wind on marble clusters of caryatids; the Tiergarten lined with flowering lindens; lanterns on the Brandenburg Gate; the monstrous apparitions of black swans; the ruby reflection of the sun on the murky waters of the Dnieper; the spell of white nights; the magical eyes of Circassian women; a dagger plunged to the hilt in the ribs of a wolf on the steppes; the spinning of an aeroplane propeller; the caw of a crow in early twilight; a snapshot (bird's eye view) of the terrible panorama of ravaged Povolozh; tractors and threshers crawling through golden wheat on the plains; the black shafts of Kursk coal mines; Crimean towers in an ocean of air; the purple velvet of theatre boxes; spectral forms of bronze statues in the glare of fireworks; the sweep of ballerinas spun from foam; glorious petrol flames from a tanker in the harbour; the horrible narcosis of rhymes; a still life with teacup, silver spoon and drowned wasp; the violet eyes of a harnessed horse; the optimistic grinding of turbine engines; Commander Frunze's head on the operating table with the heady reek of chloroform;[83] bare trees in the courtyard of the Lubyanka; the hoarse baying of village dogs; the wondrous poise of concrete piles; a cat stalking a bullfinch in the snow; cornfields under a barrage of artillery fire; lovers parting in the valley of the Kama; the military cemetery near Sevastopol. . . .

After glimpsing Darmolatov's literary milieu in Petrograd in 1921, distressed by the execution of Gumilev (the first major writer executed by the Soviet regime), the narrative finds the poet in 1930, employed as a translator, thanks to one B. D. Novsky. After Novsky's arrest, Darmolatov prepares to disappear in his turn. The next photograph, dating from August 1933, shows him aboard a ship with a party of writers, visiting the White Sea canal. He is on the brink of mental collapse: "he washed his hands in methyl alcohol and saw an informer in everyone". Hospitalised at the end of the year, he sleeps for five weeks "and from that time on it was as if *the clamour of the world* could never reach him again." He lives on, suffering elephantiasis of the testicles, and is seen for the last time in 1947, in Montenegro.

In a Postscript, Kiš mentions a last photograph of Darmolatov, this one of the poet's immense scrotum, "the size of the biggest collective farm pumpkin". The image is reprinted in medical textbooks, he adds, "and as a moral for writers, that writing requires more than just balls."[84]

––––––––––

Subtitled "Seven Chapters from a Shared History", *A Tomb for Boris Davidovich* was meant to be a political shocker and a piece of enduring literature.

The catalyst was Kiš's experience in Bordeaux in 1973 and 1974. He had not lived in France since 1964 and was dismayed by the new generation of radical students. "The spirit of Stalinism was very much present," he recalled. "I was like a man from another planet." When he challenged the students' opinions, they

---

83 Mikhail Frunze was Trotsky's successor as Commissar of War. He died in 1925 following (in the words of a historian) "a simple operation for a stomach ulcer, leaving the suspicion that he had been assassinated by his physicians on Stalin's orders".

84 Was this grotesquerie influenced by Rabelais, his favourite author?—"Others swelled up so enormously in the substance of their bollocks that three of them easily filled a fifty-gallon cask." And was Kiš then behind Salman Rushdie's mention of "men with elephantiasis of the balls" in *Midnight's Children*? And did he inspire novelist Geoff Dyer's glimpse of a man in Varanasi, "pushing a barrow in which he seemed to be carrying some kind of gourd. . . . what I had taken to be a pumpkin were actually his testicles"?

called him "a fascist, an imperialist . . ." Pascale Delpech, then one of his students, recalls how Kiš spent many evenings "trying to convince people who would not be convinced." These nice young French bourgeois—raised with all the Western freedoms of travel, expression, and access to information—were just as prone to intolerant dogmatism, just as blinkered by ideological prejudice as communists in Yugoslavia. Refusing to accept that his experience granted him any greater insight into communism, they waved away his descriptions of Soviet oppression. "We really were a generation formed of clichés and commonplaces," Pascale remembers. "I saw him with working-class communists in Bordeaux, and there was no difficulty: their beliefs were real personal convictions, the outcome of their experience. What he couldn't bear were the commonplaces and ignorance of *intellectuals*."

He became friends with another Yugoslav teaching in Bordeaux: Slobodan Vitanović, a professor of French from Belgrade. Vitanović recalled heated arguments with local leftists about Aleksandr Solzhenitsyn, whose *Gulag Archipelago* was published in France at the very end of 1973, leading to his expulsion from the USSR the following year. In 1974, the leftists still belittled Solzhenitsyn, and their hostility sometimes veered into anti-Semitism: Vitanović heard him called a "baptised Jew". It would take two or three years for his book to crack pro-Soviet prejudice in the French left, leading the former Maoist intellectual Bernard-Henri Lévy to hail him as "the Shakespeare and Dante of our time", who "forces us to *believe* what we were satisfied with *knowing*." Kiš revered Solzhenitsyn's achievement and bought the first edition.[85]

The only way of getting through to the students was by telling stories which could not be seriously doubted. If these stories were to disabuse readers of their illusions, they had to be credible and written with sympathy for political idealism. So they had to rest upon authentic records. At the same time, they should not pretend to be works of testimony; for Kiš was not a camp survivor like Solzhenitsyn or Varlam Shalamov (author of *Kolyma Tales*, published in an émigré journal in New York between 1970 and 1976), or Karlo Štajner, author of *7,000 Days in Siberia* (1972), and hailed by Kiš as Yugoslavia's own Solzhenitsyn.

This limitation could be turned to account. He had noticed that the sheer scale and remoteness of Stalinist crimes encouraged the French students to disbelieve them. The extent of the Gulag in time (more than two decades), space (the vastness of Siberia), and numbers (around 18 million victims) made it unimaginable—especially to people who wished not to imagine it anyway.

---

85 The title of his book nods to *One Day in the Life of Ivan Denisovitch*. Lakis Proguidis suggests persuasively that *Ivan Denisovitch* is the "counter-book" of Kiš's title story. The redemptive humanism of Solzhenitsyn's narrative—which enabled it to be published during Nikita Khrushchev's thaw—is countered by the annihilation that Boris Davidovich cannot escape.

His stories needed to harness this sense of remoteness. If the Gulag seemed too fantastic to be real, Kiš should show that the sheer reality of the Gulag was fantastic. As he put it later, "I had to find a fantastic way of writing realistically." He wanted a style to render a waking nightmare. Yet there was no question of repeating the puzzle-structure of *Hourglass*: the meaning of these stories should be self-evident. He needed different resources, a different influence to contend with.

He found what he needed in a slim volume of stories by Jorge Luis Borges. He had first read Borges in French translation in Strasbourg in the 1960s. As a literary encounter, it was second only to his discovery of Joyce. "Liberation from psychological clichés—this is what Borges means above all," he said. As well as that, his intertextuality (allusion to other literature), his use of real and fictional documents, playful erudition (invented bibliographies, quotations from non-existent works), compression, rigour, witty intelligence, detachment, eclecticism, veneration for European literature, mockery of national conceptions of literature, wonderful narrative clarity and drive: these all appealed immensely.

What Kiš made of the elderly Borges's sometimes indulgent comments on dictatorships in Argentina and Chile, or his ambiguous fondness for the violent traditions of gaucho culture, he never said. In fact, the only thing about Borges we can be sure he disliked was the title of his 1935 book about hoodlums and pirates, *A Universal History of Infamy*. What Borges called his techniques of "mismatched lists, abrupt transitions, the reduction of a person's entire life to two or three scenes" were an inspiration as Kiš composed what he called his "exemplary stories".[86]

The title was, however, an irony too far. "Borges's stories are for little children," he said; these arch chronicles of gangsters, impostors and petty villains did not merit such a billing. Worse than this, the title was dishonourable for a book published in the age of Hitler and Stalin. "I claim that the universal history of infamy is the twentieth century with its camps—Soviet camps most of all," he said. "Infamy is when in the name of the idea of a better world for which entire generations have perished, in the name of a humanistic idea, you build camps and conceal their existence and destroy both people and their most intimate dreams of that better world."[87]

The application of Borgesian technique to the Soviet system—that "indecipherable labyrinth of state offices", as Borges himself called it—was a superb invention. For other writers in Yugoslavia, where he was a cult author in the 1970s,

---

86 A second fictional tribute to Borges's *History of Infamy* was Roberto Bolaño's novel, *Nazi Literature in the Americas* (1996; published in English translation, 2008). The accolade of creative critique is always remarkable; to receive it twice, with such distinguished and varied results, is extraordinary.

87 Kiš is not the only admirer of Borges to have taken issue with his disdain for political brute facts. The Uruguayan writer Eduardo Galeano lamented that "With great delicacy and sharp wit, Jorge Luis Borges tells the Universal History of Infamy. About the national infamy that surrounds him, he doesn't even inquire."

Borges offered an escape from politicised realist conventions. For Kiš, he provided a means of writing *about* politics. In this way, *A Tomb for Boris Davidovich* pays creative homage to Borges while 'correcting' one of his faults. By slipping a grand purpose into the heart of Borges's firework show and turning all that candlepower into a searchlight beam playing on the Stalinist inferno, Kiš would do to, and for, Borges what *Hourglass* had done to, and for, Joyce, Queneau, and the nouveau roman.

Borges had researched his stories (which he deprecated as "nothing more than glosses on other books", "hoaxes and pseudo-essays"), then "amused himself" by tweaking the plots and inventing extra details to "mystify" readers. Kiš set about his task in the same way, consulting works of reference. Pascale Delpech realised that Kiš was working on a project of his own when he borrowed her copy of Louis Réau's history of Russian art. When she asked why, Kiš said he needed a description of a church for his new book. She wondered why he didn't make it up, as writers usually do. No, said Kiš firmly, writers *don't* make things up.

Drawing on Karlo Štajner's memoir, Soviet encyclopaedias, Roy Medvedev's book on Stalin, and first-hand accounts of Soviet conditions, borrowing here and there from Réau and other scholars to make his descriptions as convincing as possible, he wrote fictional biographies of a handful of characters who were destroyed by the Gulag. Anecdotes from Štajner's memoir, relating the bizarre and wretched fate of other inmates, provide the plots for five of the stories. While only one of the characters is a murderer, none is entirely innocent.

The book's style is dense, lurid, often melodramatic, sometimes terminally satirical, visionary, even scriptural (casting an ironic light on the chiliastic hubris of Marxism-Leninism). Information is conveyed with telegraphic brevity. The narratives are elliptical, often a montage of captioned scenes, like obituaries pieced from archives that are unreliable as well as incomplete, or illustrations in some infernal Book of Hours to celebrate the Soviet liturgy. Much is suggested, little explained.

Kiš keeps himself inside the narrative frame, "dynamically regulating the distance between narration and facts", as his old friend Wladimir Krysinski notes. The first-person singular is found on the first and last pages, and in-between. "At this point the reliability of the documents is suspended," is a typical interjection. When he does this, or refers to a non-existent "appended bibliography", Kiš is up to something more than Borgesian playfulness: he reminds us of the Soviet destruction of alternative accounts of history, and the shelf-miles of documents locked away until the USSR disintegrated in 1991.

Occasionally he tells us what he is doing—or wants us to think he is doing—and stresses the uncertainty of his reconstruction. "After an obvious gap in our sources (with which we don't wish to burden the reader, or we would deny him the pleasant and deceptive satisfaction of believing that this is one of those stories which, luckily for their authors, are usually equated with the power of imagination), we find him in an insane asylum in Malinovsk," and so on.

Parenthetical disclaimers may just confuse readers, or even assure them that an author so intrusive must be the sole creator of his fictional world. Kiš was aware of this risk, and in a sense the disclaimers were sheer false modesty. For he wanted to undercut his readers' illusion that they were enjoying a sovereign literary experience, unaccountable to history, yet without ceasing to seduce them with the rewards that readers want. These rewards are found in the powerful evocations of place, the intoxicating particulars, the glimpses of horror in the Gulag, lit like an El Greco painting of martyrs.

Other traditional rewards are, however, withheld. The characters have little interior life. Much is suggested, little explained. Above all, the revolutionaries' motives are hardly explored. The convictions that become the levers of self-destruction are not analysed. In one paragraph, a young man festers in a provincial town; in the next, he has dedicated his life to an all-consuming political cause. The arrests ensue automatically, by an inevitable logic; any connection to a crime is coincidental. After exploring consciousness in *Garden, Ashes* and *Hourglass*, Kiš focuses here on action and its consequences.

What these people do is so much more important than what they think, exactly because their actions are determined by an ideology of power. Although it claimed to be a scientific system, incarnating reason in its highest form, Marxism-Leninism was a cult or faith. Absorbed by ideology, indifferent to other ethical standards, the believers dehumanise themselves before the Stalinist machinery completes their destruction. Where *Hourglass* examined fascism's 'external' destruction of individuality, *Boris Davidovich* tackles communism's 'internal' effort to do the same.

While *Boris Davidovich* achieves an effect of hammering monotony remarkable for such a short book, the stories are not repetitive. There is a canny development across the span of plots. The first story, with its shtetl flavour of Isaac Bashevis Singer, turns on the flaying of the polecat.[88] What Reb Mendel knows, but Miksha cannot grasp, is that the solution was worse than the problem—a judgement that might, we infer, apply to the Russian Revolution itself. Miksha may dimly grasp that he had offended the tailor's religious propriety, but not that he had violated humane principles of any denomination. His subsequent murder of the girl—a crime committed "with self-righteous hate", as Kiš underlines—seems like a natural escalation. Both acts draw on sources of cruelty that have nothing to do with politics.

---

88 Kiš later explained that the episode with the polecat drew on boyhood experience in his father's Hungarian village.

With the second and third stories, Kiš shifts our gaze to the role played by idealistic Western supporters of the Bolshevik Revolution. Verschoyle's shrill loathing of Ireland provides a miniature portrait of extreme anti-patriotism, a prejudice no better than its opposite, which leads the young Irishman to commit everything to extreme internationalism.

Verschoyle and Edouard Herriot are deceived by their best intentions. Where the Irishman pays with his life, the Frenchman's error is paid by others—such as the chauffeur Alyosha, tortured for having allegedly mistaken a fake priest for the real thing. Kiš could have chosen another distinguished dupe, such as Henry Wallace, Roosevelt's vice president, similarly deceived during a visit to Kolyma in 1944. With his students in mind, he wanted an eminent French leftist.

The fourth story goes behind the perimeter fence. Taube's death is ordained by a game of cards between criminals in a camp. This is insane, but would any other explanation make better sense? The workings of the "criminal Olympus" in the camps parallel the Soviet power structure outside. As Tomislav Longinović remarks, the "uncanny alliance between the criminals and the Gulag masters lays bare the foundation of the revolutionary reversal of values." Kiš makes his conclusion unusually explicit: "Distant and mysterious are the ways that brought together the Georgian murderer and Dr Taube. As distant and mysterious as the ways of the Lord."

The fateful collaboration between idealism and tyranny is best worked out in the title story. The disgraced revolutionary Novsky and his interrogator are locked in struggle, mythomaniacs fighting over the perceived status (not the truth) of Novsky's life and imminent death. Fedukin's inevitable victory, confirmed by Novsky's omission from "the revolutionary chronicles", is gained by force alone. His efforts to persuade Novsky "of the moral obligation of making a false confession . . . failed completely." This is a vital point for Kiš, who has no time for the thesis (which he associated with Arthur Koestler) that some of Stalin's victims had colluded with their tormentors as a final service to the Communist Party. It is Novsky's fight to remain the author of his own legend that earns Kiš's respect. His place in history matters more than physical survival.

The story about Baruch David Neumann serves the book in two ways. By echoing the themes of persecution and forced conversion in a remote setting, the plot underscores the religious dimension of twentieth-century totalitarianism. For its antecedents are to be found in the annals of the Inquisition (with Jews, again, as archetypal victims). Thanks to this story, the book traces a genealogical thread within what Norman Cohn called the "common stock of European social mythology", namely "the urge to purify the world through the annihilation of some category of human beings imagined as agents of corruption and incarnations of evil".

Second, the story illustrates Kiš's documentary principle. Presenting himself (misleadingly) as the story's mere translator, he claims that his changes to the text were "minor deletions". This is untrue; the passages that clinch the analogies with Stalinism were added by Kiš, who also adds a few "translator's footnotes", one of which illumines the book's entire purpose. Pointing out that the Jews' relative security in Pamiers was due to a decree of the local inquisitor, the "translator" glosses: "This decree . . . shows the degree to which personal attitudes and civic courage in difficult times could change the destiny that cowards hold to be inevitable and proclaim to be fate and historical necessity."

If this were truly offered as a translation, it would be unethical. But reader, beware! *Boris Davidovich* is fiction. Kiš came across the story of Baruch the Jew in a Bordeaux bookshop (see chapter 7). Redacting the document much as he had done with his father's letter in *Hourglass*, he understated his interference in order to increase the story's plausibility and amplify its historical echo, underlining continuities between Christianity and communism (which Kiš was hardly the first to remark). The document and its resonance are real, however, regardless of Kiš's story. The bibliography in the Translator's Note is accurate.

Both a coda and an apologia, the final story has been called the most enigmatic. Unlike Miksha, Verschoyle, Taube, or Novsky, Darmolatov is a fellow-traveller of the revolution: perhaps harmless, possibly contemptible, certainly absurd. It is a tale about complicity. The arrest that he expects does not come because it would be superfluous: as Longinović says, Darmolatov "has internalised the oppressor and is performing all the necessary operations himself." The year of his death, 1968, was surely chosen as the nadir of Western leftist illusions. His story has pathos without a hint of grandeur. He is also the only poet in the book's cast. As Mirjana Miočinović has pointed out, Kiš's catalogue of tropes from Darmolatov's verses, previously quoted, is beautifully judged: a series of allusions to successive phases of Russian poetry, from Acmeism to socialist realism, which manages to be both stirring and second-rate.

On the final page, as Darmolatov embarrasses the author-when-young by clambering into Njegoš's throne, the book brings us to Yugoslavia for the first and only time. The year is 1947: the high noon of Yugoslav Stalinism. (Kiš's presence in the story is fictional, by the way; the celebrations for the centenary of *The Mountain Wreath* took place in June or July, and he did not reach Cetinje until October.) The Postscript delivers the last of the book's many shocks to the reader, and the only one that could be called facetious. Again, there is a double function. With this vulgar signing-off, Kiš pulls down the imaginative structure that he has just erected. ("My definition of literature", he said, "is an attempt at a global vision of reality and its simultaneous destruction.") By this insolence he vindicates literature over politics.

Less obviously to foreign readers, Kiš hoists a two-fingered salute to an assumption about literary creativity which stems from a nationalist myth: that, in the words of a local cultural critic, "reproductive power" is a "specific quality of the Serbian people", the undeniable proof of its "vital force". This mockery implies a pre-emptive defence of Kiš's cosmopolitan, modernist poetics of fiction. A few months after *Boris Davidovich* was published, in summer 1976, he would, as we shall see, be forced to defend his work—and his vocation—in earnest.

Apart from wanting to awaken French leftists to unpalatable truths, Kiš had another motive for writing about the Gulag. "The reality of German camps was there in my earlier books," he explained later. "The other camps were, so to say, missing." This posed "a challenge", because he "wanted those two crucial phenomena of our century to be in [his] books." Countless victims had disappeared in both kinds of camp, but only the victims of fascism were in his writing. Thematically, his books had shared the official Yugoslav fixation upon a mythic version of the Peoples' Liberation War (as the Second World War in Yugoslavia was known). For this reason, they kept company with a vast output of fiction, poetry, film and drama about the fascists and their enemies, the ultimately victorious partisans, organised by the Communist Party under the leadership of you-know-who. Inevitably, most of this output was turgid, populist, and unimaginative. As such, it may have insulated Kiš's earlier work—which was none of those things—from disapproval.

The denial of any essential difference between Auschwitz and Kolyma became a fixation for Kiš. By writing so vehemently against Stalinism, Europe's other totalitarian order, Kiš risked running afoul of Yugoslav orthodoxy, which trumpeted fascist sins while stifling criticism of communism. For he was breaking the cordons around a neuralgic topic: Yugoslavia's relationship with the Soviet motherland.

Tito's Communist Party was ardently Stalinist during and after the Second World War. Even so, it was too independent for Stalin's liking (see chapter 26). The Yugoslav regime eventually forged a separate political identity, outside the Soviet camp without being anti-Soviet. In practice, the Yugoslav elites followed Moscow when faced with the challenge of political (and therefore cultural) pluralism. For Yugoslavia and the USSR were bound by interests that no flirtation with the West could supplant. Threats to one-party rule were anathema. Hence, the long prison sentence meted out to the apostate Milovan Đilas in the early 1950s, Tito's betrayal of Hungary's reformist leadership in 1956, and the disastrous purges of so-called liberal communist factions in Serbia and other republics in the early 1970s (see the fourth interlude).

While criticism of Stalin was permitted, Yugoslav leaders were always suspicious that anti-Stalinist messages concealed anti-communist or even anti-Titoist content. Writers or artists who attacked Stalinism without praising Yugoslav communism were liable to be persecuted. Yugoslavia, after all, had had a concentration camp of its own (see chapter 33).

Karlo Štajner's book, completed by 1958, was unpublishable until the early 1970s, when Tito himself may have given the go-ahead. As late as 1985, it was impossible to publish Solzhenitsyn's *Gulag Archipelago* in Bosnia. When a Croatian publisher wanted to publish it, two men from the Soviet consulate came knocking on the door: if the publisher went ahead, the USSR would cancel its ship-building contracts with Yugoslavia. Local communist officials followed up, assuring the publisher that these were not empty threats.[89] Similar pressures delayed publication of a translation of Nadezhda Mandelstam's memoirs for a decade.

Kiš decided to approach a publisher in Zagreb with his manuscript. Zlatko Crnković at the Znanje publishing house edited a prestigious list called HIT, which had proven a success with readers and critics. Unconvinced that *Boris Davidovich* was right for HIT, Crnković offered to publish it in a different list—something he probably knew Kiš would find unacceptable.

Crnković, a distinguished editor and translator, still found the subject painful three decades later. "I made a mistake. But there it is. We live and learn. More knowledgeable men than I have made similar mistakes. After all, André Gide turned down Marcel Proust." The only extenuation he offers is that Kiš had made contact via his friend Predrag Matvejević, a committed leftist with strong opinions who provoked strong feelings. "I was surprised that Kiš, who was more than aware of his own stature, did not offer me his manuscript himself," Crnković says. "And I was worried that if I accepted Kiš's book, Matvejević would offer me something of his own, which would be difficult to turn down."

In Kiš's view, such personal frets were all too typical of provincial mentalities in Yugoslavia. Back in Belgrade, he wrote Crnković a scathing letter. Prone by temperament to react to perceived affronts "with a forcefulness of which I often repent", Kiš had waited before responding. Now he did so. "Not only was the series that you offered me inappropriate: it was humiliating, what with its anonymous, bad and amateurish writers and books, although I take it that your offer was in fact a veiled rejection exactly because of its humiliating conditions." Even inclusion in Crnković's premier list would have "troubled, not to say offended" Kiš because of the presence of certain local writers. "But I consoled myself with the thought that the list included such names as Céline, Genet, Nabokov, Boll. . . .

---

89 Solzhenitsyn's work was eventually published in Serbo-Croatian in 1988. The translator was Vidak Rajković, a librarian from Cetinje, who undertook this immense task on his own initiative. He offered the manuscript to an editor in Sarajevo. When publication was blocked by the regime in Bosnia and Herzegovina, then the most repressive of Yugoslavia's six republics, a Belgrade publisher stepped in. At that time, Serbia was relatively liberal in cultural terms.

I thought that one book by a local writer might, after all, appear on this list." After "most courteously" requesting the urgent return of his typescript, he signed off "With cordial greetings to you and your salesmen". Crnković knew no reply was possible.

Matvejević suggested approaching Miroslav Krleža, the grand old man of Croatian and Yugoslav letters. Krleža put them in touch with Slavko Goldstein, the director of Zagreb's university press. Kiš wanted a quick decision: Goldstein received the typescript on a Friday and had to answer on Monday. He read it overnight and knew at once that he wanted it. Under Yugoslav law, he needed the approval of his editorial council. "The council was very good, composed of university professors, excellent people, very open-minded." The chairman gave the go-ahead by telephone. Goldstein then agreed on terms with a Belgrade publisher for joint publication—an arrangement that Kiš approved.

Goldstein says that *Boris Davidovich* was not the most controversial title he published. Veljko Mićunović's *Moscow Diary*, Arthur Koestler's *Darkness at Noon*, and Isaac Deutscher's biography of Trotsky all drew reactions from the political

With Predrag Matvejević (l.) and Karlo Štajner, after receiving the Ivan Goran Kovačić prize for *A Tomb for Boris Davidovich* at Lukovdol, Croatia, June 1977. (Controversial in Serbia, *Boris Davidovich* won garlands in Croatia.)

237

establishment in Croatia.[90] "In the 1960s and 1970s," he explains, "if you wanted to criticise the Yugoslav system, you had to do it under cover of criticising Stalinism and the Soviet Union. *Boris Davidovich* was an example of this par excellence. Personally I preferred *Garden, Ashes* and *Hourglass*, but I thought this would be his most discussed book. Many people had such ideas [about communism], but none of them was such a good writer. *Boris Davidovich* was stronger as criticism and better as literature than anything the others wrote."

A Tomb for Boris Davidovich was published in June 1976 to press reviews that were very positive and sometimes ecstatic: "brilliantly written", something "to cure any reader's laziness", "an important and good book", "one of the necessary books of our time", "truly perfect", "full of artistic maturity", "deserves every sort of praise". Many reviewers noted the attack on Stalinism; a few generalised the point by suggesting that Kiš wanted to show "the way in which political power destroys all human and ethical values", or how "force" had been used "against mankind in the name of blind dogma". Even *The Communist*, the regime's official organ, enthused about Kiš's "mastery". Kiš was gratified; friends were amused to see him lording it at the Writers' Club in Belgrade, drinking till dawn with Mirko Kovač while the waiters dozed around them.

Sales were more than healthy: the initial run of 4,000 was repeated in December.[91] Foreign rights were quickly sold for English, French, and Italian editions. The foreign reviews were glowing. Other translations into Western languages followed in the early 1980s. Unlike Kiš's previous books, however, *Boris Davidovich* appeared nowhere else in communist Europe before 1989—or not officially: *samizdat* translations circulated in Budapest, Warsaw, and Prague. At this time of writing, it has been translated into many central and eastern European languages, including Ukrainian, but not yet into Russian.

During the 1990s, when Kiš became emblematic for anti-nationalists across the former Yugoslavia, *Boris Davidovich* gained new currency. Especially for readers in Bosnia and Herzegovina, where concentration camps were opened and scores of thousands of civilians were murdered in the name of ideologies, history seemed to reconfirm the genius of Kiš's miniature chronicles of blindness and terror.

---

90 Veljko Mićunović was a former Yugoslav ambassador to the USSR. Goldstein published his diaries in 1977. The English translation (1980) was acclaimed for its candid glimpse of Soviet attitudes to the rest of the world. However, according to Goldstein, the book was controversial in Yugoslavia for a different reason: "not because of anything he had written about Khrushchev but because it was the first time a Yugoslav had publicly discussed Tito's role in suppressing the Hungarian revolution."

91 *Boris Davidovich* appeared in paperback the following summer, with a first run of 20,000, reprinted (10,000 copies) in February 1979. These are remarkable figures for a book by a difficult writer in a middle-sized market with no exports.

From the Gymnasium I entered the University of
Belgrade, where I was the first student to graduate from
the newly created Department of Comparative Literature.

In his last year of school, Kiš applied to study literature at Belgrade university. He was accepted—not a foregone conclusion—and in autumn 1954 joined the Department of General Literature and Literary Theory, in the Faculty of Philosophy, to take the new degree course in the History of World Literature. He enrolled under the name Kiš, adopting the name definitively. It was as a student in Belgrade that literature became his homeland; that he fell in love with Mirjana Miočinović, and she with him; that life revealed itself as something which could be lived as he chose, not as the object of force and deprivation.

He had spent several months with his aunt's family near the railway station in 1948 and 1949 after failing a school exam, studying behind drawn curtains, with the city's muffled roar as soundtrack. When he arrived in late summer 1954, age nineteen, orphaned, longing to escape from provincial Cetinje, already saturated in Hungarian and French romantic poetry, he had no intention of keeping Belgrade at arm's length.

With almost half a million inhabitants, Belgrade was the only city in Yugoslavia with a complete urban ecology. After three hundred years as an Ottoman outpost, half a century as Serbia's capital, and half that time again as the capital of royal Yugoslavia, Belgrade was being remade as the headquarters of a communist federation. From its original reef above the confluence of the Danube and the Sava rivers, it had spread and morphed between the two world wars. Boulevards sliced through the lanes of the old city. Grey palaces of administration loomed over nineteenth-century tenements, two-storey shops, and older stone dwellings, still with fruit trees and livestock in their cobbled yards. To a Swiss visitor in 1953, the city had not caught up with its own growth; it was raucous, almost brutal; civility was banished to private contacts. "The streets seemed occupied rather than inhabited; the mesh of incidents, gossip, encounters was rudimentary." Reeking of engine oil, melons, black soap, cabbage and sewage, the city "was like a giant sore that had to run and stink before it could heal, and its robust blood seemed strong enough to heal, come what may."

What the Luftwaffe failed to demolish in 1941, Allied bombs flattened three years later. Tracts of the pre-war city lay in ruins, so there was much to rebuild. Reconstruction and renewal were the watchwords: more than a practical challenge, they were felt by many as a "sacred, patriotic, socialist duty". The new regime set its seal, topping public **239** buildings with red stars, renaming the main boulevard after the Red Army (until 1952, when it was changed to Revolution Boulevard). Flowers decked the graves of partisans in parks and squares; graves edged in red held Soviet soldiers who had died in the liberation. Desirable residences had been snapped up by the party elite along with their furnishings and works of art. Special shops for officials were abolished in 1951, but privileges were maintained in other ways and manifest to all.

There was a gleaming extension on the low land across the river Sava. Intended as "a showcase of socialist planning", New Belgrade was built on a regular, symmetrical grid that would supposedly avoid the class differentiation which blighted cities in capitalist societies. By summer 1953, the pace of construction had slowed and New Belgrade looked like a vast abandoned building site, with skeletal structures sinking into the soft riverside ground.

In 1954, a Western guidebook reported that Belgrade had been "almost completely rebuilt". This was untrue but faithful to the city's energetic impression on foreigners, not all of whom approved. Two French ladies regretted that "every trace of eastern influence has been mercilessly obliterated" from the architecture, while Serbia's traditional costumes could be seen only in the museum of ethnography, as if banished from the teeming pavements. Another visitor was struck by how people never mentioned the pre-war past; perhaps, he guessed, they "drew from their forgetfulness the courage to live again."

There were other reasons, too, for reticence: talking about the pre-war period was risky, and recent history was so overwhelming. During a decade, the citizens of Belgrade had undergone Nazi invasion and occupation, fascist collaboration, the destruction of the Jews, partisan resistance and Soviet-assisted liberation, then postwar violence (settling scores with political enemies, real or alleged), the communist new order, the clash with Stalin, and—finally—the charting of a Yugoslav road to democratic socialism. A British visitor in 1954 grew accustomed to the radio loudspeakers in Kalemegdan Park, "relaying the latest speech or drenching us in the ecstatic melancholy of Serbian folk music." There were so few cars that Belgrade had no traffic lights. "All manufactured articles were scarce." There was a shop where people could sell goods that their relatives in America had sent. Arriving from Poland in spring 1958, on the other hand, the economist John K. Galbraith found himself "reveling in the luxury of life".

Late in 1948, when Tito was still hoping to regain membership of the Cominform, "pictures of Lenin and Stalin were conspicuous in many streets". Charlie Chaplin's *The Great Dictator* (1940) was showing in the cinemas. The confrontation with Stalin peaked in 1950 and by the end of 1951 was winding down. No longer fearful of invasion by the Eastern bloc, the regime broke with the Soviet model of communism. Western admiration of the "Yugoslav experiment" in more democratic single-party governance soon followed, along with grudging Soviet bloc acceptance a few years after Stalin's death in 1953. The break with Stalinism opened new space for cultural autonomy. Petar Lubarda's exhibition in 1951 was one landmark. A Montenegrin member of the Central Committee argued that the break had created unique freedom for Yugoslav writers, who should chart the "most progressive" course between the vulgar Marxism of Soviet theorists and Western capitalist decadence. Both alternatives were equally "shallow and foreign"; an "authentic Yugoslav art" would shun both.

The case was made with more subtlety by Krleža to the Yugoslav Writers' Congress in 1952. Denouncing both the "aesthetic Puritanism" of Stalinist art and Western models of artistic freedom, he called on Yugoslav writers to stop "imitating" the literature of Western Europe, which was erected "on the bones of conquered peoples, to whom we ourselves unfortunately belonged". Unlike the Western Europeans, whose "victories in battle ensured victories of the spirit", the Yugoslavs "belong to the category of civilisations whose material and moral right to exist has been denied by foreign powers." The urgent task, he said, was to overcome the effect of "centuries of defeats" and achieve a new "synthesis", founded not on "romantic verbiage" but on "authentic, poetically presented facts . . . to explain and affirm the tragedy of our mutual negations." Krleža's call for an anti-nationalist literature, rooted in actuality, would be answered within his lifetime by Kiš's art, albeit in terms that condemned Yugoslav communist cultural production.

———

Comparative literature—a component of literary studies in Belgrade before the war—was in eclipse for several years after 1945; it was suspected of ideological collusion with 'cosmopolitanism'. The rift with the Cominform created an opportunity that was ably seized by Vojislav Đurić (1912–2006). Born in central Serbia in 1912 (his earliest memory was of an Austrian shell hitting the family home), Đurić was appointed minister of education in the new People's Republic of Serbia. But he did not want a political career. In 1949, he joined the university to lecture on world literature, the field of his prewar doctoral studies. A charismatic teacher, Đurić offered a course on "The Origins of Poetry and the Sources of Its Development" that impressed students who were unused to engaging critically with myth. Another course considered the poetry of ancient Mesopotamia, Egypt, India, and China, noting the analogies with Yugoslav folk poetry. A third focused on the Bible and Homer, which he treated as the twin pillars of world literature. (He had to lobby the authorities for permission to include the Bible.)

In the early 1950s, Đurić pressed the university to promote world literature to a full degree. Literary theory in the university was still heavily influenced by Leonid Timofeyev's *Theory of Literature* (published in Belgrade in 1950), a Soviet tract which stated that "Marxist-Leninist teaching in art is the highest level of aesthetic thought yet achieved in the world, its new phase which is qualitatively different from the whole of history until now." Literary form, Timofeyev argued, must be "democratic", meaning accessible to the broad masses.

To strengthen his case, Đurić appealed to influential figures for support, but only Isidora Sekulić, the *grande dame* of Serbian letters, answered the call. (When I asked why nobody else had replied, the ninety-one-year old Đurić waved a contemptuous hand: "Because of the slave mentality in Serbia! Five hundred years under the Turks!") Nevertheless, the loosening of cultural and educational policy worked in his favour, and he got his way. In 1954, he was appointed to resurrect the pre-war Department of General Literature and Literary Theory, with the new degree in World Literature as its centrepiece.

The syllabus led students from the Song of Songs, the Psalms, and the Book of Job to Joyce and Kafka, via the Greeks and Romans, Dante, Rabelais, Shakespeare, Cervantes, Jean Racine, John Milton, Voltaire, Goethe, Dostoevsky, Tolstoy, and Flaubert, with excursions into ancient Egyptian, Indian, Chinese, Arabic, and Persian literatures. Students had to learn two or three languages as part of the degree, for Đurić insisted that nobody can know the literature of their own language without knowing foreign literatures as well. A three-year course in literary theory was also compulsory. Recruiting talented younger staff, blending the French historical conception of comparative literature with the new American critical (or 'great books') approach, and offsetting Marxist methods with other modes of interpretation, Đurić designed a course that was broadminded, undogmatic, pluralist, and devoted to literature as "an art with its own specific expressive possibilities" rather than a vehicle of social or political meaning. Given the situation in Yugoslavia at that time, his syllabus was remarkably free of political or ideological undercurrents.

The first intake for the World Literature degree numbered about twenty students, older than the average. They and their successors often felt like an elite compared to the other literature students, partly because their degree was so grandly ambitious and partly because—as Đurić warned each intake—it would not make them easily employable. (Kiš: "It was known as a useless degree, but I didn't care what came next.") Graduates were bound by camaraderie and affection for Đurić himself, known fondly but nervously as Zeus.

Kiš was a superlative student. When Marko Špadijer arrived from Cetinje to study World Literature in 1957, Kiš was "already a legend" at the faculty. Some of his essays were still mentioned ten or twenty years later as standard-setting achievements. Kiš was, said Đurić when I met him, "incomparable". He had never had a better student. He was a very courageous man, with an "inner radiance", but "sensitive as a child", taking offence very easily. He sat in the back row at lectures, where he was easily seen because he was tall. One of Đurić's assistants remembered Kiš as solitary and independent, self-possessed enough to attend only the lectures which interested him. For years afterwards, when irritated by idle or facetious elements in a class, Đurić reproached them that his first and best student was so poor that he slept rough in the park and still came out top in everything.

As an academic discipline, comparative literature dates from the second half of the nineteenth century. The subset of world literature has been controversial from the outset. The scholar who pioneered comparative methods disapproved of world literature categorically because it represented "the severance of literature from defined social groups".

In other words, it split literature from nations. This was exactly what its supporters approved, beginning with Goethe, who had coined the term in 1827: "National literature does not mean much nowadays; the age of world literature [*Weltliteratur*] is at hand, and everyone must strive to hasten its approach." World literature kept its idealistic aura—its aspiration to identify "the best which has been thought and said in the world".

Anti-nationalism was part of the ideal, and it still is. During and after the Second World War, as David Damrosch observes, many scholars held out "messianic hopes for world literature as the cure for the ills of nationalistic separatism, jingoism and internecine violence". In the United States, courses in world literature spread after 1945 until they were offered by "virtually all of our major universities". This flowering was in part a gift from displaced Central European Jewish humanists to the New World. At Yale, René Wellek defined world literature as "the study of literature in its totality" based on "an ideal of the unification of all literatures into one literature where each nation would play its part in universal concert". In 1952, Erich Auerbach—also at Yale—summoned prophetic tones to express a more sombre vision: "our philological home is the earth: it can no longer be the nation. . . . We must return, in admittedly altered circumstances, to the knowledge that prenational medieval culture already possessed: the knowledge that the spirit [*Geist*] is not national." The courses inspired by these teachers focused on foreign writing in English translation—even though the third of the Central European triumvirate, Leo Spitzer at Johns Hopkins University, believed literature had to be studied in its original language, or at least with a strong awareness of that language—and were, a recent scholar points out, "unlike the separate study of 'literature', intended to introduce future citizens to cultural experiences 'outside' their own society".

(The Soviet version, meanwhile, was enshrined in Moscow's Institute of World Literature, founded by Maksim Gorki in 1933, whose members—according to one admirer—"put to practical use the theoretical premises well established in Soviet literary studies" and found their "philosophical basis" in "historical monism, [rooted] in the works of Marx, Engels and Lenin." Not much scope there for idealism, pluralism, or inspiration.)

Sceptics have faulted world literature because it poses a challenge of selection that cannot be answered. They mocked the typical American syllabus for following "without method the random Homer-to-Arthur-Miller zigzag through Western literature." Another concern was covert Eurocentrism; for world literature courses were more truly, as one eminent critic observed, courses "in the literary and intellectual tradition of the West, what is called the Judaic-Hellenic-Christian tradition." While this was not quite true of Đurić's syllabus, Kiš's own affinity, despite allusions in his student essays to Persian and Indian myths, was for European literature.[92] His objection to Eurocentrism was

---

92 In *Boris Davidovich,* Kiš associates his fictitious Russian poet, A. A. Darmolatov, with "the Acmeists' cosmopolitan program, their 'yearning for European culture', thanks above all to the influence of another poet, Mandelstam". But Mandelstam had famously defined *Acmeism* as "a yearning for world culture", *toska po mirovoi kulture.* The slip was surely due to these two terms being interchangeable, in Kiš's mind.

different; he regretted that it really signified half a dozen literatures at most. A *true* Eurocentrism, he argued, would make room for Europe's smaller languages and their literatures. He believed "the inequality of the world literary system" (Franco Moretti's phrase) had denied recognition to his compatriots and masters—Andrić, Krleža, and Crnjanski. He deplored this injustice in print and speech, especially after moving to France, though he knew it was beyond remedy. "If I bring up these three," he said in 1984, "it is not only because I believe them to be great European writers but also because, unlike many French writers, they took literature seriously and experienced it tragically."

Since the 1970s, the rise of cultural studies centred on multiculturalism has sometimes had the effect of denying people's right or ability to explore outside their given ethnic, racial or sexual identity. With postcolonial and postmodern literary theory meanwhile dismantling not just the Western literary canon but 'literature' as such, world literature became an "abstracted construct", a narrative that elided difference in the name of would-be universal values: human nature, cosmopolitanism, rationality, enlightenment, and other ciphers of occidental oppression. Instead of being rethought, Eurocentrism was denounced and disowned—without anyone quite knowing how to replace it as a structuring principle of comparatism, and so achieve both "global reach and textual closeness." As a result, according to one American academic, world literature has "become a category reserved for the leftovers of an international literary market on the one hand, and the leftovers of our 'national language'-based curricula on the other." What Đurić and his most famous pupil would think of this decline may be imagined.[93]

Kiš had a keen nose for political agendas in cultural dress, and from the early 1980s he denounced anti-humanist trends in literature and criticism. Literature, he insisted, is "one and indivisible, good or bad", and must not be co-opted by struggles for political rights. "I'm horrified by books about minorities, by the sectarian success they often parade, by the minority alibi that lends them extra-literary qualities and public acclaim," he said in 1984. "If the only reason to read a book is that it deals with blacks, Jews, homosexuals or—forgive me—women, then I'm not interested."

The scope of the syllabus, as well as the high-minded commitment of Đurić and his staff, answered a deep need in Kiš. He loved the wide horizons of the syllabus, the generic connections and poetic correspondences he was encouraged to explore. A second-year essay on the Prometheus myth began with Aeschylus and covered Goethe, Shelley, and Friedrich Nietzsche before ending with Albert Camus on "the revolt of mankind in

---

93 Their Department of General Literature and Literary Theory appears to be standing firm. According to its website, "If current global trends in comparatism persist, Belgrade will soon be the only place on the planet where the Bible, Homer, Dante and Proust can be studied comparatively, as part of our universal literary heritage".

the atomic age". An essay on comedy elaborated a comparison between Rabelais, whose laughter is "elementary and pure", and Cervantes, whose Don Quixote, "the last knight errant", is, "like so many heroes in literature, deeply national and also international at the same time." The syllabus gave him the history of literature as antithesis to history as such.

His student essays show a mind discovering and testing itself, alert to the metaphysical appetites that drive good writing, without mistaking literary seriousness for philosophical solemnity or political significance. For literature, he already believed, was an artificial paradise, in Baudelaire's sense. When Kiš graduated in 1958 with the highest marks, Đurić thanked him for proving that the new degree was possible: "You have saved me!" Kiš stayed at the faculty to do postgraduate research for two years (now with a grant: his first), but when Đurić offered a permanent teaching position ("You can have one tomorrow if you want"), Kiš's reply was firm: *I have chosen another path. I would rather write myself than lecture about people who have done their writing.* He had published reams of essays and reviews, a dozen poems, and half a dozen stories. At the end of the decade, he was ready to try something longer.

He paid for a berth in a student dormitory in New Belgrade (four or five beds with a washbasin), but spent all his time in the city centre, across the river Sava, and disliked the long tramp home after missing the last bus; so he often slept wherever he could at the end of the night, "dossing in someone's room with people I'd just met." After he joined the board of a literary magazine, *Vidici*, he "slept in their offices for two years. I had a key." When a chance came along to take digs in the city centre, late in 1957, he did not need to be asked twice.[94] As there was space for a second student, he invited Boško Mijanović to join him. This is how they came to lodge with Nikolai Aleksinski (see chapter 29). When he had to leave Aleksinski, he found a rented room in Skadarska Street. Then, after a year or two, he moved into a garret. (This was late in 1960, months after he had completed *The Garret*.) What mattered was to be in the centre.

Kiš had only his father's small pension, so he was always hard up. For clothes, he depended on packages from his Aunt Gabriella in Trieste (wife of Uncle Adolf). At the end of the summer, he would cut cardboard insoles to make his shoes a little more weather-proof. (He had done this since 1942. "When you take off your shoes, the insoles are *papier-mâché*.") Wrapping newspaper around his feet, under his socks, also helped with insulation. Around 1960, when Kiš was finally getting a stipend, Mirko Kovač remembers him smoking "voluptuously, almost lasciviously" in cafés in winter, sipping tea with rum, running his fingers through his mane of hair, confessing that his coat and shoes were borrowed, and wrapping sheets of newsprint under his jumper to keep warm.

---

94 In this same year, 1957, the young Georges Perec followed a hopeless *amour* to Belgrade, where he got very drunk and challenged her consort to a fist fight. This happened shortly after Perec had completed a pastiche of Gide's *Paludes* (see first interlude: *The Garret*), which he gave in tribute to the object of his passion. The intersections and analogies between Kiš and Perec—their lives and works—deserve an essay or, better, a story.

Hunger was another problem. Food was hardly more plentiful than in the provinces. The students had vouchers for the university canteen; if they wanted cigarettes or drinks, they sold a few vouchers. For eating out, the option favoured by Kiš and his Cetinje friends was a cheap restaurant that served them boiled cabbage with a slice of bread, followed by cabbage salad. They also dined contentedly on bread, margarine, and tins of yellow Dutch cheese. At night, they might scour the pavements for banknotes mixed up with litter and find enough for another litre or two of wine.

A new friend from Montenegro was Milan Popović, who remembers Kiš as gaunt, lanky, rather dishevelled; blue-eyed, impulsive, hot-tempered, charming, with an air of mischief; "broadminded and accessible, but no less quarrelsome and impatient". Their friendship was not particularly intellectual, or even talkative: Kiš knew how Popović disliked the verbal sparring that clever students love. He supplied other things that Kiš

The Montenegrin quartet in Belgrade: Pavle Đonović, Boško Mijanović, Milan Beli Popović, and Kiš

valued as the supreme virtues of friendship: warmth, understanding, and loyalty. Kiš was highly strung, easily overwhelmed by emotion, and when they went out together, Popović—two years older—made sure there was a spare drink to hand, in case his friend needed diverting from the brink of tears or blows. Kiš had a sixth sense for careerists and culture-snobs among their contemporaries and was merciless towards them, whatever the numerical odds. When he went too far, Popović intervened like an older brother to save him from a beating. Kiš was independent in other ways as well, shrugging off the pressure to join 'volunteer' projects to clear bombsites or dig the foundations of new buildings.

Boško Mijanović, who had come from Cetinje in 1953 to study mathematics and economics, marvelled at his friend's ability to spend all night in bars and then all day in the library. Boško joined the others at their faculty lectures when his schedule allowed. With Popović, the quartet was inseparable. According to Pavle Đonović, who was study-ing Yugoslav literature, Montenegrin students had a cachet; they had been well taught, were quick-witted, and easily trumped any expectation—created by their distinctive accent—that they could be patronised as country cousins. With this asset, their social life flourished, leading to contact with a whirl of random characters and acquaintances: in Kiš's case, painters, writers, landlords, barflies, waiters, and professors, as well as his aunt and cousins, and other students. Milan Popović was struck by his extraordinary openness to unexpected encounters. In their favourite cafés, a procession of larger-than-life people wandered along in the course of an evening, filling their eyes and ears with more human variety than they could absorb. To the end of his life, Kiš defined happiness as sitting at a café table with a drink.

Reading with avid intensity, writing in concentrated bouts until the library closed at 8 p.m., and then escaping from print to drink and sing with friends; watching French films (he even looked like Jean-Paul Belmondo in *Breathless*); smoking two or three packs of cigarettes a day: student life suited Kiš so well that it set a lasting pattern. Ever since, he has been linked with Belgrade's postwar scene: "*le personnage emblématique de la bohème belgradoise*", as a recent critic writes.

At the time, this life was imposed by poverty. "We weren't 'bohemian', we were poor," he explained long afterwards, with a touch of asperity, to correct a sentimental misunderstanding. "Even if you don't have a place to stay or anything to eat, or much to wear—you can always afford a drink." He saw "Belgrade's Montmartre" in the 1950s as another symptom of cultural belatedness, a pale shadow of Paris or Moscow before the First World War; the afterglow of a tradition that was about to be extinguished by pop music, drugs, and affluence. In his eyes, *poètes maudits* like Paul-Marie Verlaine, Ady, or Ujević had remained true to themselves, rejecting false responsibility (to career, institutions, income, politics) and its attendant vanities in order to embrace freedom—the freedom for commitment to what mattered: art, love, family, and friendship. The risk of drifting into alcoholic squalor never worried him; he trusted in the discipline of his emerging vocation. "I drank a lot," he once said of his student days, "on an empty stomach, to the limit, 'down in one', but always sticking to my secret recipe for survival."

This recipe came from the Croatian poet Tin Ujević, who once explained with disarming simplicity how he had written so much and so well when his companions were foundering in seas of booze: "I drank at night and worked by day." To his friend Filip David, Kiš was never a true bohemian: his boozing and carousing were escapes from solitude and "inner demons".

Wine comes in at the mouth
And love comes in at the eye

W. B. Yeats

After the dreary confinement of Cetinje, Belgrade meant liberation. As well as the cafés and social life, it had a cultural scene that was neither overshadowed by a heroic, folkloric past nor tyrannised by provincial communists. Three theatre companies offered classical and modern repertories. The cinemas showed foreign films, albeit with long delays; 1953 saw the release of Esther Williams's 1944 musical *Bathing Beauty*, one of the first Hollywood movies to get distribution after the war. Kiš and his friends preferred the Jugoslovenska kinoteka, a new venue that showed art films, including the masterpieces of Marcel Carné and Jacques Prévert. A decade later, Kiš remembered the kinoteka as a magic box, an Aladdin's lamp, "a haunt for girls with long black hair *à la* Juliet Gréco and 'existentialists'—scruffy young men with beards—where we sat in the dark, either terribly alone or holding hands, enchanted, listening to the dialogue in those marvellous films whose words sank into our hearts and convinced us, if only for a moment, that the world was made of love and love would save the world like some new Messiah."

This nostalgic vision paid tribute to a particular young woman with long black hair. During his first term, Kiš told Boško Mijanović he had to come and see a beautiful girl at his lectures. This turned out to be Mirjana Miočinović, who would become his wife, soulmate, anchor, and Platonic other half, so deeply involved in his work as well as his life that she is woven into it as a scarcely perceptible pattern of absoluteness.

Mirjana was born in Belgrade at the end of 1935. Her father came from the Banija region of Croatia, home to a large community of Serbs (until the wars of the 1990s); her mother was born near Užice in central Serbia. Another student, who also fell for Mirjana and later became a friend of the couple, remembered her as "more than beautiful, a little eccentric and exceptionally clever." Kiš was quickly smitten. Boško says that he has rarely seen anyone so enamoured. Mirjana was, Kiš wrote to Đonović, *moja neminovnost*: "my inevitability". But it was not to be, and could not have been, a simple affair. A year passed before Mirjana recognised Kiš's attention. "He misunderstood my reserve as the haughtiness of a 'well brought up girl'," she recalls. "We saw each other in classes, in the library, sometimes at concerts, which he came to mainly on my account; and at the cinema."

Her parents had doubts about the scruffy young man. Eventually he was allowed to take Mirjana out once a week, on Thursdays; Pavle and Boško spruced him up before these occasions. They had no contact during her two-year absence for study in France (1957–1959), and then picked up where they had left off, overcoming Kiš's infatuation with another woman. When Kiš went off to do his military service in March 1961, he was head over heels in love. (He spent half his year in the wilds of Herzegovina and half in a remote Croatian town between Zagreb and the sea.) During a spell of leave early in 1962, the couple became engaged. Having nowhere else, he slept in the *Vidici* offices for two months before their marriage in June. Her parents were by now very fond of him and he of them.

The newlyweds moved into a room in a flat behind Serbia's parliament. Their landlord was Mirjana's uncle. As the room was only 2.5 by 3.5 metres square, Kiš worked on the bed, cross-legged, the typewriter on his lap. That October, they went to Strasbourg for his first stint as a lector in France (see chapter 31). When they returned in June 1964, they moved back into the room behind the parliament. Mirjana started work at the new Institute for Literature and Art (an independent research centre, another of Đurić's initiatives), so they had one regular salary, however modest. In 1971, she moved to the Faculty of Drama in Belgrade.

In November 1966, they finally moved into a flat of their own, in Ranko Tajsić Street. Kiš was not delighted: "We shan't be staying here long." It turned out to be their last address. He remained there for fifteen years, moving out only after the divorce in 1981. An uxorious Don Juan, devoted both to Mirjana and to womanising, Kiš had a commitment to marriage that was as complex and paradoxical as his relationship to fiction. He never wrote about their private life; she will never do so ("Not everything has to be written"). "Meeting him was my destiny," she has said. "However pathetic that may sound, I really don't have other words for a bond that has endured more than fifty years."

It was a union of similar opposites. When they met, Kiš looked and acted like a free spirit; not so Mirjana. Yet her inner resources for defying convention and compromise proved as sturdy as his. Kiš's friends saw her as providing discipline that he needed; guarding his privacy at home, creating calm conditions for him to write, gently discouraging his wastrel habits. She demurs, seeing their harmony as entirely natural and spontaneous. Helped by Mirjana, Kiš came to be at home in Belgrade. For her part, she overcame insecurities of her own, with his support, to become a respected author and teacher. "He was a person of passions," she says, "while I am a person of loyalty." If so, it is loyalty raised to the pitch of passion; for the alterations of divorce and Kiš's death have not weakened it.

The other reason why Kiš could feel at home in Belgrade was down to historical luck. Mirjana recalls Yugoslavia's exhilarating freedom in the 1950s compared with the rest of communist Europe. "We already had translations of Proust, Joyce, Broch, Gide, Faulkner. We were not cut off from the world of ideas, from the history of ideas and

"She is my inevitability."—The wedding, Belgrade, 10 June 1962

of styles." Milan Popović also recalls how "warm currents of knowledge from the wide world" reached them as students. Đonović, too: "We read Camus, Sartre, Hemingway, Faulkner . . . people we'd had no chance to read in Cetinje." Of Kiš, herself, and their circle, Mirjana says that this openness was their "priceless and essential advantage compared to the countries of the Eastern bloc." And they knew how to value their "margin of freedom for inquiry and expression". Without this, Kiš would not have become the writer that we know.

The standing of Kiš's beloved Joyce is evidence of this margin. Joyce had been a butt of Stalinist criticism since the early 1930s, when Karl Radek described *Ulysses* as "a dung heap swarming with maggots and photographed by a movie camera through a microscope". This primitivism never dominated in Yugoslavia, thanks largely to Krleža and the former Surrealists around Tito, led by Marko Ristić, Koča Popović, and Oskar Davičo. Ristić argued against a Soviet critic that culture and ideology were not identical, and socialist countries should not simply "be against Western culture"; indeed there was no cultural "opposition" between East and West. As for Joyce, he was indeed the product of a given society, but "he is also, at the same time, the product of a long evolution of literature itself."

From time to time, Đonović and Kiš walked down to the railway station late at night and watched the trains pulling in and out. Although Kiš said little, Đonović had the impression that he was deep in thought about his childhood and his father, the railway inspector. The early poem about his father (see chapter 2) was probably written soon after Kiš arrived in Belgrade; yet it appears that his mind and imagination were not burdened at that time by the loss. We infer as much from his reaction in 1960 to Alain Resnais's film *Night and Fog*, when he spoke up for our "right to oblivion". (*Psalm 44,* also written in 1960, was a range-finding effort to measure his distance from Jewish and family tragedy.) Mirjana's remark that she knew very little about Kiš's earlier ordeals before they married, points to the same conclusion. These were years of reprieve from the traumas of childhood and early youth.[95] When he returned to them or they to him, as a married man in Strasbourg, he had the emotional distance and literary resource to lend them the grace of form.

95 This reprieve was helped by the wider indifference to the Holocaust during the 1950s. (The indifference was particularly coarse and coercive in communist countries, where Holocaust victims were assimilated with other "victims of fascism", whose martyrdom had paved the way for Marxist-Leninist redemption by the Red Army.) Eva Hoffman (b. 1945) has noted that "the so-called latency period, when the Holocaust seemed to recede from public consciousness, coincided with our own developmental latency . . . when the processes of one's own psychic past tend to be put on hold, or to go underground."

{SIXTH INTERLUDE}

The Anatomy Lesson (1978)

Nothing comes of nothing, Thieflet; no story comes
from nowhere; new stories are born from old—it is
the new combinations that make them new.
                    Salman Rushdie, *Haroun and the Sea of Stories*

Several weeks after *A Tomb for Boris Davidovich* was published, literary Belgrade
was abuzz with rumours that Kiš's new book was derivative, full of passages lifted
from other writers. These rumours reached the gossip columns, but the accusations were not formalised until November, when a Zagreb magazine ran an article
called "A Necklace of Other People's Pearls". The author, Dragoljub Golubović,
a minor journalist from Belgrade, alleged that two of the most praised stories in
Boris Davidovich had been pasted together from a French history of Russian art
and from Roy Medvedev's book on Stalinism. All the stories, he added, were about
Jewish rebels.

Kiš challenged the journalist to substantiate his charges and called on the
grey eminences behind the attack to come forward; for he was convinced that the
journalist had been put up to it. Golubović's reply was half-hearted, but the affair
snowballed. For the next two years, newspapers and magazines around the country
joined the quarrel. It became the loudest and most significant literary scandal in
postwar Yugoslavia.

Kiš's supporters included writers and scholars from Serbia, Croatia, Bosnia
and Herzegovina, and Slovenia. They argued that his use of non-fictional material from other books was warranted by the purpose of 'documenting' his stories;
it could not, they said, be dismissed as "copying" (Golubović's word). For it was a
widely accepted narrative method and had nothing to do with stealing credit. On
the contrary, the double-echo of Kiš's prose in *Boris Davidovich* was fully intended.
Readers were meant to feel trapped, as in a prison or a nightmare; to see that the
characters existed in commonplaces—the 'received ideas' of the revolutionary; and
to grasp that nothing in the stories was new, on the contrary it was—or should
be—horribly familiar. ("I expected readers to question the facts in the book," Kiš
explained much later, "and I prepared myself—very naïvely—to be able to say,
'Pardon me, *nothing* in the book is made up.'")

As well as the Belgrade journalist, other figures rumoured to be prominent
among the book's detractors, such as the Montenegrin novelist Branimir Šćepanović
and a French teacher of Slavic languages, Jean Descat, also showed little appetite for

the spotlight.[96] The vacuum was filled by a professor of literature at the University of Belgrade, one Dragan M. Jeremić, whose solid shoulders were ready for this burden. As a prominent member of the cultural establishment, and president of the Association of Writers of Serbia, Jeremić sat on juries that awarded prominent literary prizes. (An incredible number of literary prizes were given in Yugoslavia, though only a handful were taken as indicators of genuine merit.) The press quoted Jeremić, in his capacity as juror, as having proposed that Kiš's book should be excluded from one of these prizes on "moral" grounds. Drawn in to the affair, he responded at length and with ineffable pomposity, setting up as a champion of "the dignity of the literary word".

Jeremić was an author as well as an academic, specialising in aphorisms. His most recent collection happened to win a prestigious prize as the affair over *Boris Davidovich* came to the boil. The chairman of the jury praised Jeremić's work as "a Marxist book" with an "undogmatic", humanist outlook. Other jurors agreed that Jeremić had sought to infuse "aesthetic questions with Marxist values". Predrag Matvejević—one of Kiš's most able supporters—tore gleefully into Jeremić's book, which did not present an elusive target: "In marriage, an institution that should secure love, love sometimes gets forgotten amid a sea of obligations and duties." "The worst thing one could hope for is not a difficult life, but stupid and limited readers." "From wittiness to triviality and frivolity is often but a single step."

Vexed by this gadfly, Jeremić dedicated himself to exposing Kiš as a full-blown impostor. Despite some sanctimonious disavowals ("in war the Muses remain silent, and I prefer the Muses' song to the rumble not only of cannons but of curses and insults"), Jeremić knew how to wield a poisoned pen. Kiš was uncreative, sterile, lacking a vision of the world; an author of "harlequin literature, made of bits taken from other's creations"; a mechanical imitator of techniques discovered in successive "masters" from Bruno Schulz to Hermann Broch to Borges. *Boris Davidovich* contained innumerable "factual errors". Kiš himself was arrogant and vulgar. His theoretical self-defence was shallow, incompetent, and pretentious, blending "ignorance and hatred", a case of critical dilettantism rather than "systematic criticism". His vaunted "erudition" highlighted a lack of originality; for "erudition may fan the flame of inspiration but cannot substitute for talent", and "knowledge cannot be imitated".

---

96 Descat had translated *Garden, Ashes* into French (1971). He and Kiš were colleagues at the University of Bordeaux from 1973 to 1976. When Descat was commissioned to translate *Boris Davidovich*, Kiš directed him to the French texts that he had used. He became convinced that Descat started the campaign against his book by gossiping to Šćepanović (whom Descat also translated, and who was bound to Kiš with complex—and easily resented—ties of obligation; for Kiš had given Šćepanović detailed help with his writing). Descat's later translations included the collected speeches of Slobodan Milošević.

These quotations come from Jeremić's book, *Narcissus without a Face* (1981), a 380-page chronicle of wounded vanity that tried to rebut *The Anatomy Lesson*, Kiš's own book about the *Boris Davidovich* affair, published in 1978.

Written in a mere month, *The Anatomy Lesson*—Kiš's longest book—glows with the speed of composition and authorial rage. It may be the angriest book published by a great writer in the past half-century. Kiš's position was that the scandal had been manufactured as an "attempt to liquidate a book and a writer"; and that it reflected the "decadence of taste, collapse of (literary) values and aesthetic criteria" in Serbia, and by implication all of Yugoslavia. He would explain the structure and concept of *Boris Davidovich* in order to lay bare this wider corruption within the literary culture. "Given the condition of our literary criticism, a condition that shows no promise of improvement, writers are duty-bound to speak out about their texts from a theoretical perspective." His lecture-room techniques would serve this double purpose, exposing the stupidity of his enemies and enlightening the public.

After summarising the course of the affair since November 1976 and caricaturing his attackers, Kiš singled out the accusation by Serbian novelist Miodrag Bulatović—then a well-known figure, widely translated—that he, Kiš, had insulted "our people". Noting that this was a nationalist complaint, he defined his primary target as political or ideological. This wrong-footed his critics (who expected the fight to start on other grounds) and bolstered his contention that the campaign against his book was not really about plagiarism at all.

Nationalist interpretations of literature, Kiš argued, "follow logically from the kind of psychological, irrational, paranoid instability that sees phantoms everywhere, the kind of psychological and moral degeneracy that reduces everything to the common denominator of *for us* versus *against us*". This degeneracy depends on ignoring the mythical nature of the loyalties at stake, and the relative nature of the myths in question. His own early awareness of "the relativity of all myths" was the outcome of painful experiences in childhood, namely the "repeated, sudden, incomprehensible uprootings" that forced him to grasp the resemblance between Hungarian and Montenegrin national myths.[97]

When his family moved home from one part of Novi Sad to another, the six-year-old Kiš had been terrified because the boys in *his* street were sure that the boys in the *other* part of town were cruel and wicked. But no harm befell him in the new street, and he "realised with astonishment verging on incredulity that here, too, in this new neighbourhood the same laws held sway, the same myths of community /

---

97 *En passant,* Kiš calls for "a theory of historical relativity". If it could only be discovered, this theory "would have repercussions no less fundamental than Einstein's theory of relativity"; for it could "resolve countless misunderstandings and prevent countless tragic blunders" without "disturbing the discrete constant of national characteristics. Quite the contrary!"

strength / fidelity, the same hatred of the 'enemy' whose territory began three streets away. . . ." A year later he moved again, farther afield:

> living in the Hungarian countryside as a farmhand and village pauper yet with the outlook and habits of a city boy (that is, aware of not belonging, of being out of my element), I soon, both at school and among the peasant families who took me in out of curiosity, absorbed various local Hungarian myths and commonplaces or oral traditions: counting rhymes, proverbs, sayings. "Hungarians are the most hospitable people in the world", the hardest working, the most religious; Hungarian soldiers are the most valiant and loyal; *Talpra Magyar, hi a haza!* (Arise, O Magyar, your country calls!); the Hungarian plain is the most beautiful sight in the world (according to objective witnesses, foreign travellers), mountains being harsh and inhospitable. . . . Hungarian history is the bloodiest, the most heroic, the most just; Hungarian rulers are the noblest and most civilised, though constantly betrayed by perfidious allies; Hungary was the rampart that held back the Turkish invaders; Hungarian is the most beautiful language on earth. . . . I accepted it all with the trust and innocence of a child in spite of certain doubts, vague notions, in spite of my experience and a presentiment that this was no place for me, for us, that we were here only for the interim, that we were war refugees, foreigners, exiles living the hard life of exile in the shadow of death.

Then he moved to Montenegro, where his mother's family included him in the Orthodox rituals and he soaked up the local (national) lore:

> Turkish heads soared through the air like ears of wheat (my grandfather had actually fought at Taraboš in 1912–13), horses neighed as in Homer, Christians pursued the infidel "as far as Skadar and even farther", victory was honoured with great feasts. . . . Everyone was a hero, each more intrepid than the last, and Montenegro and the seven hills had never been taken by the Turks, never surrendered. I could have sworn I had heard it all before—the poems, the stories from my school textbook (Jagoš Jovanović's *History of Montenegro*), the same heroic exploits with the same moral, the same Homeric hyperbole; I could have sworn I had plucked the blood-soaked peonies of Kosovo in other patriotic odes in another language, under the name of *bazsarózsa*.[98]

---

98 According to legend, red peonies covered the battlefield in Kosovo where the Serbian empire was defeated in 1389. *Bazsarózsa* is "peony" in Hungarian.

These pages have the force of allegory. Kiš does not claim that his mixed ethnic origins led to this crucial lesson: it was displacement that opened his eyes.

Just as our experience of national myths is arbitrary and subjective, so it is with languages: "all that I can conclude from the fact that I write solely (and therefore best) in my own language is the self-evident fact that I write solely (and therefore best) in my own language. That is what makes it the sole (and best) language for me. That and nothing more."

He accused his opponents of supporting the nationalist manipulation or subversion of literature. For criticism in Yugoslavia was, he said, anti-individualist and sociological, bent on accumulating literary power. Writers of the same generation were assimilated to each other, ignoring differences. Crude psychological and political interpretation was favoured over the analysis of literary systems or structures, and the ways in which these generate meaning.

Worst of all, local critics were *anti-literary*. Misunderstanding the nature of tradition, they encouraged the view that writers could and should invent themselves, needing no relationship to the "European cultural heritage" that formed their true patrimony. This myth of self-creation has, Kiš suggested, profound political consequences. If a writer does not find and make an identity in literature, he will (in Yugoslavia, at least) have to take one from "history and local myth". This in turn leads writers to see "their nationality as a *spiritual* dowry, as if a writer were born with a tradition, as if one's cultural heritage were sucked in with mother's milk, as if spiritual nobility did not come exclusively from the *spirit*." Far from being ethnically bestowed, a proper relationship to literary tradition has to be achieved.

Taken to an extreme, the romantic notion of originality nourishes cultural and political reaction. Against the veneration of a single culture and language, Kiš sketches his ideal of world literature, with influences intersecting and interacting, an "astrological" vision of a polycentric heritage "with no Sun as its Centre and Tyrant", where "all the zones of influence are equally important and predominant and only the relationships change, the triumph of one influence is only a transient adventure, which is suddenly and unexpectedly replaced by another. . . . For in this *system*, all the particles act on each other". These relationships bear no correspondence to the borders around "states, centuries, schools, nationalities, epochs, literary connections, individual talents, or the Zeitgeist". On the contrary: by virtually demolishing those borders, these relationships of influence "create constellations that endure at the confluence of centrifugal and centripetal forces, sustaining themselves by the logic of the logos and the unique spirit of written words", thanks above all "to the spirit of him who, right here, put the words in this new and unrepeatable order, with a single clear spiritual centre—my own!" It was a beautiful elaboration of the case being made around the same time by Milan Kundera and others, that fiction is individualism's natural habitat.

257

This went over the heads of Kiš's detractors, who alleged that his relationship to Borges, for example, was one of simple derivation. (This obsession with originality straddled Yugoslav politics as well as culture; the boast that Tito's regime had invented the only authentic democratic socialism in the world was forced on every schoolchild.) Kiš branded this as "genetic reductionism"—as if literary works worthy of the name could be grasped by crumbling them into attributable elements. As if, having identified the parents, we knew everything about the child. On this view, "the writer has no right to be what he is . . . a creator, a demiurge, a *Dichter*, unique, irreducible, irreplaceable; and the work cannot be what *it* is—a miracle!"

The Anatomy Lesson has scintillating digressions on *Boris Davidovich*, the poetics of quotation, *The Garret*, Borges, Ivo Andrić, testicular writing (practised by Balkan nationalists who despise "dubious erudition, Western influence, the Cartesian decadence that depletes an author's ballsy spontaneity"), Judaism ("as in my previous books, Jewishness serves only as a mark of defamiliarisation"), and "schizopsychology".[99] Kiš elaborated his ideas about the inadequacy of "psychological approaches" in literature for treating, not the enormous questions of our time, but ordinary experience, which has been changed by the "fantastic" and "occult" enormities of the twentieth century. "Hiroshima is the focal point of that fantastic world, whose contours could first be discerned at about the time of the First World War" with the collapse of continental empires, the rise of Bolshevism, and the first shoots of fascism.

It followed that writers should cease to "approach their heroes with an eye to interpreting their actions psychologically, in terms of moral consistencies or violated taboos"; for our models of psychological interpretation are anachronistic, reflecting moral codes that no longer exist. Instead, writers should respect the "obligation to put that paranoid reality on paper", which calls for the use of "documents, probes, investigations", and the avoidance of "personal, arbitrary diagnoses or prescriptive medicines and cures."

In the final section, Kiš climbs off the dissecting table and applies his scalpel to the prose of Jeremić and Šćepanović. These satirical readings confirmed his diagnosis of the officially approved, prize-winning literature in Yugoslavia. For he found advanced degeneration of language, enfeebled metaphors, sickly conformism, sclerosis by folklore, aggressive monolingualism, and nationalist myopia. After analysing one of Jeremić's long, laudatory, and ill-written reviews of a well-established Serbian author,[100] Kiš perorated fiercely:

---

99 Kiš adapted this word from "schizophysiology", which was coined by Arthur Koestler in an attempt to account for mankind's "chronic, quasi-schizophrenic split between reason and emotion" in terms of evolutionary physiology.

100 This was Antonije Isaković, who would play a disgraceful role in Serbia's nationalist delirium of the 1980s and early 1990s.

And all this accumulates on paper, word by word, page by page, day after day, year after year, layer on layer, like guano, in our newspapers and magazines, then gets bundled together as books, so it turns into a 'work', an *oeuvre*, an *opus*, and then these selfsame books win prizes and praise, they get written up in the selfsame coprophagic hackwork, and so it goes on, and these selfsame books gather on library shelves, unneeded and forgotten in the dimness of dank stockrooms (but looming large in Jeremić's bibliography, one after another, like steps in a staircase ascending to the Academy and Immortality), without anyone ever asking our public, loud and clear, why books like this are written at all, and who benefits from Jeremić's illiterate and harmful exertions.

Demolished by Kiš, Dragan Jeremić made a virtue of necessity. In *Narcissus without a Face*, he parades his inability to refute the allegations of banality and kitsch as evidence of noble self-restraint (contrasting with his unhinged assailant). The rictus of professorial equanimity was a mask for Jeremić's dismay that, after industrious decades in the state-subsidised comfort of Serbia's literary community, he would be known to posterity as a 24-carat buffoon or, worse still, an emblem of sinister and overweening mediocrity.

Jeremić made no distinction between the views of E.S. in *Hourglass* and Kiš himself. He was unable to consider E.S. as a fictional character. He portrayed Kiš as a consistent and conspiratorial plagiarist, building a career by forging literature. So primitive was his conception of originality, and so complete his inability to understand intertextuality and the poetics of montage, that his denunciations hold no interest except as symptoms of the cultural belatedness that Kiš and his supporters saw as a hallmark of Yugoslav provincialism. After all, a century had passed since Edmond de Goncourt denigrated Flaubert's supposed lack of creativity and a full half-century since T. S. Eliot and James Joyce were accused of similar offences. What would Jeremić have made of Lawrence Sterne's playful purloining in *Tristram Shandy*? What about Igor Stravinsky's reworkings of Bach and Tchaikovsky, or Pablo Picasso's ransacking of world culture? What about Georges Perec's 1967 work, *Un homme qui dort*, "an autobiographical novel of which practically every phrase had already been written by someone else"?[101] Did Jeremić truly believe that citing a non-fictional text to obtain a literary effect in a work of fiction was ethically indistinguishable from passing off another writer's efforts as one's own?

---

101 Including Kafka, Melville, Joyce, and Dante, according to Perec's biographer, David Bellos. But Perec published in Paris, not Belgrade.

It is easy to share the scepticism of a French scholar who cannot believe that Jeremić and the others really meant their accusations of plagiarism. But they were in earnest. Kiš's exasperation was not feigned: he could scarcely believe the stupidity of his accusers or the leaden insolence of their accusations. Yet this would not by itself have spurred Kiš to such anger. (At least one of his supporters, Velimir Visković, publicly regretted his furious, all too "Balkan" mode of self-defence.) To understand his reaction, we need to keep in mind the ulterior threats that came to rival and even dwarf the original allegations.

The nationalist dimension in Jeremić's attacks was lightly coded. For he accused Kiš of denigrating "local traditions and contemporary currents in our literature". During his furious exchange with Matvejević, early in the affair, Jeremić remarked that matters which had begun in Serbia could hardly be monitored from Zagreb, "400 kilometres away". Warnings to people in another republic to mind their own business carried a powerful charge. In this case, the warning had pointed implications. If Croats had better keep their noses out of Serb quarrels, what right had an "ethnographic rarity" to criticise? Especially if he was "uniquely unoriginal", a contriver of fragments that could not "grow into an organic whole . . . incapable of spiritual reproduction"? While Jeremić expressed no anti-Semitic opinions, he disparaged Kiš in terms that were a hand's breadth from the familiar prejudice that Jewish artists were innately sterile.

Jeremić adapted this prejudice to the fixations of communist Yugoslavia. Hence Kiš was not only uncreative: he was anti-socialist. In contrast to the "wonderful optimism and faith in the future" that, as he claimed, shone from the writings of camp survivors, *Boris Davidovich* preached resignation in the face of injustice. In other words, Kiš was an enemy of progress, guilty of moral quietism, encouraging us to "lose faith in the possibility that man can be free and achieve peace and social justice". This insight led Jeremić to contend with a dialectical flourish that, far from opposing the horrors described in his book, Kiš really advocated "fatalistic reconciliation with evil in general and Stalinism in particular."

"Creativity should be the banner of new, socialist culture and of socialism as such", Jeremić concluded; for creativity belonged properly to "our resolve for a better future". Pandering to Titoist paranoia about Yugoslavia being forever menaced by foreign powers, which were only kept at bay by communist vigilance, Jeremić claimed that Kiš's servile attitude to "a series of foreign writers, many of whom would not merit a leading place in our literature, means in fact perpetuating our literature's former relationship towards foreign literature as the relationship between a colony and its metropole." Bent on undermining Serbia's or Yugoslavia's literary independence, what else was Kiš but a rootless cosmopolitan—a figure from anti-Semitic mythology (see chapter 22)—gnawing at the foundations of organic culture?

With this in mind, it is easier to see why Kiš reacted so strongly. Yet his friend Miroslav Karaulac wondered, in hindsight, if he should have defended himself at all, "because he had done nothing wrong. The accusations were comical: they simply revealed the aesthetic ignorance of his opponents." But not reacting was out of the question. Slobodan Vitanović, Kiš's colleague in Bordeaux, believes the attacks hit him "as proof that his worst fears were true": he too was destined for exclusion and victimisation—like his father, and like Jews down the centuries.

Some of Kiš's friends tried to discourage him from reacting. Borislav Pekić urged him not to be provoked by "intrigues" whose only purpose was to drag him into "provincial literary politicking". Mirjana, on the other hand, was adamant: he must respond with all guns blazing. When the journalist's attack was about to be published, Filip David was tipped off and advised to let Kiš know. Expecting that it would be "just the usual gossip", he decided not to bother. When David mentioned this at a later stage, Kiš was upset: "Why didn't you warn me?" he said. "I've got nothing but my writing. If they compromise me as a writer, I'll have nothing left." He had never built an institutional career; unlike Jeremić, he had no safety net. He was upset again when David relayed a message from Miodrag Bulatović that he, Kiš, was taking it all too seriously. Other friends, too, were warned bluntly to break any contact with his opponents. For Kiš, everything was at stake: his honour as a writer and a man, but also his status in his own country. He *would* be defiant, and he would *not* be a scapegoat. Like B. D. Novsky, he would fight for the integrity of his name.

Any time in the 1970s might have been politically inopportune for *Boris Davidovich*, but 1976 was unmistakably so. Tito's rule was in its last, phantasmagoric phase. The reform communist movements of the late 1960s had been scotched and a numbing orthodoxy had taken their place. Drained of idealism, the political system was turning into a simulacrum of itself—its own effigy or death-mask. Stagnation was the norm across communist Europe: in Czechoslovakia, a "bureaucratic order of grey monotony" stifled all individuality. "What prevails", wrote Václav Havel, "is *order without life*." In Poland, the Solidarity movement had not yet emerged. The United States was licking its wounds after Vietnam. Everywhere, the end of the Cold War was still unimaginable.

November 1976 brought an official Soviet visit to Yugoslavia. Led by the ailing Leonid Brezhnev, a month shy of his seventieth birthday, the visit was a reminder that bilateral relations were as sensitive as ever. Although the joint communiqué after the visit underlined "comradely voluntary co-operation", the Yugoslav elite still worried that Moscow would try to force the country back under the Soviet yoke as soon as Tito died. For the partisan generation that had lived through the war and the 1948 break with Stalin, these fears were ineradicable.

A story has circulated for decades—Kiš was aware of it—that Brezhnev criticised *Boris Davidovich* during his visit. At the end of a meeting with Tito, he supposedly brandished a copy of the book and complained that "anti-socialist writers" were published in Yugoslavia. Tito supposedly replied that statesmen had no need to concern themselves with writers, who could be safely left to their affairs; then, after the visitors had left, he approved a campaign against the troublesome author. As the scandal erupted in early November and Brezhnev left Belgrade on 17 November, the dates work out. It is easy to conjecture that the Soviet embassy fed this titbit to Brezhnev's team as something timely to use against the Yugoslavs.

A glance at the Yugoslav state archives found ample evidence that Brezhnev did indeed make much of the "anti-Soviet" views expressed by Yugoslav journalists and intellectuals. Tito calmly rebuffed the allegations. When his security officers swept the Soviet delegation's premises after their departure, they found a planted list of this material, complete with quotations. Kiš is not mentioned in the list, but this does not mean that evidence will not turn up. Brezhnev mentioned at the first formal meeting, on 15 November, that he had already discussed the "anti-Soviet" problem with Tito; so it is possible that *Boris Davidovich* was raised on that occasion.

Be this as it may, Kiš came to believe that his book's real offence was its refusal to concede any redemptive or consolatory gleam in the suffering and death inflicted by the Gulag system, and thus in communism as such. Whatever the truth, there might not have been a hostile reaction if someone else had written it. For Kiš's entire curriculum vitae invited attacks by reactionaries, envious writers, and uncomprehending professors. ("They haven't forgiven you for your talent," Miroslav Krleža had warned him in 1973, meaning by *they* the crowd of mediocrities who flourished in Yugoslavia's cultural institutions. The country's most prestigious literary figure, Krleža valued Kiš as the best writer of his generation, but when Kiš begged frantically for advice as the *Boris Davidovich* affair was brewing, the other man was brusque. "You deliberately goad the world around you with your pen, so what's there to be surprised about now?" Instead of "dramatizing" an escalation that was "completely natural and logical", Kiš should let the storm-in-a-teacup blow itself out. As the veteran of countless polemical battles, the survivor of three dictatorships, and Tito's intimate, the eighty-three-year-old Krleža was either too tired or too canny to get involved.)

The scandal fixed Kiš's reputation among Serbia's political elite as a shady character, esteemed in the West, probably unpatriotic. In the mid-1980s, Yugoslavia's Minister of Defence Nikola Ljubičić—soon to be a co-conspirator of Slobodan Milošević against Yugoslavia's constitutional order—opposed a move to award Kiš a prestigious prize "because he was an émigré, some kind of enemy". A senior communist wrote in his memoirs that he did not care for *Boris Davidovich* "either as literature (though it is not worthless from that point of view), or for the perspectives that it expresses. Its anti-Stalinism is sheer anti-socialism. Apart from that, it is burdened with very explicit Zionism (so it seems to me)."[102] The mud stuck. In 2003, the authorities in Subotica quashed a proposal to name a street after Kiš, apparently because someone in the city hall claimed to have heard from "a friend in Paris" that Kiš was "a mere plagiarist".

Even if the hostility of such people meant nothing to Kiš, he was too sensitive to slights, too easily stirred by injustice, and too insecurely placed in his own culture not to be shaken. He neither forgot nor forgave. And in a sense, he won. *The Anatomy Lesson* became a cult book, reprinted and loved especially by younger readers. It ranks alongside Laza Kostić's *Book about Zmaj* (1902) and Krleža's *Settling Scores with Them* (1932) and *Dialectical Antibarbarus* (1939) at the summit of polemical literature in the language.[103]

The book gained a prophetic lustre a decade or so after its publication, when the nationalist-communist nexus that Kiš detected in his assailants came to define Serbia's official, public identity. How could his analysis of "genetic reductionism", for example, not strike readers in the 1990s as a prevision of evil times when genealogy (the scrutiny of surnames and bloodlines) would once again—as in the Second World War—be used by demagogues and warlords to enact the Day of Judgment on millions of Yugoslavia's citizens? By Kiš's own definition, "the greatest and rarest of writers" are those "ahead of their time", whose "perfect pitch detects the tremors of history like the approach of a mighty earthquake, whose sensitivity registers phenomena in embryo" that are "barely perceptible to others". Whether or not such writers really are the rarest and greatest, Kiš himself was among their number.

Yet, simply by taking part in the fight, he also lost. The excellence of his style, the lucidity of the theoretical sections (which have led *The Anatomy Lesson* to be acclaimed as "our first serious book on intertextuality"), the courage of his self-analysis, and the zest of his attacks cannot stifle a feeling that Kiš dignified his opponents with his attention; that—worst of all—he sank into the native mire for the only time in his writing life. In this sense his opponents won, and it gives the book an acrid taste.

"*The world is too brutal for me*": Kiš had copied the poet John Keats's statement of defeat into a student notebook, in English, long before. With this book,

---

102 This was Dragoslav Marković (1920–2005), who played a key role in the removal of Serbia's liberal reformist leadership in 1972. Four years later, he compiled a catalogue of Serbia's grievances with its position in Yugoslavia: a move that helped pave the way for Serbia's putsch a decade later.

103 Kiš's copy of Kostić's book is thickly scored and scribbled with admiring exclamations. To leaf through it is to hold the (countervailing) literary tradition of a nation in one's hands. Krleža's polemics, famous in their day, have become almost unreadable, less because their occasions are so remote than because their garrulous, pleonastic style has become hard to bear.

and then with his self-defence in court (see chapter 32), he faced up to the brutal world and won. He gambled everything on trumping his opponents with a book that had to be cleverer and more truthful and ruthless than anything they could produce. The fact that *The Anatomy Lesson* is his only book with a happy ending, yet he still left Belgrade, seemed to confirm his bleak view of history's power over literature, whose victories are beautiful and unavailing.

Let the last, fittingly wrathful words come from Mirjana Miočinović, speaking in 1999—the year when NATO states bombarded Serbia over the persecution of Albanians in Kosovo, a policy overwhelmingly supported by Serbian intellectuals. The scandal over *Boris Davidovich* was, she said,

> the first time this secret collusion between communism and nationalism showed itself very openly. . . . There was and still remains a fatal bond between Orthodoxy and the revolutionary myth, "pan-Slavism and Dostoevsky" as Kiš himself described this typically Serbian characteristic in 1986, ten years after the "affair".[104] That affair made me realise something that I at least consider to be a fact: namely, that the Serbian intelligentsia is the worst part of the Serbian people; that it carries within itself all the worst mental traits; that it is poisoned by the prejudices it transmits to others through the institutions it runs (culture, education, media); that it is the intelligentsia which made a principle out of hostility and contempt for the Other, behind which there actually lurks a fear of the Other. In my opinion it is guiltier than anyone else for causing all the events that led to what it now pathetically calls the "martyrdom" of the Serbian people.

---

104 The quotation is from Kiš's essay "Variations on Central European Themes" (1986), discussed in chapter 4.

As a lector for Serbo-Croatian language and literature
I have taught in Strasbourg, Bordeaux and Lille.

In 1962, Kiš applied successfully to be a lector at the University of Strasbourg. (As he was not a party member and had no family connections in high places, Vojislav Đurić's support was decisive.) He took up the appointment in the autumn and rented a small flat on the outskirts of the city.

Kiš liked to say that nothing in a writer's fate is accidental. This can be true only for writers who weave dense patterns from their own experience, as Kiš did; and even so, it is easy to see an elective affinity in this case. Strasbourg lies at the crossroads of history and language, with an identity as complex and conflicted as Kiš's own. It had changed hands five times in the space of a century, as France and Germany fought for supremacy.

Yet, when Kiš arrived, the city had embraced a peaceful future as the symbol and showpiece of (Western) Europe's new commitment to abandoning the annihilatory logic of nationalism. This rupture had been heralded by bright moments in the city's cultural history. Goethe, the proponent of world literature, had marvelled at the Gothic splendour of Strasbourg's cathedral. In 1882, the Yugoslav scientist Nikola Tesla built and successfully tested an induction motor here. The artist Hans or Jean Arp was born here in 1886 and grew up bilingual. And the Lithuanian-born philosopher Emmanuel Lévinas (1906–1995) began here the studies which led to his insight that "the self is only possible through recognition of the Other".

No city could have been better suited to stimulate Kiš, a passionate Europhile then coming to terms with the violence in his own history. His two years here were happy and productive. As well as translating poetry by Verlaine and Ady, he wrote a dozen poems of his own. He translated the *Exercises in Style* by Queneau, the *Le Cid* of Pierre Corneille, and, with Mirjana, the *Maldoror* of Lautréamont. Above all, he found his voice in *Garden, Ashes*. A photograph shows him, spruce and cool, with a rockabilly haircut, at a café table with a colleague from the university's Slavic Institute. This was Wladimir Krysinski, the Polish language lector, who had arrived in Strasbourg a few months earlier. The two men became friends. Krysinski took note of Kiš's "impressive hair" and enjoyed his jokes about Tito. (The marshal visits an art exhibition. His entourage knows that he knows nothing about painting, so they wait anxiously for him to comment. Eventually Tito gestures at part of a canvas and says: "The green dominates **265**

With Wladimir Krysinski, coffee, and cigarettes. Strasbourg, 1963

here.")[105] As they got to know each other, Kiš told Krysinski about his translations, especially about Ady. He also introduced him to Mandelstam, as well as to Andrić and Krleža. "Danilo explained that he admired both writers but had a slight preference for Andrić. In particular, he seemed to like his sensitivity and simplicity. In his opinion, Krleža's expressionism was an excellent tool to narrate modern life as well as the bestiality and cruelty of war. And he was impressed by Krleža's erudition, which was always helpful in understanding the complexity of modern literature and philosophy." When Kiš was invited to lecture at the university's Institute of European Studies, he concentrated on Andrić (*Ex Ponto,* an early volume of poetical prose) and Krleža (*The Return of Filip Latinowicz*).

Krysinski introduced Kiš to another Polish student, Georges Krygier, who was studying dentistry. The three men worked hard all day and then relaxed in the cafés, spending their bit of disposable money on Alsatian wine. Krygier remembers Kiš as an 'eternal student', gregarious but unworldly, and "absolutely not materialistic. Charming and charismatic, not shy, yet remote. I had the feeling he lived in his own world." Krygier was impressed by Mirjana: "She was so beautiful, physically and as a person. She kept Kiš from smoking and drinking too much, but very discreetly. They were very careful with money, as we all had to be."

A Polish Jew, born in 1935, Krygier had survived the Warsaw ghetto. After the failed uprising of 1944, he lived in hiding with his father until early 1945. "Kiš and Krysinski were the only people I could talk with about the war," he recalls. "My story was so fantastic, French people thought I must be making it up." Kiš listened with deep attention. When his turn came to speak, his face twisted in dislike and he would shake his head, "as if he wanted to chase the bad memories away"; it was a sort of tic, Krygier says.

---

105 This joke was probably caused by Tito's speech in early 1963 attacking abstract art as a bourgeois deviation. (Soviet leader Nikita Khrushchev had done the same with more vehemence a year earlier.)

Krygier the victim of fascism became a naturalised Frenchman in 1965, while Krysinski chose not to return to Poland after his lectorship; today he is a professor of comparative literature in Montreal. Krygier became a distinguished dentist, a visiting professor at American universities, who still works long days in his Paris clinic.

Early in 1973, soon after *Hourglass* had won Serbia's prize for the best novel of the previous year, Kiš applied to be the language lector in Paris. When this was rejected, he applied for the University of Bordeaux. This time he succeeded.

One of the dozen students who enrolled for his class was Pascale Delpech, then in her second year studying Russian, with Serbo-Croatian as a second language. Kiš was shocked, she says, at how little they knew or had read; it was his first contact with the first post-literate generation. The students, in turn, were fascinated by their teacher's flamboyance and seriousness. When he arrived, he bore bruises from a fist fight in Belgrade. She learned later that an old acquaintance had 'revealed' one of Kiš's affairs to Mirjana in a letter; when the men met at the opening of the Belgrade book fair, Kiš went for him. They were surrounded by journalists covering the fair, so the scandal was very public. At the same time, Kiš was gloomy because—as he admitted to Pascale—the affair in question had ended.

While the students were taking the measure of this "strange apparition", in Pascale's phrase, they had to buckle down. "Danilo was an extravagant person in many ways, but he was a very serious teacher. Severe, punctual, never missing a lesson, respecting the university institutions, always telling us how ignorant we were, and how impolite. Sometimes he shouted at us. He was dismayed by our manners! But if you were interested, he was patient—and excellent." Lessons were followed by a drink in the café next to the faculty building. After a few months, with the class whittled down to five or six, he transferred the lessons to the café. Other teachers looked askance, but the students loved it.

Kiš was required to teach language only, but it was unthinkable to separate language from literature. His method was to inculcate grammar and vocabulary through poetry but also through stories, "lots of stories about writers, literature, larger-than-life characters," as Pascale recalls. Soon he had them translating verses by Crnjanski and sometimes by his friend Predrag Čudić. Towards the end of the first year, Kiš urged the students to apply for scholarships for language seminars that were organised along the Yugoslav coast. He prepared them for the beaches and cafés of Dalmatia by teaching them swearwords and songs. His guitar came with him to lessons.

There was another reason too why Kiš reached Bordeaux in a particular frame of mind. Before he left Belgrade, he told an old friend that his book-writing was over. He always felt this emptiness after finishing a book. The despair ran deeper after *Hourglass* because it left him with nothing more to say about his family. (Presumably this was why he applied, around this time, for a full-time post to teach translation studies in Novi Sad.) The theme he had explored for a decade was exhausted; who could say if another would ever take its place? He was racked with doubt for many months, before the stories that make up *A Tomb for Boris Davidovich* crystallised in his imagination.

He became close to Pascale, who was a gifted pupil as well as his smitten admirer. Born in Baden Baden (her father was an army officer), she moved to Bordeaux with her parents when she was twelve and began to learn Russian at fourteen. Compared to Kiš, she was conventional enough and no better read than the other students ("just a few poems of Baudelaire"). In other ways, she was strikingly different. It mattered that she was immune to the unthinking leftism that many students shared. When their liaison became more serious, Kiš said that he was married and would never leave his wife. She made no objection: would take what he had to give.

By the time Kiš applied again for the lectorship in Paris, in 1979, his life had been turned upside down, first by the scandal over *Boris Davidovich* and then by the defamation case brought by the journalist who had triggered the scandal. That case was thrown out by the court in March 1979 (see chapter 32).

The triumph in court was shadowed by a looming crisis in his personal life. The relationship with Pascale had endured. When he returned to Belgrade from Bordeaux in 1976, she followed and spent the next three years in Novi Sad. Mirjana was aware of Pascale as one of Kiš's admiring ex-students, probably a former or occasional girlfriend who was now his translator, bringing his work to the wider world. In that capacity, she had helped the younger woman in practical ways.

This arrangement was both convenient and torturous for Kiš. The relationship with Mirjana, his mainstay for decades, had easily weathered earlier infidelities. She had not questioned him about his affairs; for his part, he had not misled her before about their importance. In the past, confession on his part had sometimes been answered with sympathy and even advice. Intellectually they were as close as ever; she had been steadfast and implacable during the *Boris Davidovich* scandal, urging him to give his critics no quarter. Now Pascale was involved with his writing: a form of intimacy that had been Mirjana's unique privilege. He was tormented by the unfairness of keeping her in ignorance of Pascale's place in his life, and by the certainty of hurting her terribly if he admitted that she had a rival. If something was missing from the marriage before Kiš met Pascale, it was nothing that Mirjana had felt to be fundamental.

When the application for Paris failed, again, he applied for the lectorship in Lille, near the border with Belgium, and got it. Between walking free from the courtroom in March and leaving for France in October, he told Mirjana the truth. She was shattered. The stress of the situation was increased by the fact that her father Đura, much loved by Kiš, was stricken with cancer. (He died in December.)

He and Pascale moved to Paris, where they rented tiny flats in adjacent buildings in the tenth arrondissement. According to the American writer Edmund White, Kiš lived "alone in a working-class district. In his room there are a desk, a chair and a bed, nothing more—the Platonic room. Or, better, the room of a writer who has embraced simplicity to ensure his freedom." The flat was a short walk from the Gare du Nord. Lille was an hour away by train. Kiš had little enthusiasm for teaching but he needed the money. Perhaps, too, in his mid-forties, he resented having to work at a level so far below his abilities and achievements, trying to enthuse students whose real interest lay elsewhere (usually in learning Russian), leaving him to drum the elements of Serbo-Croatian into their heads. Interviewed on television in Belgrade in 1982, he shook his head in bafflement: "None of my French students knows a single poem by heart, in French. None!" This disaffection coloured a story that he wrote while he was still there:

> On Friday I went to Lille, for my teaching. I had about ten students; I talked about "an idiom from the great family of Slavic languages, which along with Russian and Polish . . .". I tried to use Madame Yourcenar's tumultuous admission to the Academy to introduce them to Serbian folk poetry, which Mme Yourcenar appreciates, as witness her *Oriental Tales*. They had not read Marguerite Yourcenar. So I tried love poems. Sonnets. They didn't know what a sonnet is. Then alexandrines, as in Racine. They didn't know what an alexandrine is. (Some sort of bourgeois con-trick, for sure.) Then I shifted to palatalisation and assibilation. This seemed to catch their interest. They wrote it all down in their exercise books. So I had to mug up on palatalisation and assibilation in the train. . . .

There was at least one exception. Alain Cappon, a student of Russian, took Kiš's course in his last year and went on to become a noted translator from Serbo-Croatian. He remembers Kiš as always soberly dressed, a satchel over his shoulder, taking any opportunity to reach for his cigarettes. The students knew he was a well-known writer and admired his simplicity—not like French writers, with their airs and graces. When Cappon tried his hand at translating, Kiš was complimentary but warned him to beware, for translation is addictive. Cappon invited him to dinner; he came, approved the choice of vodka ("Stolichnaya: it's a good one"), and finished the bottle.

To his students, Cappon says, Kiš was "the perfect Yugoslav". He was employed as "lector for Serbo-Croatian language", with no reference to literature. In a report on his first year, however, Kiš said that he taught Serbo-Croatian language and grammar, and *Yugoslav civilisation*, a poignant term. Cappon recalls no broad discussions about civilisation, but remembers very well how Kiš insisted that he was teaching them Serbo-Croatian, not Serbian or Croatian, and "flew into a rage" if he thought a student was mocking or questioning the duality of the language.

Kiš was not given to discussing Serbo-Croatian in print, but it seems likely that he saw this language as the foundation of Yugoslavia's unity as a state. By defending the one, he upheld the other. He was also defending himself: his hybrid origins, his refusal to opt for the sectarian identities that were available (Serbian, Montenegrin, Jewish). He wrote the Ekavian variant of Serbo-Croatian, which is the more Serbian vowel form; but he used the Latin alphabet, which is more Croatian than the Cyrillic alphabet. His language is syntactically pure with a Flaubertian purity but lexically impure, laced with artful colloquialisms, occasional Montenegrin words, and Hungarian and Germanic (Habsburg) words, phrases and proper names which bring a flavour of Vojvodina, and very few of the Turkisms that enrich the language in the old Ottoman territories of Serbia and Bosnia.

What was called the "Serbo-Croatian language space" extended from Istria in the northwest to the Albanian, Macedonian, and Bulgarian marches in the south and south-east. This space encloses a variety of dialects and usages, as well as two alphabets. The anomalous oddity of Serbo-Croatian was not lost on Kiš; to the contrary, he liked its inauthenticity: the very feature that offended nationalists. As he told a conference in France, in spring 1989, "I was a lector for a long time, but I never managed to explain to my students which language they were learning! I told them it was the language spoken in Yugoslavia, but I was devious enough not to add that it isn't the only language spoken there." Indeed not; only some 70 per cent of Yugoslavs had Serbo-Croatian as their mother tongue. The remainder had Slovenian, Macedonian, Albanian, Hungarian, or one of a dozen minority languages.

Although language policy in communist Yugoslavia tried to ensure equality among the country's major languages, Serbo-Croatian was first among equals, the lingua franca. The name dates from the mid-nineteenth century, when writers and intellectuals agreed to form a unified language. In 1954, the year Kiš went to Belgrade, linguists and writers met in Novi Sad to affirm that the "national language of Serbs, Croats, and Montenegrins

The Platonic room. Paris, February 1989

is one language." It would be called Serbo-Croatian in Serbia, and Croato-Serbian, or 'Croatian or Serbian', in Croatia. This compromise did not mollify cultural nationalists in either republic, who refused to commit themselves to a single linguistic standard. Croatian writers in particular insisted on the primacy of the Croatian literary language.

Kiš publicly despised this linguistic nationalism. "The reputation of certain Yugoslav writers rests entirely on sectarianism," he remarked. "They are first and foremost Serb or Croat (depending on their programme) and only then writers: the adjective counts for more than the noun." Nationalist writers freely choose their identities—even or especially if their choice is to deny that they have any, due to some fateful genetic birthright or ethnic pre-emption. He was astonished that writers from Yugoslavia could not see how their own interest lay in promoting a single Yugoslav literature. The wider world had no curiosity about the literatures of peoples whose names they could barely say, let alone remember. In 1989, probably the year when Yugoslavia's violent demise became inevitable, he was introduced at a conference as a Serbo-Croatian writer. His jokey response acknowledged the genuine problem of definition: "I am not a Serbo-Croatian writer, I am more a Montenegrin, if I'm not a writer from Vojvodina, to some extent a Jewish writer, with a completely Hungarian surname. . . . My surname means 'small', although I'm 1.85 metres tall. . . . I am not South African or Czech, I am a *Yugoslav* writer. Many Yugoslav writers don't accept that designation. They prefer to be Serb or Croat, but never both at the same time. . . ."

He is being provocative in the *Birth Certificate* when he mentions Serbo-Croatian literature in the singular. In the 1950s, it was still possible to speak of Yugoslav literature as a single entity. This changed during the 1960s to "Yugoslav literatures", a usage that Kiš accepted. This was reasonable because of literature written in Slovenian and Macedonian, not to mention the minority languages. By the 1970s at the latest, it was standard to refer to Serbian and Croatian literatures, plural—and Kiš sometimes did so too. But he believed that all literature in Serbo-Croatian formed a whole. In his own translations, he took the entire language area and its literary heritage as his diapason. To replicate the colloquial dialogue in Molière's *Don Juan*, he drew on the Croatian renaissance drama of Dubrovnik, mixed with modern slang from the same city. For Juan himself, Kiš looked to the comedies of Jovan Sterija Popović (1806–1856), a Serbian playwright from Vojvodina. He was pleased with the result, rightly seeing it as an innovation.

His particular targets were Serb and Croat intellectuals who made cults of their respective languages—"so alike in structure, so different in aroma". These cults defined each language against the other, maximising the mutual differences regardless of the price. Yugoslav linguistics and lexicography were always the continuation of politics by other means. As Yugoslavia spiralled down to its terminal crisis, dictionaries of national differences within Serbo-Croatian began to appear. When one of these was published in Belgrade in 1989, Kiš annotated its errors. According to this lexicographer, *zrcalo* is the Croatian word for "mirror" (*ogledalo* in Serbian). In the margin, Kiš scribbled a famous phrase from Njegoš's *The Mountain Wreath*—the jewel of Serbian and Montenegrin literature—about a monkey gazing upon its image in a *zrcalo*. Endeavours to differentiate the national components within Serbo-Croatian were worse than futile: they might—as they ultimately did—succeed, which would destroy the unified communication space. This was deplorable for literature, because it diminished the range of available expression; writers who encouraged this process were cutting off the branch they sat on. And it was politically ominous, for national differentiation by language foreshadowed the territorial definition of nations.

Around 1990, the new constitutions of Croatia and Serbia declared that Croatian and Serbian, respectively, were their official languages. In Bosnia and Herzegovina, both languages were recognised along with a third: Bosnian. By 1993, a historian relates, "the Serbo-Croatian / Croato-Serbian language ceased to exist on the political and on the legal levels. On the personal level, this meant that for official purposes (school enrolment, population census, job applications, etc.) the option of naming one's language Serbo-Croatian no longer existed." Kiš's mother tongue ceased to exist.

Official language policy has continued to codify the Croatian, Montenegrin, Serbian, and Bosnian variants, institutionalising regional differences as national. Yet patriotic intellectuals are still frustrated by the endless difficulty of separating the languages, with their two or more heads but a single heart and pair of lungs. And they are still driven to vituperative distraction by sceptics who refuse to accept that dialectal differences amount to a sovereign entity. By a painful if appropriate irony, the only international institution which still upholds the unity of the "Serbo-Croatian language space" is the War Crimes Tribunal in The Hague, which adds insult to the injuries of its martyred detainees—all bar one or two innocent in their own eyes—by sticking to "BCS", meaning Bosnian-Croatian-Serbian, in all of its workings, from indictments to sentences. (Some people insert an M for Montenegrin, making BCMS, presumably to reassure the indictees from Montenegro that they have equal status.)

Kiš loved his language with insubordinate devotion. Erich Auerbach once wrote that a critic's greatest asset is his own national language and culture; for this asset to become "truly effective", however, the critic must be separated from this heritage and then "transcend" it. Kiš underwent this schism and transcendence by moving to Hungary in 1942 and then to Montenegro in 1947, when he relearned his mother tongue. He invested everything in the remastered language, and by the mid-1960s may well have come to believe that *Garden, Ashes* had secured his permanent acceptance in Belgrade. If so, this belief did not survive an experience in 1968, when he joined a tour to Russia with the Atelije 212 theatre (see chapter 29). As the company caroused during the long train journey home, Kiš started to sing a favourite folk-song. One of the company snapped at him: "Why are you singing that Croatian song? We've let you write in this language. . . ." The message was clear: you are still an outsider, don't abuse our hospitality. Mirjana Miočinović (the source of the story) believes this may have been Kiš's first real encounter with Yugoslavia's internal nationalist bickering. That Kiš was shocked is clear from the opening stanza of a squib written some time afterwards:

So you let me write in this language?
And which other would I write in but
Our own? In "Biblical" perhaps—Hebrew?
When this is the language I think and breathe in,
Dream in, hold in my little finger. . . .

The baffled hurt is explicit, as is the *esprit d'escalier*—the wish that he had not been dumbfounded in the train. "Our own" is the pointed riposte, before venting his anger at the tacit anti-Semitism. That incident was surely in the back of his mind a decade later when he set down his credo as a counter-attack against critics who had accused him of writing derivative, second-hand literature:

> I believe that every work of value is an act of revolt against the writer's own and only language. . . .
>
> Which is why I wish to state here and now to those who would fear for my soul that I have no need for them to absolve me of my sin, which is to write in the language I write in, no need for their firmans or ukazes, because I do not recognise them, no need for their bulls or indulgences, because it is my language! And if we fail to understand one another . . . it is not because the authors of the firmans and ukazes do not understand what I say and write: no, our misunderstandings are of an entirely different nature: they take place on the intellectual and moral level, and I refuse to allow them to impose their standards—be they linguistic or literary or moral—on me. We simply do not speak the same language. Thanks be to the Lord God of Sabaoth!

Yet the traditionalists who never accepted Kiš were not wholly mistaken. Their pack instinct told them he was different; and so he was; he did not share their aspirations and affiliations, or their mode of belonging. (Jewishness was a label for that difference, as he acknowledged by capping his defiance with a Hebrew word.) And he had no secure alternative base between his fellow writers in the language that bound them together, for better or worse, and the wider world's indifference to all their divisive obsessions. In a fragment dating from 1986 and then discarded, presumably for being too raw and personal, he dramatised the pressures on a writer in his position: living abroad, working in his native (Central European) language while resisting powerful currents within it:

> He is around fifty years old—certainly no less—and lives in exile (like Kundera), writing in his mother tongue: Czech, Slovak, Polish, Hungarian, Serbo-Croatian, perhaps Yiddish (though he seems too young for that). Whichever it is, he writes it like a dead language, which only makes it more precious. He still speaks and reads French, German, Hungarian, Russian, he's been bilingual since birth and learned the others later, but everyone asks him—this solitary (as it

seems to him) guardian of his far-off and close-up mother tongue, they all want to know why he doesn't write in French, German, English—and he's already explained a hundred, a thousand times that one does not write with language but with one's whole being: with myths, traditions, consciousness and subconsciousness, with entrails, memories, and everything else that turns into automatism at the stroke of a hand: into random metaphors, associations, literary allusions, idiocies, unintended or deliberate quotations. For he—and this is truly what Central European writers do—drags around a terrible burden of linguistic and musical melodies; he hauls a piano and a dead horse behind him, along with everything that has been played on that piano and everything that the horse once bore into battle and to defeat—marble statues and bronze bearded busts, pictures in baroque frames, words and melodies that nobody can understand outside that language, *realia* which in other languages need to be explained with long footnotes—the wide world of unknown allusions, wars, epic poems, epic heroes, historical and culturological data, Turkisms, Germanisms, Magyarisms, Arabisms each with its clear and precise semi-tone. . . . For he (unlike a Russian, Frenchman, Englishman, or German) cannot allow himself not to learn and know any other language than his own. . . Idioms, expressions, proverbs, riddles, fables, synonyms that must be used selectively, for synonyms are not the selfsame word or sound or colour: "*kara-tamna noć*", with its resonant Turkism "*kara*", is not the same as "*crna noć*" or "*tamna noć*", for that "*kara*" stirs historical associations, it implies some ethnographic, ethnological, indeed national, heavy, thick, impasto darkness, filled with cries and screams, horses neighing, children weeping, mothers wailing: this is black darkness like blood, like a raven [*gavran*], like the two "black ravens" [*vrana gavrana*] in the epic poem,[106] where the new synonym "*vran*" [black] is, if not quite a new colour or a new shade of blackness, then a new adjective which goes with a new noun. "*Vran*" is the colour of a girl's hair, for example, and it isn't the same as "black hair", not merely black but pitch-black or inky, just as the night can be "*tavna-tavna*", which is, again, no longer that same Turkish, bloody night filled with screams and horror, but rather the night at moonrise, lilac-scented, serene and. . . lyrical.[107]

And he knows that all this, all these sounds, the entire instrumentarium of his language, gets lost in translation. He knows that "*black*" is not the same as "*kara*", "*vran*", "*taman*" or "*tavan*", he knows that the French "*noir*" is actually a

---

106 "*Vrana gavrana*" occur in the cycle of folk poems about the battle of Kosovo in 1389, which Kiš would have heard at his mother's knee. In the nineteenth century, nation-building intellectuals acclaimed these poems as the foundation of Serbian literature, and not only literature.

107 In the Serbian language, *kara* (black) is an undeclined adjective of Turkish origin. *Taman* (f. *tamna*) means dark, dim, murky. *Noć* means night. *Crn* (f. *crna*) means black or dark. Raven is *gavran*. *Vrana* is a crow, and *vran* (f. *vrana*) means jet-black, black as crow or raven feathers. *Tavan* (f. *tavna*), meaning murky or sombre, is another adjective of Turkish origin.

lighter hue, as Mallarmé said it was, and that "*jour*", with its muffled, drawn-out "*-ou-*" would really be a better word for night, as if language toys with meaning, sticking a white label on the night and a black label on the day without rhyme or reason, and he knows that "*schwarz*" and "*Nacht*" are by dint of their brevity, their staccato, not the same as "*crn*", or "*tavan*", "*taman*", "*kara-taman*", or "*noč*", "*noćca*", and "*kosa vrana*".[108] And he knows that no translation, not even the finest, can catch all the meanings, all the levels of his language, all its historic, literary, national, confessional, ethnographic, poetic associations; and he smiles sadly when critics say his books sound better in French than in the original, where it goes without saying that the original was written in some barbaric language or other, and the meaning of all that incomprehensible barbaric stuttering only becomes clear, intelligible and justified in translation.

Which is why he smiles a little bitterly when they say "Do write in French, you speak such beautiful French!", for they don't know that speaking beautifully and writing are not the same, they don't know that a writer's language is his destiny and every attempt at foreign intervention, every violence against that destiny is like a surgical procedure or genetic mutation from which one cannot emerge intact or unchanged.

---

108 *Noćca* is the untranslatable hypocorism of *noć*. *Kosa vrana* means raven hair, jet-black hair.

17922/233

Kao lektor za srpskohrvatski jezik i književnost boravio sam
u Strazburu, Bordou i Lilu. ~~Trenutno~~ *Poslednjih godina* živim u Parizu, ~~~~ u desetom
arondismanu, i ne bolujem od nostalgije; ~~~~ kad se probudim,
ponekad ne znam gde sam: čujem kako se našijenci dozivaju, ~~i piškara~~
~~ju,~~ a iz kola parkiranih pod mojim prozorom ~~~~ sa
kasetofona, trešti harmonika.

(1983)

For the last few years I have been living in Paris, in the tenth *arrondissement*, and am not homesick; sometimes I wake up not knowing where I am: I hear our countrymen calling to one another, and an accordion blaring from the cassette player in a car parked under my window.

Kiš's departure for France at the end of summer 1979 was the climax of a tumultuous year. The previous September, he had faced charges brought by the Belgrade journalist who had accused him of plagiarism in 1976. Golubović alleged criminal defamation: in *The Anatomy Lesson*, he was described as "militantly ignorant" and "scandal-mongering". He claimed damages of 1 million dinars. (The court estimated Kiš's monthly income as 5,000 dinars.) Bizarrely, the plaintiff offered to drop the action if Kiš submitted to a psychiatric profile and was found to be "mentally incompetent" or suffering from diminished responsibility. If the profile found Kiš to be fully *compos mentis*, the journalist would demand a prison sentence. He took similar action against Kiš's ally Predrag Matvejević in Zagreb. The novelist Miodrag Bulatović, meanwhile, demanded that *The Anatomy Lesson* be banned (even though its first print-run of 4,000 copies had almost sold out) and blustered to journalists that he would demand 10 million dinars in damages.[109]

Court proceedings in a one-party state are a perilous business. Kiš told Boško Mijanović that the police had come to his flat and pressed him to leave Yugoslavia. He had replied that he refused to become a dissident: he would not leave the country unless he could return whenever he chose. The prosecution twice approached Karlo Štajner for a statement against Kiš. Štajner refused. When his sister Danica begged Kiš to hire a lawyer, he refused.

In October 1978, before a crowded public gallery, Kiš demonstrated the strict accuracy of his characterisation. The plaintiff had, he argued demurely, misunderstood the genre of polemical literature. He had not attacked the plaintiff in any personal way; rather, he had presented him as a "type" of the ambitious, malicious journalist who meddles in matters beyond his comprehension. This was why Golubović was nowhere named in *The Anatomy Lesson*. (The plaintiff was outraged by the suggestion that not he but his literary double was Kiš's target.) Everyone is free to choose his or her affinity and tradition, Kiš declared; for himself, he was proud to link his name with the anti-obscurantist tradition from Voltaire to Baudelaire, Laza Kostić, Krleža, and Vinaver.

---

109 Bulatović went on to become an outspoken nationalist and supporter of Slobodan Milošević.

Turning the tables, he told the court how shameful it was that practically nobody had objected to the plaintiff's "open and unambiguous racism" when his attacks on Kiš and his book were published, for example when he alleged that all the stories in *Boris Davidovich* centred on "Jewish rebels". For the plaintiff had set himself up not only as a literary expert "but also as an *expert on racial purity*, appealing to *everyone who shares a concern about the national culture*. This was and is a racist *and Nazi* programme," Kiš stated dramatically. Other accusations were just as malignant, such as that Kiš's choice of American publisher for *Boris Davidovich* could "only serve Cold War tendencies", because this publisher supposedly favoured anti-communist books.

The curtain fell on the *Boris Davidovich* affair on 22 March 1979, when the court dismissed the case. A higher court rejected the journalist's appeal. Meanwhile, the court in Zagreb suspended the case against Matvejević.

While Kiš's literary vindication was complete, his private life was in disarray. When he flew to Paris, it was understood that the separation from Mirjana would be a kind of estrangement. They still shared an address and continued to meet when Kiš visited Belgrade. In early summer 1981, Mirjana told him that she could not carry on like this, and they should get a divorce. *If that's what you want*, Kiš said quietly. It was not what she wanted—quite the opposite: mention of divorce was a desperate gamble to get him back. Once uttered and answered, the words were not recalled. Kiš's compliance may have been motivated by a sense of guilt (a divorce was the least he could give her), or by realism (the marriage was over anyway). It is impossible to be sure.

The divorce was quickly arranged. On 2 July 1981, a broiling summer day, the couple went to the district court to sign the papers. Mirjana remembers that they looked so miserable, the judge suggested kindly that they might be reconciled one day. The proceedings were brief. It so happened that the trial of a writer was scheduled to begin that day, elsewhere in the building; the poet Gojko Đogo stood accused of spreading "enemy propaganda" and defaming the person and works of Tito in his book, *Woolly Times*. Kiš was interested in the case and hurried off to observe the trial. Mirjana found herself alone on the steps outside the court building. This, of all fates, she had never expected after twenty-seven years. Belgrade shimmered like a desert. She went home, collected all her letters from Kiš, and destroyed them.

———

When journalists asked why he had moved to Paris, Kiš answered in terms of cultural history and literary affinity, avoiding personal detail. "My generation marks the end of a long tradition of Yugoslav intellectuals in France. This is closely bound up with language. Nowadays everybody speaks English, but in my day we mostly learned French at school. For us it was Paris, only Paris." The account of his first trip to Paris, in August 1959, confirms that he really had expected it to be the metropole of world culture.

Pascale (who learned of Kiš's divorce only after the fact) believes the principal reason behind his decision was the scandal over *Boris Davidovich*. A mixture of disgust at the treachery of old acquaintances like Šćepanović and Bulatović, and disappointment at the lukewarm support from other quarters, had made Belgrade intolerable. His old friend Pavle Đonović thought he was driven by spite. Others saw it as a natural step by an ambitious writer in pursuit of wider fame. He may have told another friend that he had to get away from Serb and Croat nationalists, "or he would go mad".

What's clear is that he kept one foot in Belgrade. He remained a Yugoslav citizen with a passport, which he used often. He was not a dissident and refused to be characterised as an opponent of the Yugoslav regime. If he was in exile, it was in an ironic, voluntary, "Joycean" sense. Belgrade became another source of recrimination and self-reproach, turning on the wronged figure of Mirjana. For "no one abandons a community without regret", as he would write a few years later.

The complexity of this tie to his homeland is captured by this long sentence in the *Birth Certificate*; if the assurance that he is "not homesick" comes too quickly to convince, the next clause deepens our doubts (and makes us wonder where he was before he awoke; "I dream about what I've been reading more often than about any other experience", he once said). He clinches the matter by framing an image of, precisely, homesickness, or circumstances that generate homesickness. The image is so lucid that it almost hurts. Kiš heightens the tension between his narrator-double's declaration ("am not homesick") and the undertow that pulls the reader in the opposite direction by dropping in a dialect word with an aroma of Montenegro, pungent as garlic. This is *našijenci*, meaning "our countrymen". The word occurs nowhere else in his work.

"Homesick" translates Kiš's cardinal word *nostalgija*. Nostalgia is memory's brooding double, the twin that saps the energy of recollection, channelling its creative juice into stagnant sumps. As remembrance was his literary element, nostalgia was a perennial temptation, impossible to disown. "And so, gradually and quite unconsciously, my mother poisoned me with memories," says Andi in *Garden, Ashes*, "nurturing a passion for old photographs and mementoes, soot and patina." What he calls "the preciousness of memory" is never quite safe from the false currency of nostalgia.

Political nostalgia is just as toxic. There is an extraordinary passage in the account that he wrote after that first trip to Paris, in 1959, with a group of students. Kiš is sitting in a café when his ears prick up.

> At the next table, facing me, a group of middle-aged people including a woman are huddled desperately together, talking in "our language", and, as far as I can gather from random fragments, holding a more or less mystical séance to conjure up memories. I know them all so well, with their feverish eyes, crippled or deeply scarred, old and young alike. . . . The émigrés of the world are all the same. Those from the Twenties who abandoned Mother Russia under the Red

invasion, those who fled across the Stone Bridge from the people's terrible justice around nineteen forty-five,[110] those who escaped from Budapest in October '56, those young people who tossed their passports off the top of the Eiffel tower with a flourish to signal their western European emancipation—they are all the same. They all gather year after year in this or that café, packed fearfully together like conspirators and missionaries for Eternal Justice and Vengeance; there they sit packed together over their plates of native Serbian *ćevapčići* and beans, or Russian *pirozhki*, or Hungarian *pörkölte* and paprikash, and day after day, year after year, they perform rituals of nostalgic remembrance and political backbiting over their spicy native dishes, in the name of Eternal Justice, the People, the Emperor and King by God's grace and the people's will. . . . But all these Quixotic storm-troopers, tilting at their windmills (symbolised by the static *Moulin Rouge* in Pigalle) in a vengeful pandemonium of thwarted Justice, whose eyes are tightly bound as if her head is throbbing: all these eternal émigrés and Don Quixotes suffer—insofar as they have not lost all trace of human feeling—from acute or chronic nostalgia . . . the sole remaining emotion that still keeps them warm, and stops them putting a bullet in their own brains, or opening the taps on the gas ovens in their one-star hotel rooms.

This savage comedy catches the apocalyptic tone of émigré polemics; but there is an overflowing animus against these nameless figures. Kiš is disgusted by the futility of their lives, by the bleeding solidarity that holds them captive in their echo chambers. It is practically a vision of hell.

By an irony that would never have trapped the older Kiš, this attack on the émigrés' lack of individuality collectivises his own prose. Anyone growing up in Tito's federation knew that Yugoslavia had always generated waves of political emigration: democratic, anti-communist, nationalist, pro-fascist. Some were war criminals; a few were liberal intellectuals. Collectively, they formed a standard target of communist propaganda. In this passage, uniquely, Kiš comes across as a callow Yugoslav patriot.

The strength of emotion measured his vulnerability. For Kiš was so nearly an émigré himself, and the generic fate of émigrés could so easily have been his own. They are separated by a hair's breadth, and he feels their bitter and deluded, artless condition as a threat. Only literature had saved him from damnation by historical misfortune. By 1959, he had established himself in Belgrade, academically and socially; the bond with Mirjana was maturing into a foundation. This passage shows how precarious his inward security really was.

When he returned to this theme at the other end of his writing life, his stance was different. In "Nabokov, or Nostalgia" (1986), he contrasts Nabokov's abstention from "traditional political struggles" with the endeavours of his fellow Russian émigrés:

---

110 *Stone Bridge* alludes to a town in Slovenia, Zidani Most, where a large number of pro-Axis Yugoslavs and others swept up in the retreat from Tito's vengeful partisans were killed in May 1945.

In both Berlin and Paris he had seen countless talents burn themselves out in the flames of political passion and nostalgia, in polemics, feuds, poverty and madness, escape into messianism, pan-Slavism, Occidentalism, Spiritist evocations of the Russian past, Orthodoxy, nationalism, anti-Semitism, treachery, espionage, palmistry and Nirvana, or else, driven by nostalgia and equating Bolshevism with populism, return to "Russia" and spiritual slavery, judicial murder, or suicide.

Turning to the other, private meaning of nostalgia, Kiš suggests that Nabokov's art draws its splendour from a childhood that let memory and nostalgia be one and the same, undivided. The "master-magician" was nourished all his life by this childhood, which he experienced at the time and ever after as "a world of kindness, beauty and love. . . . The Russia of his childhood is his lost paradise, his Paradise Lost, its images and archetypes (*pardon, maître!*) feeding his writing to the end of his days, with exile merely stimulating his nostalgia." The glories of Nabokov's fiction are what they are, beyond dispute; and yet there is a price: "Where civilisation and culture have ceased to exist, where man's spiritual and moral qualities have been destroyed, there is no place for Nabokov's characters or for parody, for games or memory." Is this price worth paying for a "world of illusion", where "the terrible tumult of history barely reaches"? Kiš is too discreet to reply, and these matters are hardly subject to conscious choice. We get the childhoods that we get. Yet one feels, behind the question, his awareness of the price he had paid for his own childhood and, more recently, for bringing that terrible tumult into his work.

{SEVENTH INTERLUDE}

The Encyclopaedia of the Dead (1983)

History is written by the victors. Legends are woven by the people. Writers fantasise. Only death is certain.

Once settled in Paris, Kiš began to write stories. Some took the form of legends; others treated episodes from his past life in Belgrade or his new life in France. By 1980, he wanted to select some of these stories for a book, unlike anything else he had published. He played with possible titles: Parables, The East-West Divan, The Encyclopaedia of the Dead . . . The book appeared at the end of 1983 as the last volume in his collected works.

Comprising nine stories of various lengths, *The Encyclopaedia of the Dead* fills only two hundred pages. Within these dimensions, Kiš included pastiche fables, literary criticism, the account of a harbour whore's funeral, a historical investigation, a tale of the supernatural, and a Borgesian composition about an infinite library. The settings range from biblical Samaria to Stalin's Russia. The book's unity is thematic (love and death) and stylistic; for the prose is patterned as densely as poetry, written against the grain of fictional luxuriance. Every detail and angle tells, and every shift between lyrical flight, erudite allusion, and granular aphorism adds meaning. The inane repetitions and incoherence of History are corrected by accountable form. Objects are always on the point of enlarging into archetypes or allegories of themselves. An interplanetary chill emanates from this constellation; its remote utterances and unfamiliar vistas grant the reader no consent to feel at home.

The first story is "Simon Magus", the name of a central figure in the heretical doctrines gathered under the term Gnosticism. These doctrines included belief in a higher God other than the Creator; disbelief in the humanity of Christ and in the Resurrection; and—in the words of a Victorian expositor—a will "to secure for the human spirit that liberty which is implied in its very nature." Gnosticism posed a threat to the early Church, which responded forcefully. "To check the inroads of Gnosticism the Church had to prohibit freedom. Dogma was made rigid; the idea of new revelation was forbidden; ecclesiastical government became official and oppressive." One scholar has traced "all Gnostic doctrines to the heresy of Simon Magus, the Samaritan Messianist and sorcerer mentioned in Acts 8.9–24." More than this: Simon may even "lie at the root of the ancient and medieval legends from which evolved the story of Faust". He was still dangerous enough in the 1470s to be depicted in a Florentine church fresco as heresy personified: aquiline in his robes, fluent and wicked before the aghast disciples, Peter and John.

It is a few years after the crucifixion of Christ, in Palestine, where the roads are thronged with disciples, "gentle, blue-eyed young men" who perch on wobbly barrels and flare with rage when contradicted. Simon wanders from village to village, denouncing Christ's followers as charlatans and their god as "a tyrant, a vindictive tyrant, and as cross as a crotchety old man". Encountering Peter, and challenged to perform a miracle, Simon declares that he will fly up to the sky. He flaps his arms, stays earthbound, is mocked, and redoubles his efforts. Concentrating on diverse evidence of earthly suffering, he then rises into the air.

As Simon dwindles to a dot below the clouds, Peter stands "petrified" by the threat of metaphysical pluralism: if what he witnesses is real, "then His miracles and the truth of the Christian faith were *but one of the truths of this world* and not the sole truth, then the world was a mystery and truth an illusion." He prays for help, and God answers: Simon has been allowed "to tempt Christian souls with his miracles, that I might show them there is no miracle without me, no power but mine." Shortly after, Simon plummets back to earth. "On the ground lay a heap of crushed, shattered bones and mangled flesh".

Kiš then gives a variant legend. Instead of trying to fly, Simon offers to be buried in the ground for three days. Far from emerging triumphantly from his coffin, however, his exhumed corpse is "a mass of leprous corruption". In each version, Simon's companion, the prostitute Sophia, sees the outcome as proof of his teaching: "Man's life is decay and perdition, and the world is in the grip of tyrants."

In 1984, a year after the story was published, Kiš was in contention for the prestigious Njegoš Prize. He lost to the Serbian poet Desanka Maksimović, mainly because a conservative juror was convinced that "Simon Magus" prophesied the collapse of communism. If the story does carry a political meaning, it concerns the vanity of artistic dissidence. For the story is an allegory of the enchantment of reading, or of art's relationship to history and force. Art's triumphs are epiphanies: spectacular and transient, absolute in their way but incapable of competing in worldly impact with faith or ideology. (Remember Kiš's definition of *literature*: "an attempt at a global vision of reality and its simultaneous destruction.")

The title story is told by an unnamed female narrator, an academic. Seeking distraction from grief for her father, recently deceased, she has accepted an invitation to Stockholm, where one evening her host escorts her to the Royal Library. There, in a room "like a dungeon", filled with volumes of a nameless encyclopaedia, she spends the night reading the entry about her father, which recounts his life from first to last in miraculous detail and a matchless style. For the Encyclopaedia provides nothing short of perfection: "suddenly, as if by magic, the reader's spirit is overwhelmed by the radiant landscape and swift succession of images. . . . Each item [of information] has its own paragraph, each period its own poetic essence and metaphor." The story consists of the narrator's paraphrase of her father's biography: "The countryside of his native region is rendered so vividly that as I read, or rather flew over the lines and paragraphs, I felt I was in the heart of it . . ."—Kiš is describing any reader's ideal experience, in which a conviction of truth serves the discovery of truth itself.

The Encyclopaedia is produced by "a religious organization or sect whose democratic program stresses an egalitarian vision of the world of the dead", an "odd caste of erudites" with "members all over the world". Only people who do not feature in any other encyclopaedia are admitted. "The principle is clear, yet the erudition, the need to record it all, everything a human life is made of, is enough to take one's breath away." The point of the Encyclopaedia is its inclusiveness, which is conjured in Kiš's stringent prose. The narrator insists that her summary is a dismal substitute for the radiant original.

> Nothing, as I say, is missing: the clay caking the rubber boots bought from a drunken soldier; a bad case of diarrhoea caused by some spoiled cabbage rolls eaten at a dive in Inđija; an affair with a Bosnian woman, a waitress, in Sombor; a bicycle accident near Čantavir and the bruised elbow that came of it; a night ride in a cattle wagon on the Senta—Subotica line; the purchase of a plump goose to take home for a New Year's celebration. . . .

And so on, to the terminus: her father dies of cancer (see chapter 7). At the end, the narrator reveals that the story has been a dream: "I awoke drenched in sweat."

This story and *Hourglass* are Kiš's best inventions. He was always in search of reflexive structures which grant the rich specificity that any fiction dies without, along with scope for the involuted patterning of motifs, and a vantage point above a landscape of themes, ideas and traditions. In this case, the specificity was devoted to the representation of an 'ordinary' existence in Yugoslavia before, during, and after the Second World War. The pathos of the biography is made palatable by refraction through an elaborate narrative construct.

The plot was a gift from Mirjana, the story's dedicatee; for the dream of an encyclopaedia was hers, and the father figure, "Đ. M.", was based on her father, Đura Miočinović (1910–1979). He and Kiš were close and shared certain convictions; according to Mirjana, her father "never had a good word to say about any nation, beginning with 'his own' (the Serbs)".[111]

---

111 But Kiš's own father was also, as ever, in his mind and art. When he writes that the Encyclopaedia "records every motion that cleared a brick from the ruins", we remember E.S. in the focal scene of *Hourglass,* with a labour brigade.

On one level, the story paints an elegiac vision of Yugoslavia—the only such in his work, made possible because he had left (lost) the country. The fact that fatal tumours of nationalism were growing within Yugoslavia when the story was published has lent it an aura of prophesy and commemoration. On other levels, the purpose is redemptive. For critic Julia Creet, the story is about hypermnesia, "the dream of complete knowledge". Politically, this democratic fantasy of total recapitulation judges the totalitarian yearning of communist regimes to spy out every detail of their subjects' lives.

In literary terms, too, the story has a redemptive angle. The Encyclopaedia is an *Aleph*: a finite object that contains infinity. Yet Kiš's purposes are not those of Borges. Compare the Library of Babel, with its despairing vision of infinity as a structure of hexagonal galleries where the inclusion of "all that it is given to express, in all languages" creates a sense of human exclusion and futility, omniscience feels like punishment, the librarians are rancorous and defeated, and, as a critic points out, "no one expects to discover anything". Kiš corrects this Olympian nightmare with a compassionate and grateful vision of books as support amid our losses, redeeming a particular life, which can be any life. Borges avers with a shrug that details are interchangeable, as are lives; Kiš responds that each life is itself.

Or compare the modest compilers of Kiš's Encyclopaedia with the "secret society" that invents the Borgesian world of Tlön, "guided and directed by some shadowy man of genius." Nothing democratic or egalitarian penetrates Borges's concept: the imagination of the blind librarian is sovereign.

Kiš's story takes its place in a tradition of Jewish meditation on letters and redemption.[112] The scholar Gershom Scholem mentioned a school of kabbalists for whom the redeemed Messianic world brings the devotee blissful knowledge of "the restoration of the original coexistence and correlation [*apokatastasis*] of all things." Scholem's friend Walter Benjamin proposed that "a chronicler who recites events without distinguishing between major and minor ones acts in accordance with the following truth: nothing that has ever happened should be regarded as lost for history."

"I too want the International of good men," wrote Isaac Babel in Soviet Russia. "I want each soul to be taken and registered. . . ." In Cynthia Ozick's imagined paradise, the deceased can call up "the lost, the missing, the wished-for. The unfinished and the unachieved." In Grace Paley's story, "Debts", an unknown woman asks the author to write about her grandfather, "a famous innovator and dreamer of the Yiddish theater," using family archives. Paley first refuses, but then reflects:

---

112 Filip David perceived "kabbalistic foundations" beneath the story, with its theme of forbidden knowledge. This surprised him: "we had often discussed Jewish matters, but never the Kabbalah."

"Actually, I owed nothing to the lady who'd called. It was possible that I did owe something to my own family and the families of my friends. That is, to tell their stories as simply as possible, in order, you might say, to save a few lives."

"The Book of Kings and Fools" is a documentary fiction about the *Protocols of the Elders of Zion*, which purports to outline a Jewish conspiracy to achieve world domination. In fact, the *Protocols* was plagiarised from a nineteenth-century French pamphlet, satirising the ambitions of Napoleon III. Although the forgery was exposed as early as 1921, its potency for stirring anti-Semitic prejudice was undiminished; the *Protocols* was probably more responsible for the Holocaust than any other book, *Mein Kampf* not excluded; and it retains its currency in Middle Eastern and Arab politics, the former Soviet Union, and post-communist Central Europe.

The preface to a Serbian edition, published in Belgrade in 2001, which I found on a bookstall in Podgorica, states that anyone who claims the *Protocols* is a forgery needs to produce the original, "because you cannot forge something that does not exist"—as though the original had not been revealed decades before. "As long as there are people who challenge the authenticity of the *Protocols*," the preface adds smugly, "there will be others who discover and publish them." Amazon.com preserves a disclaimer on its pages that sell the *Protocols*: "a hoax e-mail has been circulating widely that falsely claims Amazon.com has favorably reviewed this book. This allegation is, of course, absolutely untrue." The *Protocols of the Elders of Zion* cannot, it seems, be drained of its poison.

It was a natural, almost an ineluctable subject for Kiš, for nothing else united so many of his obsessions. The power of books to do harm, the nexus of fiction and atrocity, the mysterious byways of plagiarism, the persistence of anti-Semitic prejudice, the wilful credulity of readers. Above all, the career of the *Protocols* was proof that nothing is more fantastic than reality. How can the fictional imagination rival the real story of this tsarist fabrication for improbable twists and turns, tension, drama, melodrama, and impact upon the world?

Kiš imitates a sort of ideal journalism: a piece of investigative reporting, wonderfully exact and allusive, buttressed with sources and quotations, beginning and ending with scenes of massacre, jumping cinematically from scene to scene, tracing the incredible path by which the *Protocols* achieved its effect. But unlike journalism, this story does not name real names. The only way to write fiction about the *Protocols* is never to mention them, or Jews, or Nazis: words that would embezzle the readers' trust, trading imagination for spurious significance (see chapter 11). At the story's heart is an imagined account of the moment when the imposture or plagiarism came to light in 1921. An unnamed Russian émigré in Istanbul notices similarities between Maurice Joly's satire and the *Protocols*, here called *The Conspiracy*:

a pamphlet aimed against tyranny and the amateur despot Napoleon III became a clandestine program for world domination. . . . Change a few words, add a pejorative remark or two about Christians, take away the venomously ironic sting of Joly's fantasies (ascribed to Machiavelli in the text) and divorce them from historical context—and you have the infamous *Conspiracy*.

The original text has been 'doubled' by plagiarism, with results that will prove fatal for millions.[113]

"The Legend of the Sleepers" is a piece of World Literature, tacitly reproaching the quest for national mythemes. The story of seven Roman noblemen, converts in the court of pagan emperor Decius, comes down from sundry Christian, Greek and Syriac sources, the Koran and Gregory of Tours, then via Gibbon and Goethe, Cavafy, Borges, and others. Punished for their faith by immurement in a cave, the seven fall into a miraculous sleep which endures for two centuries. They awaken—harbingers of the Second Coming—into a changed world, ruled by the Christian emperor Theodosius. Amid celebration of their reappearance, the sleepers tell their story and bless the emperor, and then pass peacefully into real sleep and death.

Kiš had abandoned a novel about this legend in 1967, and returned to the theme in Paris. "Let us imagine that someone *shows* a story instead of telling it—the story of the seven sleepers of Ephesus, say." This remark in Borges's story, "Averroës' Search", may have been Kiš's cue to evoke the impossible experience of the sleeper Dionysius; the return of sensation to stone-like limbs, the "crimson flame" of sunlight, the swirling confusion of dream and reality, the frightening hubbub of the crowd: these are presented with barely a word of explanation.

He drew on a reworking of the legend by Tawfiq al-Hakim, whose play (1933) limited the sleepers to three and made much of Decius's daughter Prisca, beloved of a sleeper. A second Prisca, daughter of Theodosius, falls in love with her namesake's ancient admirer and joins him when the sleepers are walled up again. In Kiš's story, Prisca is doubled only in the sleeper's mind, which is haunted by "the image of two women conflated by time and memory into one, without limits or bounds, for they were made of the dust and ashes of two memories, the clay of two successive creations into which sleep had breathed a soul, his soul. And the two images mingled in his consciousness, his memory, and he kneaded the clay of which

---

113 A much more famous work of fiction involving the *Protocols* is Umberto Eco's copious novel, *Foucault's Pendulum* (1988). Comparing them, critic Svetlana Boym concludes: "If for Eco conspiracy theory is interesting as a problem of interpretation, for Kiš it is an actual historical threat. Kiš's characters cannot afford the playful and ambiguous repertoire of Eco's computer games."

they were made, and in the end he could no longer distinguish two women, two dreams, but only one . . ."

The final vindication of faith is absent from Kiš's version. His sleepers simply find themselves back in the cave, objects not subjects of their untellable tale. Dionysius's reprieve from darkness becomes another layer of memory. "Vainly calling to the Lord his God", only Prisca's name brings comfort, stirring "a vague and distant elation".

"Red Stamps with Lenin's Head" is the last story in the book, and it was the last to be written. When he was finishing the other stories, probably late in 1982, his old friend Svetlana Termačić rebuked him for never having written a love story. She could not have known that Kiš was indeed ready—having lost Mirjana—to write about her, just as—having emigrated in 1979—he had written about Yugoslavia in "The Encyclopaedia of the Dead". (In each case, an interval of a year and a half elapsed between loss and composition.) One night, he knocked on Svetlana's door with a typescript in his hand and read the story to her and Franjo. He revised it over several months, completing it in May 1983.

The story has the form of a letter to an unnamed scholar from a woman who does not reveal her name. The letter concerns Mendel Osipovich, a Russian poet who wrote in Yiddish between the 1920s and the 1940s.[114] The woman claims to have been the poet's lover and muse for several decades; as such, she can answer questions that the scholar had posed at a lecture (which the woman attended, without identifying herself). One question in particular impelled her to write: "you asked, 'What has become of Mendel Osipovich's correspondence?' and stated that the *Collected Works* published by Chekhov House in New York must be considered incomplete." She alone can, she says, solve this mystery, and in order to do so, she recounts the untold story of their love, from the first meeting in a magazine office ("I put my hands under the desk to keep him from seeing them tremble") to her last sight of him "at a rally, reading a proclamation. He was a broken man by then; he sensed his end was near."

Their union was literary as well as erotic: "I personally typed or copied out all Mendel Osipovich's works; I was, sir, the midwife to his literary labours." The climax of the narrative is her chance discovery in 1949 that Osipovich was corresponding with a woman who translated his poems into Russian. "I believe I could have forgiven him an infidelity of the flesh—with poets as with gods, anything is forgivable. But the fact that he wrote to the young woman about his poetry, his soul, the mysterious sources of his inspiration . . . that, sir, is what shattered me, shook my very being". In a pitch of jealous despair, she fetches the packet of his letters, bound

114 Osipovich's name and details of his biography suggest Osip Mandelstam (1891–1938).

with a black velvet ribbon he bought me when we first met. . . . As soon as I tore the first letter, I knew I could not retreat, and this despite the realisation running through me like a knife that I would regret my action, that I already regretted it. . . . And that is how Mendel Osipovich's *Collected Works* were deprived of their fifth volume and his correspondence reduced to twenty notes to publishers and friends. What the terrible "sword of the revolution" failed to destroy was destroyed by the frenzy of love.

The setting reflects Kiš's literary entanglement with the Russian poets whose work bridged the 1917 revolution and witnessed its monstrous results. The emotional substance, however, has private sources, which he never discussed. For they lie within the triangular maze that led to his divorce.

"Red Stamps" pays tribute to the immense gift of Mirjana's loyalty and the tenacity of her love. It even foresees her long and devoted viduity. It might almost be called Kiš's *Marriage Certificate*. It was the only story in the book that he did not give her to read before publication. The nameless narrator destroys Osipovich's letters, just as she had destroyed Kiš's letters on the day of their divorce. Yet the narrator is no more to be identified with Mirjana than with Nadezhda Mandelstam.[115] The narrator is herself, and Kiš undercuts the pathos of the plot by making her complex, difficult, even deluded. She reads everything published about Osipovich and mocks far-fetched interpretations of his work, particularly those with a Freudian bent. Yet she has left the critical field wide open for such "utter nonsense"; hoarding her unique experience and knowledge, she creates a vacuum that silly critics rush to fill. Jealous, possessive, and self-effacing, she may herself be a psychopathic case, ripe for therapy or analysis.

And her account is laced with odd anomalies. If the poet's friends knew about their liaison, why have scholars of his life and work never suspected her existence? Would his young translator into Russian have known nothing about the liaison— and stayed silent about it after Mendel's death? Might the narrator be a self-dramatising fantasist? Above all, there is the tragicomic moment when she wonders how the poet would have described the scene when she destroyed his letters, and pictures herself as "the young woman" in that scene, although she was then in her fiftieth year. At other times, her insight and wisdom are moving: "What is done is

---

115 Nadezhda Mandelstam's memoirs influenced Kiš's characterisation of Mendel Osipovich's lover. Here is *Hope Abandoned:* "If it were not for my faith in a future meeting I should never have been able to live through all these many years of loneliness. I laugh at myself and do not dare believe, but my faith never leaves me. We shall meet, and there is no parting. Thus it was promised, and this is my faith." And this, from Kiš: "Since dreams are an image of the other world and proof of its existence, we shall meet in dreams . . . Fate has been well disposed toward me, and I seek no reparations. . . . why shouldn't I too, all materiality aside, hope that we shall meet in the other world?"

done. The past lives on in us; we cannot blot it out." As Guy Scarpetta says, by the end of the story, we do not know which account of the poet's life and work is true: the 'official' version, or the narrator's counter-version.

———

Reviewers were nonplussed by *The Encyclopaedia of the Dead*. What were they meant to make of these disparate subjects and ways of telling?

Kiš sat back and watched. Usually he primed the critics with well-timed interviews, explaining what his latest book was about. On this occasion, still resenting the literary establishment's uncertain support over *Boris Davidovich*, he kept silent. The results of this experiment were, he recalled, "disastrous". Deprived of authorial guidance and also of the anti-fascist or anti-Stalinist compass that had steered them through *Hourglass* and *Boris Davidovich*, the reviewers did not know how to respond. Was the new book perhaps reactionary? Yes, they decided, it was probably reactionary, what with its mysteries, religious settings, and archaism. Not that there were many reviews anyway; as Filip David says, "reviewing was connected to politics, and if someone was politically out of favour, then. . . ."

When he did discuss the book, Kiš said the title story and "Red Stamps" were the best. He was proud of his female narrators: they were "the result of a quest for change, for a new psychological register and a new voice." He called it a book about love and death, adding that he had tried to exclude politics, but in vain.

There was another reason too for the reviewers' indifference. As Kiš knew, space for the non-national reception of literature was shrinking; amid the "nationalist euphoria" that was rising in Yugoslavia, though it was still modest compared with the insane dimensions it would achieve a few years later. So Kiš was not surprised if his stories appeared trivial. This was ironic, as the book contains the best meta-critique of Yugoslavia's slide into mythomania and mass paranoia, which was itself a precondition for the decline towards genocidal violence.

The Encyclopaedia of the Dead appeared in a country that contrived to be jittery and paralysed at the same time. Tito's long-anticipated death in 1980 had left a besetting and insidious sense of uncertainty. The ideology of Yugoslav unitarism had expired, unmourned, in the 1960s. Communism in Europe was weakening, but Yugoslavia had generated very little liberal or democratic energy to exploit or accelerate this trend. Instead, the initiative lay with nationalist intellectuals—such as Dobrica Ćosić and Gojko Đogo (see chapters 22, 32 and 33)—who saw neighbouring nations as the enemy. The 1980s saw the creation or resurrection of nationalist myths, drawing on the traditionalism and authoritarianism that were deeply rooted in Yugoslav society. This process went fastest and farthest in Serbia where, in the words of one analyst, the development of nationalism was "marked by an attempt to hijack and manipulate History in order to mobilise Serbian public opinion against fresh dangers. These themes were conveyed by the entire Serbian intellectual and artistic scene."

For the cultural critic Svetlana Slapšak, one proof that Yugoslavia was going off the rails was the chorus of official support for "a Mexican car-dealer and hotelier called Roberto Salinas Price", who announced in 1985 that the true location of ancient Troy was not in Asia Minor but in Herzegovina. This was ridiculous, but no worse than other myths, usually of ethnogenesis, being peddled by Yugoslav intellectuals with better credentials:

> A Slovenian poet proclaimed Venetians the direct ancestors of Slovenians, which would put them in the position of having generated the Etruscan and Roman civilisations; Croats chose an Aryan origin in ancient Iran; Serbian impostors simply declared that the Serbs were the most ancient nation on earth, and the craziest of them saw "Serbian knights" on ancient Egyptian bas-reliefs. Albanians declared Illyrians their ancestors, which, by a miracle of continuity, would make them the most ancient possessors of the territory; Macedonians simply proclaimed Alexander of ancient Macedonia their king. . . .

Not to be left out, a sect of Montenegrin nationalists claimed that Troy's true location was near Lake Skadar. With Yugoslavia's political landscape as arid as biblical Samaria, and equally populated with dubious prophets and apostles, these newfangled myths of identity had a dire effect, mobilising popular emotions behind sectarian goals, foreclosing debate about other aspirations and horizons.

In this febrile climate, Kiš's tales of deception and manipulation, false prophesy, conspiracy, the anticipation of mindless murder, the link between language and atrocity, all lit by blood-red shafts of irremediable loss, could not have been more apt: a handful of counter-myths, so well-crafted and packed with matter that they outlast the political madness and intimate misery which informed them. "Even though there are not many stories in the book," the Hungarian novelist Péter Esterházy told me, "you feel it *is* an encyclopaedia. You feel it is complete. This was his greatness." More recently, the Bosnian writer Miljenko Jergović praised it as a wonderful book, but one that seems to be losing the battle with silence and "the impossibility of writing".

(1983)

> For exile is a negative condition: one is not living
> in a place so much as not living in a place.
>
> Anthony Burgess

Publication of his collected works in Belgrade and Zagreb at the end of 1983 in ten volumes, handsomely bound in orange cloth boards with gold lettering, sealed Kiš's status as one of Yugoslavia's pre-eminent writers.

Yet, as before, finishing a book plunged him into despair and self-doubt, leading to a long period of what he called "chronic idleness". He wrote to his German translator, "I'm not working at all. (Reading isn't work, reading is therapy.)" The crushing sense of mortality could only be relieved by jettisoning the discipline of work, crawling from bar to bar night after night with any available company. Friends were dismayed by the utter lack of discrimination, which contrasted so sharply with the refinement of his literary taste. When Stanko Cerović asked how he could spend so much time with empty people, Kiš shrugged: it really didn't matter, wasn't worth discussing. "He was happy when he was writing," Stanko recalls, "desperate when he wasn't." If time away from his desk was worthless, it might as well be spent recklessly.

Still rankling over the *Boris Davidovich* affair,[116] eaten by remorse over Mirjana and perhaps another lost love, and perhaps too, at times, over his childlessness, he coped with his inner demons as well as his material insecurity, staunchly supported by Pascale and a small circle of true friends in Paris, such as Franjo and Svetlana Termačić and their teen-aged daughters, who were a surrogate family, as Stanko was almost a younger brother. He was also a frequent visitor at the elegant flat of the Serbian artist Vladimir Veličković, a founder of the Mediala group, and his wife Maristella, who remembers endless discussions of communism and democracy. Kiš once pounded the dining table so hard with his fist, emphasising "the absolute evil of communism", that it toppled over. He refused to accept that communism had produced any benefits to mitigate its black record. Nor would he grant distinctions between the Soviet and Yugoslav brands. His condemnation was unbounded.

But not everything was politics. Maristella remembers when she invited him to watch a documentary program on television about the 1942 massacre in Novi Sad. (Kiš did not own a television set.) During the program he threw himself out of his chair, to-

---

116 "He talked about it obsessively," according to Gabi Gleichmann. "He hated very few people, but he hated *them:* the children of Stalinism, still living in the structures of Stalinism."

wards the television, exclaiming "I saw my father!" Much moved, she wished she could repeat the program for him. "His deepest obsession was with his father."

The Penguin edition of *Boris Davidovich* appeared in 1980 as part of Philip Roth's series 'Writers from the Other Europe', with Joseph Brodsky's preface, bringing Anglophone fame on a new scale. Publication in the *New Yorker* in 1982 also helped. Susan Sontag lauded him with memorable absurdity as one of the three best writers in the world. Translations into other languages also proliferated: more than a dozen in the first half of the 1980s.

Despite this growing reputation, he did not keep famous company or cultivate useful contacts. He was too much of a rebel, too proud, and too committed to literature as the antithesis of careerism, wherever he found himself. During the early 1980s, he was guest of honour at a luxurious private dinner in Manhattan, overlooking Central Park. The host was Nina Rosenwald, a Sears and Roebuck heiress, politically and philanthropically *engagée*. Others at the top table included novelist Philip Roth; Aryeh Neier, the director of Human Rights Watch; David Rieff from Farrar, Straus and Giroux; and Linda Asher, fiction editor at *The New Yorker*, who published "The Encyclopaedia of the Dead" in Ammiel Alcalay's translation.

Alcalay was also invited, but found his seat among the artisans. He recalls a chilly evening that became convivial only after the VIPs' departure: "Danilo wanted us to stay, have a few drinks, and let his hair down a bit. It became very hilarious when he inspected all the closets, drawers and other contents of the apartment, trying to figure out what its exact function was. Finally, in the great one-liner of the evening, sitting on the couch, it dawned on him: it was a *shtup plats*, a place for fucking." Alcalay, Rieff, and Neier cannot recall who organized the evening, or with what motive. The film-maker Dušan Makavejev remembers another dinner (or the same one?) above Central Park, "where the flowers alone, I found out, cost $2,000!" Perhaps these lavish events belong to the cultural history of the cold war; after the American publication of *A Tomb for Boris Davidovich*, Kiš may have been seen as a useful anti-communist asset, worth subsidizing until it became clear that he could not be tempted by dissidence.

This, after all, was a man who, as his friend Gabi Gleichmann remembers, "was invited only once to all sorts of places". He routinely offended hosts by his extravagant manner—what Susan Sontag diagnosed tartly as "the exhibitionism of the drunken Balkan male". For he drank like a fish, especially when bored, as happened easily; loosened by alcohol, he would curse *bien-pensant* leftists, still in plentiful supply, and French condescension. He was most comfortable sitting and smoking at a café table, playing elaborate word-games with friends. Language was sacred. Miroslav Karaulac watched him scold a *clochard* who hailed him as he took cash from an ATM: "Hey, mister, have you got a few francs for me?" Kiš ticked him off: "Why are you asking when you just saw me take out some money? Say it properly: 'Give me a few francs, mister!'" Still annoyed by the tramp's gentility, he dug in his pocket for coins.

The irony of this story is that Kiš himself was readily seen as a vagabond by Western Europeans and Americans. His editor in New York, David Rieff, noticed the impression he made on admirers who knew nothing about the Balkans. *They expected Kafka*, Rieff recalls, *and what they got was 'Boudu Saved from Drowning'*—Jean Renoir's comedy about a vagrant or free spirit who wreaks havoc in a bourgeois family that tries to 'save' him. Gabi Gleichmann brought the same expectations to their first encounter and was duly dismayed.

> He challenged my preconceptions of how a cosmopolitan intellectual should act. I assumed a Jewish intellectual must be very sophisticated, not just in ideas but in manner; and Danilo appeared to be anything but sophisticated. My *petit bourgeois* being was offended by the way he drank, ate, and swore. So, I was fascinated by his writing, but not by him. When I met him at conferences over the next few years, he would greet me familiarly, but he was always drunk, it was embarrassing. He claimed intimacy without having any intimate relationship with me. These reservations disappeared over time, when I came to see his humility, his gentleness and unpretentiousness, and his generosity.

Sontag thought his rackety ways misled people who did not know him well, and may have been meant to do so. "Some people can do it all—drink and be famous and write as well—but Danilo couldn't. He was much more delicate than he seemed."

Kiš soon grew disillusioned with French writers and intellectuals. Having revered French culture all his life, mostly from afar, and done much to make it known in his own language, he was bound to find daily contact with its living embodiments disappointing. Better read in French than most of them, refusing to be tagged as a pro-Western dissident, bristling at Parisian ignorance of Europe's smaller literatures, Kiš was unsuited to the role of grateful acolyte. As Edmund White observed, Kiš "lives in Paris but he's certainly not part of Paris literary life." When people asked at parties where he came from, he wearied of trying to explain and said curtly "Africa centrale", pronounced Italian-style, *chentRARlay*.

"Being a Yugoslav writer in Paris," as he told an interviewer, "means being alone." Yet no other role was available. He satirised French prejudices and his own lost illusions in a pair of scathing essays. "We are exotica, we are a political scandal, we are—in the best case—noble memories of the Marne," he declared, evoking Serbia's hallowed First World War alliance with France. Yugoslav writers could gain a hearing abroad only if they stuck to political themes; they were effectively barred from writing about "poetry, suffering, history, mythology, the human condition".

Characteristically, he put the onus of blame not on French vanity but on his own culture. "Have we deserved our fate? Indeed we have. We are guilty and must bear the consequences in silence." For Yugoslav writers had been the first to politicise their

"You've made me look like Sophia Loren!" he teased Maristella Veličković after this photo shoot. Paris, May 1981. Photo by Maristella Veličković

literature, insisting on ethnic identities that meant little to the outside world. "We have failed to resist the temptation of exporting our minor (or major—what's the difference?) problems of nationalism and chauvinism and shouting from the rooftops that we are not primarily Yugoslavs, no, we are Serbs or Croats, Slovenes or Macedonians or whatever, listen carefully, it's very important, ladies and gentlemen, you mustn't get us mixed up. . . ." The narcissism of local nationalists meshed with the indifference of the outside world. He saw how anti-communist energy in Yugoslavia, but not only there, was absorbed by "national feelings and nationalist impulses", auguring the triumph of values remote from his own liberal pluralism. By the late 1980s, he called himself "the only Yugoslav writer in the world" and predicted that smaller national or ethnic identities would never win recognition in the wider world.

He felt most comfortable with his compatriots, of whom there were many in his arrondissement. Pascale remembers that the company he kept was "very Yugoslav. He used his own language all the time, buying Yugoslav newspapers, socialising with Yugoslavs." At Pascale's urging, he renewed contact with Mirjana and kept in close touch with her and his old friends in Belgrade, returning every few months. His favourite place in Yugoslavia, however, was Dubrovnik, the walled city on Croatia's southern coast, only a short drive from his sister's home in Montenegro. He had always loved Dubrovnik, surely drawn to its cosmopolitanism and its Renaissance beauty, and its historic role as a bridge between Western (Venetian, Italian) and Eastern (Slavic, Byzantine, Ottoman) cultures. He and Pascale dreamed of having enough money to live between Paris and Dubrovnik. Lacking those means, they took a room in the Hotel Argentina whenever they could afford it, even chambermaids' quarters in the attic if nothing else was free, and spent their days with the writer Milan Milišić and his wife Jelena Trpković, who were close friends.

By 1985, Kiš was ready for a new project, and wondering if he could write a novel about a Renaissance poet who lived in Dubrovnik. Diogo Pires (1517–1599) was a Portuguese Jew who fled the Inquisition in his homeland, converted to Christianity, studied medicine in Salamanca and then fled to Antwerp and later to Italy. In 1555, the persecution of Christian converts in Ancona drove him across the Adriatic Sea to Ragusa, now Dubrovnik, where a ban on Jews had been repealed. He reverted to Judaism, taking the name Isaiah Kohen or Koen, and lived as a teacher and writer, penning Latin works in praise of his lost birthplace and adoptive home. He spent his last years in the ghetto and was buried in the Jewish cemetery. Pires was also known as Didacus Pyrrhus Lusitanus and Jacobus Flavius Eborensis; in Serbo-Croatian, his name is Didak Pir.

It was "a dream project", in Pascale's words, combining exile, language, Dubrovnik, persecution, Judaism, and poetry. Yet we have no idea how Kiš would have approached it. He left nothing but a few pages of jottings in Serbo-Croatian and Hungarian, a solitary translation (of Pir's poem, "To a Flea"), and a little inventory of images from Pir's verses: "Jewels, a pearl, rare wood; medicinal herbs; dill: flowers; grass, lentils, fruit and other fruits of the earth; different kinds of drink and food from animals: placid livestock and wild beasts; chickens; a raven; a reed; a fly; *ligna acapna*;[117] ice and snow; a handkerchief; a gauntlet; munitions; a liar and disabled people; items for social pastimes; fever and gout; deep old age at seventy; Jesuit lodgings in Dubrovnik." Untransposed by the imagination, this list pulsates faintly on the page. Would he have found a solution, animated those motifs, and written a kind of fiction that he had never attempted before? Could he have constructed a novel on a scaffold of so few documents? Mirjana Miočinović believes his creative cycle would have resumed if illness had not struck in 1986. Others are less confident; a Japanese critic suggests that "the price of 'Joycean exile' was high—he could not continue writing novels."

At the end of June, he and Pascale joined a dinner party at the house of Ljuba Popović, a former Mediala artist from Belgrade. According to another guest, novelist Slobodan Selenić, Kiš was cheerful and charming, the centre of attention, talkative as ever, almost euphoric as he joked about a diagnosis of tuberculosis which his doctors had made, to explain a recurrent cough. TB in this day and age, "like a romantic poet!" They should put him in a glass case, he boasted, and show the medical students. Later in the evening, he said how sorry he was that he would never be a best-seller with an income to match. Selenić asked what he would do if he were. "I'd sit in front of the café La Coupole," Kiš said at once, "sipping Courvoisier, smoking Gauloises and watching

With Pascale Delpech at a café table, smoking Gauloises, watching the world go by. Paris, 1981

117 Firewood that burns without smoking.

the world go by." That's what you do already, said Selenić. "When I have the money, yes," Kiš admitted, "but even then I'm not carefree."

The following year, he was awarded a Bosnian prize for work "inspired by the national liberation struggle, the socialist revolution, and the postwar reconstruction". (The individual liberation struggle, the literary revolution, and ethical reconstruction would have been a fitter tribute.) The ceremony was at Kozara in northern Bosnia, site of a much-mythologised battle between Tito's partisans and the Germans with their local fascist allies. The writer Stevan Tontić watched as Kiš gave a speech, then read his *Birth Certificate* aloud. He looked out of place, Tontić thought: too urbane for these wild surroundings, a cosmopolite among the mountains. As a habitué of city cafés and bookshops, immune to the fascination with communal roots and folklore, Kiš took no interest in Yugoslavia's rural zones. That same year, he published an essay about Ivo Andrić which contains his only remarks about Bosnia, that "exotic country at the heart of Europe . . . where the Levant and the West collide, and Balkan Christians and Ottoman warriors live together in coercive symbiosis." With hindsight, *coercive symbiosis* was ominous. Among the spectators at Kozara that September day were certainly people who would have to flee in spring 1992, when thousands of Muslim Bosniak and Croat civilians were killed or herded into concentration camps, becoming "ethnographic rarities" in their own land.

Kiš's next journey was to Stockholm, where Gabi Gleichmann was waiting to discuss a joint project. Earlier in the year, he had urged Kiš to leave his French publisher, Gallimard, which was more prestigious than generous. He persuaded Bernard-Henri Lévy, an ex-Maoist turned *nouveau philosophe* and all-round intellectual celebrity, to mediate on Kiš's behalf with the publisher Grasset. Persuaded by Gleichmann that Kiš was a potential Nobel laureate, Lévy applied leverage and Grasset decided to promote Kiš as the next big thing after Milan Kundera from the fashionable region of Central Europe. They offered a lavish contract for three books: a new novel, a translation of *The Anatomy Lesson*, and a volume of conversations with Gleichmann. The novel would have been about Didak Pir. The translation was to be undertaken by Pascale, with Kiš's assistance.[118] The book of conversations was to be called *Life, Literature.*

The collaboration was Gleichmann's idea. "Danilo said he hated interviews. I said, let's experiment, using two voices: a book in dialogue form. Between the fifth and sixth drinks, he agreed—while complaining that he was not that sort of a writer." The two men made a start in May and June 1986. Kiš still had mixed feelings: "He thought it would be a good way to express certain very important experiences that might be sentimental if written in a novel, such as the death of his mother, but that might work if addressed in conversation. But he didn't like to work every day. He was a *bon vivant*, he liked to have a good life even if his idea of the good life was plain and boring."

---

118 Pascale remembers a tense meeting at Grasset to discuss the completed draft translation. When senior executives urged him to moderate the furious language of *The Anatomy Lesson,* Kiš was inflexible: gentlemen, let us be clear: I won't change a single comma or full stop.

There was another problem, too: the contract with Grasset could not easily be squared with his ingrained pessimism and self-doubt. "His basic attitude was that life is a failure. With that attitude, one looks for the bad in good things," Gleichmann says. "His contract gave him, I think, 7,000 francs a month for five years: in effect, a salary. For a man who was used to living on almost nothing, this was a revolution. He had never had a proper contract before; now he felt the pressure. He was a bit haunted by the fact that he'd been paid for something he hadn't written yet. As it turned out, without that money from Grasset, he would have starved after he got sick."

Gleichmann was disappointed that Kiš had done nothing with their project over the summer, but did not let this cloud the visit, which marked the publication of *Hourglass* in Swedish. The reviews were gratifying, and all went well. On Kiš's last day in Stockholm, Gleichmann took him and Pascale on an excursion to the Åland islands. Dining on board the luxurious ship, Kiš let slip a remark: "For the first time in my life, I'm happy." It was a magical moment: "I felt that *he* felt he was saying the forbidden words. He was using the word he should never have used, because 'happy' was what life never allowed him to be. We were speaking Hungarian. I was shocked by what he'd said; he was shocked too."

Back in Paris, Kiš had an appointment with Jack Lang, French minister of culture, who invested him as a *Chevalier de l'Ordre des Arts et des Lettres*. After graciously thanking Lang for intervening to secure his right of permanent residence in France, Kiš declared that the only chevalier who should matter to a writer was Cervantes's Knight of the Sorrowful Countenance, and as such, he welcomed his accession to the Quixotic order of dreamers and knights errant.

At the end of the month, he and Pascale travelled to New York for a PEN conference. They planned to stay for three months, but he had a persistent cough that could not be shaken off. Thinking it might be pneumonia, he went for a hospital check-up. Lung cancer was diagnosed at once. Jelena Trpković and Milan Milišić happened to be staying in the apartment opposite, and they watched Kiš pacing back and forth in his lighted room all night, after the diagnosis. He sketched the tumour for Jelena, to show her what the doctors had found on the X-ray. He cursed the French physicians who had mistaken the problem with his lungs for tuberculosis only a year before.

They returned to Paris for the operation. On 16 December, half of a lung was removed. A course of radiotherapy followed, then six months of chemotherapy. The surgeon told Pascale that the operation had failed to excise the cancer; she had to live with that knowledge, acting as if permanent remission were possible while knowing it was not.

In the first post-operative months they watched television endlessly, even children's cartoons—anything to distract him. Visiting friends were saddened to see him slumped in front of the television, channel-hopping. He stopped smoking, and Pascale stopped as well to make it easier, though she knew it was useless. "He was desperate," the writer Radoslav Bratić recalls. "He played with his fingers, waved his hands around and crossed his arms, not knowing where to put them or what to do with them." As Kiš measured the room like a caged animal, Karaulac overheard him say to himself: "I have smoked away my lungs." He had chain-smoked for decades. Like the narrator of *The Garret*, he behaved as if smoking was "the only thing in the world worth doing." His voice was smoky; his teeth were discoloured by smoke; the fingers on both hands were stained nicotine-yellow. Andrzej Stasiuk, a Polish admirer, says he can smell the smoke rising off the pages of his books. Besides Gauloises, unfiltered Gitanes were his favourite. Joking that he was a professional smoker, he would say, "A man writes *so* that he can smoke." A televised interview in 1982 showed him scouring the ashtray with each butt, a ritual that ended with lighting the next. Anyone who smokes while writing will find the two activities blending in their head. Kiš had once told Maristella Veličković that "Sometimes I don't know if I'm writing or smoking." Check-ups with his doctor in Paris would start with a ritual question: have you stopped smoking, or shall I get my gun? The doctor would reach for the desk drawer where he pretended to keep a pistol. No, doctor, came the calm reply, it's still three or four packs a day. His dentist in Paris was his old friend from Strasbourg, Georges Krygier; during an appointment a year or so before the diagnosis, Kiš started coughing uncontrollably. "You've got to stop smoking, it's ridiculous," Krygier protested, but Kiš would not hear of it.

Maristella saw the fear in his eyes, the first time he came for dinner after the operation. He said he was going crazy because he could not smoke. "All his old aggression was gone. He could not bear to be alone." Before dinner, he crouched down beside a lamp and took a tiny red bundle out of his pocket. The bundle contained a miniature Chinese doll that the film-maker Chris Marker had given to the writer Claude Roy, when Roy was recovering from a cancer operation. "It will work for you too," Roy had said encouragingly to Kiš, when he visited him in hospital. When Kiš showed Maristella the little doll, she thought how diminished he looked, "like a crumb". The following day, he called to thank her for the evening—something he had never done before.

He told his oncologist that the operation had left him "spiritually castrated". When the oncologist said that Kiš should understand he was no longer the same person but, rather, a child looking for its mother, he was impressed. "Just imagine," he told Maristella, "I didn't know that!" The doctor's remark chimed with a conviction of his own that he had become a different person—"and I despise myself." He told Georges Krygier the same thing: "I'm another man now, I'm not the same person."

Suicide became an obsessive theme in conversation. "At one phase of his illness he told me that he had borrowed a pistol," Predrag Čudić remembered. He told friends that he slept with a gun under his pillow, in case the urge to end it all became overpowering. Boško Mijanović found him much changed after the operation; presentiments of death were strong. Svetlana Termačić remembers how he would curl up on their bed and repeat, wretchedly, "I'm not brave—not a brave man!"

Kiš grew convinced that words had played a part in his illness. In 1988, he told Gabi Gleichmann that he had always been good at fucking up his life. *Do you remember that moment on the ship?*, he asked. *I destroyed it, I destroyed my life by saying that.* Gabi protested, but Kiš would not budge. He also told an interviewer that he had written his cancer into existence by describing the father's tumour in "The Encyclopaedia of the Dead". For doctors had told him that his own cancer dated approximately from the time when he wrote that story. To someone with his belief in the power of language, cause and effect were all too clear.[119]

At the worst moments, Stanko Cerović says, Kiš seemed to feel that his three life-long passions—for literature, women, and politics—had all proven to be bitter illusions. He had given everything to literature, and for what? To be hounded out of Belgrade by mediocrities, then patronised or ignored in Paris. Remorse over Mirjana was biting in 1983, when he wrote the final story in *Early Sorrows*, which foretells that young Andi "will meet a girl he will love forever". The two best stories in *Encyclopaedia of the Dead* are about Mirjana. Pascale gave Kiš everything; he—seemingly haunted by a sense that he had botched the true love of his life, or missed it altogether—gave back what he could.

As for politics, his hopes for a pluralist Yugoslavia were mocked by the deepening crisis there. On a more personal level, his efforts to support Yugoslav dissidents on the basis of universal human rights were liable to rebound when the dissidents' politics contradicted his own. The weakness of liberal dissidence in Yugoslavia is too complex a theme for analysis here; suffice to mention Mirko Kovač's story about Kiš and the poet Gojko Đogo, mentioned in chapter 32. Kiš appealed to President François Mitterrand to intervene on behalf of this "young and gifted poet", and he quarrelled with Kovač when he refused to sign a petition for Đogo's release from prison. Some time later, Kiš and Kovač met Đogo in the street. Đogo glanced at Kiš and said coarsely, "I saw you at my trial, who are you working for?" He took for granted that Kiš, with his international fame, would have been reporting to the police or a foreign embassy for money or favours. Kiš was dumbfounded for a moment, then cursed Đogo and walked away. When Kovač caught up with him in a café, he was sinking vodka shots in deep gloom.[120] This was the man that Milan Milišić saw as naïve in every respect beyond literature.

István Eörsi, a Hungarian dissident writer, asked Kiš in 1988 why he did not return to Belgrade and join the struggle against nationalism. Kiš shook his head: even going back every summer, he wanted to leave after a week because he could not bear to see how the Croats and Serbs were ready to slaughter each other.

For many months after the operation, writing was out of the question. Gabi Gleichmann spent six weeks in Paris, in February and March 1987, and met Kiš often, but it was impossible to work on their book of conversations. "At some level he knew he wasn't going to write any more books," Gleichmann says. "He was somehow afraid of starting anything big." That summer, he told interviewers that he had more or less stopped reading, let alone writing. In August, he inscribed a copy of *The Encyclopaedia of the Dead* to

---

119 See chapter 7 for other occasions when he wrote about tumours or tumour-like growths.
120 Đogo's later career as a warmonger, supporting the Serbian destruction of multiethnic Bosnia, vindicated Kovač's judgement.

Mirjana. "To Mira," it said, quoting from the last story in the book, "who is the source of all my inspiration and who midwifed all my literary labours." The past tense was revealing. When friends asked what he was working on, he changed the subject. Claudio Magris heard him say, serenely, "*On a déja écrit*": the writing has all been done. But he was not always serene; sometimes he quoted Eugène Ionesco: "The only thing worse than writing is not writing." Years before, he had told Susan Sontag: "I *hate* writing. I only write when I can't stand not to write." Writing is a drug, he once explained, than which the only thing worse is when the organism demands it, and it cannot be had.

His last substantial essay took the Marquis de Sade as its subject. Written late in 1987 for a conference in Dubrovnik, it presents Sade as exploring one logical implication of universal relativism in a godless world, where "sensual pleasure is the only present". The essay is a black pearl, rolling to a sombre conclusion:

> His inflamed imagination worked with a single material, human flesh, and his covetous eyes concentrated on a single nocturnal sky, the *nox microcosmica*, which medieval anatomical atlases situated in a circle whose centre is the groin and whose circumference does not surpass navel and knees. In Sade the *nox microcosmica* grows into a vast cosmic darkness without stars and without God— into the Apocalypse.

To Stanko Cerović, Kiš's obsessions during these years became more moral than literary, as his life's work assumed a shape that was undeniably final. He was preoccupied with the immorality of intellectual self-delusion, and with the importance of doing *no harm*. "I can say for myself that I have never betrayed the true aims of humanity in any of my books." Outside central and eastern Europe, where writers lent (and sold) themselves to political causes with gusto, this sounds portentous. Within the Yugoslav context particularly, where even Krleža eulogised Tito and Ivo Andrić once called for the deportation of Albanians from Kosovo, it reflects his commitment to literature as an ethical vocation.[121] He could still translate short pieces—poems, morsels of prose—and assist many of his translators, some of whom became friends.[122] And he could keep up his profile in the literary world by accepting invitations to conferences. Although his English was too limited for public speaking or much private conversation, he had joined the elite conference circuit in the early 1980s and cut an unmistakable figure: slim, shock-headed, elegantly wasted like a Rolling Stone. At the International PEN congress in New York in January

---

121 Krleža's panegyrics to the "ideal standard-bearer of the Kantian conception of World Peace", etcetera, were collected in 1980. Andrić's betrayal of the "true aims of humanity" occurred in 1939 when, as a senior diplomat, he argued that Yugoslavia should pursue the partitioning of Albania as a means to weaken and assimilate ethnic Albanians in the province of Kosovo: "The deportation of Muslim Albanians to Turkey could then be carried out since, under the new circumstances, there would be no major impediment to such a move."

122 One of his last translations was of Goethe's mysterious ballad, "The Erl-King": "Who rides by night in the wind so wild? / It is the father, with his child. / The boy is safe in his father's arm, / He holds him tight, he keeps him warm. . . ."

1986, organised by Norman Mailer, on 'The Writer's Imagination and the Imagination of the State', an American observer noted the "flamboyant, curly-headed, French-speaking charmer Danilo Kiš", opining that "totalitarianism was an art of destruction, cruelty, and crime whose instruments were deception and the *mensonge*."

He was seen as exotic, conjured as such. And he was sometimes happy to play along, especially with female admirers. A journalist at the same congress reported that Kiš was "referred to as 'that charismatic Yugoslav' and 'the literary Jean-Paul Belmondo'." When she approached with a compliment, he replied that she was *adorable et charmante*, and kissed her hand. "Later, I returned to his corner to find him draped with pretty girls. 'You seem to have many ladies,' I remarked in French. '*Oui*,' he sighed, the smoke from his Gauloise describing a trajectory of brooding resignation, '*j'ai toujours beaucoup de femmes. Ça marche très bien au commencement.*'" Later still, Kiš vouchsafed "the longest English speech he has made all week: 'You must come to Yugoslavia. You would like it there. In Yugoslavia we have no homosexuals. We are all'—he looks around the room for the words and proudly finds them—'we are all *real boys*!'"

A conference in Lisbon in May 1988, as the Soviet imperium approached dissolution, saw sharp exchanges between Central Europeans and Russians. Kiš confessed to feeling "a little exhausted" by discussions of Central Europe, whose writers were—he agreed with the poet Adam Zagajewski—"impoverished" by being read in an exclusively political key. When Tatyana Tolstaya raised the temperature by objecting to the anti-Russianism that was, she alleged, latent in the promotion of a Central European identity, Kiš bridled at the "pedagogical tone": "I feel like a small child being lectured to." He even claimed to "feel the presence of the Soviet Army" in Tolstaya's words.

Another panel involved British writers. Salman Rushdie remembers how Kiš "watched with amusement a panel discussion during which Martin Amis, Ian McEwan and myself laid into Margaret Thatcher's government". When it was over, Kiš "gave me a slightly ferocious but very accurate caricature he had done of me which is now among my proudest possessions." Kiš asked Rushdie about his forthcoming novel, *The Satanic Verses*, which would be published in London a few months later. He "seemed genuinely interested in what I'd set out to do," Rushdie recalls.

Someone else on whom he made an impression in Lisbon was the Hungarian novelist Péter Esterházy. Before they met, Esterházy had assumed from Kiš's reputation that he must be a fairy-tale figure: garbed in a huge fur coat, drunk, with a girl under each arm. Instead he was like a tall French gentleman in a bad mood. Within minutes of their meeting, Kiš confessed that he had not written a word for two years. Esterházy was taken aback by his candour. "It was a very intense encounter, like flirting. We agreed that literature isn't important: life is important, women are important, and everything is form."

A year later, in May 1989, the Iranian *fatwa* against Salman Rushdie was an all-consuming topic. In that month, making one of his last appearances, Kiš shared a platform in France with Michael Ignatieff, the Canadian writer and broadcaster. Like many liberals at that time, Ignatieff tied himself in knots over the affair, taking refuge in the

anguished "difficulty" of locating a tolerant position and upholding "a principle of tolerance that grits its teeth, where you hear ideas that make you sick but that you treat with
the minimum of human respect." Instead of hiding behind moral certitudes or accusations of fascism, we should, he urged, try to think like ethnologists.

This was too much for Kiš. "You have to be an imbecile to see things that way and
say you are an ethnologist," he rudely declared. "I am no kind of ethnologist, but I do
have political experience that you don't have."

"You can't say that!" Ignatieff protested. "I have the right to say it," Kiš replied inex-
orably, "because only a man with no political experience whatever could say such things,
could say that one cannot make a hard and fast judgement. In a case like the Rushdie affair, we can certainly speak of a fascist attitude, and even worse than fascist. . . ." Ignatieff
left the platform.[123]

Kiš was appalled to see Western cultural values undermined from within. From
his point of view, Ignatieff's scruples were worse than misplaced; they betrayed the
values which they meant to defend. Common courtesy should, in this emergency, be
optional. It was, anyway, less important in his native Yugoslavia; and although he had
lived in France for years, Kiš never grasped that a lapse of manners in the West can be
unforgivable.

Collecting the Premio Tevere in October 1988 before the Italian television cameras,
his baritone voice was barely audible. At the end of the year, he spent a day with Milan
Popović, one of his oldest friends. Popović had just seen him on television, receiving a
Yugoslav prize, and been dismayed by his "corroded" appearance and "squeaky voice".
He hurried from Cetinje to Belgrade, bearing a bottle of *rakija* as a gift. As they talked,
Kiš finished half the bottle. Popović asked when he would get something new to read,
and Kiš said he was not writing at all, his head was empty. Then how did you write all
those books in the past, Popović asked, trying to rally his friend. "By accident," said Kiš
mischievously, "the way you got your children." It was their last meeting.

In March 1989, he spent two weeks in Israel. His chief reason for making the trip
was to keep a promise made in 1986 to Ženi Lebl and Eva Panić Nahir, Yugoslav Jewish
immigrants who wanted to tell him about their experiences as survivors, decades before,
of Yugoslavia's brutal prison camp, a stony island in the Adriatic Sea. The interviews were
to be filmed as a documentary.

The camp on Goli otok (Bare Island), was established on Tito's orders in summer
1948, following Yugoslavia's expulsion from the Cominform. Although the island was
not far from the coast, it was uninhabited and inaccessible except by boat. In all, as many
as quarter of a million people may have been imprisoned on Goli otok or elsewhere as
'Cominformists', 90 per cent of them sentenced for "verbal offences".

---

123 Meeting Ignatieff several years after this incident, I asked him about it. "I didn't know Kiš was so ill,"
Ignatieff said with a regretful smile. An eminently political reply.

According to Milovan Đilas, the senior communist who set up the camp, "the vast majority of Cominformists would never have been sent to Goli otok had the proceedings been the least bit legal". Prisoners carried out "socially useful labour", such as carrying stones from one place to another, as part of their "re-education". The penal system on the island was ingenious. Prisoners knew their only chance of release lay through beating and tormenting the other inmates, so proving their love of Tito and the Communist Party. Stalinist methods were applied in the fight against Stalinism. Goli otok came to be seen, Đilas admitted later, as "the darkest and most shameful fact in the history of Yugoslav Communism." An open secret for decades, the prison was closed only in 1988.

Initially, Kiš had resisted the women's request; Goli otok had become almost a fashionable theme, and he shied from adding to the flood of publications. He changed his mind, perhaps because the women's Jewishness confirmed his sense of Jewish identity as a fateful brand. Having survived the Second World War against the odds, these women were sentenced a few years later in a travesty of justice to the hell of Goli otok. Working with the film-maker Aleksandar Mandić, Kiš proved an excellent interviewer despite a hollow cough which he could not shake off (it punctuates the soundtrack). Self-effacing in pursuit of the facts, he keeps a narrative thread, not crowding the interviewees as he focuses on their ethical decisions and the orgiastic brutality of the camp regime. These films, called *Goli život* (Bare Life), address his perennial themes within—for the first time—Yugoslavia, using a new form, documentary film; they make a fitting testament.

A month later he was back in Dubrovnik, guest of honour at a conference about postmodernism and giving an interview to a Croatian magazine. The interviewer, Jas-

With Aleksandar Mandić and Ženi Lebl (Jennie Lebel) on the beach at Tel Aviv, March 1989

mina Kuzmanović, was a young agency reporter "in awe of the greatest living Yugoslav author." She was impressed by his courtesy, dissembling boredom with questions he must have heard many times before; and "struck by how elegantly he spoke, with no preparation, and by how little vanity he showed, surrounded by all those academic admirers." He looked tired, and people talked about how he had cancer, "but nothing about him revealed that he had just a few months left."

In his replies, the old chestnuts were done to a turn. "I want my books to be more credible than the so-called realist novel," he said. "The point-of-view in the classic novel is god-like, the writer is omniscient, and I myself, probably due to a *déformation professionelle*, don't believe a writer who knows everything. . . . Even with the greatest writers, psychology is their weakest point. I don't want to know, and I don't know, what my hero thinks, let alone guess what my heroine's thinking." His practical alternatives were these: either to create "a first-person narrator who is credible, or [to write] so-called documentary prose that has to convince readers that what they read is authentic fact." As for postmodernism, Kiš shrugged: he did not really know what the term meant. If it included the search "not to be anachronistic", however, he was ready to accept that it might have a bearing on his work.

Meeting Kiš for the last time, in Paris, that spring, Gabi Gleichmann was struck by his tenderness with his (Gabi's) new-born son. "He kept running into the bedroom to see the baby. At one point he showed us the galley proofs of a new paperback edition of his *Family Circus*, in French.[124] He had been checking them, and he said *I'm feeling proud of myself. It's good work. I didn't cheat. There's nothing in it that's not solid. I'm happy.* He looked at me, and I at him, and it took a thousandth of a second to realise *that's the wrong word, don't say that.*"

He continued to give interviews. Terrified as he was of dying and racked by self-doubt, his pessimism darkened into cosmic despair. "Communism is eternal", he said near the end. "Nothing can be done. It's too late." When asked about Yugoslavia, he admitted that disintegration and civil war were possible, "but I want to be optimistic. . . . We have to endure and not forget our European matrix." If he had to write a book about his homeland, he would, he said, attempt a Rabelaisian satire about a conference where experts and officials jabber at each other in a language that not even they can understand, let alone the public outside. Arriving in Belgrade in July with Pascale for their usual extended summer visit, he seemed in good form. Filip David was impressed when he ran up the stairwell to prove his good health. But he soon developed pains in his back, and his right arm weakened alarmingly. He told Mirko Kovač to shake his hand; Mirko found that it was inert. Yet even in this condition, he was animated about politics. He told his friend László Végel—a Hungarian writer from Vojvodina—that they should organise a movement of Serbian writers against Milošević. When Végel asked whom else they could

---

124 The *Family Circus* comprises *Early Sorrows, Garden, Ashes,* and *Hourglass.*

invite to join, Kiš was stumped for an answer. It was probably around this time that he met the Bosnian veteran poet, Izet Sarajlić, for the last time, and asked rhetorically "How can I get well in a city that's sick?"

Before he left for Montenegro and Dubrovnik in early August, Kiš wrote a poem in memory of his friend Mira Trailović, who died of cancer on 7 August. A legendary figure in Belgrade's theatre world, Trailović was fondly known as *buldožer u bundi*, 'the bulldozer in furs'.

On news of the death of Madame M.T.

What work well done, Death,
what a feat—
razing a fortress like that!
Gobbling that much meat,
grinding that much bone
so quickly.
Devouring that much energy
so fast, like burning up a cigarette.
What a job there, Death,
what show of force.
(As if you wouldn't've been
taken at your word.)

The poem appeared in *Politika* newspaper on 12 August. It was to be his last published work.[125]

By this time, Kiš was in Cetinje. In the past, his annual visits had brought high-spirited reunions with dear friends. This time, illness and foreboding could not be escaped. Family and legacy were on his mind. He told Pavle Đonović's wife Sonja, "You are a lucky woman. You have two sons." As always, he called on the artist Dimitrije Popović, born in Cetinje in 1951. Popović saw how much weaker he looked than at their previous meeting, a few months earlier. Clutching his lower back from time to time, Kiš explained in a whisper that he must have caught a cold and asked if he could watch television: he featured in a documentary that was to be repeated, and he wanted to see what he used to look and sound like. Watching the image of Kiš on television, comparing it with the ailing man in front of him, Popović had a premonition of Kiš's death.

Kiš and Pascale left that afternoon for the coast under a thundery sky. Strolling through Herceg Novi with Marko Špadijer, he told his old friend that this was probably

---

125 "Word" also ends Samuel Beckett's last work, "What Is the Word" (1988). Beckett, another contender with silence and maker of fundamental sounds, died in December 1989, two months after Kiš.

their last walk together. He talked about committing suicide, though he feared that he lacked the courage. They moved on to Dubrovnik and the Hotel Argentina. At the end of the month, by chance, Maristella Veličković arrived at the same hotel. She found Kiš in the television room, gloomy and defeated, staring at the screen. "I'm sick," he said, without even greeting her. He went to the military hospital in Herceg Novi, a few miles away, for an examination on 5 September. Afterwards he asked a question: "*La commedia è finita?*" The doctor nodded. He and Pascale were due to fly back to Paris on 17 September, but they left early. Back in Paris, the oncologists found metastases in his spine and proposed experimental surgery. Kiš refused. On 17 September, he wrote out his will in a large, shaky hand.

A few days later, Susan Sontag called to tell him he had won the Bruno Schulz Prize, endowed by the novelist Jerzy Kosinski and worth $10,000. But Kiš was beyond reach of good news. From the start of October, he refused further treatment, and even food. Danica remembers Pascale's account of this decision: "I *won't* take more medicine, I *won't* live as an invalid," Kiš declared. "I was born healthy and I want to end as I began." The fascination with circular form that had shaped his writing restored a measure of control over his end. Pascale, who had tended and encouraged him tirelessly, entreated him to swallow something, a little yoghurt, anything. In vain. When Karaulac telephoned, for the last time as it turned out, Kiš announced matter of factly, "Well, I'm dying." He added a line from a famous romantic Serbian poem: "'Comes the time for me to go to the tomb', as they say." Pascale was forbidden to mention his condition in his hearing; when Danica telephoned from Montenegro, she was given bland assurances that he was sleeping and eating well. Stanko Cerović was the only friend he wanted to see. A few days before the end, he said: "I dreamed that I'd died. It was fantastic." Death came at home on 15 October at 6 in the evening. He was fifty-four, his father's age when he was taken away to Auschwitz.

In his will, Kiš specified that he wanted to be buried in Belgrade with Orthodox rites. In her heroic consistency, Mirjana has included the cargo manifest for the flight that carried his corpse to Belgrade on 18 October, in her CD of documents pertaining to Kiš. SPARE PARTS, HUMAN REMAINS, FILTERS, VARIOUS GOODS. . . . He would have approved. It is his final document and inventory.

The funeral took place in Belgrade's New Cemetery on 19 October.[126] It was a warm autumn day, as still as glass. His sister Danica and many of his friends were shocked: how could he—never a believer—have wanted an Orthodox funeral, especially at a time when the Serbian Orthodox Church was playing such a grisly role, stoking the fires of ultranationalism? But there is no mystery. It was his final vindication of the individual and personal over the collective and the political. For the debt to his mother's faith, which had saved him from Auschwitz, had to be honoured. Even so, many mourners were dismayed by

---

126 Kiš was buried beside Petar Lubarda, the artist who had interviewed him forty-two years before in Cetinje.

the Church's pitiless exploitation of the opportunity, packing the cemetery with senior clerics and ignoring Kiš's testamentary instruction that the service should include "no speechifying".

A few months later, after returning from a journey, Milan Milišić jotted down a poem about Kiš:

I saw an image of your lungs
on the aeroplane's wet porthole glass
The clouds: pale billows from all
the cigarettes you smoked
floating motionless

Milišić was to die on 5 October 1991, the first civilian casualty when the Yugoslav army and navy bombarded Dubrovnik. (As the son of a Bosnian Serb father and a Montenegrin mother, devoted to the Croatian city of his birth, he personified the cosmopolitan spirit that was targeted by the warmongers.)

Mirjana Miočinović resigned from Belgrade University soon afterwards, in protest at its leaders' failure to denounce Serbia's war against Croatia. As well as editing Kiš's posthumous publications and collected works, she became an important voice of civic conscience throughout the 1990s, articulating the same principles that Kiš had expressed in literature.

Pascale Delpech persevered with translating Kiš's work into French while she worked for international peacekeeping missions to the former Yugoslavia, and eventually as director of the French cultural centre in Belgrade. As an interpreter with the United Nations, she took part in marathon wartime negotiations with the Bosnian Serbs. Once, during a cigarette break, she found herself on a terrace with General Ratko Mladić, already known as the 'Butcher of Bosnia'. Mladić bent down to pluck a sprig of clover pushing up between the paving of the terrace. He then awarded the clover to Pascale with a gallant gesture.

Safet Zec dedicated his last prewar exhibition—where else but in Dubrovnik—to Kiš. The following year, in 1992, he abandoned his home in besieged Sarajevo and took his family to Italy, where they live to this day. Mirko Kovač left Belgrade in disgust at the nationalist take-over in 1991, moving to Croatia, where he still lives. Borislav Pekić died in London the following year, also of lung cancer, leaving only Filip David in Belgrade of the original quartet.

———

A month after Kiš's funeral, the Yugoslav Writers' Union disintegrated; its last president, Slobodan Selenić, resigned, saying the fate of the union was inextricably linked to that of Yugoslavia as a state. During the remaining months before war began in summer 1991, tributes were paid to Kiš as a distinctly Yugoslav figure. The Croatian poet Jure Kaštelan said finely that his best books were "a precious inheritance for all the Yugoslav literatures."

As Yugoslavia crumpled into bloodshed, intellectuals on all sides trumpeted their nations' primordial uniqueness. The more they did so, the more alike their nations became. Kiš, by contrast, admitted far-flung influences on his work, yet the result was entirely his own. Amid the extreme grievances, zero-sum demands, media manipulation, and fake democracy, his sentences rang true. His quest for identity through literature was incomparably more honest and humane than the boasting about identity that defiled the public space. People spoke of him with sad pride, as if he represented their best selves and they had let him down. In particular, his 1973 broadside against nationalism became a standard reference for anti-war activists.

He was the last in the trio of great Yugoslav artists:

—The sculptor Ivan Meštrović (1883–1962), who—in his early work—represented
  Yugoslavia in terms of heroic synthesis, as a unitary myth.
—The writer Ivo Andrić (1892–1975), who represented Yugoslavia in terms of
  a tragic but still unitary history.
—Danilo Kiš, who represented Yugoslavia by analogy, in terms of a formalism
  that reconciles plural identities and unique influences.

Facing the multiplicity of Yugoslavia, with all its actual and potential clashes and contradictions, as well as its improbable interactions, an artist could be either inclusive or exclusive—could aim for epic or epitome. There are no giant frescoes or historical syntheses in Kiš's writing. He was in search of the communicable universality within childhood, the family crucible, the growth of imagination, persecution, and the maddening delusions of ideology—beneath or beyond the narratives of national victimhood and oppression. (This is why Muharem Bazdulj, a young writer from Bosnia, calls him *the metaphysician of Yugoslavia*.) His work implies that what was crucially or explosively denied in communist Yugoslavia was not one or another nationalist self-description. It was, rather, a space where those accounts could be aired and investigated in all their intricacy, tragedy and lunacy.

"Along with his books," Bazdulj says, "Kiš gave us the entire *terra incognita* of world literature, where they are at home and to which they belong." International criticism of Kiš (such as there is) agrees he was "the most cosmopolitan and innovative Yugoslav writer of the post-World War II period." In Serbia, he has become a touchstone in the study of recent literature. During the 1990s, innovative critics took up the cause of Kiš and Borislav Pekić because their work allowed contemporary approaches to be used and to challenge the traditional canon of Serbian literature. In particular, Aleksandar Jerkov launched the study of the poetics of fiction, metafiction, intertextuality, and other modes of reading that subvert the "dangerous narratives of History, Nation and Territory". More recently, a feminist critic, Tatjana Rosić, presented Kiš as the father of new literary paradigms; *Hourglass* stands to Serbian literature, she suggests, much as Eduard Kis's letter stands to *Hourglass*: a fertile source of fictional possibilities. But Rosić also accused Kiš of "macho self-promotion", patriarchalism, and renewing the "phallocentic narrative of Serbian culture".

Yet others in Serbia still see him as an impostor, a Trojan horse inveigled within the bastion of national culture by hostile forces. In 2005, a fresh assault on his reputation was mounted by one Nebojša Vasović, a Serbian émigré living in Canada. Incensed not only by Kiš and his reputation but also by his vocal admirers, Vasović accused the writer of milking his Jewish identity for sympathy as a universal victim, among other offences, which included a culpable (unpatriotic) fondness for the Croatian writer Krleža. One critic remarked drily that at least the anti-Semitism of Vasović's book was explicit.

Younger writers continue to revere him throughout the area where the Bosnian, Croatian, Montenegrin, Serbian, and even the Slovenian languages are spoken: for his writing, for his shining and combative integrity, and because he personified the road not taken to a different future for their countries. Someone said, rightly, that Kiš became a metaphor of nostalgia for Yugoslavia. Since *Boris Davidovich*, his books have not sold in large numbers, but they stay in print. His publisher in Croatia reported in 1996 that "readers thank us by phone and letter for publishing Kiš, who is a cult author here, with a bigger public than all the members of the Society of Croatian Writers put together"—a taunt that may well have been true. It is wonderful that this isolated, ungovernable man—Milišić called him "irreplaceable and, truth to tell, scarcely conceivable"—provides a consummate standard of responsibility to language and society, beyond his status as, to quote Nadine Gordimer again, "the genius of a particular time, experience and place". This is why Milišić added that "for many of my generation, Kiš grew to be more than a dear man and a writer we valued—he became an institution, a norm." And why Aleksandar Hemon calls him "a role model for a whole generation of young writers of the former Yugoslavia, whose morality illuminated the gloom of nationalistic cultures." There isn't a cheap moment in his books, not a jot of cynicism or exploitation. "There are better story-tellers than Danilo," said Joseph Brodsky, "but there are no better stylists."

Central European writers, Kiš wrote in a fragment, are fated to drag a piano and a dead horse behind them wherever they go (see chapter 31). The piano holds, ark-like, the heritage of Western art, while the dead horse signifies the leaden legacy of local "battles and defeats", "words and melodies that nobody can understand outside that language". Kiš's dreamlike insight came to mind one day in the Serbian Academy of Sciences and Arts. During the 1980s, the academy came to be seen as Serbia's heart of intellectual darkness, breeding murderous resentment against Yugoslavia. Nevertheless, just as he wanted an Orthodox funeral, this was where Kiš wanted his books and papers to be deposited.

After a few hours leafing through his books, I was invited into the head librarian's office. As a Serb from Kosovo, she was keen to challenge Western misconceptions about Serb–Albanian relations in that contested province. When my attention wandered to a trolley loaded with huge leather tomes next to her desk, she smiled for the first time.

"Diderot's Encyclopaedia," she said proudly, "a first edition." It had been bequeathed by Marko Ristić, a surrealist poet from Belgrade who was Tito's first ambassador to Paris. This was a fine coincidence, for Diderot had mattered to Kiš from first to last.[127] As a student, he approved Diderot's thought that distance from loss is essential for creating art about loss; and his last book ends with Diderot's vision of posthumous love, "commingling" a couple's ashes.

From Kosovo's ethnic tyranny to Diderot's enlightenment and beyond—to Joyce, Borges, and a reunited Europe—is almost too far to measure; but it is there, along that spectrum, that Kiš's writing shines most brightly.

---

127 A double coincidence, in fact, for Kiš also admired Marko Ristić (who had, with Serbian insouciance, inked his initials on the title page of volume one of the Encyclopaedia).

Acknowledgements

This endeavour has benefited from the generous assistance of Marina Abramović, Ammiel Alcalay, Linda Asher, Davor Beganović, Neil Belton, Branislav Borilović, Kenneth Brown, Alain Cappon, Cathie Carmichael, Dragana Čitlučanin, the late Norman Cohn, Gordana Crnković, Zlatko Crnković, Predrag Čudić, Helen Darbishire, Filip David, the late Pavle Đonović, the late Vojislav Đurić, Péter Esterházy, Gabi Gleichmann, Slavko Goldstein, Vesna Goldsworthy, Malcolm Hardy, Charles Hebbert, Aleksandar Hemon, Peter Inkei, Alan Jenkins, the late Miroslav Karaulac, Boro Krivokapić, Georges Krygier, Wladimir Krysinski, Jasmina Kuzmanović, Renate Lachmann, John Lyon, Louis Mackay, Dušan Makavejev, Divna Malbaša, Milena Marković, Robyn Marsack, John McCourt, Boško Mijanović, Danica Mitrović, the late Krsto Mitrović, Vida Ognjenović, Sasha Pajević, Milan 'Beli' Popović, Alexandre Prstojević, Regina Rácz, the late Radomir Reljić, David Rieff, Mirjana Robin, Salman Rushdie, Ines Sabalić, Tripo Simonutti, the late Susan Sontag, Marko Špadijer, Eva Spitzer, Ivo Tartalja, Franjo Termaćić, Svetlana Termaćić, Tatijana Termaćić, Bato Tomašević, Sonja Tomović-Šundić, Jelena Trpković, Joanna Trzeciak, Maristella Velićković, Velimir Visković, the late Slobodan Vitanović, Andrew Baruch Wachtel, Eric Beckett Weaver, Ivo Žanić, and Dragomir Zupanc.

In particular, John Ackerman, Ivo Banac, Wendy Bracewell, Aryeh Neier, Peter Palmer, and Dubravka Ugrešić helped and advised in decisive ways. Christina Pribićević-Zorić drafted the translations of "The Lute and the Scars" and Vida Ognjenović's memoir. Vesna Domany Hardy, Celia Hawkesworth, Jim McCue, Marija Mitrović, and Ian Thomson commented valuably on drafts. Nebojša Čagorović, Stanko Cerović (who also introduced me to Josef Holoček), and Ivana Đorđević were companions in this project over many years.

I am obliged to the Open Society Institute, the Society of Authors, and the Leverhulme Trust. Without their support, the book would not have been brought to completion. I am grateful to the Carcanet Press Ltd. for permission to publish excerpts of *Homo Poeticus*. Two short stories from *The Lute and the Scars* ("The Lute and the Scars" and "A and B") are published here with the permission of Dalkey Archive, which published John K. Cox's translation in 2012. Thanks to Faber & Faber for permission to reprint excerpts from *Garden, Ashes*, translated by William Hannaher (1985). I also thank Librairie Arthéme Fayard and Kiš's estate for their kind permission to translate and publish excerpts from Kiš's hitherto untranslated writings.

Above all, my thanks go to Mirjana Miočinović and Pascale Delpech for their patience, trust, and encouragement over many years, despite questions that veered between the intrusive and the banal, and continual requests for practical assistance. My gratitude to them—as more broadly to the dedicatees—is inestimable.

Notes

Introduction: Great and Invisible

xi *Epigraph*: Sontag [2002]. xi *"the genius of a particular time, experience and place"*: Gordimer [1991]. xi *despite admirers . . .* : Nadine Gordimer: "the best of that outstanding group of Eastern European writers [including Kundera and Skvorecky]". Susan Sontag [2002]: "one of the handful of incontestably major writers of the second half of the century". Claudio Magris: "an incomparable writer". Joseph Brodsky: "*Garden, Ashes* [is] a veritable gem of lyrical prose, the best book produced on the Continent in the post-war period." Edmund White [1994]: "*Hourglass* is the most convincing account we have of the Jewish experience in the Second World War." John Bayley: "the remarkable Danilo Kiš, who adds to the other ways in which he cannot be categorised his origins on the borders of Hungary and Yugoslavia, a place where systems, nationalities, and languages meet on what has to be called a permanently temporary basis." Josef Škvorecký: "an extraordinary writer". The critic Harold Bloom counts *A Tomb for Boris Davidovich* among the canonical works of Western literature. xi *"great and invisible"*: Kundera [1999]. xi *"the only one who never sacrificed . . ."*: Kundera [1999]. xi *Rushdie listed a baker's dozen . . .* : Rushdie [2002], 52. The list in full: Albert Camus, Graham Greene, Doris Lessing, Samuel Beckett, Italo Calvino, Elsa Morante, Vladimir Nabokov, Gunter Grass, Aleksandr Solzhenitsyn, Milan Kundera, Danilo Kiš, Thomas Bernhard, and Marguerite Yourcenar. xi *only Kiš was and is out of print in Britain . . .* : Sales figures in the United Kingdom from 1998 to May 2003 make cheerless reading: *Early Sorrows* 6, *Garden, Ashes* 2, *Homo Poeticus* 20, *The Encyclopaedia of the Dead* 97, *Hourglass* 98, *A Tomb for Boris Davidovich* 199 (statistics from BookScan). The publishers were Faber & Faber and Carcanet in the United Kingdom, and Farrar Straus & Giroux and Northwestern University Press in the United States. xi *"You think my Wednesday people . . ."*: The novel is *The Messiah of Stockholm* (Ozick [1988], 14). Lars Andemening, the protagonist in Ozick's novel, is a book-reviewer, here being upbraided for his devotion to unmodish Central European writers. xii *"He was a very rooted writer, but also completely cosmopolitan"*: Susan Sontag to the author, Tuzla, 20 October 1995. xiii *"vast area of tribes and nationalities . . ."*: U.S. Assistant Secretary of State Richard Holbrooke, quoted in the *Financial Times*, 21 February 1996. The Second World War and the Cold War did not begin in the Balkans; the point is, this region is seen as a perennial source and spawning-ground of bad things. xiii *"I don't have close ties . . ."*: V, 489. Please see the bibliography for the abbreviations used for Kiš's works. xiii *"the permanent search for form"*: HPEI, 197. xiii *He printed the text elsewhere . . .* : IPDK, 570; *ARS* [2009], 201.

Birth Certificate

1 Translated by Michael Henry Heim: ES, 115–18; HPEI, 3–5.

Chapter 2

5 *"Miksha looked up at that portrait . . ."*: TBD, 14. 6 *"nothing in a writer's life is accidental"*: GTI, 238. 7 *These three poems about his mother, father, and sister . . .* : P. Čudić makes this point at PP, 18. 7 *His ancestors may have been . . .* : GTI, 248. 7 *"The wood in the forests he owned . . ."*: GTI, 249. 7 *"a rare encounter . . ."*: Skl, 339. 8 Danilo / male / Jew *reads the entry . . .* : Krstić, 31. 8 *"to cut*

short his suffering...": HPEI, 239. 9 *After reading up on psychopathology and anxiety...:* HPEI, 248. 9 *"the son of a 'writer', of an authentic...":* HPEI, 209. 9 *as Danilo would tell a friend...:* Krygier in conversation with the author, 22 April 2010. 9 *We get on the train with our absurd baggage...:* ES, 91. 11 *memories of his father "are negatives...":* HPEI, 238. 11 *"the father who appears in my works...":* HPEI, 238–39.

Chapter 3

13 *"when we're among metaphors...":* GTI, 142; also GTI, 171. 13 *"non-narrative I"* ("svoje nepripovedačko ja"): Skl, 159. 13 *"the maker's invisible and unseen mark", etc.:* Skl, 159.

Chapter 4

15 *Epigraph:* Balašević, 154. 15 *"contact zone between Illyrians...":* Mócsy, 5. 16 *The Pannonians do not live in towns...:* Mócsy, 21. 16 *"one of the last and most difficult conquests...":* Gibbon, vol. 1, ch. 5. 16 *"became attractive to many easterners...":* Mócsy, 5. 16 *"the tame resemblance of Roman provincials":* Gibbon, vol. 1, ch. 5. 16 *"paralysing economic life...":* Gibbon, vol. 2, ch. 20. 17 *"retaliated on the Avars,...":* Gibbon, vol. 9, ch. 49. 17 *"the outside world: a great, almost cosmic deluge...":* Czigány, 37. 17 *"unknown and forgotten.... waiting more than 400 years...":* Krleža [1963], 176. 17 *"a cultural space whose boundaries...":* Snel [2004], 355. 18 *If a man endowed with a dog's hearing...:* H, 26–27. 18 *"anthropological novel":* HP, 203 ff. 18 *Ulysses has been called...:* by novelist Anthony Burgess [1990]. 18 *Today as I was riding towards Kalibunar...:* Andrić [1992], 105. 19 *"situated geographically in the centre...":* Kundera [1984], 108. 19 *"development of a Pannonian consciousness...":* Fitz, 30. 20 *"Miłosz as well as Kundera naming him...":* Zagajewski, xii. 20 *he was giving up hope that Yugoslav writers...:* Babić, 65. 20 *"a Europeanwriter in the first place":* GTI, 264. 20 *"if there is a style and a sensibility...":* GTI, 264. 20 *he pointed out that foreign readers...:* GTI, 173. 21 *"Variations on Central European Themes":* quotations are from this essay, which is included in HPEI, 95–114. 22 *"we have come to the era of post-art":* Kundera [2010]. 22 *When Wittgenstein explained...:* Monk, 300–301. 22 *Claudio Magris from Trieste, when he commented...:* Thompson [1992]. 22 *Guy Scarpetta finely remarks...:* Scarpetta [1996], 180–81.

Chapter 5

23 *"As a result, until 1942...":* HPEI, 244.

Chapter 6

25 *"according to Jewish encyclopaedias...":* Levi, 47.

Chapter 7

27 *"an alchemical process":* HPEI, 59–60. 27 *"self-immanence":* HPEI, 178. 28 *"If a story attains the grace of form...":* V, 511. 28 *"a polyphonic whole"...:* HP, 205–6. 28 *"Any biography, especially...":* GTI, 236. 28 *"dreams of Paris...":* V, 452. 28 *"the crowd of characters...":* M, 83. 28 *"failed to attain the grace of form":* ED, 119. 28 *Some time in February-March 1976...:* Skl, 136–39. 29 *"when you blew on the downy surface...":* ES, 89. 29 *"The damp had covered the walls...":* M, 19. 29 *"The moisture on the ceiling...":* BP, 29. 29 *It culminates in* Hourglass, *where...:* H, 100–101. 30 *"in the pale glow of the oil lamp":* BP, 179. 30 *"The room was like the hold...":* M, 19. 30 *"The waves of night dash...":* H, 3, 4. 30 *"The guard escorted me to an...":* ED, 40. 30 *"awareness of the relativity...":* HPEI, 29. 30 *"a woman with an eternal...":* ES, 85. 31 *"Clusters of lilac that disintegrate...":* PP, 41. 31 *"so they can be afflicted...":* HP, 254. 31 *"to kill this unnecessary, tongue-*

tied . . .": IPDK, 567. 31 *"like a tumour"*: HP, 43. 31 *"it's multiplying, even . . ."*: HPEI, 226. 31 *or the schematic drawing of a plant* . . . : ED, 64–65. 31 *"We are haunted by twin phantasmagorias . . ."*: Adair, 152–53.

Chapter 8

35 *"only way to convey knowledge . . ."*: HPEI, 266. 35 Hourglass *could not have been written* . . . : GTI, 131. 36 *"comprehensive vision of the world . . .*: HPEI, 135, 136. 36 *Borges's impossible objects* . . . : Manguel, 58. 36 *"courting a dead end . . ."*: Kenner, xiii. 36 *"narrative omniscience and . . ."*: ŽL, 59. 36 *"no writer tried, with more success . . ."*: Cheyette, 56. 36 *Saul Bellow deprecated Joyce* . . . : Bellow. (See Bluefarb for an argument that Moses Herzog, Bellow's most famous creation, shares many traits with Joyce's anti-heroic hero.) 37 *the loss of the father created* . . . : Davison, 204. 38 Joyce *"was abstemious during . . ."*: Ellmann [1977], 693. 38 *"atmosphere of spiritual effort"*: quoted by Nadel, 224. 38 *"excitement, movement, arguments . . ."*: HP, 177. 38 *"a sort of encyclopædia"*: Ellmann [1977], 535. 38 *Kiš's literary "ideal"* . . . : GTI, 19. 38 *"should never write about the . . ."*: Ellmann [1977], 470. 38 *"the outcome of a passion . . ."*: Ellmann [1977], 588. 38 *what he called "belated" Ireland*: Joyce [2000a], 50. 38 *"The hands on our literary clock tower . . ."*: Krleža [1963], 16. 38 *called Europe "his spiritual father"*: Ellmann [1977], 737. 38 *"our European matrix"*: GTI, 305. 38 *nationalist "trolls" in Ireland* . . . : Joyce [2000a], 62. 39 *"You have to be in exile . . ."*: Ellmann [1977], 706. 39 *"We moderns all came not . . ."*: GTI, 56. 39 *"Joyce's wonderful defeat . . ."*: HP, 110. 39 *Virginia Woolf, who had called* Ulysses. . . : V, 208. 39 *Kiš explained that by "defeat"* . . . : Skl, 176. 39 *"no true art" can be "without a strong dose of banality"*: Cioran, quoted by Pavel, 26.

First Interlude: *The Garret*

41 *Epigraph*: Johnson. 42 *"I started writing it . . ."*: V, 492. 43 *"the popular image of the artist . . ."*: Berlin [2001], 204. 43 *"in the lightest, most Parisian way . . ."*: White [1998]. 43 *we know that Gide was on his mind in September 1959* . . . : V, 546. 43 *He said it had a trippy feel* . . . : GTI, 104; Skl, 343. 44 *Daviĉo responded generously* . . . : IP, 31–34. 44 *One reviewer objected* . . . : Skl, 343. 44 *his new book* The Garret . . . : Krysinski [2010]. 45 *"national Serbian literature . . ."*: Pantić, 15. 45 *"fatal lack of ironic detachment . . ."*: HPEI, 249.

Chapter 9

47 *"Israelite inhabitants of the country"*: quoted by Braham [1981], 3. 47 *Unlike in Austria, however* . . . : McCagg. 47 *seeing the Jews' best prospects in a liberal Magyar state*: Barany. 48 *By 1910, Hungary had the third largest* . . . : Braham [1981], 2. 48 *"hundreds of thousands of Jews"*: Ozsváth, 338. 48 *"more intelligence and more industriousness"*: Katz. 48 *"The anti-Semite is a man . . ."*: Poliakov [2003], 40. 49 *several thousand Jews were murdered* . . . : Ozsváth, 338, cites an estimate of 5,000 to 6,000. 49 *Joseph Roth noted in the mid-1920s* . . . : Roth, 89.

Chapter 10

51 *Owners of the very widespread name Kohn* . . . : Krstić, 43. 51 *"a disguised but none the less . . ."*: Nadel, 143. 51 *"A proper name is an extremely important . . ."*: Flaubert, 333. 51 *E.S.'s "nightmarish memory"* . . . : H, 39.

Chapter 11

53 *their failure "to settle the Jewish question"*: Arendt [1985], 140. 53 *"a lovely Sunday morning in Budapest"*: Levi, 23. 53 *although some 60,000* . . . : Deák. 53 *The Hungarian regent, Admiral*

Horthy . . . : Cesarani, 5, 16; Bullock, 877. 53 *"had absolute proof . . ."*: Braham [2000], 122. 53 *Preparations for a huge influx . . .* : Vrba. 53 *Eichmann explained that his orders . . .* : Eichmann, quoted by LeBor and Boyes, 282. 53 *"like a dream"*: Arendt [1985], 140. 53 *"the entire state apparatus . . ."*: captions in the Holocaust Museum in Budapest. 53 *"probably the greatest and most horrible . . ."*: Cesarani, 38. 54 *They had not been ghettoised . . .* : LeBor and Boyes, 176. 54 *"strict and conscientious"*: from the "Appeal to Hungarian Jewry" published in the official *Journal of Hungarian Jews*, 23 April 1944, quoted by LeBor and Boyes, 261. 54 *"matching the regional organisation . . ."*: Cesarani, 16. 54 *"deluged with protests . . ."*: Arendt [1985], 201. 54 *"in daily terror of their lives"*: Szép, x. 54 *his mind did not flinch . . .* : P, 281. 55 *84 per cent of the Jews from Zala died . . .* : Braham, ed. [1969], 179. 55 *eventual "loss of Jews from the Hungarian-annexed . . ."*: Tomasevich, 591. 55 *Zalaegerszeg, where the guards . . .* : Braham [1981], 670, 671. 55 *By early July, the ghetto held 3,209 . . .* : Braham [1981], 670, 671. 55 *"small single room in the depths of the ghetto"*: BP, 137. 55 *"In Auschwitz, we . . ."*: NM, 119. 55 *"his treacherous bowels"*: ES, 82. 56 *"painted a triptych entitled . . ."*: Francis Bacon, quoted by Sylvester, 344. 56 *"When I was writing my own long poem . . ."*: Szirtes [2008]. 56 *his only published comments on art and the Holocaust . . .* : V, 90–93.

Chapter 12

57 *"a crucified wilderness"*: Đilas [1966], 14. 57 *he slew more than eighty "Turks"*: Đilas [1966], 213. 57 *Like the Spartans of old, Marko . . .* : Holeček; Herodotus, 487. 57 *so small that not even a dead man . . .* : Đilas [1966], 183, 334. 57 *intrigued against him in 1882*: Holeček, 156–57. 57 *"had no more than 100 . . ."*: Roberts, 261. 57 *"handwriting was square and firm . . ."*: HPEI, 243. 58 *"Generosity is shown in small . . ."*: Cerović [2008], 115. 58 *the Plutarch of Montenegrin patriarchalism*: Dvorniković, 411. 59 *Marko asked the Czech how people lived in Europe . . .* : Cerović [2008], 117–23. 59 *"there was no harmony . . ."*: Cerović [2008], 123–24. 59 *"My point of departure . . ."*: HPEI, 275–76. 60 *"No longer are there only commissars . . ."*: review of *Typhus* by Erih Koš, V, 396. 60 *He once defined the "essence" . . .* : GTI, 202. 60 *praised the physical and moral healthiness . . ."*: Skerlić, quoted by Čolović [2000], 138. 61 *"Here was his home—in the thick of battle"*, etc.: Borges [1985], 149, 231.

Chapter 13

63 *"strange race"*: GTI, 308. 63 *"has an ardent desire . . ."*: Cvijić, quoted by Carmichael, 65. 63 *As for the Macedonians . . .* : Carmichael, 75. 63 *"the worship of authorities . . ."*: Živković's paraphrase. 64 *"their cold egoism . . ."*: Cvijić, quoted by Banac [1988a], 311. 64 *For Cvijić, it has been said, "the higher the altitude . . ."*: Živković. 64 *Hence the Serbian government's decision . . .* : Wachtel [1998], 257. 64 *"dynamism, rhythm, strong temperament . . ."*: Dvorniković, quoted by Wachtel [1998], 94. 64 *"fighting strength" and "love of freedom" . . .* : Dvorniković, quoted by Žanić, 411. 64 *"the outstanding theorist of Serbian imperialism"*: Dinko Tomašic, quoted by Živković. The full quotation: "the outstanding theorist of Serbian expansionism, attempts to establish the superiority of the Dinaric race and the necessity of transforming other Yugoslav types into subordinate groups under the leadership of Serbia". Tomašic, 53. 64 *"lowlanders could be seen . . ."*: Živković. 64 *"fairly accurate"*, etc.: Joel Halpern and Eugene Hammel, quoted by Živković. 64 *verged, quite logically, into eugenics . . .* : Wachtel [1998], 260. 65 *If I were to rummage . . .* : Skl, 190–91. 65 *"my eschatological conviction . . ."*: GA, 77. 65 *Medical confirmation of infertility . . .* : From Kiš's unpublished correspondence, disclosed to author. 65 *titled "Golden Rain" . . .* : PE, 36–40. 66 *"an attempt at a global vision of reality"*: HPEI, 266. 66 *"She shakes the snow . . ."*: H, 14. 66 *"he was wrapped up in a scarf . . ."*: ARS [2009], 101. 66 *"I remember seeing him . . ."*: Goldsworthy, 169.

Chapter 14

67 "quite disproportionate role" . . . : Katzburg, 96. 67 *the government said there would be no further . . .* : Katzburg, 104. 67 *"capital in Hungary should work under Christian direction"*: Katzburg.

63 *If this bill becomes law . . .* : quoted by Cesarani, 57.   68 *"We cannot kill the cow that we want to milk"*: Katzburg.   69 *"I am half-Jewish, or Jewish . . ."*: HPEI, 257.   69 *"I am a Jew insofar as others . . ."*: GTI, 346.   69 *an "inauthentic Jew" who . . .* : HPEI, 217.   69 *"in a Jewish family in which. . ."*: GTI, 345.   69 *"fear, hunger and injustice"*: HPEI, 204.   69 *"My fate is to be a wandering Jew"*: GTI, 333.   69 *the seal of his "troubling dissimilarity"*: HPEI, 233–34.   69 *The policy on national identity . . .* : Handbook, 129.   69 *"In contrast to all former states . . ."*: Jews in Yugoslavia, 127.   69 *Having lost 80 per cent . . .* : Sekelj et al., 84, 93.   70 *"A year before she died . . ."*: GTI, 227; HPEI, 205.   70 *to denounce anti-Semitic outbursts . . .* : V, 597–607.   71 *one of his stories*: "The Story of the Master and the Disciple", ED, 119.   71 *"an important element in Jewish mysticism"*: Séronya, 25.   72 *"never 'loved' any people or collective"*: Kirsch.   72 *"To confine them [Jews] within . . ."*: Benbassa, 113.   72 *"does at least create identity . . ."*: Benbassa, 181.   72 *"something inadvertently Jewish . . ."*: HPEI, 266.   72 *Scarpetta agrees, seeing Hourglass as . . .* : Scarpetta [1996], 203.   72 *"witty poetical conceit" to . . .* : Boyarin, 2.   72 *what Cynthia Ozick termed . . .* : Ozick [1991], 223.   72 *a form of story which "Jews tell well" . . .* : Berman, 253.   72 *"self-questioning and uncomfortable . . ."*: Judt.   72 *"playing the Creator . . ."*: GTI, 290.   73 *"power of abstraction, profound . . ."*: Cox.

Chapter 15

75 *There had been cases of organised anti-Semitism . . .* : Milentijević.   75 *Anti-Jewish legislation followed . . .* : Tomasevich, 582.   76 *Did it take you two hours . . .* : H, 172–73.

Chapter 16

77 *"one who himself, or at least . . ."*: Katzburg.   78 *Kiš had no doubt . . .* : GTI, 202; Horvath, 109. ("I survived mainly thanks to having been Christened in the Orthodox faith": Tel.)   78 *transformation for flight, that is . . .* : Canetti [1981], 395.

Chapter 17

79 *Kiš told an interviewer . . .* : HPEI, 238.   79 *"every barbershop window . . ."*: HPEI, 238.   79 *As Sava Babić points out . . .* : Babić, 22.   79 *Hitler issued orders . . .* : Bullock, 770.   79 *"liberate Southern Hungary"*, etc.: Sakmyster, 256.   79 *kissing the ground . . .* : LeBor and Boyes, 176.   79 *Further south, inside Serbia proper . . .* : Milentijević.   80 *may have been supported by the Germans . . .* : Macartney, 69.   80 *"while stipulating that no 'superfluous' . . ."*: Macartney, 71.   80 *"the final solution of the Jewish question"*: Wannsee Protocol, quoted by Roseman, 108.   80 *Novi Sad was sealed off . . .* : Macartney, 71–72.   80 *Some 7,000 suspects were rounded up . . .* : Braham [1981], 209.   80 *Groups were executed at street corners . . .* : Braham [1981], 210.   80 *"was carried through with unbelievable . . ."*, etc.: Macartney, 72.   81 *The "pacification" in the Vojvodina . . .* : Jaša Romano (1980), Jevreji Jugoslavije, 1941–1945, 159–60, quoted by Tomasevich, 590.   81 *"a haven for Jews . . ."*: Arendt [1985], 139.   81 *were branded collectively as "partisans"*: Braham [1981], 212.   81 *The officers were tried . . .* : Sakmyster; Macartney, 254.   81 *"Although we destroyed the occupying . . ."*: Cseres, 19–20.   81 *Accounts by survivors are as harrowing . . .* : Ludányi; Cseres.   81 *"my father was following the logic of his financial ruin"*: HPEI, 236.   81 *"torn from sleep one night . . ."*: HPEI, 235–36.   82 *"by a miracle"*: GTI, 117.   82 *Kiš's account differs slightly . . .* : HPEI, 238, 244, 245.   82 *"How disappointed she must have been . . ."*: HPEI, 236.   82 *According to his son . . .* : GTI, 224.   82 *"I saw death very close up, and I was afraid"*: GTI, 307.   82 *"At the time I was completely cut off . . ."*: HPEI, 236.   82 *the beginning of his "conscious life"*: Tel.   83 *Very early one morning, my mother . . .* : BP, 55–59.

Second Interlude: *Garden, Ashes*

86 *"within a chapter, even within the same phrase . . ."*: Ferenczi, 91–92.   86 *"un effet de simultanéité . . ."*: Prstojević [2005], 50.   86 *Rilke's* Doppelbereich . . . : see the ninth of Rilke's "Sonette an Orpheus",

the Sonnets to Orpheus (1922). 87 *"Every time I read this passage . . .":* Hemon [n.d.]. 89 *"magical memories of a Holocaust childhood":* Sicher, 155. 90 *"I wanted to show someone saving himself . . .":* V, 486. 90 *"in spurts" as he said . . .* : V, 493. 90 *"Why, they are one and the same . . .":* V, 493. 90 *"I am convinced that it is me . . .":* V, 486. 91 *"old enough to remember but too young . . .":* Suleiman, 278, 277, 286, 291, 294. 91 *"there was almost always the reparative urge . . .":* Hoffmann, 68, 16. 91 *Freud's theory that mourning . . .* : Hoffmann, 72. 91 *"Passengers were requested to bring . . .":* Appelfeld, 11. 92 *"The sliding door was closed on us . . .":* Kertész [2005], 71. 92 *"For even there, next to the chimneys . . .":* Kertész [2005], 262. 93 *Miroslav Krleža's memoir . . .* : V, 489. 93 *Kiš had helped Filip David . . .* : Raca; David [1999]. 93 *to these friends, who were dazzled:* David [1999]

Chapter 18

95 *. . . a dark, low-ceilinged room . . .* : BP, 66. 96 *Nothing in the world would make him . . .* : H,164–66. 98 *"undulating" just as Kiš wrote . . .* : H, 12. 98 *". . . our new home, 'servants' quarters' . . .":* GA, 56. 98 From the outside: *The hut is screened . . .* : Skl, 271–72. 100 *. . . Those who knew / what was going on here . . .* : Szymborska. 100 *According to Kiš, this teacher was . . .* : NM, 7. 100 *One of the essays she set . . .* : Tel. 101 *"the frightful burden" of his sins:* GA, 80. 101 *All the lyrical pathos of the Catholic Church . . .* : HPEI, 26. 101 *so I imagined myself trembling . . .* : GA, 71. 102 *loaded "with all the seed of living things . . .":* Dalley, 122. 102 *Andi sees "the descendants of Noah . . .", etc.:* GA, 110, 115. 102 *"endlessly repeated, . . . reduce themselves . . .":* H, 15. 102 *a conviction "that it will survive us . . .":* H, 51. 102 *swimming in deep water, in total darkness . . .* : H, 74–75. 103 *Let my body be my ark and my death . . .* : H, 262–63. 103 *When the Mesopotamian source of the Flood myth was discovered . . .* : quotations in this paragraph and the next are from Cohn, 15; Ryan and Pitman, 249, 237, 250, 246; Dalley, 50.

Chapter 19

105 Dissimilarity *was Kiš's favourite word. . .* : quotations in the first three paragraphs are from GTI, 184, 183, 238, 187. 106 *"preserve the disintegrated condition . . .":* GTI, 43. 108 *"those mysterious disappeared people . . .":* GTI, 225. 109 *Noah's Ark (From Mr Poppy's notebook):* V, 44–47. 112 *"For Kiš," as his friend Predrag Čudić . . .* : P. Čudić, 18. 113 *to "recreate life out of life":* James Joyce, quoted by Diment, 112. 113 *Why Kiš defined literature as a parallel life . . .* : GTI, 226, 287. 113 *"evil is never 'radical' . . .":* Arendt [1978a], 251. 114 *"The nationalist fears no one, 'no one but God' . . .":* HPEI, 19. 114 *"The subject of self-censorship . . .":* ŽL, 100. 114 *"the philological jousts between Zagreb and Belgrade . . .":* HPEI, 31. 114 *"a barrier . . . that from humanity divorced / Humanity . . .":* Wordsworth (1850), *The Prelude* 7, 388–91, quoted by Hartman, 447. 115 *"gazing at its own narcissistic likeness . . .":* Skl, 170. 115 *"everyone we meet invents us . . .":* Phillips, 7. 115 *"magical and self-fertilising transformation . . .":* ČA, 157. 115 *"a book is the product . . .":* Proust, quoted by Kundera [1995], 267. 115 *or Aleksandr Solzhenitsyn . . . or Roland Barthes . . .* : Solzhenitsyn, quoted by Fitzpatrick; Barthes, quoted by Sontag [2007a], 152. 116 *"It was by way of imitation . . .":* Adorno, 366. 117 *"He moved through the fields . . .":* GA, 88. 116 *Mr Sam was sitting up stiff and straight . . .* : GA, 132–34. 117 *the belief "that children . . .":* Crawley. 117 *"the double of the Demiurge":* Skl, 337. 117 *"the body of his father . . .":* this and other quotations in this paragraph, Crawley. 118 *"the dialectics of interdependent points . . .":* Krysinski [2010]. 121 *Kafka's tale, "The Hunter Gracchus" . . .* : Kafka, 90, 92, 87. 122 *"a soundless solitary dialogue":* Arendt [1978b], 190. 122 *"talking with oneself . . . hence also inwardly listening":* Kant, quoted by Arendt [1978b], 186. 122 *"this duality of myself with myself" . . .* : Arendt [1978b], 185. Emphasis added. 122 *A man stands before a window . . .* : HP, 146. 123 *"familiar compound ghost" . . .* : Eliot [1978], 193, 195.

Third Interlude: *Early Sorrows*

128 *"l'homme ne vit pas l'Histoire, il vit dans l'histoire":* GTI, 270. 128 *"images" that "could not be worked into":* GTI, 128. 131 *"weighed down by snow":* H, 64. 132 *How I want to leave, go far away . . .* : with

thanks to Eric Beckett Weaver for finding and translating this untitled poem by Dezső Kosztolányi. Written in 1910 and known by its first line, "Másként halálos csend és néma untság" (A different deadly silence and silent boredom), the poem was published in Kosztolányi's collection, *A szegény kisgyermek panaszai* (Complaints of a Poor Child). 132 *Ivana Vuletić has explored with finesse* . . . : Vuletić, 117–52.

Chapter 20

135 *One autumn evening (if the reader* . . . : BP, 198–99; GA, 167–68. 135 *He confirmed to an interviewer in 1985 that* . . . : GTI, 169. 136 *"the first post-Party, post-Partisan generation"* . . . : ARS [2009], 314. 136 *will recur in the last story* . . . : Vassileva noticed this.

Chapter 21

137 *Then, in a long lyrical monologue* . . . : BP, 179. 138 *"in long rhythmical lines without a break* . . .": BP, 177. 139 *"our history, our ethnography, our psychology* . . .": ŽL, 121. 139 *"dreamed of collecting folk poetry like Vuk Karadžić"*: HPEI, 28. 139 *what he called "the pleasure of narration"*: TBD, 31. 140 *Without realising it, my mother had created* . . . : ES, 89. 140 *"I can't write at all without two conditions* . . .": HPEI, 268.

Fourth Interlude: *Hourglass*

141 *The difference between a story and novel* . . . : Skl, 133. 141 *"as if it were an opening* . . .": GTI, 27–28. 141 *"I simply did not have the information* . . .": Tel. 141 *"300 or 400 pages, two or three versions* . . .": Pekić [2002], 96. 141 *"pushing ahead millimetre* . . .": Pekić [2002], 109. 141 *"at least a thousand pages"*: Kovač [1994], 126. 142 *Kiš reckoned—not without pride* . . . : Pekić [2002], 120. 142 *"kept fewer than 300* . . .": HP, 230. 142 *"Every word of that is balm* . . .": Karaulac [2007]. 142 *"Is my father alive?' I asked* . . .": Schulz [1980], 116. 145 *a canvas of Plato's cave*: Motola. 145 *Leopold Bloom's list* . . . : Joyce [2000b], 855. 148 *"Half of a Jew's life," Joseph Roth* . . . : Roth, 68. 148 *This bullying interrogator is* . . . : Charles Newman, an American reviewer, noticed this: "By the end of the book, we realize that it is we, the readers, who are doing the interrogating". 150 *Joyce's* Ulysses *both is, and is more than* . . . : see Ellmann [1986], xiii, 116. 150 *Kiš praised "work that has the courage* . . .": Lévy [2007]. 150 *"The letter was necessary"* . . . : Tel. 150 *critics have taken him at his word*: for example, Barańczak; Gordimer; Newman; Proguidis [1996b]; Prstojević [2003b]; Scarpetta [1996], 185. Motola, a rare sceptic, refers to the letter as "ostensibly written by Kiš's father". 151 *"I believe that literature must correct History* . . .": HPEI, 206. 151 *"you can remain the friend of the sufferer* . . .": Arendt [1978b], 188, 192. 151 *Kiš liked to say that literature is freedom*: HP, 280. 152 *"When they meet,* anything *is possible* . . .": Sartre [1955], 22–23. 152 *"Why does this deception* . . .": Berlin [2005], 339. 153 *"a Jack-in-the-box, a Fabergé gem* . . .": McCarthy, 20. 153 *"no masquerade of plot, no hero* . . .": HP, 60–62. (The novel was *Pustolina* [The Desert] by Vladan Radovanović.) 154 *Scarpetta, the book's best critic* . . . : Scarpetta [1996]. 154 *"I tried to replace the monotony* . . .": HPEI, 163. 155 *"barely transparent darkness"*: V, 42. 155 *"the kind of prohibition* . . .": Hoffman, 15. 156 *"I feel the issue is not so much moral as literary"*: HPEI, 263. 156 *"a combinatorial game* . . .": Calvino, 22. 156 *"the most convincing account we have* . . .": White [1994]. 156 *"it is precisely when the author's work* . . .": Sontag [1993], 187. 156 *"there are no cracks in it"*: HP, 241. 157 *the fictional equivalent of twelve-tone music* . . . : V, 368. 157 *Yet he wondered if he had muted the emotion* . . . : Tel. 157 *made a mistake by putting the Letter at the end* . . . : Cerović [1992], 132. 157 *"What mimetic power, what metamorphic strength!* . . .": Albahari [1992], 73. 158 *self-styled "revolutionary democrats"* . . . : Lakičević, 135. 158 *Ritually accused in the press* . . . : Perović [2000a], 11. 158 *"a broad coalition of Stalinists and nationalists"*: Perović [2000a], 95. 158 *"Do you really have to go?"*: Nenadović, 157. 158 *"incorrigible opportunists and cynical power-seekers"*: Nenadović, 159. 159 *either "Europeanisation" or "the ethnic state"* . . . : Perović [2000a], 74, 97. 159 *"traditionalist, positivist, sociological"* . . . : HP, 91–92.

Chapter 22

161 *"a rubbish bin of cities writ large . . ."*: GTI, 188. 161 *"put on the Index by the new order . . ."*: GA, 41. 161 *"the significance and magnitude . . ."*: GA, 37. 162 *"vulcanological, Zionistical, zoogeographical . . ."*: BP, 45–47. 162 *". . . to know the truth more fully . . ."*: Rabelais, 506. 162 *aspires to something absurdly unattainable while . . .* : Viktoria Radics makes this point at 137. 162 *The avant-garde, Kiš concluded, "has sought . . ."*: HP, 58. 163 *"the broad masses can learn nothing . . ."*: Lukács, quoted by Lunn, 82. 163 *"a poem that was nothing more . . .* : GTI, 187. 163 *"Human and animal debris: nail parings, . . ."*: Mihailovich [1994]. 165 *what Guy Scarpetta calls "a liberated imagination" . . .* : Scarpetta [1996], 194–97. 165 *"strive to (re)construct a (lost) totality"*: Rakusa [1992], 78. 165 *"born in 1899 in Esztergom, Hungary . . ."*: TBD, 56. 165 *I see Verschoyle retreating from Malaga . . .* : TBD, 20–21. 166 *"the ineffable joys of enumeration"*: Perec, 198. 166 *"rather too perfectly astonishing" inventories of Borges*: Perec, 196. 166 *"A notebook and fragments of Pilsudski's proclamations . . ."*: Babel, 193. 166 *"And images that are invented by poets . . ."*: ARS [2005], 268–71. 166 *"work of writing is always done . . ."*: Perec, 133. 167 *cosmopolitanism was the primary attribute . . .* : V, 202. 167 *"cosmopolitan and autochthonous, European and Hungarian"*: V, 290. 167 *acclaimed Borges as cosmopolitan*: Skl, 337. 167 *"For I had already soared above Belgrade . . ."*: V, 530. 167 *"marked with shameful 'cosmopolitanism' . . ."*: GTI, 183. See also HPEI, 102. 168 *"a form of malicious though illusory . . ."*: Anderson, 75. 168 *"a free circulation around the globe . . ."*: Damrosch [2006], 105. 168 *the text is available elsewhere*: HPEI, 15–19; Thompson [1993], 338–41. 169 *"notorious"*: ČA, 30. 169 *a blow-by-blow account to their mutual friend*: Pekić [2002], 355–59. 170 *According to Mirjana, the quarrel also left Kiš shaken . . .* : GTI, 123; Miočinović [2007]. 170 *a vociferous advocate of Serbian nationalist opinions . . .* : Mihailović, cited in Popov, ed. [1996]. 170 *"actively engaged in promoting Serbian nationalism . . ."*: Slapšak, Snel, and Neubauer, 408. 170 *as Andrew Wachtel has shown . . .* : Wachtel [1998]. 171 *"Danilo was practically the only Serbian . . ."*: Tolnai. 171 *"Dobrica has opened the Serb . . ."*: Tolnai. 171 *in May 1968, when Ćosić caused a stir . . .* : Wilson, 188.

Chapter 23

173 *"All that matters is convincing the reader," he would say . . .* : HPEI, 199, 198. 173 *"Unfortunately the modern novel is quite unable . . ."*: V, 486. 174 *"the heroine of a future book"*: V, 485. 175 *Kiš's most dogged critic complained . . .* : Jeremić, 173. Elsewhere he accused Kiš of being "wholly insensitive to historical accuracy": Jeremić, 205. 175 *"Metalanguage remains the same . . ."*: Riffaterre, xvi. 175 *According to the archives, the victims . . .* : see the Yad Vashem database of Shoah victims, http://www.yadvashem. org/wps/portal/!ut/p/_s.7_0_A/7_0_FL?last_name=Frojd&first_name=Maksim&location=Novi%20 Sad&next_form=results (accessed July 2011); Golubović, 318; BAJKA.org, a Serbian online forum, http://www.bajka.org/viewtopic.php?f=59&t=21 (accessed July 2010). 175 *"The finer the line distinguishing fact from fiction . . ."*: Ní Mheallaigh. 175 *When Karlo Štajner faulted the accuracy . . .* : HPEI, 256–57. 175 *"facts in literary form" . . .* : Tel. 175 *date back two thousand years . . .* : Ní Mheallaigh. 175 *"that it was really like that (more or less) . . ."*: Skl, 336. 176 *"Once again I pull out . . ."*: Sansom. 176 *He once copied out some samples . . .* : Skl, 164. 176 *"divine or godlike point-of-view"*: Skl, 335. 176 *"a vision and sense of a time-honoured . . ."*: Beckett [1995]. 176 *"In the presence of extraordinary reality . . ."*: Stevens, 165. 177 *for "more and more readers" . . .* : Sontag [1979], 74. 177 *"I don't write so-called fantastic tales" . . .* : Skl, 353. 177 *"Whereof we cannot dream" . . .* : HP, 64. 177 *In 1983, Kovač published an excerpt . . .* : ARS [2009], 88–89, 102–6.

Chapter 24

179 *As many as 50,000 Montenegrins would die . . .* : Roberts, 31, 393. 179 *"The other two went over to the Partisans . . ."*: Tomašević, 270–73. 179 *By October, Tito's partisans controlled . . .* : Morrison, 55, 62–63; Tomašević, 273. 179 *"The same day they entered Cetinje," a witness remembers,*

"the Partisans . . .": Tomašević, 314. 179 *The card reached Jakov, who had assumed . . .* : Tel. 180 *"more noisily than in Moscow"*: Đilas [1985], 140. 180 *"starting a new life in a second language"*: Tolnai. 180 *He contributed to* Republika . . . : P. Čudić, 13. 180 *He wrote a scrupulous monograph . . .* : Banac [1988a], 281. 180 *Danilo discovered Risto's private library . . .* : GTI, 226. 180 *"Le Petit Larousse Illustré, 1923 edition . . ."*: HPEI, 243. 181 *Kiš wrote only once about Dragićević family life . . .* : ČA, 42–43. 181 *a splendid tribute in* Garden, Ashes: BP, 180. 182 *"One may expect anything from such a people" . . .* : Đilas [1966]. 182 *according to Marko Miljanov . . .* : Đilas [1966], 214. 182 *"So something had to be done . . ."*: Đilas [1966], 451. 182 *"done nothing notable"*: Đilas [1966], 449. 183 *"the whole Serb race" and its "national spirit"*: Skerlić, quoted by Čolović [2000], 139. 183 *cult was lavishly promoted . . .* : Wachtel [1998], 105, 104. 183 *"the complete expression of our fundamental . . ."*: Andrić, quoted by Carmichael, 24. 183 *"Though most of them were illiterate . . ."*: Tomašević, 215. 183 *Now it was acclaimed as a Montenegrin masterpiece . . .* : Wachtel [1998], 145. 183 *the words of another enthusiast . . .* : Salko Nikezić, quoted in Njegoš, 7, 18, 20, 12. 184 *the Dubrovnik poet Milan Milišić . . .* : Milišić [1996], 173. 184 *the protesters carried banners with lines from Njegoš . . .* : Žanić, 39. 184 *Karadžić boasted in 1991 . . .* : Karadžić, quoted by Rasim Kadić in* Mladina *(Ljubljana), quoted by Thompson [1993], 331. 184 *a British journalist saw . . .* : Glenny, 133. 184 *Karadžić told a sympathetic interviewer . . .* : Karadžić, interviewed by Patrick Besson, quoted by Coquio. ("Quand la guerre a commencé, je pensais tout le temps à Njegos car les choses arrivaient telles qu'il les avait prédites. Je savais *La Couronne de montagnes*, son grand poème épique, par coeur.") 185 *"a true breviary of interethnic hatred"*: Mirko Grmek, Marc Gjidara, and Neven Šimac, quoted by Carmichael, 24. 185 *"reading Njegoš, our folk poetry, and listening . . ."*: ČA, 59. 185 *a recent French critic's claim . . .* : Coquio. 185 *"not so much books to be read . . .* : Brković [1995], 83. 186 *"Njegoš's pessimism was cosmic . . ."*: Dvorniković, 971. 186 *a study of his work . . .* : Cerović [1996]. 186 *"Thanks be to Thee, O Lord . . ."*: this translation of Njegoš's "Testament" is adapted from Michael B. Petrovich's translation in Đilas [1966], 431–32. 187 *"I wish to go to my death with dignity . . ."*: H, 262. 187 *In 1982, he told an interviewer . . .* : Tel. 187 *others, too, guessed that it was on his mind*: P. Čudić, 13. 187 *"a petrified world, and very difficult for literature"*: GTI, 275. 187 *"cruel moral climate"*: PE, 166. 187 *"the inherent presence of culture by way of allusion . . ."*: HPEI, 111. 188 *"our patriarchal petrifaction"*: BP, 35. 188 *"a white road descending in ribbons cut out of the rock"*: H, 98. 188 *a short text which features the road from Kotor*: Skl, 270–71. 189 *one of Danilo's chieftains evokes . . .* : the speaker is Serdar Radonja. 190 *"The fiery reflection of the sun on the glass front . . ."*: H, 105.

Chapter 25

191 *When Lubarda and Milunović . . .* : Brajović, 47–48. 191 *Montenegro's first School of Fine Arts . . .* : Simeonović Ćelić, 230. 191 *"we can't know" who the nameless . . .* : Labov [n.d.], 20. 191 *"old German woman who sells boiled sweets" . . .* : BP, 10. 191 *"heated by flames from the hearth of memory"*: V, 46. 191 *"Yugoslavia's half-million-strong German community . . ."*: Schindler. 192 *"very difficult for literature"*: GTI, 275. 192 *another relative died in an accident . . .* : Tomašević. 192 *"fairness and justice, and the chance to participate . . ."*: Đilas [1985], 67. 192 *Nevertheless, the new regime was suspicious . . .* : the Arte Media website alleges this, http://www.arte.rs/sr/umetnici/petar_lubarda-83/biografija/ (accessed February 2010). 192 *One of his admirers . . . "Soviet-style socialist realism" . . .* : Brajović, 55, 56. 192 *His exhibition in Belgrade in May 1951 . . .* : Madžarević, 60–61. 192 *"And he found stone in everything . . ."*: Đilas [1966], 14. 192 *"a pure socialist realist artist"*: Simeonović Ćelić, 232. 193 *Kiš compared the two painters in a short essay . . .* : SVMM. 193 *"a gentle, peaceable and tolerant man"*: Đorić, 38. 193 *"large watery eyes"*: the artist Ljuba Popović, quoted by Madžarević, 131. 193 *"a small iridescent sphere" . . .* : Borges [2000], 129–30. 193 *"function of contemporary painting" . . .* : Šejka, quoted in Đorić, 12, 13. 193 *an aesthetic of rubble and rubbish dump in 1960s Yugoslavia*: Đorić, 36. 194 *Meret Oppenheim, of the legendary . . .* : Đorić, 17. 194 *The two men spent much time in Belgrade cafés . . .* : Miočinović [2007]. 194 *"He was stoical, with a strange cheerfulness . . ."*: Tel. 194 *"that offers most joy, like the old masters . . ."*: Đorić, 46. 194 *Šejka's "striving for totality" . . . According to Mirjana*

Miočinović . . . : V, 495, 568. 194 *Pascale Delpech, his partner in the last decade of his life, recalls . . .* : Delpech, cited by Tolnai. 194 *One of his last stories . . .* : Skl, 241–47. 195 *he was even introduced to others . . .* : Kovač [1992], 17. 195 *"I preferred the company of painters . . ."*: Tel. 195 *"the only alternative to the governing nomenklatura . . ."*: Đorić, 17–18. 195 *"graveyard of dead styles and aborted –isms"*: Mediala member Miro Glavurtić, quoted in Đorić, 25. 195 *"tremendous feeling of shame"*: Abramović, http://spikyart.org/nationstate/thesis5.htm (accessed January 2010).

Chapter 26

197 *"There were excellent teachers, including White Russians"*: Tel. 197 *The sense of liberation from fear was something he never forgot*: GTI, 226–27; Đonović. 197 *"we looked more like prisoners than teenagers"*: Đonović. 197 *He later said that he spent the time reading . . .* : GTI, 9. 198 *One of the teachers, Zorka Vukčević, recalled much later . . .* : recalled by Boško Mijanović in "Povratak vremena" [The Return of Time], http://www.cetinje-mojgrad.org/?p=4062 (accessed August 2011). 198 *The virtues of "revolutionary folklore" were proclaimed . . .* : Sekulić. 199 *"intoxicated with their successes, which are not so very great"*: Jelavich, 325. 199 *"healthy members of the CPY"*: Banac [1988b], 126. 199 *In 1949, Tito announced that Yugoslavia . . .* : Roberts, 41. 199 *"I do not know what all this is about . . ."*: Banac [1988a], 171. 199 *Some 9 per cent of known 'Cominformists' were Montenegrins . . .* : Banac [1988b], 150. 199 *The brutality of this suppression troubled . . .* : Banac [1988b], 167. 199 *"I will shake my little finger and there will be . . ."*: Banac [1988b], 117. 199 *"Stalin. Stop sending assassins to murder me . . ."*: Medvedev and Medvedev, 62. 200 *"History was repeating itself"*: AMM, 206. 200 *"The worst thing was, she suffered so much . . ."*: AMM, 205. 200 *"This is how I reasoned . . ."*: GTI, 334. 200 *"Stars how much further from me fill my night . . ."*: Empson, 24.

Chapter 27

201 *"decided that I had an 'ear' . . ."*: AMM, 206. 201 *"a wonderful old gentleman"*: Tel. 202 *"What do you mean?" said the singer . . .* : Karaulac, 2007. 202 *On a sluggish Sunday afternoon towards the end . . .* : from Ognjenović, slightly abbreviated.

Chapter 28

205 *"Even in Cetinje, I was beginning . . ."*: Tel. 205 *"I kept myself for something harder—prose . . ."*: ŽL, 192. 205 *He came to think it was also a valve . . .* : HP, 256. 205 *A poem is a semantic event, not a record of transcendent experience . . .* : V, esp. 262. 206 *According to the poet Predrag Čudić . . .* : Predrag Čudić, in *ARS* [2005], 119. 206 *"not a single translator but several translators . . ."*: Babić, 15, 40. 206 *only ones that let readers of Serbo-Croatian know how great a poet Ady was*: Babić, 41. 206 *Kiš was fascinated by Ady . . .* : V, 288–89. 206 *"poisoned me with yearning", he wrote in 1959 . . .* : V, 520. 206 *"I thought, what is there left for me to write?"*: GTI, 309–10. 206 *Happy New Year—World/Light—Edge/Realm— Haven! . . .* : Brodsky. 208 *"opened up a new poetic continent for us"*: Predrag Čudić, in *ARS* [2005], 119. 208 *he wondered if his translations from Hungarian had not nourished . . .* : GTI, 315. 208 *"that foreigner with 'barbarous pronunciation', that infatuated nomad . . ."*: V, 520. 208 *"this poet" who "had a monument and streets . . ."*: MNC. 208 *"Rose of imagination, thought's narcissus . . ."*: Juhász, 141. 208 *"a complete stock list of Hungarian 'dead capitalism' . . ."*: V, 284–85. 208 *"the light skull's broken bubble of bone" . . .* : Juhász, 142, 158. 209 *"the brain of Dr Freud . . . an intelligence torn from its cranial husk . . ."*: H, 58. 209 *"gutted Rose rooted in Freud's heart"*: Juhász, 156. 209 *"the stylistic, cultural and other diktats that they wanted . . ."*: Petri [1992]. 209 *"Poetry as ugly as reality", was Kiš's approving . . .* : HPEI, 100; also ŽL, 218. 209 *"unrelieved barrenness and despair" . . .* : Kleinzahler. 209 *"All that can save us now, all that can save, / is absolute distrust"*: Petri, 71. 209 *Queneau's "combinatorial art"*: HP, 101. 209 *"The Exercises du style would have lost nothing . . ."*: ŽL, 71.

Chapter 29

211 *The first refugees from Russia's civil war . . .* : information about Russian émigrés in Yugoslavia from Jovanović, 43–45; Bondarev; Ludmila Seliverstova, *Voice of Russia World Service,* http://www.ruvr.ru/main.php?lng=eng&q=28940&cid=59&p=27.06.2008 (accessed February 2010). The quoted passage ("Russians moved to Serbia . . .") is from Vladislav Maevskii (1893–1975), cited by Bondarev. 211 *had stabilised at 20,500*: Wachtel [2006], 257. 211 *"a sizeable group of Russian émigré families" . . .* : Tomašević, 105. 212 *When Soviet forces joined Tito's partisans . . .* : Normand and Acker, 19. 212 *"There's no human consideration there . . ."*: Đilas [1985], 186. 214 *a prose-poem by the Belgian poet . . .* : quoted by Koprivica [2005]. 215 *"Danilo marvelled at that tree's tenacity . . ."*: Ibrahim Hadžić in *ARS* [2009], 153. 217 *Opposing the "widespread regimentation, registration . . ."*: Serapion Brothers' manifesto of July 1922, cited in Hayward and Labedz, 31.

Fifth Interlude: *A Tomb for Boris Davidovich*

223 *"Our revolution does not devour its children!"*: Đilas [1985], 186. 228 *"a simple operation for a stomach ulcer . . ."*: Polonsky, 16. 228 *"Others swelled up so enormously . . ."*: Rabelais, 17; Rushdie [1995], 81; Dyer [2010], 276. 228 *"The spirit of Stalinism was very much present . . ."*: Tel. 229 *"the Shakespeare and Dante of our time" . . .* : Lévy [1979], 154. 229 *Lakis Proguidis suggests persuasively . . .* : Proguidis [1996b]. 229 *hailed by Kiš as Yugoslavia's own Solzhenitsyn*: GTI, 296. 230 *"I had to find a fantastic way of writing realistically"*: GTI, 210. 230 *"Liberation from psychological clichés . . ."*: Tel. 230 *"mismatched lists, abrupt transitions, the reduction . . ."*: Borges [1998], 3. 230 *"Borges's stories are for little children"*: Tel. 230 *"I claim that the universal history of infamy . . ."*: GTI, 153. 230 *"With great delicacy and sharp wit . . ."*: Galeano. 230 *"indecipherable labyrinth of state offices"*: Borges [1999], 163. 231 *"dynamically regulating the distance between narration . . ."*: Krysinski [1988]. 232 *the revolutionaries' motives are hardly explored*: G. Crnković, 32–34. 232 *the episode with the polecat . . .* : ČA, 110–11. 233 *"uncanny alliance between the criminals and the Gulag . . ."*: Longinović, 116. 233 *the thesis (which he associated with Arthur Koestler) . . .* : GTI, 170. 233 *His place in history matters more than physical survival . . .* : Longinović, 117. 233 *"common stock of European social mythology" . . .* : Norman Cohn, quoted by Lay. 234 *the final story has been called the most enigmatic*: Motola, 608. 234 *"has internalised the oppressor . . ."*: Longinović, 126. 234 *As Mirjana Miočinović has pointed out, Kiš's catalogue . . .* : Miočinović [2001]. 234 *"My definition of literature", he said . . .* : HPEI, 266. 235 *"reproductive power" is a "specific quality of the Serbian people" . . .* : Čolović [2000], 116. 235 *"The reality of German camps was there . . ."*: Tel. 236 *When a Croatian publisher wanted to publish it . . .* : Z. Crnković. 236 *Solzhenitsyn's work was eventually published . . .* : Lovrenović. 236 *"I made a mistake. But there it is . . ."*: Zlatko Crnković to the author, 27 October 2004. 236 *"with a forcefulness of which I often repent . . ."*: Kiš to Zlatko Crnković, 12 October 1975. 238 *"not because of anything he had written . . ."*: Interview with Slavko Goldstein, Zagreb, 14 September 1996. 238 *friends were amused to see him lording it . . .* : Pekić [2002], 506.

Chapter 30

239 *"The streets seemed occupied rather than inhabited . . ."*: Bouvier, 26. 239 *"was like a giant sore that had to run and stink before it could heal, and its robust blood seemed strong enough to heal, come what may"*: Bouvier, 42. 239 *"sacred, patriotic, socialist duty"*: Đilas [1985], 22. 240 *renaming the main boulevard after the Red Army . . .* : Norris, 138. 240 *Intended as "a showcase of socialist planning" . . .* : Norris, 213–14. 240 *New Belgrade looked like a vast abandoned . . .* : Bouvier, 20. 240 *By 1954, a Western guidebook reported . . .* : *Nagel Travel Guide,* 125. 240 *"every trace of eastern influence has been mercilessly obliterated"*: Normand and Acker, 16, 17. 240 *"drew from their forgetfulness the courage to live again"*: Bouvier, 30. 240 *A British visitor in 1954 . . .* : Tennyson, 52, 43. 240 *"reveling in the luxury of*

life": Galbraith, 81. 240 *"pictures of Lenin and Stalin were conspicuous in many streets"*: Gunther. 240 *A Montenegrin member of the Central Committee argued . . .*: Puniša Perović, cited by Sekulić. (The quoted phrases may or may not be from Perović himself.) 241 *"aesthetic Puritanism" of Stalinist art . . .*: Krleža, [1963], 56. 242 *"an art with its own specific expressive possibilities"*: "Katedra . . .". 242 *"It was known as a useless degree, but I didn't care what came next"*: Tel. 242 *Đurić himself, known fondly but nervously as Zeus*: P. Čudić, 9. 242 *Kiš was "already a legend" at the faculty*: Špadijer. 242 *Đurić reproached them that his first and best student was so poor that he slept rough . . .*: P. Čudić, 9. 242 *"the severance of literature from defined social groups"*: Hutcheson Macaulay Posnett, quoted in Weninger, 106. 243 *"the best which has been thought and said in the world"*: from Matthew Arnold's celebrated 1869 definition of *culture*: "a pursuit of our total perfection by means of getting to know, on all the matters which most concern us, the best which has been thought and said in the world, and, through this knowledge, turning a stream of fresh and free thought upon our stock notions and habits, which we now follow staunchly but mechanically". 243 *"messianic hopes for world literature . . ."*: Damrosch [2003], 282. 243 *"virtually all of our major universities"*: in Block, 1. 243 *"the study of literature in its totality"*: Wellek, quoted in Lawall, 49. 243 *"an ideal of the unification of all literatures into one literature . . ."*: Wellek, quoted by Pizer. 243 *"our philological home is the earth: it can no longer be the nation . . ."*: Auerbach. 243 *"unlike the separate study of 'literature' . . ."*: Apter; Lawall, xi. 243 *"put to practical use the theoretical premises well established . . ."*: Vipper, 545, 546. 243 *"without method the random Homer-to-Arthur-Miller zigzag . . ."*: Clements, 186. 243 *"in the literary and intellectual tradition of the West . . ."*: Lionel Trilling, quoted in Block, 3. 243 *"the Acmeists' cosmopolitan program . . ."*: TBD, 131. 243 *"a yearning for world culture"*, toska po mirovoi kulture: Mandelstam, quoted by Cavanagh [1995], 6. 244 *A true* Eurocentrism, *he argued . . .*: V, 513–15. 244 *"If I bring up these three," he said in 1984 . . .*: HPEI, 192. 244 *"abstracted construct"*: Djelal Kadir, quoted in Weninger, 94. 244 *"global reach and textual closeness"*: Apter, 44. 244 *"become a category reserved for the leftovers . . ."*: Vellenga Berman. 244 *"If current global trends in comparatism persist . . ."*: "Katedra . . .". 244 *"one and indivisible, good or bad"*: ŽL, 87. 244 *"I'm horrified by books about minorities . . ."*: HPEI, 183. 244 *"the revolt of mankind in the atomic age"*: V, 120. 245 *Don Quixote, "the last knight errant", is, "like so many heroes . . ."*: V, 136–37, 142. 245 *"dossing in someone's room with people . . ."*: Tel. 245 *In this same year, 1957, the young Georges Perec . . .*: Bellos, 172–78, 160. 245 *Mirko Kovač remembers him smoking "voluptuously . . ."*: Kovač [1992], 17. 247 *he even looked like Jean-Paul Belmondo in* Breathless: Tolnai. 247 *"le personnage emblématique de la bohème belgradoise"*: Prstojević [n.d.]. 247 *"We weren't 'bohemian', we were poor . . ."*: Tel. 247 *In his eyes,* poètes maudits *like Paul-Marie Verlaine, Ady, or Ujević had remained true to themselves . . .*: V, 75–79. 248 *"I drank at night and worked by day"*: HP, 211. 248 *his boozing and carousing were escapes . . .*: David [1999]. 248 *release of Esther Williams's 1944 musical . . .*: Ugrešić [2003], 177. 248 *"a haunt for girls with long black hair . . ."*: HP, 124. 248 *"more than beautiful, a little eccentric . . ."*: Tvrtko Kulenović, quoted in Miočinović [2007]. 248 *Mirjana was, he wrote to Đonović,* moja neminovnost: "my inevitability": Đonović. 249 *head over heels in love*: Tolnai. 249 *Kiš worked on the bed, cross-legged, the typewriter on his lap*: P. Čudić, 10. 249 *"Meeting him was my destiny," she has said . . .*: Miočinović [2007]. 250 *"priceless and essential advantage compared to . . ."*: Miočinović [2007], 62, 65–66. 250 *"a dung heap swarming with maggots . . ."*: Karl Radek, quoted by Figes, 479. 250 *Ristić argued against a Soviet critic . . .*: Ristić. 251 *our "right to oblivion"*: V, 90–93. 251 *Mirjana's remark that she knew very little . . .*: Miočinović [2007], 63. 251 *"the so-called latency period . . ."*: Hofmann, 77.

Sixth Interlude: *The Anatomy Lesson*

253 *"I expected readers to question the facts in the book"*: Tel. 254 *one of these prizes on "moral" grounds*: ČA, 24. 255 *insulted "our people"*: ČA, 29. 255 *"a theory of historical relativity"*: ČA, 45. 255 *"realised with astonishment verging on incredulity . . ."*: ČA, 29. 257 *"all that I can conclude from the fact that I write solely . . ."*: HPEI, 32. 258 *"chronic, quasi-schizophrenic split . . ."*: Koestler [1978]. 259 *He portrayed Kiš as a consistent and conspiratorial plagiarist . . .*: Jeremić, 367. 260 *a French scholar who cannot believe . . .*: Mertens. 260 *"uniquely unoriginal", a contriver of fragments . . .*: Jeremić, 349,

321–22. 260 *"wonderful optimism and faith in the future"*: Jeremić, quoted in HP, 31. 260 *"lose faith in the possibility that man can be free . . ."*: Jeremić, 323, 242. 260 *"fatalistic reconciliation with evil in general . . ."*: Jeremić, 241. 260 *"Creativity should be the banner of new, socialist culture . . ."*: Jeremić, 374–76. 261 *Borislav Pekić urged him not to be provoked . . .*: Pekić [2002], 126. 261 *"What prevails"*, *wrote Václav Havel . . .*: Havel, 25. 261 *The Yugoslav elite still worried that Moscow would try . . .*: Koprivc. 262 *"They haven't forgiven you for your talent," Miroslav Krleža had warned . . .*: according to Koprivica [2009]. 262 *Krleža valued Kiš as the best writer . . .*: according to Matvejević [1992], 122. 262 *Instead of "dramatizing" a development . . .*: IP, 36. 262 *"because he was an émigré, some kind of enemy"*: Stambolić, 102. 263 *"either as literature (though it is not worthless . . ."*: Quoted in ŽL, 207. 263 *This was Dragoslav Marković (1920–2005) . . .*: Sell, 77. 263 *"a friend in Paris" that Kiš was "a mere plagiarist"*: Pančić . 263 *the greatest and rarest of writers . . ."*: HPEI, 174. 263 *"our first serious book on intertextuality"*: Delić. 264 *his only book with a happy ending . . .*: Cerović [1992]. 264 *the first time this secret collusion . . .*: Miočinović [1999].

Chapter 31

265 *nothing in a writer's fate is accidental*: HPEI, 234. 265 *"the self is only possible through the recognition of the Other"*: Lévinas, quoted in Kapuściński, 5. 267 *When this was rejected, he applied for the University of Bordeaux*: Pekić [2002], 123. 267 *he told an old friend that his book-writing was over*: Kovač [1994], 123. 267 *he applied, around this time, for a full-time post . . .*: Babić, 45. 268 *"alone in a working-class district . . ."*: White [1994], 218. 269 *"None of my French students knows a single poem . . ."*: Tel. 269 *On Friday I went to Lille, for my teaching . . .*: Skl, 214. 270 *the "Serbo-Croatian language space" extended . . .*: Ranko Bugarski, in Busch and Kelly-Holmes, 24. 270 *he liked its inauthenticity: the very feature that offended nationalists. . .*: HPEI, 31, 32. 270 *"I was a lector for a long time, but I never managed . . ."*: ŽL, 123. 271 *"The reputation of certain Yugoslav writers . . ."*: HPEI, 183. 271 *astonished that writers from Yugoslavia could not see . . .*: GTI, 192. 271 *"I am not a Serbo-Croatian writer . . ."*: ŽL, 123. 271 *"Yugoslav literatures", a usage that Kiš accepted*: for example, GTI, 81. 271 *Kiš scribbled a famous phrase from Njegoš . . .*: Karaulac [2007]. 272 *"the Serbo-Croatian / Croato-Serbian language ceased to exist . . ."*: Busch and Kelly-Holmes, 8. 272 *for this asset to become "truly effective" . . .*: Auerbach. 272 *when he relearned his mother tongue*: GTI, 226. 272 *this may have been Kiš's first real encounter . . .*: PE, 176. 273 *I believe that every work of value is an act of revolt . . .*: HPEI, 34

Chapter 32

277 *Miodrag Bulatović, meanwhile, demanded . . .*: Krivokapić, 480. 277 *The prosecution twice approached Karlo Štajner . . .*: according to Matvejević [1992], 45. 277 b*efore a crowded public gallery*: Kovač [1994], 125. 277 *He had not attacked the plaintiff . . .*: Krivokapić, 497. 278 *"open and unambiguous racism" . . .*: NO, 96. 278 *Other accusations were just as malignant . . .*: NO, 98. 278 *"My generation marks the end of a long tradition . . ."*: GTI, 138. 277 *he really had expected it to be the metropole of world culture . . .*: V, 519–55. 279 *"or he would go mad"*: Eörsi [1992], 151. 279 *an ironic, voluntary, "Joycean" sense*: GTI, 219. 279 *"no one abandons a community without regret"*: HPEI, 113. 279 *"I dream about what I've been reading more often . . ."*: GTI, 129. 279 *"And so, gradually and quite unconsciously . . ."*: BP, 183. 279 *"the preciousness of memory"*: GA, 54. 279 *At the next table, facing me, a group of middle-aged people . . .*: V, 542–43. 280 *In "Nabokov, or Nostalgia" . . .*: HPEI, 149–55.

Seventh Interlude: *The Encyclopaedia of the Dead*

283 *Epigraph*: ED, 131. 283 *Kiš included pastiche scripture, legend . . .*: Rizzante. 283 *"to secure for the human spirit that liberty which is implied in its very nature"*: Scott. 283 *"To check the inroads of Gnosticism the Church had to prohibit freedom . . ."*: Scott. 283 *"all Gnostic doctrines to the heresy of Simon Magus . . ."*: Herdman, 6. 284 *a conservative juror was convinced . . .*: Špadijer interview, Podgorica, 21

September 1997. 284 *"an attempt at a global vision of reality . . ."*: HPEI, 266. 285 *"never had a good word to say about any nation . . ."*: Skl, 429. 286 *"the dream of complete knowledge"*: Creet, 275. 286 *"all that it is given to express, in all languages"*: Borges [1971], 81. 286 *"no one expects to discover anything"*: Woodall, 119. 286 *"guided and directed by some shadowy man of genius"*: Borges [1998], 72. 286 *"we had often discussed Jewish matters, but never the Kabbalah"*: David [1995]; David interview, Belgrade, 13 October 1993. 286 *"the restoration of the original coexistence . . ."*: Scholem, 224. 286 *"a chronicler who recites events without . . ."*: Benjamin, 256. (The quotation continues: "To be sure, only a redeemed mankind receives the fullness of its past—which is to say, only for a redeemed mankind has its past become citable in all its moments. Each moment it has lived becomes a citation *à l'ordre du jour*—and that day is Judgment Day.") 286 *"I too want the International of good men . . ."*: Babel, 118. 286 *"the lost, the missing, the wished-for . . ."*: Ozick [1998], 222. 286 *"a famous innovator and dreamer of the Yiddish theater . . ."*: Paley, 10. Italics added. 290 *"If it were not for my faith in a future meeting . . ."*: Mandelstam, 302. 291 *as Guy Scarpetta says, by the end of the story . . .*: Scarpetta [1992], 112. 291 *Kiš sat back and watched*: ŽL, 199. 291 *"disastrous"*: HPEI, 229. 291 *the title story and "Red Stamps" were the best*: according to Pavlović, 93. 291 *"the result of a quest for change, for a new . . ."*: HPEI, 198. 291 *a book about love and death, adding that he had . . .*: GTI, 266. 291 *the "nationalist euphoria" that was rising . . .*: ŽL, 198–201. 291 *creation or resurrection of nationalist myths . . .*: Sima Ćirković, historian, quoted by Zagorka Golubović in Golubović, Kuzmanović, and Vasović, 31. 291 *"marked by an attempt to hijack and manipulate . . ."*: de la Brosse, 32. 292 *"a Mexican car-dealer and hotelier . . ."*: Slapšak. 292 *Miljenko Jergović praised it as a wonderful book, but . . .*: ARS [2009], 314.

Chapter 33

293 *For exile is a negative condition . . .*: Burgess [1991], 345. 293 *what he called "chronic idleness"*: IPDK, 571. 293 *"I'm not working at all . . ."*: IPDK, 567. 294 *"Danilo wanted us to stay, . . ."*: Ammiel Alcalay, email to the author, 20 August 2010. 294 *"where the flowers alone, I found out, . . ."*: Dušan Makavejev, email to the author, 11 October 2009. 294 *"the exhibitionism of the drunken Balkan male"*: Susan Sontag to the author, Tuzla, 20 October 1995. 294 *"Hey, mister, have you got a few francs for me?"*: Karaulac [2007]. 295 *"lives in Paris but he's certainly not part of Paris literary life"*: White [1994], 218. 295 *"Being a Yugoslav writer in Paris . . ."*: GTI, 234. 295 *"We are exotica, we are a political scandal . . ."*: HPEI, 75 ff. 297 *"national feelings and nationalist impulses"*: HPEI, 275. 297 *"the only Yugoslav writer in the world"*: GTI, 318. 297 *Diogo Pires (1517–1599) was a Portuguese Jew who fled . . .*: Jewish Virtual Library. 298 *"the price of 'Joycean exile' was high . . ."*: Oku. 298 *"like a romantic poet"*: IPDK, 574. 298 *"I'd sit in front of the café La Coupole . . ."*: Selenić. 299 *He looked out of place, Tontić thought . . .*: ARS [2009], 201. 299 *"exotic country at the heart of Europe . . ."*: ŽL, 73–74. 300 *Kiš declared that the only* chevalier *who should . . .*: ŽL, 119–22. 300 *"He was desperate," the writer Radoslav Bratić recalls . . .*: Bratić. 301 *"the only thing in the world worth doing"*: M, 73. 301 *Andrzej Stasiuk, a Polish admirer, says . . .*: Stasiuk. 301 *Besides Gauloises, unfiltered Gitanes were his favourite*: Bratić. 301 *"At one phase of his illness he told me . . ."*: P. Čudić, 14. 302 *"young and gifted poet"*: IP, 26. 302 *Some time later, Kiš and Kovač met Đogo in the street. . . .*: according to Kovač [2008]. 302 *István Eörsi, a Hungarian dissident writer, . . .*: Eörsi. 303 *"I hate writing. I only write when I can't stand not to write"*: Sontag [2007b]. 303 *Writing is a drug, he once explained . . .*: Tel. 303 *"sensual pleasure is the only present"*: HPEI, 134. 303 *"I can say for myself that I have never betrayed . . ."*: HPEI, 277. 303 *"ideal standard-bearer of the Kantian conception of World Peace"*: Krleža [1980], 149. 303 *"The deportation of Muslim Albanians to Turkey could then . . ."*: Andrić [n.d.]. 303 *"Who rides by night in the wind so wild? / . . ."*: Goethe, 87. 304 *"flamboyant, curly-headed, French-speaking charmer . . ."*: Stern, 887, 869. 304 *"referred to as 'that charismatic Yugoslav'. . ."*: Koenig. 304 *Kiš bridled at the "pedagogical tone" . . .*: Cross Currents [1990]. 304 *"watched with amusement a panel discussion . . ."*: Rushdie [2005]. 304 *Like many liberals at that time, Ignatieff tied himself . . .*: ŽL, 126; *Cosmopolitiques*, 183–84. 305 *established on Tito's orders . . .*: Đilas [1985], 235. 305 *as many as quarter of a million people may have been . . .*: Dragoslav Mihailović, *Goli Otok* (Belgrade, 1990), quoted by Popov [1996a], 105.

306 *"the vast majority of Cominformists would never . . ."*: Đilas [1985], 240. 306 *"the darkest and most shameful fact in the history . . ."*: Đilas [1985], 245. 306 *Kiš proved an excellent interviewer . . .* : Beganović, 285–302. 307 *"in awe of the greatest . . ."*: Jasmina Kuzmanović, emails to the author, 4 and 5 February 2010. 307 *"I want my books to be more credible than the so-called . . ."*: Kuzmanović [1989]. 307 *"but I want to be optimistic . . ."*: GTI, 305. 307 *He told Mirko Kovač to shake his hand . . .* : Kovač [1994], 125. 307 *He told his friend László Végel . . .* : Zupanc [2009]. 308 *"How can I get well in a city that's sick?"*: Sarajlić [1993]. 308 *Samuel Beckett's last work, "What Is the Word" (1988) . . .* : Beckett [1988]. 308 *Popović saw how much weaker he looked . . .* : as recalled by Dimitrije Popović in "Smrt Danila Kiša" [The Death of DK], http://www.cetinje-mojgrad.org/?p=4062 (accessed August 2011). 308 *told his old friend that this was probably their last walk . . .* : Špadijer. 309 *"La commedia è finita?" The doctor nodded . . .* : Karaulac [2007]. 309 *"'Comes the time for me to go to the tomb' . . ."*: Karaulac [2007]. 309 *"I dreamed that I'd died. It was fantastic."*: Karaulac [2007]. 311 *I saw an image of your lungs . . .* : Milišić, unpublished poem provided to the author by Jelena Trpković. 311 *the first civilian casualty when the Yugoslav army . . .* : see Todorović. 311 *its last president, Slobodan Selenić, resigned . . .* : Dragović-Soso, 285. 311 *"a precious inheritance for all the Yugoslav literatures"*: Jure Kaštelan quoted in *Kiš u Dijaspori*, 108. 312 *Muharem Bazdulj, a young writer from Bosnia, calls him* the metaphysician . . . : Bazdulj. 312 *"Along with his books," Bazdulj says . . .* : Bazdulj [1999]. 312 *"the most cosmopolitan and innovative Yugoslav . . ."*: Segel. 312 *In particular, Aleksandar Jerkov launched . . .* : Jerkov's two principal contributions are *From Modernism to Postmodernity* (1991) and *The New Textuality* (1992). 312 *"dangerous narratives of History, Nation and Territory"*: Perišić. 313 *"macho self-promotion", patriarchalism, and renewing the "phallocentic narrative . . ."*: Radović [2011]. 313 *assault on his reputation was mounted by one Nebojša Vasović . . .* : Lazarević Di Giacomo [2006], 253 ff. 313 *One critic remarked drily that at least the anti-Semitism . . .* : Vule Žurić, quoted in Lazarević Di Giacomo [2006], 265. 313 *a metaphor of nostalgia for Yugoslavia*: Tolnai. 313 *"readers thank us by phone and letter for publishing Kiš . . ."*: Lucić. 313 *"a role model for a whole generation . . ."*: Hemon [2008]. 313 *"There are better story-tellers than Danilo . . ."*: Joseph Brodsky, in Wicker, 138. 313 *Central European writers, Kiš wrote in a fragment, are fated . . .* : Skl, 332. 314 *distance from loss is essential for creating art . . .* : V, 27. 314 *"commingling" a couple's ashes*: ED, 199.

Bibliography

(Details are of editions consulted, not necessarily of first publication.)

Works by Danilo Kiš

AMM: contribution to *À ma mère*, edited by Marcel Bisiaux and Catherine Jajolet (Paris: Pierre Horay, 1988), 203–6.

BP: *Bašta pepeo* (Belgrade: BIGZ, 1995).

ČA: *Čas anatomije* (Belgrade: BIGZ, 1995).

ED: *The Encyclopaedia of the Dead*, translated by Michael Henry Heim (London: Faber & Faber, 1989).

ES: *Early Sorrows*, translated by Michael Henry Heim (New York: New Directions, 1998).

GA: *Garden, Ashes*, translated by William Hannaher (London: Faber & Faber, 1990).

GTI: *Gorki talog iskustva*, ed. Mirjana Miočinović (Belgrade: Prosveta, 2007).

H: *Hourglass*, translated by Ralph Manheim (London: Faber & Faber, 1990).

HP: *Homo Poeticus* (Belgrade: BIGZ, 1995).

HPEI: *Homo Poeticus: Essays and Interviews*, edited and introduced by Susan Sontag, translated by Michael Henry Heim, Francis Jones and Ralph Manheim (New York: Farrar, Straus and Giroux, 1995).

IP: *Iz prepiske*, ed. Mirjana Miočinović (Vršac: Biblioteka Nesanica, 2005).

IPDK: "Iz prepiske Danila Kiša", *Sarajevske sveske* 17 (Sarajevo: 2007).

M: *Mansarda*, translated by John J. Cox (New York: The Serbian Classics Press, 2008).

MNC: "A Man with No Country", translated by Christina Pribićević-Zorić, in Joanna Labon, ed., *STORM 6: Out of Yugoslavia* (Manchester, UK: Carcanet, 1994), 179–88.

NM: *Noć i magla* (Belgrade: BIGZ, 1995).

NO: "Nacrt odbrane", edited by Mirjana Miočinović, *Hereticus. Časopis za preispitivanje prošlosti* 2, no. 1 (2004).

P: *Peščanik* (Belgrade: BIGZ, 1995).

PE: *Pesme, Elektra*, edited by Mirjana Miočinović (Belgrade: BIGZ, 1995).

PP: *Pesme i prepevi*, edited by Predrag Čudić (Belgrade: Prosveta, 2003).

Skl: *Skladište*, edited by Mirjana Miočinović (Belgrade: Prosveta, 2006).

SVMM: "Slikarski svet Milana Milunovića" (*Mladost*, 1958), in *ARS: Časopis za kniževnost, kulturu i društvena pitanja* [ARS: A Journal for Literature, Culture and Social Questions] 11, no. 4–5 (2009).

TBD: *A Tomb for Boris Davidovich*, translated by Duška Mikić-Mitchell (Harmondsworth, UK: Penguin, 1980).

Tel: interview with Boro Krivokapić, "Teleskopija", TV Belgrade, broadcast 12 April 1982.

V: *Varia*, edited by Mirjana Miočinović (Belgrade: Prosveta, 2007).

ŽL: *Život, literatura*, edited by Mirjana Miočinović (Belgrade: BIGZ, 1995).

Mention should also be made of two invaluable compact discs, *Ostavština* (2001) and *Sabrana dela* (2003), edited by Mirjana Miočinović and produced by Aleksandar Lazić and Predrag Jančić, with support from the Open Society Fund in Belgrade.

Other works cited

Gilbert Adair [1986], *Myths & Memories* (London: Flamingo).

Theodor Adorno [2004], *Aesthetic Theory*, translated by Robert Hullot-Kentor (New York: Continuum).

Jasmina Ahmetagić [2007], *Dažd od živoga ugljevlja* [A Rain of Fire and Brimstone] (Belgrade: TRAG).

Rabia Ali and Lawrence Lifschultz, eds. [1993], *Why Bosnia? Writings on the Balkan War* (Stony Creek, Connecticut: The Pamphleteer's Press, 1993).

David Albahari [1992], "Le rêve du Maître" [The Dream of the Master], translated from Serbo-Croatian by Mireille Robin, in Ferenczi, ed., 71–74.

Amanda Anderson [2006], "Cosmopolitanism, Universalism and the Divided Legacies of Modernity", in *The Way We Argue Now* (Princeton: Princeton University Press).

Ivo Andrić [1992], *The Days of the Consuls*, translated by Celia Hawkesworth and Bogdan Rakić (London: Forest Books).

—— [n.d.], *Draft on Albania* (1939), retranslated from the Serbo-Croatian by Robert Elsie, based on an existing English version, http://www.albanianhistory.net/texts20_1/AH1939.html (accessed November 2011).

Aharon Appelfeld [1987], *The Age of Wonders*, translated by Dalya Bilu (London: Quartet).

Emily Apter [2006], "Global *Translatio*. The 'Invention' of Comparative Literature, Istanbul, 1933", in *The Translation Zone. New Comparative Literature* (Princeton: Princeton University Press).

Hannah Arendt [1958], *The Human Condition* (Chicago: University of Chicago Press).

—— [1978a], *The Jew as Pariah: Jewish Identity and Politics in the Modern Age* (New York: Harcourt Brace Jovanovich).

—— [1978b], *The Life of the Mind. One: Thinking* (London: Secker & Warburg).

—— [1985], *Eichmann in Jerusalem. A Report on the Banality of Evil* (Harmondsworth, UK: Penguin Books).

Matthew Arnold [1869], *Culture and Anarchy,* http://www.authorama.com/culture-and-anarchy-1.html.

ARS: Časopis za kniževnost, kulturu i društvena pitanja [ARS: A Journal for Literature, Culture and Social Questions] [2005], 10 (1–2).

—— [2009] 11 (4–5).

Erich Auerbach [1969], "Philology and Weltliteratur", translated and introduced by Maire Said and Edward Said, *Centennial Review* 13 (1): 1–17.

Isaac Babel [1994], *Collected Stories*, translated by David McDuff (London: Penguin).

Sava Babić [1998], *Bokorje za Danila Kiša* [A Bouquet for DK] (Kanjiža: Umetnička radionica "Kanjiški krug").

Đorđe Balašević [1996], *Dodir svile* [The Touch of Silk] (Zrenjanin: Gradska narodna biblioteka "Žarko Zrenjanin").

Ivo Banac [1988a], *The National Question in Yugoslavia. Origins, History, Politics* (Ithaca: Cornell University Press).

—— [1988b], *With Stalin against Tito. Cominformist Splits in Yugoslav Communism* (Ithaca: Cornell University Press).

Stanisław Barańczak [1996], "La fenêtre et le miroir" [The Window and the Mirror], translated from Polish by Marek Bieńczyk, in Proguidis, ed.

George Barany [1974], "Magyar Jew or Jewish Magyar?", in *Jews and Non-Jews in Eastern Europe 1918–1945*, edited by Bela Vago and George L. Mosse (Jerusalem: Israel Universities Press).

John Bayley [1991], "Did It Flow?", *New York Review of Books*, 11 April.

Muharem Bazdulj [1999], "Prorok Danilo" [The Prophet Danilo], *Feral Tribune*, 25 October.

—— [2009], "Smrt, literatura" [Death, Literature], *Vreme*, 15 October.

Samuel Beckett [1988], "What Is the Word", http://www.online-literature.com/forums/showthread.php?t=25593 (accessed 23 May 2011).

—— [1995], "The Capital of the Ruins", in *The Complete Short Prose 1929–1989*, edited by Stan Gontarski, 275–78 (New York: Grove Press).

Davor Beganović [2007], *Pamćenje traume. Apokaliptička proza Danila Kiša* [Remembering Trauma. The Apocalyptic Prose of DK] (Zagreb-Sarajevo: Naklada ZORO).

David Bellos [1995], *Georges Perec. A Life in Words* (London: Harvill Press).

Saul Bellow [1963], "The Writer as Moralist", *Atlantic Monthly*, March.

Esther Benbassa [2010], *Suffering as Identity. The Jewish Paradigm*, translated by G. M. Goshgarian (London: Verso).

Walter Benjamin [1979], *Illuminations*, translated by Harry Zohn (Glasgow: Fontana/Collins).

Isaiah Berlin [2001], *The Power of Ideas* (London: Pimlico).

—— [2005], *Liberty* (Oxford: Oxford University Press).

Carolyn Vellenga Berman [2009], "The Known World in World Literature: Bakhtin, Glissant, and Edward P. Jones", *Novel: A Forum on Fiction*, http://findarticles.com/p/articles/mi_qa3643/is_200907?ai_n42856392 (accessed June 2010).

Marshall Berman [1995], "'A Little Child Shall Lead Them': The Jewish Family Romance", in *The Jew in the Text. Modernity and the Construction of Identity,* edited by Linda Nochlin and Tamar Garb, 253–75 (London: Thames & Hudson).

Haskell M. Block, ed. [1960], *The Teaching of World Literature,* special issue of *UNC Studies in Comparative Literature,* no. 28.

Harold Bloom [1994], *The Western Canon. The Books and School of the Ages* (New York: Harcourt Brace).

Sam Bluefarb [1976], "The Middle-Aged Man in Contemporary Literature: Bloom to Herzog", *College Language Association Journal* 20(1): 1–13.

Nikita Bondarev [2009], "Russia and Russians in Serbian History, Part 3", Russkiy Mir Foundation, http://www.russkiymir.ru/russkiymir/en/publications/articles/article0125 (accessed February 2010).

Jorge Luis Borges [1971], *Labyrinths. Selected Stories and Other Writings* (Harmondsworth, UK: Penguin).

—— [1975], *A Universal History of Infamy*, translated by Norman Thomas di Giovanni (Harmondsworth, UK: Penguin).

—— [1985], *Selected Poems 1923–1967*, translated by Norman Thomas di Giovanni et al. (Harmondsworth, UK: Penguin).

—— [1998], *Collected Fictions*, translated by Andrew Hurley (New York: Penguin Putnam).

—— [1999], *Selected Non-Fictions*, edited by Eliot Weinberger (New York: Viking).

—— [2000], *The Aleph*, translated by Andrew Hurley (London: Penguin).

Dragan Bošković [2004], *Islednik, svedok, priča. Istražni postupci u* Peščaniku *i* Grobnici za Borisa Davidoviča *Danila Kiša* [Investigator, Witness, Story. Investigative Procedures in *Hourglass* and *A Tomb for Boris Davidovich* by DK] (Belgrade: ΠΛΑΤΩ).

Orhan Bosnević [1993], "The Road to Manjača", in Ali and Lifschultz, eds.

Nicolas Bouvier [1992], *The Way of the World*, translated by Robyn Marsack (Edinburgh, UK: Polygon).

Daniel Boyarin [1990], *Intertextuality and the Reading of Midrash* (Bloomington and Indianapolis: Indiana University Press).

Svetlana Boym [1999], "Conspiracy Theories and Literary Ethics: Umberto Eco, Danilo Kiš and *The Protocols of Zion*", *Comparative Literature*, http://www.danilokis.org/boym.pdf (accessed May 2011).

Randolph L. Braham, ed. [1969], *Hungarian-Jewish Studies*, vol. 2 (New York: World Federation of Hungarian Jews).

—— [1981], *The Politics of Genocide. The Holocaust in Hungary* (New York: Columbia University Press, 1981).

——, ed. [1994], *Anti-Semitism and the Treatment of the Holocaust in Postcommunist Eastern Europe* (Boulder: East European Monographs/Columbia University Press).

—— [2000], *Studies on the Holocaust. Selected Writings,* vol. 1 (Boulder: East European Monographs/Columbia University Press).

Aleksa Brajović [2001], *Slika i misao Petra Lubarde* [The Painting and Thought of Petar Lubarda] (Belgrade: Biblioteka SVETILNICI).

Radoslav Bratić [2005], "Kišova radionica" [K's Workshop], *JAT New Review.*

Jevrem Brković [1995], *Glosarij* [Glossary] (Zagreb: Nacionalna zajednica Crnogoraca Hrvatske).

Joseph Brodsky [1987], "Footnote to a Poem", translated by Barry Rubin, in *Less than One. Selected Essays* (Harmondsworth, UK: Penguin).

Alan Bullock [1993], *Hitler and Stalin. Parallel Lives* (London: Fontana Press).

Anthony Burgess [1990], *You've Had Your Time. Being the Second Part of the Confessions of Anthony Burgess* (London: Heinemann).

Christy L. Burns [2000], *Gestural Politics. Stereotype and Parody in Joyce* (Albany: SUNY Press).

Brigitta Busch and Helen Kelly-Holmes, eds. [2004], *Language, Discourse and Borders in the Yugoslav Successor States* (Clevedon, UK: Multilingual Matters).

Italo Calvino [1997], *The Literature Machine*, translated by Patrick Creagh (London: Vintage).

Elias Canetti [1981], *Crowds and Power*, translated by Carol Stewart (Harmondsworth, UK: Penguin).

Alain Cappon [2009], "DANILO KIŠ 1989–2009", September. (From author.)

Cathie Carmichael [2002], *Ethnic Cleansing in the Balkans. Nationalism and the Destruction of Tradition* (London: Routledge).

Clare Cavanagh [1995], *Osip Mandelstam and the Modernist Creation of Tradition* (Princeton: Princeton University Press).

Stanko Cerović [1992], "La danse mystique du scalpel", in Wicker, ed.

—— [1996], *Njegoševe tajne staze* [Njegoš's Secret Paths] (Podgorica: Montenegropublic).

—— [2008], *Après la fin de l'histoire. Un regard sur les révoltes du vingtième siècle* [After the End of History. A Glance at the Rebels of the Twentieth Century] (Paris: Climats).

David Cesarani, ed. [1997], *Genocide and Rescue. The Holocaust in Hungary 1944* (Oxford: Berg).

Brian Cheyette [1992], " 'Jewgreek is greekjew': The Disturbing Ambivalence of Joyce's Semitic Discourse in *Ulysses*", *Joyce Studies Annual* 3 (summer): 32–56.

Milan M. Ćirković [n.d.], "Danilo Kiš", in "Borges: Influences and References", http://www.themodernword.com/borges/borges_infl_kis.htlm (accessed August 2000).

Hélène Cixous [1976], "Fiction and Its Phantoms: A Reading of Freud's Das Unheimliche (The 'Uncanny')", translated by Robert Denommé, *New Literary History* 7(3), http://www.yorku.ca/singram/hum6125_07/HUMA6125_readings/10_25_cixous.pdf (accessed August 2010).

Robert J. Clements [1977], "World Literature Tomorrow", *World Literature Today* 51(2): 180–86.

John M. Coetzee [2003], *Youth* (London: Vintage).

Norman Cohn [1996], *Noah's Flood. The Genesis Story in Western Thought* (New Haven: Yale University Press).

Ivan Čolović [2000], *Politika simbola* [The Politics of the Symbol] (Belgrade: Biblioteka XX vek).

Catherine Coquio [2004], "Violence et déni dans la littérature: l'ultranationalisme serbe", in *L'Histoire trouée. Négation et témoignage,* edited by Catherine Coquio (Nantes: L'Atalante), http://aircrigeweb.free.fr/ressources/bosnie/Youg_Litt_Coquio.html (accessed November 2009).

Marcel Cornis-Pope and John Neubauer, eds. [2004], *History of the Literary Cultures of East-Central Europe. Junctures and Disjunctures in the 19th and 20th Centuries.* 3 vols. (Amsterdam and Philadelphia: John Benjamins).

Cosmopolitiques. Forum international de politique [1989], Actes du colloque 'L'Europe de la pensée, L'Europe du politique', Albi, 5–6 May.

Kenneth Cox [1971–1972], "The Poetry of Louis Zukofsky: *A*", *Agenda* 9(4)/10(1).

Alfred E. Crawley [1911], "Doubles", in Hastings, ed., vol. 4.

Julia Creet [2002], "The Archive and the Uncanny. Danilo Kiš's 'Encyclopedia of the Dead' and the Fantasy of Hypermnesia", in *Lost in the Archives,* edited by Rebecca Comay, Alphabet City, no. 8 (Toronto: Alphabet City Media).

Gordana Crnković [2000], *Imagined Dialogues. Eastern European Literature in Conversation with American and English Literature* (Evanston: Northwestern University Press).

Zlatko Crnković [1997], "Publika ne voli režimske pisce" [The Public Does Not Like Regime Writers], *Tjednik* (Zagreb), 12 December.

Cross Currents [1990], "The Lisbon Conference on Literature: Central Europe and Russian Writers", *Cross Currents* 9: 75–124, http://quod.lib.umich.edu/c/crossc/ANW0935.1990.001/85 :5?didno=anw0935.1990.001;rgn=full+text;view=image (accessed May 2011).

Tibor Cseres [1993], *Titoist Atrocities in Vojvodina 1944–1945. Serbian Vendetta in Bácska* (Buffalo: Hunyadi Publishing).

Marko Čudić [2007], *Danilo Kiš i moderna mađarska poezija* [DK and Modern Hungarian Poetry] (Belgrade: ΠΛΑΤΩ).

Predrag Čudić [1996], *Saveti mladom piscu ili književna početnica* [Advice to a Young Writer, or A Literary Primer] (Belgrade: Radio B92).

Lóránt Czigány [1986], *A History of Hungarian Literature. From the Earliest Times to the Mid 1970s*, http://mek.niif.hu/02000/02042/html/index.html (accessed May 2011).

Stephanie Dalley, trans. and ed. [2000], *Myths from Mesopotamia: Creation, the Flood, Gilgamesh and others* (Oxford: Oxford University Press).

David Damrosch [2003], *What Is World Literature?* (Princeton: Princeton University Press).

—— [2006], "Rebirth of a Discipline: The Global Origins of Comparative Studies", in Weninger, 99–112.

Filip David [1995], "Paralelni zivot" [A Parallel Life], *Vreme*, 11 December.

—— [1999], "Fragmenti o Kišu" [Fragments about Kiš], *Zarez*, 15 October.

Neil Davison [1996], *James Joyce, 'Ulysses', and the Construction of Jewish Identity* (Cambridge, UK: Cambridge University Press).

István Deák [2008], "Mindless Efficacy", *Hungarian Quarterly* 49(192), http://www. hungarianquarterly.com/no192/9.shtml (accessed November 2009).

Daniel Defoe [1983], *Robinson Crusoe* (Oxford: Oxford University Press).

Renaud de la Brosse [2003], "Political Propaganda and the Plan to Create a 'State for all Serbs'. Consequences of Using the Media for Ultra-Nationalist Ends", Report compiled at the request of the Office of the Prosecutor of the International Criminal Tribunal for the former Yugoslavia by Renaud de la Brosse, senior lecturer at the University of Reims, France, http://hague.bard. edu/icty_info.html (accessed August 2011).

Paul Delaney [1989], "Soviet Bloc Writers Clash at a Conference", *New York Times*, 10 May.

Jovan Delić [n.d.], "Izložba Biblioteke grada Beograda. Povodom obeležavanja 70-godišnjice rođenja Danila Kiša", leaflet for the exhibition at Belgrade City Library 70 years after Kiš's birth [2005].

Zoran Đerić [2000], *Anđeli nostalgije. Poezija Danila Kiša i Vladimira Nabokova* [The Angels of Nostalgia. The Poetry of DK and Vladimir Nabokov] (Banja Luka: Besjeda).

Milovan Đilas [1966], *Njegoš. Poet, Prince, Bishop,* translated by Michael B. Petrovich (New York: Harcourt, Brace & World).

—— [1985], *Rise and Fall* (London: Macmillan).

Galye Diment [1994], *The Autobiographical Novel of Co-Consciousness: Goncharov, Woolf, and Joyce* (Gainesville: University Press of Florida).

Pavle Đonović [1989], "Srećna vremena" [Happy Times], *Ovdje* (Titograd), November–December.

Dejan Đorić [2007], *Leonid Šejka* (Belgrade: Službeni glasnik).

Jasna Dragović-Soso [2003], "Intellectuals and the Collapse of Yugoslavia: The End of the Yugoslav Writers' Union", in *Yugoslavism. Histories of a Failed Idea 1918–1992,* edited by Dejan Đokić (London: Hurst).

Čedomir Drašković, ed. [1993], *Bibliografski vjesnik* 23(2–3).

Vladimir Dvorniković [1939], *Karakterologija Jugoslovena* [The Characterology of the Yugoslavs] (Belgrade: Kosmos).

Geoff Dyer [2010], *Jeff in Venice, Death in Varanasi* (Edinburgh: Canongate).

Thomas S. Eliot [1978], *The Complete Poems and Plays* (London: Faber & Faber).

Richard Ellmann [1977], *James Joyce* (Oxford: Oxford University Press).

—— [1986], *Ulysses on the Liffey* (Oxford: Oxford University Press).

William Empson [2000], *The Complete Poems* (London: Allen Lane, Penguin Press).

István Eörsi [1992], "Hommage à Danilo Kiš au Centre Georges Pompidou, le 29 mars 1990" [Homage to DK at the Pompidou Centre, 29 March 1990], in Ferenczi, 117-25, 127-28, 131-67.

—— [1993], *Nezavisni* (Novi Sad), 22 October.

Georges Ferenczi, ed. [1992], *Pour Danilo Kiš. Édition spéciale dédiée à la mémoire de Danilo Kiš,* special issue of *La revue EST-OUEST internationale,* no. 3.

Orlando Figes [2003], *Natasha's Dance. A Cultural History of Russia* (London: Penguin).

Jenő Fitz [1982], *The Great Age of Pannonia* (Budapest: Corvina).

Sheila Fitzpatrick [2008], "Like a Thunderbolt", *London Review of Books,* 11 September.

Gustave Flaubert [1997], *Selected Letters,* translated by Geoffrey Wall (London: Penguin).

Hal Foster [2009], "Crack Open the Shells", *London Review of Books,* 12 March.

Sigmund Freud [1919], "The 'Uncanny'", translated by James Strachey, http://www.yorku.ca/singram/hum6125_07/HUMA6125_readings/10_25_cixous.pdf (accessed August 2010).

John K. Galbraith [1958], *Journey to Poland and Yugoslavia* (Harvard: Harvard University Press).

Eduardo Galeano [2000], "Words That Must Be Said", *The Atlantic Online,* 30 November, http://www.theatlantic.com/past/docs/unbound/interviews/ba2000-11-30.htm (accessed May 2010).

Misha Glenny [1992], *The Fall of Yugoslavia. The Third Balkan War* (London: Penguin Books).

Michael Glover [2001], "Survival of the Bleakest", *Financial Times,* 2–3 June.

Johann Wolfgang von Goethe [1983], *Selected Poems,* edited by Christopher Middleton (London: John Calder).

Vesna Goldsworthy [2005], *Chernobyl Strawberries. A Memoir* (London: Atlantic Books).

Zagorka Golubović, Bora Kuzmanović, and Mirjana Vasović [1995], *Društveni karakter i društvene promene u svetlu nacionalnih sukoba* [Social Character and Social Changes in the Light of National Conflicts] (Belgrade: Filip Višnjić).

Zvonimir Golubović [1991], *Raciji u južnoj Bačkoj* [Raids in South Bačka] (Novi Sad: Matica srpska).

Nadine Gordimer [1992], "A Race with Darkness", *The Observer,* 6 January.

Antonio Gramsci [1971], "The Intellectuals", in *Selections from the Prison Notebooks,* translated and edited by Q. Hoare and G. N. Smith (New York: International Publishers).

Irena Grubica [2007], "*Ulysses* in Croatian", *Joyce Studies in Italy 10: Joyce and/in Translation,* edited by Rosa Maria Bollettieri Bosinelli and Ira Toresi (Rome: Bulzoni).

John Gunther [1949], *Behind Europe's Curtain* (London: Hamish Hamilton).

Peter Hanak [1984], "Problems of Jewish Assimilation in Austria-Hungary in the Nineteenth and Twentieth Centuries", in *The Power of the Past. Essays for Eric Hobsbawm,* edited by Pat Thane, Geoffrey Crossick, and Roderick Floud (Cambridge, UK: Cambridge University Press).

Handbook on Yugoslavia [1987] (Belgrade: Federal Secretariat for Information).

Geoffrey Hartman [2004], "Poetics after the Holocaust", in *The Geoffrey Hartman Reader,* edited by Geoffrey Hartman and Daniel T. O'Hara (Edinburgh: Edinburgh University Press).

James Hastings, ed. [1908–1926], *Encyclopaedia of Religion and Ethics,* 12 vols. (Edinburgh: T. & T. Clark).

Václav Havel [1987], "Letter to Dr Gustáv Husák" (April 1975), in *Vaclav Havel, or Living in Truth*, edited by Jan Vladislav (London: Faber and Faber).

Max Hayward and Leopold Labedz [1963], *Literature and Revolution in Soviet Russia 1917–1962. A Symposium* (Oxford: Oxford University Press).

Aleksandar Hemon [2000], "Imitation of Life", in *The Question of Bruno* (New York: Random House).

—— [2008], "Whose Writer Is Danilo Kiš?", in *Best of Sarajevo Notebooks* 18 (Sarajevo, 2008).

—— [n.d.], "Reading Danilo Kiš", Context No. 9, Dalkey Archive Press, http://www.dalkeyarchive.com (accessed 9 January 2011).

John Herdman [1990], *The Double in Nineteenth-Century Fiction* (Basingstoke, UK: Macmillan).

Herodotus [1954], *The Histories*, translated by Aubrey de Selincourt (Harmondsworth, UK: Penguin).

Eric Hobsbawm [2005], "Benefits of Diaspora", *London Review of Books*, 20 October.

Eva Hoffman [2004], *After Such Knowledge. A Meditation on the Aftermath of the Holocaust* (London: Secker & Warburg).

Josef Holeček [2002], *Crna Gora u miru* [Montenegro at Peace] (Podgorica: CID).

Brooke Horvath, ed. [1994], Danilo Kiš, special issue of *Review of Contemporary Fiction* 14(1).

Chrissie Iles, ed. [1995], *Marina Abramović. Objects performance video sound* (Oxford: Museum of Modern Art Oxford).

Barbara Jelavich [1983], *History of the Balkans. Twentieth Century*, vol. 2 (Cambridge, UK: Cambridge University Press).

Dragan M. Jeremić [1981], *Narcis bez lica* [Narcissus without a Face] (Belgrade: Nolit).

Jewish Virtual Library [n.d.], American-Israeli Cooperative Enterprise, http://www.jewishvirtuallibrary.org/jsource/index.html (accessed May 2010).

Jews in Yugoslavia [1989] (Zagreb: Muzejski prostor Zagreb, Jezuitski trg 4).

Samuel Johnson [1751], "Advantages of Living in a Garret", *The Rambler*, no. 117, 30 April.

Miroslav Jovanović [2006], *Ruska emigracija na Balkanu 1920–1940* [Russian Emigration to the Balkans 1920–1940] (Belgrade: Cigoja).

James Joyce [2000a], *Occasional, Critical and Political Writing* (Oxford: Oxford University Press).

—— [2000b], *Ulysses,* annotated student ed., with an introduction and notes by Declan Kibberd (London: Penguin Books).

Tony Judt [2010], "Toni", *New York Review of Books,* blogpost, April 19, 12:30 p.m., http://www.nybooks.com/blogs/nyrblog/2010/apr/19/toni/ (accessed August 2010).

Ferenc Juhász [1970], *The Boy Changed into a Stag. Selected Poems 1949–1967*, translated by Kenneth McRobbie and Ilona Duczynska (Oxford: Oxford University Press).

Franz Kafka [1979], "The Hunter Gracchus", in *Description of a Struggle and Other Stories*, translated by Malcolm Pasley (Harmondsworth, UK: Penguin).

Ryszard Kapuściński [2008], *The Other*, translated by Antonia Lloyd-Jones (London: Verso).

Miroslav Karaulac [1992], "Les années strasbourgeoises" [The Strasbourg Years], in Wicker, ed.

—— [2007], "Staza kroz Kišovu baštu" [A Path across K's Garden], *Vreme* 15 February 2007, http://www.vreme.com/cms/view.php?id = 488029 (accessed June 2010).

"Katedra za opštu književnost i teoriju književnosti" [The Chair of General Literature and Literary Theory] [n.d.], Faculty of Philology, Belgrade University, website, http://www.fil.bg.ac.rs/katedre/opsta/Katedra%20za%20sajt.doc (accessed June 2010).

Jacob Katz [1980], *From Prejudice to Destruction. Anti-Semitism, 1700–1933* (Cambridge, Mass.: Harvard University Press,).

Nathaniel Katzburg [1981], *Hungary and the Jews. Policy and Legislation 1920–1943* (Jerusalem: Bar-Ilan University Press).

Imre Kertész [2005], *Fatelessness*, translated by Tim Wilkinson (London: Harvill Press).

Adam Kirsch [2009], "Beware of Pity. Hannah Arendt and the Power of the Impersonal", *New Yorker*, 12 January, http://www.newyorker.com/arts/critics/atlarge/2009/01/12/090112crat_atlarge_kirsch?currentPage=all (accessed December 2009).

Kiš u Dijaspori [1990], special issue of *Vidici* 38(4–5).

August Kleinzahler [2001], "An Apple Is an Apple", *London Review of Books*, 19 July.

Rhoda Koenig [1986], "At play in the fields of the word. Alienation, imagination, feminism, and foolishness at PEN," *New York* magazine, 3 February, 40–47.

Arthur Koestler [1978], *Janus: A Summing Up* (London: Hutchinson).

Jak Koprivc [2005], "Zli vuk koji bi da proguta Jugoslaviju" [The Wicked Wolf That Would Devour Yugoslavia], *Danas* (Belgrade), 10 January.

Božo Koprivica [2005], "Od neizlečive mladosti" [From Incurable Youth], *Vreme* 24 February.

—— [2009], "20 godina od smrti Danila Kiša. Život i smrt izgovaram s fusnotom" [20 Years since the Death of DK. I Pronounce Life and Death with a Footnote], *Vreme*, 15 October, http://www.vreme.com/cms/view.php?id=891537 (accessed May 2011).

Mirko Kovač [1992], "Nécrologie", in Ferenczi, ed., 17–25.

—— [1994], *Evropska trulež* [European Rottenness] (Zagreb: Antibarbarus).

—— [2008], "U Bosni se osjećam najbolje" [I Feel Best in Bosnia], *Dani* (Sarajevo), 12 September, http://www.knjigainfo.com/index.php?gde=@http%3A//www.knjigainfo.com/pls/sasa/bip.text%3Ftid%3D54070@ (accessed May 2011).

Boro Krivokapić [1980], *Treba li spaliti Kiša?* [Should Kiš Be Burned?] (Zagreb: Globus).

Miroslav Krleža [1963], *Eseji. Knjiga treća* [Essays. Vol. Three] (Zagreb: Zora).

—— [1967], *Eseji. Knjiga šesta* [Essays. Vol. Six] (Zagreb: Zora).

—— [1980], *O Titu* [About Tito] (Sarajevo-Zagreb: Oslobođenje-Mladost).

Boško Krstić [1999], *Potraga za ulicom divljih kestenova* [In Search of the Street of Horse Chestnut Trees] (Sremski Karlovci: Kairos).

Wladimir Krysinski [1988], "Metafictional Structures in Slavic Literatures: Towards an Archeology of Metafiction", in *Postmodern Fiction in Europe and the Americas,* edited by Theo D'haen and Hans Bertens (Amsterdam: Rodopi).

—— [2010], "Danilo Kis, Souvenirs", June. (From author.)

Milan Kundera [1984], "A Kidnapped West or Culture Bows Out", translated by Edmund White, *Granta* 11: 95–118.

—— [1995], *Testaments Betrayed*, translated by Linda Asher (London: Faber & Faber).

—— [1999], "Danilo Kis, uno scrittore grande e invisibile" [DK, a great and invisible writer], translated from French by Massimo Rizzante, *La Repubblica*, 12 October.

—— [2010], *Encounter: Essays*, translated by Linda Asher (London: Faber & Faber).

Jasmina Kuzmanović [1989], "Ne znam što je post moderna" [I Don't Know What Postmodernism Is], *Danas* (Zagreb), 9 May.

Jessie Labov [2002], "A Russian Encounter with the Myth of Central Europe", paper delivered at the conference The Contours of Legitimacy in Central Europe: New Approaches in Graduate Studies, St Antony's College, University of Oxford, 20–22 May, http://users.ox.ac.uk/~oaces/conference/papers/Jessie_Labov.pdf (accessed May 2010).

—— [n.d.], "Balkan Revisions to the Myth of Central Europe", http://www.hks.harvard.edu/kokkalis/GSW1/GSW1/02%20Labov.pdf (accessed May 2010).

Renate Lachmann [2006], "Danilo Kiš: Factography and Thanatography (*A Tomb for Boris Davidovich, Psalm 44, The Hourglass*)", *Partial Answers* 4(2): 219–38.

Mijat Lakičević, ed. [2003], *Prelom '72. Uzroci e posledice pada srpskih (komunističkih) liberala oktobra 1972. godine* [Breaking Point '72. Sources and Consequences of the Fall of the Serb (Communist) Liberals October 1972] (Belgrade: € Press).

Sarah Lawall, ed. [1994], *Reading World Literature. Theory, History, Practice* (Austin: University of Texas Press).

Paul Lay [2007], obituary for Norman Cohn, *The Guardian*, 9 August, http://www.guardian.co.uk/news/2007/aug/09/guardianobituaries.obituaries (accessed February 2010).

Persida Lazarević Di Giacomo [2006], "Una nuova polemica attorno a Kiš", *Studi Slavistici* III, 253–72, http://www.fupress.net/index.php/ss/article/view/2146/8815 (accessed January 2012).

Adam LeBor and Roger Boyes [2000], *Surviving Hitler. Choices, Corruption and Compromise in the Third Reich* (London: Simon & Schuster).

Trude Levi [1995], *A Cat Called Adolf* (Ilford, UK: Valentine Mitchell).

Bernard-Henri Lévy [1979], *Barbarism with a Human Face* (New York: Harper & Row).

—— [2007], "'A Monument of Audacity and Modernity'", *The Guardian*, 9 October.

Tomislav Z. Longinović [1993], *Borderline Culture: The Politics of Identity in Four Twentieth-Century Slavic Novels* (Fayetteville: University of Arkansas Press).

Ivan Lovrenović [2008], "Kako u Sarajevu nije objavljen *Arhipelag Gulag*" [How *Gulag Archipelago* Was Not Published in Sarajevo], *BH Dani*, 8 August, http://www.zokster.net/drupal/node/1830 (accessed March 2010).

Predrag Lucić [1996], "Dlaka na hrvackom jeziku" [Hairs on the Croatian Tongue], *Homo Volans*, Zagreb, 24 July.

Andrew Ludányi [2003], "The Fate of the Hungarians in Yugoslavia", in *Ethnic Cleansing in Twentieth-Century Europe*, edited by Steven Béla Várdy, T. Hunt Tooley, and Agnes Huszár Várdy (Boulder: Social Science Monographs/Columbia University Press).

Georg Lukács [1963], *The Meaning of Contemporary Realism*, translated by John Mander and Necke Mander (London: Merlin Press).

Eugene Lunn [1985], *Marxism and Modernism. An Historical Study of Lukács, Brecht, Benjamin, and Adorno* (London: Verso).

Carlile A. Macartney [1961], *October Fifteenth. A History of Modern Hungary 1929–1945*, Pt. 2 (Edinburgh: Edinburgh University Press).

Gradimir D. Madžarević, ed. [2006], *Mediala* (Belgrade: Službeni glasnik).

Claudio Magris [1990], "Kiš di Subotica", *L'Indice*, July 1990.

Nadezhda Mandelstam [1976], *Hope Abandoned*, translated by Max Hayward (Harmondsworth, UK: Penguin Books).

Norman Manea [1992], *On Clowns: The Dictator and the Artist* (New York: Grove Press).

Albert Manguel [2000], *Into the Looking Glass Wood* (London: Bloomsbury).

Predrag Matvejević [1992], "Hommage à Danilo Kiš au Centre Georges Pompidou, le 29 mars 1990" [Homage to DK at the Pompidou Centre, 29 March 1990], in Ferenczi, ed., 117-25, 127-28, 131-67.

William O. McCagg Jr. [1989], *A History of Habsburg Jews, 1670–1918* (Bloomington and Indianapolis: Indiana University Press).

Mary McCarthy [1973], *The Writing on the Wall* (Harmondsworth, UK: Penguin).

Zhores A. Medvedev and Roy A. Medvedev [2006], *The Unknown Stalin*, translated by Ellen Dahrendorf (London: I. B. Tauris).

Pierre Mertens [1996], "Jardin des supplices, cendre et diamant", *L'Atelier du roman*, no. 8: 20–25.

Vasa D. Mihailovich [1994], "Garbage Heap (from Papers Left Behind)", translation of Kiš's poem *Đubrište* (1966), *Review of Contemporary* Fiction 14(1): 124–27.

—— [1997], *The Mountain Wreath*, a translation of *Gorski vijenac* by Petar Njegoš (Belgrade: Serbian Europe), http://guskova.ru/˜mladich/Njegosh/1997/the_mountain_wreath (accessed December 2009).

Radmila Milentijević [1994], "Anti-Semitism and the Treatment of the Holocaust in Postcommunist Yugoslavia", in Braham, ed. [1994].

Milan Milišić [1990], "Danilo Kiš: Moral i mòra. Uz godišnjicu smrti", typescript, 7 October. (From author's widow, Jelena Trpković.)

—— [1996], *Stvaranje Dubrovnika* [Creating Dubrovnik] (Sarajevo: Bosanska knjiga).

Marko Miljanov [1901], *Primjeri čojstva i junaštva* [Examples of Humanism and Heroism] (Belgrade), http://montenegrina.net/pages/pages1/knjizevnost/primjeri_cojstva_i_junastva.htm (accessed June 2010).

Mirjana Miočinović [1999], "On the Role of the Serbian Intelligentsia and the Position of Montenegro", interview by Ljubeta Labović, *Monitor* (Podgorica), 10 September. Republished in translation in *Bosnia Report* (Bosnian Institute, London), n.s. no.11–12, August–November 1999, http://www.bosnia.org.uk/bosrep/augnov99/serbian_intelligentsia.cfm (accessed September 2011).

—— [2001], "Pisac je čovjek koji razmišlja o formi" [A Writer Is Someone Who Thinks about Form], in *Entgrenzte Repräsentationen—Gebrochene Realitäten. Danilo Kiš im Spannungsfeld von Ethik, Literatur und Politik* [Unbounded Representations—Broken Realities. DK Between Ethics, Literature and Politics], edited by Angela Richter, 97–110 (Munich: Verlag O. Sagner).

—— [2007], "Margina slobode" [A Margin of Freedom], interview with Muharem Bazdulj, *Sarajevske sveske* (Sarajevo) 17.

András Mócsy [1974], *Pannonia and Upper Moesia. A History of the Middle Danube Provinces of the Roman Empire* (London: Routledge & Kegan Paul).

Ray Monk [1991], *Ludwig Wittgenstein. The Duty of Genius* (London: Vintage Books).

Franco Moretti [2000], "Conjectures on World Literature", *New Left Review* 1(January–February), http://www.newleftreview.org/A2094 (accessed June 2010).

Blake Morrison [1993], *And When Did You Last See Your Father?* (London: Granta).

Kenneth Morrison [2008], *Montenegro. A Modern History* (London: I. B. Tauris).

Gabriel Motola [1993], "Danilo Kiš: Death and the Mirror", *Antioch Review* 51(4): 605–21.

Vladimir Nabokov [2001], "Spring in Fialta", in *Collected Stories* (London: Penguin).

Ira B. Nadel [1989], *Joyce and the Jews* (Basingstoke, UK: Macmillan).

Nagel Travel Guide to Yugoslavia [1954] (Geneva: Nagel Publishers).

Aleksandar Nenadović [1989], *Razgovori sa Kočom* [Conversations with Koča] (Zagreb: Globus).

Charles Newman [1990], "How It Feels to Cease to Be", *New York Times*, 7 October.

Karen Ní Mheallaigh [2008], "Pseudo-Documentarism and the Limits of Ancient Fiction", *American Journal of Philology* 129(3): 403–31.

Petar Petrović Njegoš [1990], *Gorski vijenac* [The Mountain Wreath] (Sarajevo: Svjetlost).

Suzanne Normand and Jean Acker [1956], *Yugoslavia*, translated by Jean Penfold (London: Nicholas Kaye).

David Norris [2008], *Belgrade. A Cultural and Literary History* (Oxford: Signal).

Vida Ognjenović [2007], *Nasuprot proročanstvu* [The Opposite of Prophecy] (Belgrade: Arhipelag).

Ayako Oku [2008], "Danilo Kiš and Central Europe: A Reading of His Incomplete Story 'Apatrid'", *Slavic Studies*, no. 55: 61–90, http://www.ceeol.com (accessed December 2009).

Cynthia Ozick [1988], *The Messiah of Stockholm* (New York: Vintage).

—— [1991], *Metaphor and Memory* (New York: Vintage International).

—— [1998], *The Puttermesser Papers. A Novel* (New York: Vintage International).

Zsusanna Ozsváth [2006], "Trauma and Distortion: Holocaust Fiction and the Ban on Jewish Memory in Hungary", in *The Holocaust in Hungary: Sixty Years Later,* edited by Randolph L. Braham and Brewster S. Chamberlin (Boulder: East European Monographs/Columbia University Press).

Grace Paley [1975], "Debts", in *Enormous Changes at the Last Minute* (London: André Deutsch).

Teofil Pančić [2003], "Kidnaperi mrtvog pisca" [Kidnappers of a Dead Writer], *Vreme* (Belgrade), 18 December.

Mihajlo Pantić [2002], *Kiš* (Belgrade: Filip Višnjić).

Thomas Pavel [2010], "Save Us from Saviours", *London Review of Books*, 27 May.

Jelena Pavlović [1990], "U traganju za Kišom" [In Search of K], in *Kiš u Dijaspori* [1990], special issue of *Vidici* 38(4–5).

Borislav Pekić [1990], "Danilo ili život kao bol" [Danilo or Life as Pain], in *Kiš u Dijaspori* [1990], special issue of *Vidici* 38(4–5).

—— [2002], *Korispondencija kao život* [Correspondence like Life] (Novi Sad: Solaris).

Georges Perec [1997], *Species of Spaces and Other Pieces*, translated by John Sturrock (London: Penguin).

Igor Perišić [2007], "Četvrta ruka. Jedan pogled na 'akademsku kritiku' u Srbiji 1991–2007" [The Fourth Hand. A Glance at 'Academic Criticism' in Serbia 1991–2007], *Sarajevske sveske* (Sarajevo) 17.

Latinka Perović [2000a], *Ljudi, događaji i knjige* [People, Events and Books] (Belgrade: Biblioteka SVEDOČANSTVA).

—— [2000b], "Yugoslavia, Serbia and the Future—Four Texts", *Helsinška povelja* 35 (December).

György Petri [1999], *Eternal Monday. New & Selected Poems*, translated by Clive Wilmer and George Gömöri (Newcastle: Bloodaxe).

—— "Modus operandi", in Ferenczi, ed., 128-31.

Adam Phillips [1996], *Monogamy* (London: Faber & Faber).

Boris Pilniak [1924], *Tales of the Wilderness* (London: Routledge).

Robert Pinget [1966], *The Inquisitory*, translated by Donald Watson (London: Calder and Boyars).

John Pizer [2000], "Goethe's 'World Literature' Paradigm and Contemporary Cultural Globalization", *Comparative Literature* 52: 213–27.

Léon Poliakov [1974], *The Aryan Myth. A History of Racist and Nationalist Ideas in Europe*, translated by Edmund Howard (London: Chatto & Heinemann).

—— [2003], *The History of Anti-Semitism. vol. 3. From Voltaire to Wagner*, translated by Miriam Kochan (Philadelphia: University of Pennsylvania Press).

Rachel Polonsky [2010], *Molotov's Magic Lantern. A Journey in Russian History* (London: Faber & Faber).

Nebojša Popov [1996a], "Traumatology of the Party State", in Popov, ed. [1996b], 81–106.

—— ed. [1996b], *The Road to War in Serbia* (Budapest: CEU Press).

Milan Popović [1993], "Uvod i riječ Milana Popovića na večeri: 'O Danilu Kišu izbliza—drugovanje koje traje', održanog 15. oktobra u 19,30 časova." [Introduction and Remarks by Milana Popović at the Meeting, 'DK from Close Up: Friendship That Endures'], typescript. (From author.)

Lakis Proguidis, ed. [1996a], *L'Atelier du roman,* no. 8 (fall).

—— [1996b], "Danilo Kiš, portrait de famille", in Proguidis, ed.

Alexandre Prstojević, ed. [2003a], *Temps de l'histoire. Études sur Danilo Kiš* (Paris: Harmattan).

—— [2003b] "Danilo Kiš : le roman face à l'Histoire", in Prstojević, ed.

—— [2005], *Le roman face à l'histoire: essai sur Claude Simon et Danilo Kiš* (Paris: Harmattan).

—— [n.d.], *Un certain goût de l'archive (Sur l'obsession documentaire de Danilo Kis),* http://www.vox-poetica.com/ecrivains/KIS/prstojevic02.htm (accessed June 2010).

Protokoli Sionskih mudraca [Protocols of the Elders of Zion] [2001] (Belgrade).

François Rabelais [2006], *Gargantua and Pantagruel,* translated by Michael A. Screech (London: Penguin).

Ana Raca [2009], "Danilo Kiš (1935–1989)", Radio B92, 15 October.

Viktorija Radič [Viktoria Radics] [2005], *Danilo Kiš,* translated from Hungarian by Marko Čudić (Belgrade: Forum pisaca).

Nadežda Radović [2011], "U srpskoj književnosti živi Kišova mačo-fantazija" [Kiš's Macho-Fantasy Is Alive in Serbian Literature]. Interview with Tatjana Rosić, author of *Mit o savršenoj biografiji* [The Myth of the Perfect Biography], Belgrade, 2008. *Danas* (Belgrade), 11 April, http://www.danas.rs/danasrs/kultura/u_srpskoj_knjizevnosti_zivi_kisova_macofantazija.11.html?news_id=213361 (accessed May 2012).

Ilma Rakusa [1992], "Inventaires poétiques" [Poetic Inventories], translated from German by Odile Vassas, in Ferenczi, ed., 75-79.

Michael Riffaterre [1990], *Fictional Truth* (Baltimore: Johns Hopkins University Press).

Marko Ristić [1958], *Politička književnost 1944–1958* [Political Literature 1944–1958] (Zagreb: Naprijed).

Massimo Rizzante [1996], "De l'idéal encyclopédique", in Proguidis, ed.

Elizabeth Roberts [2007], *Realm of the Black Mountain. A History of Montenegro* (London: Hurst).

Mark Roseman [2002], *The Villa, the Lake, the Meeting. Wannsee and the Final Solution* (London: Allen Lane/Penguin).

Joseph Roth [2001], *The Wandering Jews*, translated by Michael Hofmann (London: Granta).

Salman Rushdie [1995], *Midnight's Children* (London: Vintage).

—— [2002], "In Defence of the Novel, Yet Again", in *Step across This Line* (London: Cape).

—— [2005], letter to the author, 3 February.

William Ryan and Walter Pitman [1998], *Noah's Flood. The New Scientific Discoveries about the Event That Changed History* (New York: Simon & Schuster).

Thomas Sakmyster [1994], *Hungary's Admiral on Horseback. Miklós Horthy, 1918–1944* (Boulder: East European Monographs/Columbia University Press).

Ian Sansom [2003], "Omdamniverous", *London Review of Books*, 25 September.

Izet Sarajlić [1993], "Pisac i domovina" [The Writer and the Homeland], *Ratni kongres pisaca Republike Bosne i Herzegovine* [War Conference of Writers of the Republic of Bosnia and Herzegovina], Sarajevo, 30 October.

Jean-Paul Sartre [1955], "François Mauriac and Freedom", in *Literary and Philosophical Essays*, translated by Annette Michelson (New York: Criterion Books).

Guy Scarpetta [1992], "Hommage à Danilo Kiš au Centre culturel yougoslave (Paris, octobre 1989)" [Homage to DK at the Yugoslav Cultural Centre, Paris, October 1989], in Ferenczi, ed. 105-13.

—— [1996], "La diaspora du sens" [The Diaspora of Meaning], in *L'age d'or du roman* [The Golden Age of the Novel] (Paris: Grasset).

—— [2007], "Danilo Kiš ou l'art de mentir vrai" [DK or the Art of Lying Truthfully], in *Le Monde diplomatique*, June, http://monde-diplomatique.fr/2007/06/SCARPETTA/14860 (accessed September 2009).

John R. Schindler [2003], "Yugoslavia's First Ethnic Cleansing: The Expulsion of the Danubian Germans, 1944–1946", in *Ethnic Cleansing in Twentieth-Century Europe,* edited by Steven Béla Várdy, T. Hunt Tooley, and Agnes Huszár Várdy (Boulder: Social Science Monographs/Columbia University Press).

Gershom Scholem [1974], *Major Trends in Jewish Mysticism* (New York: Schocken Books).

Bruno Schulz [1980], *Sanatorium under the Sign of the Hourglass*, translated by Celina Wieniewska (London: Picador).

Ernest F. Scott [1913], "Gnosticism", in Hastings, ed., vol. 6.

Harold B. Segel, ed. [2003], *The Columbia Guide to the Literatures of Eastern Europe since 1945* (New York: Columbia University Press).

Laslo Sekelj et al. [2002], *Antisemitizam* [Anti-Semitism], special issue of *Nova srpska politička misao* [New Serb Political Thought], no. 1.

Snežana Sekulić [n.d.], "Kulturna politika u Crnoj Gori poslije Drugog Svjetskog Rata" [Cultural Policy in Montenegro after the Second World War], http://www.montenegrina.net/pages/pages1/politika/kulturna_politika_u_cg_poslije_2svj_rata.htm (accessed February 2010).

Ludmila Seliverstova [2008], "Church Bells Cast in Voronezh for Montenegro", *Voice of Russia World Service*, 27 June, http://02varvara.wordpress.com/2008/06/27/church-bells-cast-in-voronezh-for-montenegro/ (accessed June 2012).

Louis Sell [2002], *Slobodan Milosevic and the Destruction of Yugoslavia* (Durham: Duke University Press).

Slobodan Selenić [1990], "Poslednji susret sa zdravim Kišem" [The Last Meeting with Healthy Kiš], in *Kiš u Dijaspori* [1990], special issue of *Vidici* 38(4–5).

Henri Séronya [1972], *La Kabbale* (Paris: Presses universitaires de France).

Efraim Sicher [2005], *The Holocaust Novel* (New York: Routledge).

Ivana Simeonović Ćelić [1997], *Milo Milunović* (Belgrade: Srpska akademija nauka i umetnosti/ Crnogorska akademija nauka i umetnosti).

Josef Škvorecký, "Light in Darkness", *New Republic*, 10 April 1989.

Svetlana Slapšak [1994], "Memory vs. 'History'" *Erewhon* 1(1): 144–51.

Svetlana Slapšak, Guido Snel, and John Neubauer [2004], "Serbia: The Widening Rift between Criticism and Literary Histories", in Cornis-Pope and Neubauer, eds., vol. 3.

Guido Snel [2004], "The Return of Pannonia as Imaginary Topos and Space of Homelessness", in Cornis-Pope and Neubauer, eds., vol. 2.

Susan Sontag [1979], *On Photography* (Harmondsworth, UK: Penguin).

——, ed. [1993], *A Roland Barthes Reader* (London: Vintage).

—— [2002], "Danilo Kiš", in *Where the Stress Falls* (London: Vintage).

—— [2007a], *At the Same Time* (London: Hamish Hamilton).

—— [2007b], "Literature Is What You Should Re-Read: An Interview with Susan Sontag", *Spirit of Bosnia. An International, Interdisciplinary, Multilingual, Online Journal* 2(2), http://www.spiritofbosnia.org/volume-2-no-2-2007-april/literature-is-what-you-should-re-read-an-interview-with-susan-sontag/ (accessed June 2011).

Marko Špadijer [1993], "Danilo Kiš—urbani vitez" [DK—Urban Knight], *Pobjeda,* 16 October.

Ivan Stambolić [1995], *Put u bespuće* [Journey into the Wilderness] (Belgrade: Radio B92).

Edwin D. Starbuck [1911], "Double-Mindedness", in Hastings, ed., vol. 4.

Andrzej Stasiuk [2009], *Fado,* translated by Bill Johnston (Champaign: Dalkey Archive).

Richard Stern [1988], "Some Members of the Congress", *Critical Inquiry.* 14(4): 860–91.

Wallace Stevens [1957], *Opus Posthumous* (New York: Knopf).

Branislava Stojanović [2005], *Spomenica Danila Kiša. Bibliografija Danila Kiša* [A Memorial for DK. Bibliography of DK] (Belgrade: Srpska Akademija Nauka i Umetnosti).

Susan Rubin Suleiman [2002], "The 1.5 Generation: Thinking about Child Survivors and the Holocaust", *American Imago* 59 (3): 277–95.

David Sylvester [1997], *About Modern Art. Critical Essays 1948–97* (London: Pimlico).

Ernő Szép [1994], *The Smell of Humans. A Memoir of the Holocaust in Hungary* (Budapest: Central European University Press).

George Szirtes [2008], "God on Trial Revisited," blogpost, Monday, September 8, http://georgeszirtes.blogspot.com/search?q=ravensbruck (accessed August 2010).

Wisława Szymborska [1997], "The End and the Beginning", translated by Joanna Trzeciak, in *Threepenny Review*, no. 70, summer, at http://www.threepennyreview.com/samples/szymborska_su97.html (accessed February 2012).

Ivo Tartalja, ed. [1992], *Zbornik u čast Vojislava Đurića* [Proceedings in Honour of Vojislav Đurić] (Belgrade: Filološki fakultet/Filozofski fakultet / Institut za književnost i umetnost).

Hallam Tennyson [1955], *Tito Lifts the Curtain. The Story of Yugoslavia Today* (London: Rider).

Mark Thompson [1992], "Between Devil and Sea", *The Guardian,* 16 October.

—— [1993], *A Paper House. The Ending of Yugoslavia* (London: Vintage).

Aleksandar Tišma [1998], interview with Luka Mičeta, *Biblioteka Alexandria,* 1(1).

Dragoljub Todorović [2003], "Procesi, presude i ubistvo Milana Milišića" [The Trials, Sentences and Killing of Milan Milišić], *Hereticus* (1), http://www.hereticus.org/arhiva/2003-1/procesi-presude-i-ubistvo-milana-milisica.html (accessed September 2011).

Oto Tolnai [2003], "Nežnije" [More Gently], *Rukovet* (Subotica), nos. 1–3.

Bato Tomašević [2008], *Life and Death in the Balkans. A Family Saga in a Century of Conflict* (London: Hurst).

Jozo Tomasevich [2001], *War and Revolution in Yugoslavia, 1941–1945. Occupation and Collaboration* (Stanford: Stanford University Press).

Dinko Tomašić [1941], "Sociology in Yugoslavia", *American Journal of Sociology* 47(1): 53–69.

Marina Tsvetaeva [2009], *Bride of Ice: New Selected Poems,* translated by Elaine Feinstein (Manchester, UK: Carcanet).

Dubravka Ugrešić [1992], "Parrots and Priests", *Times Literary Supplement,* 15 May.

—— [2003], *Thank You for Not Reading,* translated by Celia Hawkesworth (Chicago: Dalkey Archive).

Maria Vassileva [2010], "Stellar Cannibalism: Stars, Mandelstams, Stamps and Stalin's Camps in 'Red Stamps with Lenin's Picture' by Danilo Kiš," senior thesis, Department of Comparative Literature, Harvard University, http://issuu.com/mvassileva (accessed May 2010).

Yuri B. Vipper [1985], "National Literary History in History of World Literature: Theoretical Principles of Treatment", *New Literary History,* 16(3): 545–58.

Rudolf Vrba [1998], "Preparations for the Holocaust in Hungary: An Eyewitness Account", in *The Nazis' Last Victims. The Holocaust in Hungary,* edited by Randolph L. Braham and Scott Miller (Detroit: Wayne State University).

Ivana Vuletić [2003], *The Prose Fiction of Danilo Kiš, Serbian Jewish Writer. Childhood and the Holocaust* (Lewiston, N.Y.: Edwin Mellen Press).

Andrew Baruch Wachtel [1998], *Making a Nation, Breaking a Nation. Literature and Cultural Politics in Yugoslavia* (Stanford: Stanford University Press).

—— [2006], "The Legacy of Danilo Kiš in Post-Yugoslav Literature", *Slavic and East European Journal* 50(1): 135–49.

Robert Weninger, ed. [2006], *Comparative Literature at a Crossroads?,* special issue of *Comparative Critical Studies. The Journal of the British Comparative Literature Association* 3(1–2).

Edmund White [1994], "Danilo Kiš: The Obligations of Form", in *The Burning Library* (New York: Knopf).

—— [1998], "On the Chance That a Shepherd Boy …", *London Review of Books,* 10 December.

Antoine Wicker, ed. [1992], *Le Désir d'Europe. Les Cahiers de Strasbourg* (Strasbourg: Carrefour des Littératures Européennes).

Duncan Wilson [1979], *Tito's Yugoslavia* (Cambridge, UK: Cambridge University Press).

James Woodall [1996], *The Man in the Mirror of the Book. A Life of Jorge Luis Borges* (London: Hodder and Stoughton).

Adam Zagajewski [1987], *Tremor,* translated by Renata Gorczynski, preface by Czesław Miłosz (London: Collins Harvill).

Ivo Žanić [2007], *Flag on the Mountain. A Political Anthropology of War in Croatia and Bosnia,* translated by Graham McMaster with Celia Hawkesworth (London: Saqi).

Marko Živković [1997], "Violent Highlanders and Peaceful Lowlanders. Uses and Abuses of Ethno-Geography in the Balkans from Versailles to Dayton", *Replika* 2: 107–19, http://www.c3.hu/scripta/scripta0/replika/honlap/english/02/08zivk.htm (accessed January 2010).

Dragomir Zupanc [2009], *Danilo Kiš: Uspomene, sećanja* [DK: Memories, Recollections], a film produced by Radio-Television Serbia, broadcast 15 October, http://www.youtube.com/playlist?list=PLB434A7066C1E3729 (accessed June 2012).

Index

Italicized page numbers indicate photographs. Page numbers followed by n indicate notes.